British financial markets and institutions

British financial markets and institutions

An international perspective

SECOND EDITION

JENIFER PIESSE
BIRKBECK COLLEGE, UNIVERSITY OF LONDON

KEN PEASNELL
UNIVERSITY OF LANCASTER

CHARLES WARD
UNIVERSITY OF READING

PRENTICE HALL

London New York Toronto Sydney Tokyo Singapore
Madrid Mexico City Munich

First published 1985
This edition published 1995 by
Prentice Hall Europe
Campus 400, Maylands Avenue
Hemel Hempstead
Hertfordshire, HP2 7EZ
A division of
Simon & Schuster International Group

Typeset in 9½/12pt Melior
by Keyset Composition, Colchester, Essex
Printed and bound in Great Britain by
Redwood Books, Trowbridge, Wiltshire

Library of Congress Cataloging-in-Publication Data

Piesse, J. (Jenifer)
    British financial markets and institutions / J. Piesse,
K. V. Peasnell, C. W. R. Ward — 2nd ed.
        p.   cm.
    Includes bibliographical references and index.
    ISBN 0-13-647165-X (pbk. : alk. paper)
    1. Finance—Great Britain.   2. Financial institutions—Great
Britain.   I. Peasnell, K. V.   II. Ward, C. W. R. (Charles W. R.)
III. Title.
HG186.G7P54   1995
332′.0941—dc20   95-8631
                                                   CIP

British Library Cataloguing in Publication Data

A catalogue record for this book is available from
the British Library

ISBN 0-13-647165-X

---

2   3   4   5   99   98   97   96

In memory of my parents

Contents

PART I: The structure of the financial system

PART II: Analysis of UK financial markets

PART III: The financial institutions

PART IV: Governance and regulation

PART V: International perspectives and future trends

List of figures

List of tables

Preface

It seemed appropriate that on the tenth anniversary of the first publication of *British Financial Markets and Institutions* a new edition should be written. But the task of updating this volume was rather more daunting than had at first appeared. There have been major changes in every aspect of the financial sector, from the structure of the markets and trading practices to the introduction of new securities and regulations. There is also an entirely different economic environment, especially in terms of the relationship of Britain to Europe and the rest of the world. Finally, to add complexity to any attempt at consistency with the first edition, new definitions of key statistical data have been developed and reporting procedures revised.

Therefore, rather than attempting to maintain the old structure and simply include current data and other information, a more systematic revision was undertaken. Some of the chapters have barely changed. Those parts of the book which describe the flow of funds in the economy and the process of matching investment and saving through financial intermediation remain, as do the sections on the characteristics of markets, the theory of interest rate behaviour and the valuation of assets. The major changes are in the descriptions of securities trading, mostly prompted by what is known as 'Big Bang' and other regulatory reforms and the introduction of new financial instruments.

The major additions to the book can be divided into two groups. The first is a fuller discussion of markets which were in existence when the first edition was published but which have now assumed a greater importance, for example, derivatives and eurocurrency markets. The second is to approach the UK markets from an international perspective, both in terms of Britain's membership of the European Union and the future of that relationship, and from a position of international competitiveness. Thus, while this book does not claim to address directly issues of international finance, it does take into account the reality that British and foreign financial markets have long been interdependent.

In writing this second edition, the original intention has been upheld: to provide a broad and balanced book which introduces the principal British financial markets and institutions in the framework of the national economy. The analysis is firmly from the UK perspective, with other markets incorporated into the discussion.

This book can be used as the main text or as a supplement to a corporate finance or business economics text. It is designed for use in business and finance courses at undergraduate level, and for students undertaking courses in accounting, business economics, and management. Typically, these courses are attended by a wide variety of students, many of whom will take no further finance courses. In this case, students are best served by a course of study which provides an overview of the system as a whole. The flows of saving and investment and the markets and institutions which facilitate these flows are the object of study, rather than the financing and investment decisions of individual firms.

It is not possible to include everything in a single text, especially an introductory one. Also, with very few exceptions, specific institutions or incidents are not referred to as these very quickly become history and their significance is no longer remembered; they also have very little meaning to overseas readers. Further readings are suggested at the end of each chapter, although since the financial sector is subject to continual changes in practice and regulation, articles from academic journals, professional magazines and the financial press are considerably more current than textbooks and students should be directed towards appropriate works.

With respect to revised data and financial statistics, detailed sources are given to enable the reader to update series without too much difficulty. The complexity of the financial system is such that huge amounts of data exist. By presenting the financial theory early in the book, followed by the individual market information, it is hoped to integrate the institutional and analytical aspects of finance from the outset. The reader is then able to learn some detail of the markets as well as their significance in the overall institutional structure. The numerical data will help to illustrate aspects of the system and the markets within it, although only a small subset of the available information has been included.

The appendices include some of the more formal financial mathematics as well as details of markets which are secondary to the text. Questions and problems are included in the book, most of which have been developed and classroom-tested in undergraduate courses in accounting and finance, and a glossary includes definitions of many commonly used terms. A separate *Teacher's Manual* providing solutions is available from the publisher.

Jenifer Piesse
Birkbeck College
University of London

Acknowledgements to first edition

We acknowledge with gratitude the helpful comments of our colleagues, as well as current and former students in the Department of Accounting and Finance, University of Lancaster. In particular we thank Patricia Berry, David Brown, John Cope and Paul Taylor who made a number of useful suggestions. Professor Edward Stamp suggested many improvements for which we are grateful. We also thank the following for their helpful comments on the institutional aspects of the text: Jonathan Miller (Fielding Newson-Smith), Stewart Millman (De Zoete and Bevan), David Revie (Legal and General Group), Paul Richards (Samuel Montagu & Co.) and David Salisbury (H. Schroder Wagg). We thank the *Financial Times* for permission to reproduce extracts.

Finally we are grateful to the Department of Accounting and Finance (University of Lancaster) and Department of Accounting (University of Sydney) for providing typing resources, and personally to Valerie Goulding, Rosemary Timperley, Susan Unsworth and Sheila Markham for their help in producing the typescript.

Acknowledgements to second edition

Several acknowledgements are in order. David Brown and David Hadley helped to compile the current data, and to construct updated and consistent series, with financial support provided by HMV Group Ltd. I am also grateful to the *Wall Street Journal*, the *Financial Times*, the *Guardian* and the Bank of England for permission to include information from their publications. A number of students in the Management Department at Birkbeck read some of the new chapters and made useful contributions, and the library staff at the Bank of England were especially helpful. Robin Jarvis, Bob Perks, Colin Thirtle and Margaret Woods have all read and commented on this new edition, suggesting further material and correcting errors, for which I am very grateful. Finally, I would like to thank Rob Townsend for his help in the preparation of the final manuscript and Toireasa McCann for producing the Teacher's Manual.

Introduction

The City of London is one of the world's great financial centres. It is an agglomeration of institutions and individuals involved in the activity of trading financial assets. This book sets out the structure of these markets and institutions in broad terms, while avoiding excessive technical detail.

The book is divided into five parts. Part I provides the foundations for the study of financial markets by outlining the function of the financial system, its relationship to the real sectors of the economy and the characteristics of financial claims. The flows of funds between sectors provides the motivation for saving and investment. The interaction of borrowers and lenders is achieved through the process of intermediation. Chapter 3 discusses the mechanisms for this process and the conflicts that exist between the government and borrowers and lenders, and how these are resolved within the context of a marketplace. Given the financial system exists in the context of the national economy, a background to monetary policy and the theory of interest rates as the price of funds is to be found in Chapter 4. The fundamental techniques of financial mathematics are developed in Chapter 5 and used to explain the general principles of security pricing. Part 1 concludes with a perspective on the international financial system, and the implications for monetary control for those countries within the European Union.

Part II examines the money and capital markets. It begins with an introduction to the markets in which securities are traded. The characteristics of markets for long-term assets are outlined and the major types of securities described. This examination is not exhaustive, but the general features of debt and equity issues are included, along with those securities which derive their value from underlying assets. Securities denominated in sterling and foreign currencies, as well as eurocurrencies are traded in London, and therefore all are covered in this section. Short-term money markets are discussed both in terms of their importance in maintaining the stability of the financial system and in foreign exchange transactions.

Financial institutions are the subject of Part III. These include the retail and wholesale banks, many of which are non-UK organisations, other deposit-taking

1

institutions and the insurance companies and other investing intermediaries. These chapters outline the specific activities carried out by these institutions, and the competitive forces which have shaped the sector.

Part IV considers three topics which have had a considerable impact on the UK financial markets over the past few years and will no doubt continue to do so. The first is the growth in importance of small and medium-sized firms, and the sources of funding available to them. Chapter 17 addresses the topic of raising funds, by means other than through the capital markets, or direct borrowing from the financial institutions. Chapter 18 explores the relationship between the financial sector and industry, and the effects of the impact of the major investing institutions on corporate ownership structures. The final chapter in Part IV considers the regulation and supervision of the financial sector as a whole. It is acknowledged that the approach to regulation of the financial system is determined by traditional legal structures and norms established by individual nation states. In the UK, the laissez-faire approach taken by the financial community has been replaced by a formal structure of self-regulation, overseen by government agencies, and with the central bank continuing to exert a major influence in terms of prudential supervision and authorisation. Furthermore, increased international investment has made regulatory harmonisation necessary to ensure the integrity of the financial sector as a whole.

The global nature of the London financial markets is a recurring theme in this book, and the international financial community is now integrated to a large extent. However, national differences still remain in terms of structure and practice. Each national system developed, influenced by historical, political and cultural characteristics and the resulting variations persist in spite of the common objective of providing low-cost funds in the most efficient manner. The evolution of existing markets and the emergence of new ones highlight these differences, as choices are made about the nature of systems now being implemented. This topic, plus some concluding comments about the future of the financial system, make up Part V.

The structure of the financial system

Introduction to Part I

Part I begins by clarifying the role of the financial system in the economy, defining the nature of financial claims and assessing how aspects of government policy affect the creation and allocation of national wealth.

We also introduce the idea of a market for financial services, including the intermediary nature of the institutions involved. Before defining the role of individual market participants, the structure of exchange mechanisms in both primary and secondary securities is outlined. These markets are numerous and complex, as well as being subject to innovation and change, so students are urged to follow readings from the materials suggested at the end of the chapters and also from the financial press.

One aspect of the financial services industry which makes it different from other industrial sectors is the way in which government interacts with the financial institutions to implement monetary policy. This is illustrated by the Bank of England's role in the financing of public sector expenditure and the control of the money supply. We shall examine this. The effects of interest rate changes and the level of inflation on the valuation of financial assets are shown, with the technical aspects of compound interest calculations in the appendix to Chapter 5.

Part I concludes with the wider view of the UK as part of the global economy, and particularly of the European Union. This role has important implications for all aspects of the economy, such as the provision of financial products and services at a competitive level at home and abroad, but also raises questions about the effectiveness of monetary policy at a national level in the future.

CHAPTER 1

Introduction to the financial system

1.1 Introduction

This chapter begins by presenting simple models of a hypothetical economy to illustrate the role served by the financial sector in the economy. The characteristics of money, and the special properties of financial assets, money and credit in the measurement and creation of national wealth are outlined at the individual sector level. The chapter concludes with a brief discussion on the ways in which the government's actions affect the financial system.

1.2 Simple model of the economy

A first step in constructing a simple model of the economy is to consider how an economy would function without a financial system. This is a somewhat artificial device because the financial system did not develop in its present form overnight. On the contrary, various features of the financial system, particularly the concept of money, came into being at the earliest stages of specialisation. Thus the *financial* and the *real* parts of the British economy have grown up together, unlike the situation in many developing or transitional economies today. Nevertheless, we do take our financial markets and institutions for granted, so it is worthwhile considering how people would go about their daily business in the absence of a financial system.

For our purposes it is sufficient to divide this simple economy into two parts or sectors. The first sector, businesses, produces goods and services wanted (directly or indirectly) by the second sector, households. The household sector exchanges the resources under its control (property and labour) for the goods and services created by the business sector. The definition of a household can, of course, differ between societies, and households are assumed in this analysis to be the ultimate owners of all resources. Finally, in this simple model, we exclude the government sector and assume the UK is a closed economy. This requires that we ignore

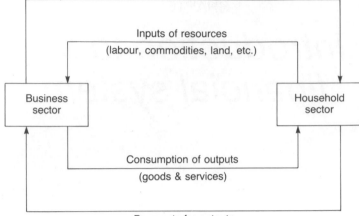

Figure 1.1   Flows in a simple two-sector economy.

government borrowing and expenditure, as well as any international trade of goods and services. The inner loop in Figure 1.1 depicts the flows in this imaginary two-sector economy. Consider the choices open to a household in this economy.

Commodities can be consumed now, or exchanged for other commodities currently owned by other households. Alternatively, some or all of its commodities can be put to productive use in order to create other commodities which will be consumed in their turn. In the former case, exchanges have to be made by bartering with other households. If the choice is to transform resources through production, the household will have to create a business in which it can employ its resources or make them available to another enterprise in exchange for some of their output. Only this latter group of productive exchanges are captured in the inter-sector real resource flows shown in Figure 1.1.

The difficulties involved in trying to exchange commodities in mutually rewarding ways are considerable, and are based on the economic concept of the *double coincidence of wants*. Certainly the time and effort which must be devoted in a barter economy to searching out other households with whom trades can be done are prohibitive. The problems multiply in the case of production. A household which provides labour inputs to a business will often have to take the outputs received in exchange and try to trade them for more desirable commodities. It is inevitable that pressure will grow to employ one or more widely circulating commodities as a standard unit of exchange, or numeraire, into which all commodities can be converted, in order to ease the search and divisibility problems which pure barter necessarily entails. The numeraire must be widely accepted as a means of settling obligations, and this means it must be in fairly fixed supply and homogeneous in quality if confidence is to be maintained in its exchange value.

Precious metals are ideal numeraires in these respects. If uncertainties concerning the quality and quantity of the money commodities persist to a great degree then it is very likely that barter exchanges will continue alongside monetary ones. Money will be used to complete exchanges in those situations where the problems and costs of barter activity are so great as to outweigh the uncertainties involved in accepting money in settlement.

The outcome of introducing monetary exchanges into the system is to create monetary as well as real flows in our simple model of the economy. Households can exchange their goods for those of other households and settle the transactions in cash. Equally, businesses can buy inputs from other businesses in exchange for cash. Although such intra-sector flows are important, ultimately all inputs come from the household sector and final outputs are consumed by households. These inter-sector real flows are settled in a monetary economy by using money. Thus monetary flows have to be included along with the real ones, and these monetary flows are shown as inter-sector income and payment paths in Figure 1.1.

In the case of simple, instantaneous-production enterprises there are no difficulties. The worker provides labour power and in return is paid in cash directly out of the revenues from (instantaneously) selling the firm's output. These wages can be exchanged for real goods and services immediately, if desired. Similarly, owners of land receive rents from farmers and other business users as and when it is used.

However, in a more sophisticated, highly productive economy, exchanges of money and goods will take place on a large scale. In particular, difficulties arise when the firm has to *invest* in order to produce output. Production is a continual process taking place over multiple time periods, so considerable amounts of time may elapse between the time of buying or hiring inputs and when revenues flow in. Examples of investment are to be found in agriculture where land has to be ploughed and sown months before harvest. Similarly in mining, tunnels are dug with tools and machines which were previously created by the prior investment of labour and other resources, while the ore is quarried and sold to other firms for further processing. In industry generally, machinery and materials have to be bought weeks or months before goods are manufactured and sold. Stated simply, investment involves waiting.

Fortunately, the preferred consumption pattern across individuals varies, and all that is required is a sufficient number of wealthy individuals who are willing and able to wait for the return on their investment. The providers of real inputs (labour, land and raw materials) who are unable or unwilling to wait for payment are paid out of capital funds provided by the wealthy individuals for whom waiting does not pose a problem. These capitalists or entrepreneurs take a share of the ultimate sale-proceeds because they are wealthy enough to be able to defer consumption since they have more than they need, and are willing to bear the risks involved in doing so. But they require a profit in return.

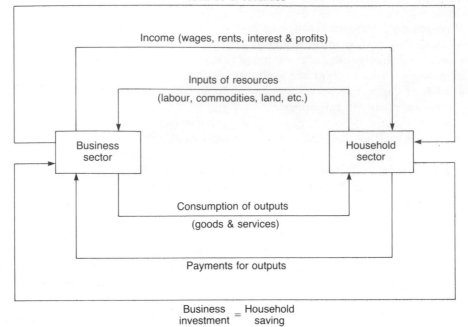

Figure 1.2 Flows in a simple two-sector economy, including investment.

The greater the scale of investment required, the fewer the number of individuals able to act independently as entrepreneurs. The greater the time between commitment of investment funds and the benefit gained, the greater the risks involved. Large-scale projects and the riskiness of investment require that capital is pooled. Sole proprietorships give way to partnerships, and partnerships to joint ventures, cooperatives and other forms of business organisation. The financing process has clearly become more complex.

Our simple model is now insufficient and has to be augmented by the addition of a capital market to facilitate investment. The savings of households are made available (lent) to the business sector and used to finance investment. In exchange for these funds, the business sector issues securities, which are a financial claim on future benefits. These can take two basic forms: debt, accompanied by a promise to make regular interest payments and to repay the principal of the loan; or equity, associated with a claim to a share of the after-interest profits and ultimately the resources of the business after loans have been paid off if the enterprise ceases to trade.

Figure 1.2 adds the necessary investment loop to our model, and illustrates the economy as consisting of three connected subsystems. First, there is the real subsystem representing the flows of commodities between sectors; secondly, the monetary (or factor payment) subsystem charting the flows of incomes and payments for commodities; and thirdly, the investment subsystem which allows for the process of multi-period production. The financial system reconciles the monetary and investment subsystems, through a collection of institutions and markets, and this is broadly the topic of this book.

1.3 Balancing financial claims

The previous section focused on production in the real sector and the short-term exchange of financial claims in the financial sector. We then extended this to cover multiple time periods and included investment and saving as well. Another way of looking at a financial system is in terms of the quantities and types of individual financial claims in existence at a single point in time. Clearly these two approaches are directly related, since a cash flow over time measures the change in the stock of claims between the beginning and the end of the period, while properly separating the stocks and flows in the process.

A balance sheet is a useful means of depicting both assets and claims on assets. The balance sheet may be constructed for a household, a company or indeed any institution in the economy. Generally, the term *entity* is used to refer to any unit which owns or issues claims on any asset. If the asset under the control of an entity can be defined, measured and somehow expressed in terms of money in a consistent way, these money values can be added together to yield a measure of the wealth of the entity.[1] It is convenient for our purposes to distinguish here between real assets (RA) and financial assets (FA); the total worth of the entity is therefore the sum of both kinds of assets:

$$RA + FA$$

There will certainly be claims against this wealth. The entity may owe money to others, i.e. it has financial liabilities (FL). The balance belongs to the owner of the entity and is denoted as net worth (NW). These relationships can be combined to form the following balance sheet equation:

$$NW + FL = RA + FA \tag{1.1}$$

or as

$$NW = (RA + FA) - FL \tag{1.2}$$

A balance sheet is simply a financial statement on which assets are shown on one side and financial claims on the other, with the two sides totalling to the same amount in accordance with the balance sheet equation.

In principle, every entity in the country could be instructed to draw up a balance sheet at a specified date, say at the end of the calendar year (31 December) or at the end of the tax year (5 April). In practice, only the government and corporate businesses normally do so, while households and many small or

Table 1.1 Personal sector assets and liabilities, 1987–92 (£bn)

	1987	1992	Annual % change over 5 years
Tangible assets	846.7	1,213.2	8.7
Intangible non-financial assets	131.0	178.2	5.3
Financial assets	831.1	1,393.0	13.5
Financial liabilities	283.2	487.9	14.5
Net financial wealth	547.9	905.1	13.0
Net total wealth	1,525.6	2,296.5	10.1

Source: CSO, *The Blue Book*, UK National Accounts, Table 12.2, 1989, 1993.

unincorporated businesses do not. However, if all economic entities did submit a balance sheet it would theoretically be possible to add together reported assets and claims from the millions of households and thousands of businesses to obtain sector-level balance sheets. The absence of balance sheet data for households makes the exercise a much more difficult undertaking in practice, although government statistical departments do produce this information for each sector at intervals.[2]

The sector balance sheet data collected by the government Central Statistical Office currently available reveal a number of interesting facets of the British financial system. The household sector is the ultimate owner of all private wealth; more interesting is the fact that it holds over half of all its wealth in the form of financial assets held directly or indirectly, through their ownership of equity claims. Also, financial assets are greatly in excess of liabilities, making the household sector a net provider of funds to other sectors. Table 1.1 shows the components of personal sector wealth in 1987 and in 1992.

It is important to recognise when comparing changes in levels of wealth, that sometimes this is the result of the creation of new wealth, and sometimes simply a reflection of price changes. Certainly during the twelve-year period 1975 to 1987, when personal sector wealth rose by over £1,200 billion, a large proportion of this was due to price changes of tangible assets, in particular, houses. This means that the amount of new assets was small compared with the growth in net worth. The effects of price changes on the valuation of assets will be discussed in the section on inflation in Chapter 4.

A comparison of the nature of wealth in the various sectors is worth noting. Personal sector wealth is largely comprised of houses and the savings referred to above. Consumer durables such as cars are too difficult to measure and therefore not included as part of tangible assets, although they may be significant.

Table 1.2 Personal sector balance sheet, 1992 (£bn)

Financial liabilities		Financial assets	
Net wealth	2,296.5	Tangible assets	1,213.2
Financial liabilities	487.9	Intangible assets	178.2
		Financial assets	1,393.0
	2,784.4		2,784.4

Source: CSO, *The Blue Book*, UK National Accounts, Table 12.2, 1993.

Table 1.3 Industrial and commercial sector balance sheet, 1992 (£bn)

Financial liabilities		Financial assets	
Net wealth	107.6	Tangible assets	737.5
Financial liabilities	1,103.1	Intangible assets	473.2
	1,210.7		1,210.7

Source: CSO, *The Blue Book*, UK National Accounts, Table 12.3, 1993.

The data in Table 1.1 can also be restated and presented in conventional balance sheet format, shown as Table 1.2. This is done in order for it to be comparable with the other sectoral balance sheets, which we will examine now. In contrast, Table 1.3 shows that assets in the business sector are generally property and plant and machinery used in production, and inventories of both raw materials and finished goods. Liabilities represent net wealth and debt of various kinds. This sector has borrowing greatly in excess of financial assets and thus are net borrowers.

The assets of the monetary and financial sectors are shown in Tables 1.4 and 1.5. Common between them are their high financial assets and liabilities, and low net wealth. This is not surprising given that their role is to assist in the flow of funds between sectors. Also, it is to be expected that the sectors' financial assets are approximately equal to their financial liabilities, since financial institutions exist to channel funds from savers to lenders by issuing securities and acquiring financial assets with the proceeds.

The real assets of the financial sector arise largely from property, and account for the vast branch networks of the retail banks and building societies. The rationalisation of some of the banks will close a few of the branch offices, but these will be replaced with technology, so the balance sheet may not change a great deal.

Table 1.4 Monetary sector balance sheet, 1992 (£bn)

Financial liabilities		Financial assets	
Net wealth	33.8	Tangible assets	17.2
Financial liabilities	1,362.1	Financial assets	1,378.7
	1,395.9		1,395.9

Source: CSO, *The Blue Book*, UK National Accounts, Table 12.5, 1993.

Table 1.5 Financial companies and institutions balance sheet, 1992 (£bn)

Financial liabilities		Financial assets	
Net wealth	35.5	Tangible assets	93.5
Financial liabilities	2,710.8	Financial assets	2,652.8
	2,746.3		2,746.3

Source: CSO, *The Blue Book*, UK National Accounts, Table 12.4, 1993.

Table 1.6 Public sector balance sheet, 1992 (£bn)

Financial liabilities		Financial assets	
Net wealth	199.7	Tangible assets	373.8
Financial liabilities	365.0	Financial assets	190.9
	564.7		564.7

Source: CSO, *The Blue Book*, UK National Accounts, Table 12.12, 1993.

Finally the public sector is listed in Table 1.6. The public sector is a combination of public corporations, local and central government which has in total decreased its share of the aggregate national wealth. This is due both to the privatisation of the public utilities and other corporations and the policy of selling public sector housing during recent years, which have affected central and local government respectively. We will return to this topic briefly in Chapter 4.

1.4 The nature of money and credit

Money is the most basic financial claim, the one in which all others are usually denominated. Changes in the supply of and demand for money have immediate impacts on the prices of other financial claims. Money can be thought of as serving three functions:

- As a unit of account, both for the present and over time.
- As a store of value.
- As a means of payment.

In developed market economies, money is used in all three ways, and we shall now consider these in more detail.

A unit of account

The role of money as a unit of account must be regarded as the most fundamental. Indeed, it is hard to see how any but the most simple of societies could do without unit-of-account money. This function is central to quantification and measurement in economic affairs. Even in a barter economy it is highly convenient to identify at least one commodity which can be used in the calculation of exchange values. The idea of money as a unit of account over time serves as a standard of deferred payment, and may be useful in providing information about the future repayment of a loan.

Although it is convenient to have a commodity which can serve as a means of payment, it is possible to use money passively as a unit of account without using it to settle transactions. In the early days of the colonisation of America and Australia merchants would often buy the produce of farmers at agreed money prices and settle the debt not in cash but by providing goods of equivalent money value. If the goods provided were not equal to the monetary value of those purchased, the balance would be carried over either as a trading balance or deposit or as an overdraft with the merchant. The problem was not generally the lack of a money commodity – in practice, several different currencies were often employed – but the lack of an adequate supply of notes and coins in circulation. However, this is no longer a barrier to transactions. The only difficulty now is if there is rapid devaluation of the currency and it does not hold its value.

A store of value

Money is also important as a store of value. The availability of a convenient store of value serves to promote saving. Households save in order to enhance future consumption and achieve this by forgoing current spending for future spending. If money is not a good store of value, for example if the currency is likely to be devalued or if inflation is expected in the future, then they must acquire real goods now and exchange them for cash for purchases in the future. But this incurs transaction costs, both in storage and search costs for a buyer in the future, and the possibility of spoilage or depreciation of the non-money asset. The more stable the purchasing power of money, the lower are the risks of saving.

A means of payment

The importance of money in the economy as defined in the previous discussion has changed dramatically in recent years. The function of money as a unit of account is often simply a proxy valuation process based on comparable assets, or simply on a judgement if the asset is not a tangible one, or where no market prices exist. The use of money, in the form of cash, as a means of payment has decreased considerably since the widespread use of credit and debit cards for purchases, while household expenses can usually be met directly by standing arrangements with banks and building societies. The use of money as a store of value is still valid, and is flexible. This can be arranged to allow for future consumption if the timing is known and to be more easily converted into purchasing power if future requirements are uncertain.

1.5 Monetary aggregates

Our discussion of the changing use of money in the economy does not cause any theoretical conflicts, since money can be defined in a number of ways. These definitions are known as monetary aggregates, and formally range from M0 to M5. In practice, M0 and M4 are those most commonly reported by the Bank of England currently, and are indicators of general economic conditions as well as measuring the effectiveness of monetary policy.

Figure 1.3 illustrates the relationship between the various definitions of money. M0 is the wide monetary base consisting of notes and coins in public circulation, money held in banks' tills and the balances held in their accounts at the Bank of England. M1 is defined as notes and coins in circulation with the public, plus current account bank balances in sterling held by UK residents. M2 is the measure of narrow money, that is money that can be readily used for transactions purposes. However, the constituents of M2 now include funds held by building societies and banks since both offer interest on demand accounts. This financial innovation, plus the change of Abbey National plc from building society to bank status in 1989 involving the switch of more than £32 billion, has resulted in a restructuring of the definition of M2.

Other definitions involve time deposits which are known as *near money*. M3, which was known as sterling M3, includes these. Thus M3 is M1 plus sterling time deposits and certificates of deposit of the private sector and the deposits of public sector entities such as local authorities. M4 is a measure of broad money, and includes all of the previous definitions, plus time deposits, investment accounts and various wholesale funds. In many of its published reports and analyses, the Bank of England separates M4 into wholesale and retail, as there are significant differences in the behaviour of the sectors.

One final monetary definition we should note is M3H. This was introduced in December 1992, and includes foreign currency deposits held by UK residents and

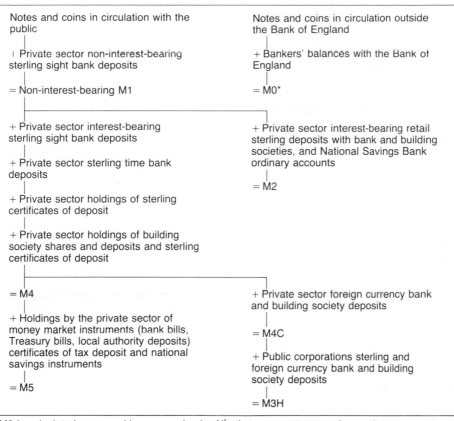

Notes and coins in circulation with the
public
|
+ Private sector non-interest-bearing
sterling sight bank deposits
|
= Non-interest-bearing M1
|
+ Private sector interest-bearing
sterling sight bank deposits
|
+ Private sector sterling time bank
deposits
|
+ Private sector holdings of sterling
certificates of deposit
|
+ Private sector holdings of building
society shares and deposits and sterling
certificates of deposit
|
= M4
|
+ Holdings by the private sector of
money market instruments (bank bills,
Treasury bills, local authority deposits)
certificates of tax deposit and national
savings instruments
|
= M5

Notes and coins in circulation outside
the Bank of England
|
+ Bankers' balances with the Bank of
England
|
= M0*
|
+ Private sector interest-bearing retail
sterling deposits with bank and building
societies, and National Savings Bank
ordinary accounts
|
= M2

+ Private sector foreign currency bank
and building society deposits
|
= M4C
|
+ Public corporations sterling and
foreign currency bank and building
society deposits
|
= M3H

*M0 is calculated on a weekly average basis. All other aggregates are observations at month end.
Note: (Source: *Bank of England Quarterly Bulletin*, February 1992, vol. 32, no. 1).

Figure 1.3 Relationships between the components of monetary aggregates.

public corporations in UK institutions. The motive for this format was to provide
a broad monetary aggregate similar to that used by other member states of the
European Union, and a harmonisation of reporting procedures is clearly preferable
to individual, and possibly non-comparable, definitions.

Although it is possible to be precise about the functions of money, it is far from
clear in practice which assets should be included in the definition of money.
There are a large number of assets which fulfil some but not all of the functions of
money. Examples include land, antiques and old paintings which can serve as
stores of value but are not means of exchange; food stamps and welfare vouchers
and other tokens which can be used as a means of exchange, and even as stores of
value, but are not units of account; and bank deposits and short-term money
instruments which are not media of exchange but can easily be turned into cash.

Table 1.7 Money definitions in the UK. Amounts outstanding (£m), March 1994

M0	(1) Notes and coin in circulation outside Bank of England	20,724
	(2) Banker's operational deposits with Bank of England	82
	(1 + 2) Wide Monetary Base	20,806
M4	(3) Cash and retail deposits in banks and building societies	399,996
	(4) Wholesale deposits in banks and building societies	154,305
	(3 + 4) Broad Money Aggregate	554,301
M3H	M4 + UK foreign currency deposits by UK residents (EU measure)	620,794

Notes: Seasonally adjusted data. M0 is calculated on a weekly averaged basis. All other aggregates at the end of each month.

Source: Bank of England Quarterly Bulletin, vol. 34, no. 3, Tables 2 and 6.2, 1994.

An indication of the relative volume of funds involved in measures of liquid and illiquid money is given in Table 1.7. In the standard definitions of money such as M0 and M4, the criteria of inclusion are the speed and ease of conversion of the asset into currency in the form of notes and coins, that is, its liquidity. All other assets vary in the degree of their liquidity. Financial claims are usually more liquid than non-financial assets, but there are many exceptions. Shares in private companies, for example, are less readily turned into cash than are precious metals, or even many property assets. It is helpful for some purposes to array assets along a liquidity spectrum, with notes and current account balances at the most liquid end, through to specialised kinds of business equipment for which there is a very limited market, at the other.

The borrowing and lending process can be thought of in terms of individuals and organisations varying their liquidity positions. Lending involves the surrendering of a liquid asset in exchange for a less liquid one. Since money can be used to buy an enormous range of goods and services whilst a promise to pay money in the future may not be acceptable to the existing owners of those goods and services, giving up liquidity implies a loss of flexibility. This sacrifice on the part of the lender is usually recompensed by a promise from the borrower to return a greater quantity of money in the future than was lent initially. Thus there is a price associated with loanable funds, known as the rate of interest.

The significance of the monetary system in general, and interest rates in particular, on the workings of the financial system is discussed further in Chapter 4. A technical appendix on compound interest is at the end of Chapter 5.

1.6 The role of government

In this introductory chapter it is important not to neglect the role of government in the operation of the financial system, although the impact of particular policies will be discussed in more detail in later chapters. However, there are three major areas of responsibility associated with government: regulation and supervision; a system of taxation; and monetary and fiscal policy. We shall comment on these briefly now, and return to them again.

Regulation and supervision

In the UK, government has authorised the financial markets and institutions to be self-regulating in many areas of their operations. The crucial aspect for any government is to maintain the public's confidence in the soundness and probity of the financial system.

Regulation of the financial system is based on a series of Acts of Parliament and administrative arrangements, whereas supervision is market-specific and undertaken directly by institutions such as the Bank of England, the Department of Trade and Industry, the Securities and Investment Board, the Occupational Pensions Board, and the Registrar of Friendly Societies.

European Union directives on a number of issues relevant to the financial system are increasingly important to the British markets and institutions, since a single market does require some harmonisation of standards and practices. Similarly, the emerging market economics in Central and Eastern Europe and elsewhere are keen to develop regulatory structures which harmonise with the established systems in the West, when they liberalise their own financial systems. The international central banks are one group seeking to reconcile regulation and supervisory control.

It should be recognised that regulation has been instrumental in shaping the financial system, but not always in the ways intended by the regulators. Perhaps the most striking example of the influence of regulation is provided by the number of new financial instruments which were introduced, where the incentive to innovate is based on the desire to evade newly imposed restrictions. It has been suggested that innovation of this kind has made the financial markets more unstable and prone to volatility.

Taxation

The UK taxation system has had a marked influence on the country's patterns of savings and investment over the years. The tax rules are not neutral, and they have stimulated the flow of savings into certain forms of investment at the expense of others. Investments which seem to be of comparable attractiveness on a pre-tax basis can look very different when tax is taken into account. The financial innovation briefly discussed above has also been a response to the tax position of investors.

Monetary and fiscal policy

Government attempts to influence the behaviour of the economy have direct effects on the financial system. A distinction can be drawn between monetary policy and fiscal policy. Monetary policy is concerned with controlling the money supply, whereas fiscal policy is concerned with the aggregate levels of expenditures and taxes. The significance of government macroeconomic policies for the financial markets and institutions is discussed further in Chapter 4.

1.7 Summary

The simple model of the economy with no government or international trade is very limited. The various functions and definitions of money allow the disaggregation of financial flows between sectors and the analysis of the use of funds. Government has an important role to play in creating a formal structure in which the financial system is managed.

Notes

1. There are a number of ways to value real assets. These include: 1. the estimated amount raised if it were sold; 2. the original purchase price; 3. the current purchase price, a combination of the above, and several others. This is an important issue, but outside the scope of this book.
2. An early attempt at measuring the wealth of the country was ordered by William the Conqueror in 1086. The results of this census were published in the Domesday Book and provided a basis for assessing tax liability.

Further reading

Bryant, C. (1987), 'National and sector balance sheets 1957–85', *Economic Trends*, no. 403, May, pp. 92–119.
Clarke, M. (1986), *Regulating the City*, Open University Press.

Useful introductions to the City are:
Coakley, J. and L. Harris (1983), *The City of Capital*, Blackwell.
McCrae, H. and F. Cairncross (1984), *Capital City*, 2nd edn, Eyre Methuen.

For a general introduction to economics:
Begg, D., Fischer, S. and R. Dornbusch (1994), *Economics*, 4th edn, McGraw-Hill. Chapter 23 gives considerable detail on the role of money in the economy.

Statistical Sources
The sources of data used are quoted at the foot of each table. However, useful information about statistical publications can be found in *Government Statistics. A Brief Guide to Sources*, CSO Press and Information Service, Great George Street, London SW1P 3AQ. This is a free booklet listing the most important official publications.

Publications from HMSO Books, PO Box 276, London SW8 5DT:

Guide to Official Statistics. Now in the 5th edition, this lists all official government statistics.

Financial Statistics. Monthly publication, with five years' historical data.

National Income and Expenditure. Annual publication, with ten years' historical data (*The Blue Book*).

UK Balance of Payments. Annual publication, with ten years' historical data (*The Pink Book*).

Questions

1.1 What is the relationship between saving and investment, on the one hand, and lending and borrowing, on the other?

1.2 In what ways are financial claims like other assets, and in what ways are they different?

1.3 What is a balance sheet? What can you learn about inter-sector financial relationships from sector balance sheets?

1.4 Try to recall the main monetary transactions you have been involved in during the past month. Describe the steps you would have had to take if the economy was a barter-based (rather than monetary) one.

1.5 Describe the three main functions of money. Discuss how well or badly each of the following assets would serve as a form of money:

(a) cigarettes

(b) cattle

(c) jewellery

(d) IOUs issued by a major company.

1.6 Explain the reasons why an increasing share of the savings of the household sector in the UK is being channelled through financial intermediaries.

CHAPTER 2

Flow of funds in the economy

2.1 Introduction

This chapter is intended to serve two separate but interrelated ends. The first is to explain simply the logic of funds flow analysis. The second is to present quantitative data about the savings–investment process and show how the official financial statistics are put together to enable readers to make sensible use of these sources in their own work.

2.2 Measurement and analysis of the flow of funds

The flow of funds accounts are of recent origin. The United States were the first to develop this form of financial statistics in the early 1950s, an example followed subsequently by many other countries. The impetus in the UK was provided by the Radcliffe Committee in 1959, and flow of funds accounts at the sector level have been published on a quarterly basis in the *Bank of England Quarterly Bulletin* since September 1963.

The flow of funds accounts are generally regarded as an integral part of the national income and expenditure accounts. Like the national accounts, the flow of funds analysis is presented for a few, highly aggregated sectors. The choice of sectors greatly affects the use that can be made of the analysis because any intra-sector flows are generally omitted and only those transactions which pass across sectoral boundaries are presented. The four main categories employed in the national income and expenditure accounts are similar to those discussed in Chapter 1, although for these purposes the business and financial sectors are included together. However, as so much financial business is done through specialised financial intermediaries, these institutions are distinguished from the company sector in the flow of funds accounts to form two sectors of their own: the *monetary sector*, comprising largely of UK banks, and the *other financial institutions sector*. In addition, the overseas sector is added.

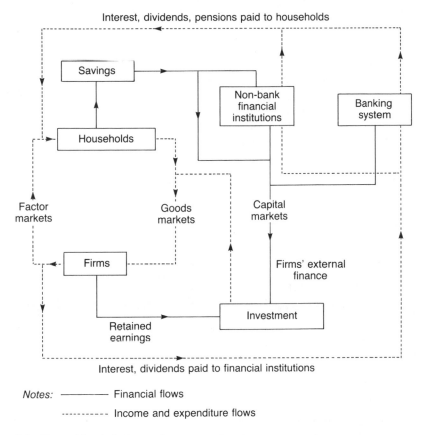

Figure 2.1 Flow of funds between the personal and company sectors.

Thus in the flow of funds analysis, the sectors are defined as follows:

- The personal sector consisting not only of households but, due to the limitations of the statistics, including also unincorporated businesses and charities.
- The company sector covering industrial and commercial companies, the banks and other financial institutions.
- The public sector consisting of public corporations, local and central government.
- The overseas sector comprising the imports, exports and financial transactions with foreigners.

Figure 2.1 illustrates the direction of flows between the personal and company sectors. This has its origins in the simple flows between sectors represented in Figures 1.1 and 1.2 in the last chapter, now shown on the left of the figure.

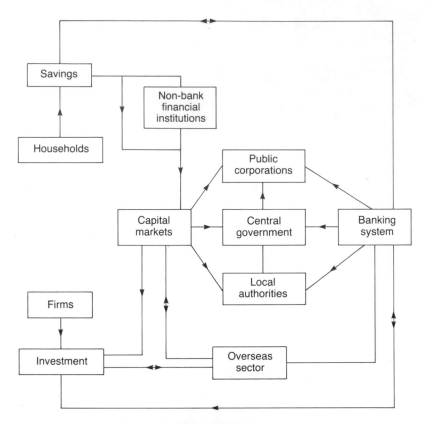

Figure 2.2   Flow of funds between the personal, company, public and international sectors.

However more detail about the bank and non-bank institutions, as well as the capital markets, is also included.

Finally, when we wish to include the public and overseas sectors as well, the interconnections are becoming fairly complex. In Figure 2.2, we have simplified the original two sectors, and the factor and goods markets associated with them, in order to add local and central government and the international sector. The analysis of inter-sectoral capital flows is discussed below, while the mechanisms that facilitate these flows, and the role played by the financial sector in this distribution of funds, is fully addressed in Chapter 3.

Flow of funds accounting provides a means of tracing the financial transactions of the different sectors, to determine the source of the cash flows and the uses to which it is put. It tracks financial transactions by recording the receipts that each sector obtains from the other sectors and the payments it makes to them. This exercise is done routinely in companies, but here it is undertaken at a national level and includes all sectors. The information gained from each sector is integrated to provide a flow of funds matrix for the economy as a whole.

A sector-specific flow of funds statement could be constructed in a variety of ways, depending on the definition of funds chosen for the analysis. The most straightforward conceptual approach uses cash only, meaning cash-in-hand plus bank balances. In this case, a cash flow statement would be prepared for each sector, recording the cash receipts from, and payments to, other sectors. Borrowing would be recorded as a financial source and lending as a financial use of funds.

Using a much broader definition, funds could mean net assets. Following the analysis in Chapter 1, net assets are the excess of the value of all assets owned over liabilities outstanding and are equal to the net worth (NW) of the sector. Any transaction that increases net worth is a source of funds, and anything that decreases it is a use of funds. Sources of net worth are income, and in the case of the business sectors, new inputs of equity finance. Uses of net worth follow from the payment of taxes, dividends and other transfer payments, and from consumption. Financial transactions concerned with the acquisition of financial assets or the incurring of financial liabilities are excluded because they have no impact on net worth. This concept of funds provides the basis of the national income and expenditure accounts.

The funds concept employed in practice is called net financial assets, and is identical to that used in Chapter 1. Net financial assets (NFA) are equal to money and other financial assets (FA) less financial liabilities (FL). Net financial assets are wider in scope than cash but narrower than net worth. They serve to place primary emphasis on the workings of the financial sector of the economy.

The connection between the flow of funds accounts and the national income accounts can best be appreciated in terms of the sector balance sheet equation (1.1) in Chapter 1. At a single point in time, the stock of assets under the sector's control consists of real assets (RA) and financial assets (FA) and is exactly equal to the financial liabilities (FL) and net worth (NW).

$$RA + FA = NW + FL \tag{2.1}$$

Since net worth is the residual, it can be written as such

$$NW = RA + (FA - FL) = RA + NFA \tag{2.2}$$

Net worth can increase from one period to the next in two ways. First, the sector can save some of its income (Y), that is, there can be an excess of income over consumption (C). Secondly, the sector could have received dividends or other transfer payments from other sectors (T), where transfer payments consist of gifts and other payments made without any corresponding product or service being received. Or both of these may occur, as in

$$\Delta NW = (Y - C) + T \tag{2.3}$$

where Δ implies the change from the previous time period $(t - 1)$ to the present (t).

Increases in real assets (ΔRA) are described as real investment or simply as investment (I). In the absence of investment to replace used-up capital, the value of the stock of real assets will decline over the expected life of the asset, and certain amounts of investment are necessary simply to maintain the value of the asset. Investment in excess of that required for replacement purposes is called net investment. Replacement and net investment taken together are called gross investment, which is the meaning of the term as used here.

We are now in a position to explain the change in balance sheet values during an accounting period. Subtracting the earlier balance sheet from the later one we get

$$\Delta NW = \Delta RA + \Delta NFA$$
$$= I + \Delta NFA \tag{2.4}$$

By substituting the expression for ΔNW, in both (2.3) and (2.4), we have

$$(Y - C) + T = I + \Delta NFA$$

and rearranging, the flow of funds (ΔNFA) is equal to

$$\Delta NFA = (Y - C) - I + T \tag{2.5}$$

This can be expressed clearly in words:

$$\text{lending} - \text{borrowing} = \text{saving} - \text{investment} + \text{transfers}$$

The reconciliation between the sector flow of funds and sector income accounts is now complete. The real volumes of savings and investment, obtained from the income and expenditure accounts, serve as the starting-point for the flow of funds analysis.

The reconciliation is performed at an aggregate level by collecting the individual sector statements into a flow of funds matrix for the economy as a whole. Assuming a single case with three domestic sectors:

- the personal sector
- the company sector
- the public sector

and a sector representing the rest of the world:

- the overseas sector.

Then, let Y_1 be the factor incomes earned by individuals (wages and salaries, rent, etc.), Y_2 company profits, and Y_3 the profits of public corporations, C_1 be consumers' expenditures and C_3, government expenditures on goods and services; I_1, I_2 and I_3 are investment expenditures of the three sectors; transfer payments, in the form of interest, dividends, grants and taxes between sectors are denoted T_1, T_2, T_3, and T_4. Finally X and M are the aggregate exports and imports, respectively.

The results are given in the first half of Table 2.1. The inter-sector transfers sum to zero, as logically they must. Similarly, the sum of the financial surplus and

Table 2.1 Flow of funds matrix for the whole economy

	Personal sector	Company sector	Public sector	Overseas sector	Total
Income	Y_1	Y_2	Y_3	$-X+M$	$Y-X+M$
Transfers (net)	$+T_1$	$+T_2$	$+T_3$	$+T_4$	0
Consumption	$-C_1$		$-C_3$		$-C$
Investment	$-I_1$	$-I_2$	$-I_3$		$-I$
Financial surplus/deficit	ΔNFA_1	ΔNFA_2	ΔNFA_3	ΔNFA_4	0
Notes and coin	ΔMA_1	ΔMA_2	ΔMA_3	ΔMA_4	0
Treasury securities	ΔTA_1	ΔTA_2	ΔTL_3	ΔTA_4	0
Company securities	ΔCA_1	ΔCL_2	ΔCA_3	ΔCA_4	0
Totals	ΔNFA_1	ΔNFA_2	ΔNFA_3	ΔNFA_4	0

deficits is also zero, since the financial liabilities of one sector must be the financial assets of another.

The final column of Table 2.1 can be rearranged into the conventional national accounting identity:

$$Y = C + I + X - M \tag{2.6}$$

This expression states that national income is equal to domestic consumption and investment plus the balance of foreign trade.

The task that remains in constructing a sector sources and uses of funds statement is to analyse the changes in financial assets and liabilities which go to make up the financial surplus or deficit for the period. Consider again the simple four-sector case. Suppose both the public and the company sectors issue financial claims. The change in government liabilities consists of treasury securities, such as government bonds (ΔTL_3) and money, i.e. notes and coin. Company securities of all kinds are not differentiated, and simply denoted as ΔCL_2. These changes in liabilities have their counterbalancing changes in assets, ΔTA, ΔMA and ΔCA and are shown in the lower half of Table 2.1.

The changes in holdings of a particular kind of financial asset or liability sum to zero, as can be seen by reading across each row. For a particular sector, the changes in net financial assets can be decomposed into the changes in its holdings of the financial assets of other sectors and in the financial claims it issues.

The introduction of the financial sectors into the analysis is consistent with the previous methodology.

2.3 **Flow of funds matrix**

The Bank of England and the Central Statistical Office (CSO) publish a great deal of flow of funds data. Included in this is the all-sectors flow of funds matrix, which is more formally called the financial transactions matrix, and is reported annually in the *Bank of England Quarterly Bulletin*, in the article on sector financing.

The financial transactions matrix for 1992 is presented in Table 2.2. Although the table is larger and more complex than the hypothetical one shown in Table 2.1, the structure is the same. There are five sectors but, owing to data inadequacies, the monetary sector and other financial institutions are merged together in the top part of the table. The public sector is divided into central government, local authorities and public corporations, as in the first three columns. The top and bottom parts of the table reconcile in the sense that the numbers in line 5 are equal to the sum of lines 39 and 40. The totals of each of the first five lines correspond to those in the national income statistics prepared by the CSO. Each line in the financial assets and liabilities part of the matrix, lines 6 to 38, should sum to zero. However, this is not always the case.

There are many deficiencies in the data used to compile the national income and flow of funds accounts. Not all bookkeeping systems contain complete records of all financial transactions, and government does not have access to all those that do. Instead, a variety of sources of greatly differing coverage and quality are used to compile the most complete set of statistics possible. The result is a number of gaps and errors.

The column named *residual error* and the *balancing item* row (40) in Table 2.2 are the direct consequences of these data deficiencies. The figure for national income should be equal to that for national expenditure but, in practice, the two do not match. The unexplained difference constitutes the residual error.

The differences between the sector surpluses and deficits and the corresponding identified financial transactions are shown as balancing items for the various sectors. The residual error is the sum of these, and arises largely from the imprecise measurement of the national income and expenditure accounts. It is hoped that the financial transactions are more reliable than the sizes of the balancing items seem to warrant. For every financial asset there is a financial liability elsewhere and, where the data sources provide different numbers, those considered most reliable are used. It is therefore generally safer to use the figures for financial transactions, line 39, than those for financial surplus/deficit, line 5, as a measure of net borrowing or lending for a particular sector.

An examination of the financial assets and liabilities section reveals a bewilder-ing variety of financial claims being traded in the markets. The lines are grouped in order of the sector which issued the financial claims: the public sector, consisting of the various instruments issued by the central government and the securities of local authorities and public corporations; the borrowings and lending of the monetary sector, that is, banks and other financial institutions; the liabilities of the company sector; the private sector, limited to the net savings channelled into life assurance and pension funds plus miscellaneous domestic instruments; and investment flows into and out of the country. The final line (line 38), labelled accruals adjustment is a 'pseudo security' in the sense that it represents outstanding but not yet invoiced liabilities to income tax, interest, etc., rather than financial claims issued by a particular sector.

The table can be used to glean a number of interesting details about the flow of funds in 1992, shown in line 39:

1. The public sector is the biggest borrower, with a deficit of £38.7 billion to finance.
2. The corporate sector is traditionally a net borrower, and continued to be so in 1992, to the extent of nearly £15 billion.
3. The personal sector provided funds amounting to £34.7 billion for the year.
4. The overseas sector, on the other hand, is a net lender.

It is helpful to examine each column in turn in order to ascertain the borrowing and lending profiles of the sectors. A large part of the public sector deficit is accounted for by the issuance of British government securities valuing £21 billion (line 8). This is generally a major item. The other major item is £10 billion used to purchase sterling with foreign currency (line 16). This is accounted for by the attempt on 16 September, Black Wednesday, to maintain the value of the pound prior to the UK leaving the Exchange Rate Mechanism of the European Monetary Union, which turned out to be unsuccessful.

Personal sector savings are invested in a variety of instruments most notably in the form of deposits in banks and building societies (lines 21–2) and in life assurance and pension funds (line 33). The personal sector borrowed £17.677 billion for house purchase (lines 27.1 and 27.2), with building societies taking the major share of the mortgage market.

The company sector withdrew £2.4 billion (lines 21.1–21.3) from the banks, offset by bank lending over £4 billion (lines 24.1 and 24.2). Issues of new securities were £10.5 billion (line 31). Outflows of company funds abroad were more or less exactly balanced by direct investment in the UK from abroad.

The overseas sector is a bit more complicated. In the year currently under consideration it is in surplus, but international flows are highly volatile from one year to the next and are responsive to interest and currency exchange rate differentials between countries.

It can be instructive to read across the rows as well as down the columns. Of the £21.4 billion increase in issues of British government securities (line 38), 76% was taken up by financial intermediaries.

A difficulty with a flow of funds matrix containing the amount of detail of Table 2.2 is that the level of detail may make analysis difficult. It is possible to simplify

Table 2.2 Flow of funds matrix, 1992

	Line	Public sector			Financial sector			Corporate sector	Personal sector	Overseas sector	Residual error
		Central government	Local authorities	Public corporations	Banks	Building societies	Other financial institutions	Industrial and commercial			
Capital Account											
Saving	1	-22,726	2,629	2,319		9,214		39,403	48,782	11,625	
Taxes on capital and capital transfers	2	-10,483	6,960	1,972		-100		-277	1,928		
Less:											
Gross fixed capital formation at home	3	7,104	5,439	4,291		4,869		48,565	21,018		
Increase in value of stocks and work in progress	4	-12		42				516	67		
Financial surplus +/deficit −	5	-40,301	4,150	-42		4,245		-9,955	29,625	11,625	-653
Changes in financial assets and liabilities											
Assets: increase + /decrease −											
Liabilities: increase − /decrease +											
Notes and coin	6	-1,400		-148	153	121	4	463	736	71	
Market Treasury bills	7	4,423	-5	20	-1,906	-986	-789	1	-758		
British government securities	8	-21,378	2	-24	1,059	994	14,148	-689	3,793	2,095	
National savings	9	-5,049	1	33	2	2	3	20	4,991		
Certificate of tax deposit	10	448		1	-97	1	2	-304	-51		
Net government indebtedness to Banking Department	11	235			-235						
Northern Ireland central government debt	12	34			2				-36		
Government liabilities under exchange cover scheme	13	28	-15	-27				14			
Other public sector financing:											
Non-marketable debt	14.1	-67									
Short-term assets	14.2		648	67							
Issue Department's transactions in commercial bills	15	4,469			-186	-686	55	-1,996	-13	-1,859	
Government foreign currency debt	16	-10,026			4,729		-428			4,935	
Other government overseas financing	17	93					362			-93	
Official reserves	18	-1,200								1,200	

Item	Line									
Local authority debt:										
Temporary	19.1		305	−46	−2	71	−975		−15	662
Foreign currency	19.2		74							−74
Sterling securities	19.3	−118	−5		−12	73				
Other sterling debt	19.4	−5,817	4,239	27	1,169	170	−23			
Public corporation debt:										
Foreign currency	20.1		514				−24			−514
Other	20.2	1,321	13	−1,283	−42				23	−8
Deposits with banks:										
Sterling sight	21.1	126	−56	−100	−3,925	620	1,343	−1,151	3,055	708
Sterling time	21.2	61	297	172	−4,173		−2,433	657	2,291	2,508
Foreign currency	21.3	57	21	19	−27,267		7,670	−1,862	147	21,215
Deposits with building societies	22			290	−14,415		1,467	235	10,642	1,781
Bank lending (excluding public sector):										
Foreign currency	24.1				12,965		1,600	1,197	346	−16,108
Sterling	24.2				7,621	−849	−287	3,031	−484	−9,032
Credit extended by retailers	25							146	−146	
Identified trade credit:										
Domestic	26.1			11			210	−221		−160
Import and export	26.2			29				131		
Loans for house purchase:										
Building societies	27.1		−310		13,869			−13,869	−13,869	
Other	27.2	−122	502	100	5,818		−1,574		−3,808	
Other public sector lending	28			21	−4	9	−909	−64	−177	−370
Other lending by financial institutions	29			3	91	895	−280	−640	539	
Unit trust units	30								280	
UK company securities	31	−7,560		−4	1,469	−1,125	5,194	−10,577	−1,206	13,609
Overseas securities	32				11,836		13,164	3,931	222	−29,153
Life assurance and pension funds	33	321					−24,569		24,248	
Misc. domestic instruments	34	151	−2	2	24	1,253	−19,795	−4,328	584	22,111
Direct and other investment abroad	35				260		234	5,857	32	−6,363
Overseas direct and other investment in United Kingdom	36				−282		−249	−5,295	−121	5,947
Misc. overseas instruments	37	188	102	−18	35	73	13,123	−4,262		−9186
Accruals adjustment	38	−1,063	−2,048	−645	9,477	339	65	893	1,759	2,682
Financial transactions	39	−41,343	3,280		−11,876	262	6,382	−14,827	34,733	8,943
Balancing item	40	1,042	870	604				4,872	−5,108	11,625
	39 + 40	−40,301	4,150	−41	9,477		6,382	−9,955	29,625	11,625
LINE	5	−40,301	4,150	−42	4,245		6,382	−9,955	29,625	

this by adding together some or all of the within sector lines. An example is provided in Table 2.3.

In this table each row represents the net increase or decrease in the financial claims issued by a sector and the net acquisitions or disposals of other sectors of the instruments created by that particular sector. A notable omission from the table is a line representing the claims issued by the personal sector, but these are hard to distinguish as purely emanating from individuals, and are unimportant to the overall result as the sector generally is overwhelmingly composed of surplus units.

A number of features of Table 2.3 warrant further comment. The extent of the public sector's reliance on financial intermediaries has already been noted above. The aggregated statistics reveal it to be almost as dependent on the personal sector, mainly because of the latter's acquisitions of government securities and national savings deposits. The monetary sector borrowed heavily from the financial and personal sectors, and a lesser amount from companies, while they lent overseas. Companies placed large amounts of money in financial institutions (monetary and other) and obtained funds from abroad.

A single funds flow statement affords limited opportunity to form views about the pattern of financing in Britain. Additional information must be used in conjunction with these data, particularly to examine trends over time, to gain any idea of the shape and direction of the flow of funds in the whole economy. The next section attempts to do this by identifying some of the clearer patterns of saving and investment in Britain.

2.4 Financing patterns in Britain

Financing patterns are a direct consequence of the trends in saving and investment. Therefore we will briefly consider these, by sector.

Saving

Average saving in the UK over the past decade is 15.5% of GDP, slightly lower than the investment average of 16.7, as shown in Table 2.4.

Disaggregate data give information on the relative share of saving and investment by sector. The personal and company sectors have traditionally generated practically all the UK's savings, but the trends in the savings of each, expressed as a percentage of GDP, follow different patterns. National saving is the total of all saving across sectors.

Personal saving is the difference between disposable income, that is, income after tax, and expenditures. In the corporate sector, saving is income after tax, interest and dividend payments, and is generally quite small, while in the public sector, it is the difference between receipts and expenditures.

Table 2.3 Financial transactions between sectors (£m)

Issuing sector	Matrix lines	Public sector	Monetary sector	Financial sector	Company sector	Personal sector	Overseas sector
Public	6–20	−29,613	4,642	12,083	−2,510	9,347	5,753
Monetary	21, 24	597	−14,779	7,664	1,872	5,355	−709
Financial (incl. building socs)	22, 25–30, 33–34	711	6,223	−43,848	−4,741	18,293	23,362
Company	31–32	−7,564	13,305	17,233	−6,646	−984	−15,344
Overseas	35–37	290	13	13,108	−3,700	−89	−9,622
Accruals	38	−3,129	73	404	893	1,759	2,682
Financial transactions	39	−38,708	9,477	6,644	−14,827	34,733	8,943

Source: Derived from Table 2.2.

Table 2.4 UK savings and investment levels

	% of Gross Domestic Product (market prices)			
	1981–5 average	1986–90 average	1991	1992
Saving	17.3	16.6	14.5	13.7
Investment	16.4	19.1	15.9	15.3

Source: Blue Book, Tables 3.5 and 3.6, 1993.

Saving in the personal sector is notoriously difficult to measure, simply because of the nature of expenditures. For example, does expenditure on home improvements constitute consumption, saving or investment? Another area of confusion is pension contributions, where payment into private schemes counts as saving and into government schemes as expenditure. However, it is clear that saving in the UK varies considerably depending on the general level of economic activity. This can be seen in Table 2.5 which gives levels of income and expenditure, and the saving ratio.

In the personal sector, all income is either consumed or saved. Some of income is used to pay taxes, including payments to central government and for the council tax (this latter charge replaced the community charge noted in Table 2.5). Added to income are any grants or transfers from government. Therefore the saving ratio is the proportion of disposable income remaining after these taxes and transfers have been included.

In the UK it does seem as though consumers are unwilling to adjust their expenditure, preferring to reduce savings when disposable income changes. It will be interesting to see the impact of higher levels of value-added tax, which is a tax on consumption rather than on earnings. This results in a rise in real prices on a selection of goods, introducing an inflationary effect on certain commodities.

Another important impact on the propensity to save is the changing demographic patterns across the country. The proportion of older people in the population is greater now than in the past, and the need to have funds for consumption beyond the usual expected working life is more commonplace. At the same time, uncertain employment and the associated disruption of workplace pension schemes, make saving patterns both more fragmented and necessary.

Price indices are published by sector to measure the change in the purchasing power of consumers, and a change in consumption patterns illustrates a desire on the part of households to maintain the purchasing power of their money balances in inflationary times. As the prices of goods and services increase with inflation it is necessary to hold larger amounts of money to pay for them. A fall in inflation could explain the subsequent decrease in the personal saving ratio. Inflation is part of the reason for the increased spending on life assurance and pensions, but it

Table 2.5 Personal income, expenditure and savings, 1987–92 (£bn)

	1987	1988	1989	1990	1991	1992
Wages	200.4	223.8	248.5	274.9	288.8	299.4
Employers' contributions	29.4	31.9	34.4	36.9	40.9	43.6
Current grants	52.5	54.1	56.8	62.0	72.1	82.6
Other personal income	78.9	92.9	103.9	115.7	116.6	124.7
Total personal income	361.2	402.7	443.6	489.5	517.9	550.3
less deductions:	43.4	48.3	53.6	61.5	63.6	64.9
Taxes on income	28.6	32.1	32.9	34.7	36.4	37.5
Social security contributions	2.1	2.4	2.4	2.6	2.6	2.7
Community charge			0.6	8.6	8.1	7.9
Personal disposable income (PDI)	287.1	319.9	354.1	382.1	407.2	437.3
Balance: personal saving	19.6	17.8	23.6	31.7	39.7	50.7
Saving ratio % (saving as % of PDI)	6.8	5.6	6.6	8.3	9.7	11.6

Source: Monthly Digest of Statistics, Table 1.5.

is not the major reason since there are considerable tax advantages to this form of investment. Equity has traditionally been regarded as a good hedge against inflation, but nevertheless the personal sector has been a steady net seller of company securities for over thirty years, perhaps reflecting the tax advantages accruing to investment in houses, life assurance, pensions and certain kinds of government securities, and the corresponding disincentive to investment in company securities which do not offer these tax benefits.

A final point about saving in the UK is the comparison between the saving ratio with that in other countries. From Table 2.6 we can see the propensity to save in the UK is less on average than other industrial countries, with the exception of the United States. Unfortunately, low savings tends to occur simultaneously with low investment, and both have proved detrimental to Britain's economic performance, whereas countries such as Japan, the Netherlands and Germany, which have a high level of savings, invested heavily.

Investment

To turn now to investment, this is divided into that required to replace used-up capital, that is, either depreciated or obsolete equipment and new additions to the capital stock. Growth is usually the result of new investment although replacement often implies a superior technology which may also contribute to growth. Total investment includes both new and replacement and is labelled in government statistics as *Gross Domestic Fixed Capital Formation*. This can take a

Table 2.6 Comparative savings levels in industrial countries, 1988–90

Country	% of Gross National Product		
	1988	1989	1990
France	21.25	22.01	21.63
Germany	25.28	26.68	27.54
Italy	21.68	21.24	20.82
Japan	32.88	33.13	33.90
Netherlands	24.39	25.55	26.33
Switzerland	28.33	29.52	29.62
United Kingdom	16.51	16.76	16.65
United States	14.93	15.35	14.51

Source: World Bank, *World Tables*, 1992.

Table 2.7 Investment by sector as a % of GDP, 1987–92

	1987	1988	1989	1990	1991	1992
Total investment	17.4	19.0	20.0	19.2	17.7	17.7
Private sector	14.3	16.3	16.8	16.0	14.6	14.3
Central government	1.8	1.6	2.0	2.4	2.3	2.6
Public corporations	1.1	1.1	1.1	1.0	0.8	0.9
Stocks and work in progress	0.3	1.0	0.6	−0.3	−0.8	−0.3

Source: Economic Trends, Tables 3 and 9, 1993.

number of forms, including domestic and business property, plant and machinery and other physical assets. Also included are stocks and work in progress. Table 2.7 shows the level of investment, at market prices, by sector, from 1987 to 1992.

The majority of investment is undertaken by the corporate sector. Investment by the private sector is mainly in property, and this was boosted by the sale of public sector housing during the 1980s. The same effect was seen as public corporations were privatised and undertook overdue investment programmes, and thereby enhanced the corporate sector figures. The remaining parts of the public sector undertake a limited amount of both saving and investment. Government expenditure is discussed in more detail in Chapter 4, but levels of investment vary depending on currency policy. Investment levels were high during the boom in the latter part of the 1980s, and then fell considerably, again during the economic recession. Equally, as we have seen, factors such as privatisation can move a large investment programme from one sector to another.

Undistributed income is an important source of company finance, but this has generally not been sufficient to fund the sector's investment in fixed assets and inventories. Investment has been a fairly stable proportion of total funds over the years, except that there was a marked decline in inventories during the recent recessions. The shortfall in finance has been made up largely by bank borrowing, particularly in recent years. Issues of ordinary shares and long-debt account for a very small proportion of new finance.

A great deal of attention has been given to the Public Sector Borrowing Requirement (PSBR) in discussions about the management of the economy in recent years. It can be thought of as a measure of the finance raised by the public sector in the markets. The PSBR is equal to the sum of the public sector's financial deficit, its lending, and certain other financial transactions not connected with the authorities' open market operations. A clear picture of which financial transactions are included in the PSBR figure and which are excluded can be obtained from Table 2.2. If the elements in the public sector in Table 2.2 are summed for lines 6 to 20.2 inclusive it will be found that they total to the amount of the 1992 borrowing requirement, £29,613 million. An examination of Table 2.3 reveals the PSBR is indeed equal to the net amount of claims issued by the public sector, confirming the definition above.

The public sector's needs for finance are far in excess of those of other sectors, and these needs are largely met by the issue of government securities. The impact of these operations on the capital markets is enormous, with trading in British government securities accounting for over 75% of the monetary value of all Stock Exchange transactions. Nevertheless, though the impact is considerable, the average value per transaction is much higher than for other securities. Thus public sector securities account for less than one-fifth of the number of transactions.

2.5 Projecting credit flows

The flow of funds accounts provide valuable data about what is happening in the financial markets, and they are widely used in the forecasting of interest rates. Official forecasts, in flow of funds form, are constructed jointly by the Treasury and the Bank of England several times during the year. These forecasts provide a view of interest rates, monetary aggregates and the financial position of the various sectors consistent with the national income forecast. This analysis is also done by economists employed in the financial community (stockbrokers, banks, etc.), and by academic researchers.

The rate of interest is the price of loanable funds, and like any other good, credit is subject to market conditions. When the demand for funds increases or the supply decreases, interest rates rise; and when demand decreases or supply increases, interest rates fall.[1] Forecasts of the components of the supply and demand for credit can therefore form the basis of forecasts of movements in interest rates. The advantage of the flow of funds matrix is that it provides a means

of keeping the component forecasts reconciled with one another, and checks can
be instituted for plausibility and consistency.

2.6 Summary

Flow of funds accounting provides a means of tracing the financial transactions
within and between different sectors. We can see that the public sector has been
the biggest borrower and that the personal sector has been the principal source of
funds. By carefully examining the flow of funds matrix we can determine what
kinds of financial claims are issued, by whom, and to whom. Not only is this kind
of information useful in determining what is happening in the financial markets
but it provides a basis for integrating forecasts.

Note

1. Interest rates as an instrument of government policy will be discussed in Chapter 4.

Further reading

Bain, A. D. (1992), *The Economics of the Financial System*, 2nd edn, Blackwell. Chapter 1
    provides a succinct flow of funds-based analysis of the financial system. The analysis is
    extended to deal with the personal, company, public and overseas sectors in Chapters
    6–9 respectively.
Polakoff, M. E. and T. A. Durkin (eds) (1981), *Financial Institutions and Markets*, 2nd edn,
    Houghton Mifflin. Concerned with the American financial system, but Chapter 2 provides
    an excellent (balance sheet-orientated) explanation of flow of funds concepts. Chapter 25
    examines the role of funds flow analysis in the forecasting of interest rates in America.
Sources of statistics used in this chapter:
Bank of England, *United Kingdom Flow of Funds Accounts*. Provides a useful account of
    the official flow of funds accounts plus detailed time series.
Central Statistical Office, *Guide to Official Statistics, No. 4*. Chapter 14 provides a detailed
    guide to the numerous published statistics concerned with the business sector and the
    financial institutions and markets.
Central Statistical Office, *National Accounts Statistics: Sources and methods*. Provides
    detailed information on the methods used to compile the national accounts. For details of
    the financial accounts, see Chapter 14.

Questions

2.1 Explain what is meant by the term *net worth*. What can cause changes in net
    worth? Why must the change in net worth be equal to the sum of real
    investment and net lending?

2.2 Must the actual real investment of an individual sector of the economy be equal to its saving? Show how, in the absence of an overseas sector, actual real investment for the whole economy must be exactly equal to its saving.

2.3 Account for the fact that the creation of internally held debt makes no difference to the wealth of the country. What happens if some of this debt is acquired by foreigners?

2.4 Discuss the following statement:

Since the financial deficits and surpluses of different sectors must be exactly offsetting, it makes no difference if the deficit of one sector (e.g. the public sector) increases.

Problems

2.5 Find the error in the following simplified matrix of financial transactions between sectors (ignore accruals and unidentified items):

	Sector		
	1	2	3
Issuing sector 1	−38	+510	−472
2	+120	+15	−165
3	−19	+62	−43
Surplus/deficit	+63	+587	−680

2.6 Using Table 2.2 describe the main sources and uses of funds for the personal and company sectors, respectively.

2.7 Using Table 2.2, determine which sectors have financial surpluses and which have deficits in 1993. Identify the major acquiring and issuing sectors of the following financial claims: company securities; investment abroad; British government securities; loans for house purchase; bank deposits.

2.8 Consider a simple three-sector economy listed below, consisting of households, companies and banks. There is no government or overseas sector. Shown below are balance sheets assumed to have been drawn up at the beginning and end of 1993, for each sector.

Income for the personal sector consists of wages of £300 for the year, of which £290 was consumed and £5 used for investment in real assets. The company sector earned £305 in sales revenues, paid out £300 in wages and the profit was paid as dividends to the personal sector. The banks made a profit of £10.

Required: Prepare a flow of funds matrix for the year 1993, and comment on the results.

	31.12.992	31.12.1993
Personal sector		
Real assets	50	55
Bank deposits	140	160
Shares in firms	50	40
Shares in banks	160	160
Net worth	£400	£415
Company sector		
Real assets	350	370
Bank deposits	60	60
	£410	£430
Bank loans	200	220
Net worth	210	210
	£410	£430
Banking sector		
Shares in firms	160	170
Loans to firms	200	220
	£360	£390
Deposits	200	220
Net worth	160	170
	£360	£390

CHAPTER 3

Financial markets and institutions

3.1 Introduction

Financial claims have much in common with other assets. In particular, they can be bought and sold in markets in essentially the same ways as cars or property. This chapter examines the general nature of markets for financial assets, and the role played by financial institutions in the promotion of saving and investment. We go on to differentiate between primary and secondary trading, and consider the transactions costs involved. Finally, we introduce some markets which have been developed specifically to reduce risk.

3.2 The demand for financial intermediation

It follows from the discussion of financial claims and sectoral balance sheets, that one function of the financial system is to improve the business and investment opportunities available to individuals and organisations. The use of money both as a unit of account and as a means of payment greatly increases the possibilities of mutually satisfactory exchanges of goods and services. By providing a store of value, money also encourages saving, thus enabling those with excess funds now to consume in the future, and to receive some benefit from this delayed consumption. Established financial markets and institutions provide the opportunity to save and invest in mutually satisfactory ways.

However, borrowers and lenders often have conflicting needs. As already seen, the business and government sectors of the economy are generally net borrowers, while individuals and households are net savers. Businesses borrow in order to buy capital equipment and property or to finance inventories. Government borrows in order to finance its deficits. Individuals and households save for a variety of reasons. They may wish to accumulate enough cash to meet large payments, maybe to buy a car, to pay a tax bill, put a deposit on a house or go to college. They may also want to transfer income for long-term future consumption, perhaps to provide for their retirement, or to meet unforeseen events such as a loss of income due to redundancy.

The savings pattern of individuals and households can be characterised by a large number of account holders saving small amounts of money. Added to this, saving does not occur evenly over the life span of individuals, but at specific periods. Traditionally, assuming a seventy-year life expectancy, the first twenty years are typically a time of negligible income and little concern for the future. These are followed by years of increasing earnings, accompanied by heavy expenditure on homes and consumer durables. Thus for many, long-term saving begins in earnest when family commitments are reduced. For those making provisions for their retirement, long-term saving may be restricted to a period of less than ten years.

Further, when savings are created to even out payment flows or for unexpected events, the horizon will be much shorter. This is a major issue at a time when employment patterns are changing and there is no longer an expectation that the labour market will provide a steady employment income throughout a normal working life. Savings patterns have changed with increased uncertainty, and although the precautionary motive implies saving continues to occur, the demand for shorter term time deposits to ensure access to liquid funds when needed is increasing.

Compared to the number of individual savers, borrowers from business and government are relatively few. But they need to borrow large amounts, and often for long periods of time. A specialised building or heavy engineering unit might cost millions of pounds and have an expected useful life of ten to fifteen years. Similarly, roads and bridges are very expensive to build and should last for many years. Sales and tax revenues which ultimately finance these investments stretch far into the future.

Apart from the size and maturity of loans to the commercial sector, a very important characteristic of business investment is the level of associated risk. Firms invest large sums in the development of new products which may either not materialise, or be too costly to produce, or for which consumer demand is limited. Similarly, unforeseen inventions might suddenly destroy the markets for established products, or newly acquired foreign assets might be nationalised. Anyone who lends money to business enterprises has to recognise that all or part of their capital might be lost. Individuals may not be willing to take such risks. If their wealth is limited, they may become severely impoverished by such losses. In the absence of mechanisms to bridge this risk gap, they are likely to prefer either to consume instead of saving or to keep their savings in less risky forms, such as cash or selected real assets.

Finally, lenders and borrowers can be kept apart because they perceive that the cost of entering the financial markets is too great. A saver can always choose to keep excess funds as cash, and is then in a position to take an investment opportunity when it arises, although they do have to take responsibility for the safekeeping of the funds. Those who do enter the financial markets as savers will always demand a positive money-return from lending, as a reward for the loss of liquidity.

But there is still the important issue of maintaining the value of the savings to be considered. It is not necessarily the case that the expected return is positive in real terms, when allowance is made for the expected changes in the purchasing power of money through time. The expected real-return in inflationary times may often be negative, with negative interest rates. An alternative would be to earn a positive real-return by buying real assets or even consumer goods which might be expected to maintain their real value in periods of inflation, but the opportunities for this type of action are limited for small savers who may not have sufficient information about potential purchasers.

The demand for funds depends on the relationship between the cost of acquiring funds and the profits which are expected to be earned by the borrowers. If the rate of interest rises, firms will be unwilling to maintain the volume of their borrowing unless the profits they expect to make from utilising the borrowings also increase. The profits must be sufficient to pay not only the interest on the debt, but also the cost of providing a marketplace for funds. A variety of financial institutions have come into being either to take advantage of economies of scale in the financial process or to reduce the uncertainties of both saving and investing. They exist to encourage and smooth the flow of savings and to intermediate between savers and investors.

3.3 The role of financial intermediaries

The institutions undertaking this role are referred to as financial intermediaries, and their role is to facilitate the flow of funds from savers to borrowers at costs lower than would be incurred privately. Financial institutions differ in a number of respects in the terms they offer to lenders, in the ways they invest and lend out their funds, and in the ancillary services they provide.

Traditionally, the main intermediaries are the deposit-taking institutions, such as commercial banks, savings banks and building societies, as well as the non-depository investment banks, and these can be seen in the centre of Figure 3.1. But many other non-bank intermediaries are increasingly involved, such as pension funds, insurance companies, mutual funds and similar organisations, through institutional saving.

There are differences in the way in which the following three groups of intermediaries operate, which has a profound effect on the balance sheet of the institution, although little relevance to the end users:

> *The deposit-taking institutions* These provide a direct link between savers and borrowers. They are the banks and building societies with whom customers have accounts for depositing and withdrawing funds.
> *The investment institutions* This group purchase assets and issue liabilities in

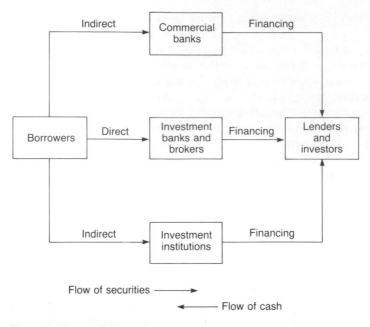

Flow of securities ⎯⎯⎯⎯▶

◀⎯⎯⎯⎯ Flow of cash

Figure 3.1   Financial intermediation.

their own right, sometimes with extended periods between receiving funds and making loans. They are the brokers and the merchant or investment banks, who frequently have to take a position in new issues, that is, invest their own funds, until they arrange a bridge between the savers and the borrowers.

The institutional investors Intermediation by this third group uses small but regular payments to acquire securities in the real sector, which provide funds to be paid as a pension in the future or as a claim against an insured loss. These are the insurance companies and pension funds with access to large amounts of funding from a pool of small investors.

Figure 3.1 illustrates the interactions which occur during the process of financial intermediation. All financial intermediaries transform funds in such a way as to make lending and borrowing more accessible. They increase the total extent of borrowing and lending and consequently raise the level of real investment in the economy. All three groups in Figure 3.1 match borrowers with lending, but only the brokers and investment banks do this directly. This is largely because they deal with the wholesale aspects of finance provision, indeed the brokers in many cases are simply facilitating the transaction. The other two groups, the commercial banks and the investment institutions both act as full intermediaries. We should now consider how they do this.

3.4 The process of financial intermediation

There are two main functions of financial intermediaries. The first is to act as a broker, bringing together borrowers and lenders. The second is to transform the funds matching maturity, volume and risk to make the funds from savers suitable to the demands of investors. This latter activity is sometimes known as the portfolio transformation aspect of intermediation, or as the transmutation of funds. We shall examine these activities in turn.

Brokerage

The brokerage aspect of intermediation is to bring borrowers and lenders together. In the absence of such mechanisms the incentive to save and the means to invest are likely to be a good deal less.

Businesses can, and do, seek funds directly from the public by advertising. They can and do approach individuals or other firms known to have excess funds. But both methods are expensive. Neither savers nor investors have sufficient knowledge of the marketplace and the cost of acquiring this information on an individual basis is very high.

Moreover, firms do not need to raise new finance every day but when they wish to start a new project or add to the funds involved in an existing one. They are essentially intermittent acquirers of funds. Equally, if there were no financial institutions, savers would be equally disadvantaged. Those with excess funds will have to look through advertisements, and contact the firms concerned directly. This is costly in time if not in money. If an individual has £50 to lend for one month the benefits of investing would not equal the costs. The existence of institutions to which savers and lenders alike can turn is likely to greatly reduce the search costs incurred by both parties. Deposit-taking institutions with many retail outlets, providing other services such as cheque-clearing mechanisms, fulfil this task very well. Commercial banks and building societies are the most common financial intermediaries, maintaining extensive networks of retail outlets.

A parallel activity was traditionally the role of the Post Office. This organisation acted as broker for the government which borrowed from individual savers in the form of savings certificates and securities. This may well have substantially reduced the transaction costs involved in financing the public sector.

Maturity transformation

One of the conflicts between borrowers and lenders is the different time horizons of investing and saving. This can be accommodated in one of two ways. First, the firm can borrow money on a short-term basis, seeking new funds as and when the existing loans are repaid. Thus, if a firm wants to borrow a specified sum for ten years, it can borrow for two years on five separate occasions, each two years apart, using the proceeds on each new loan to repay the old one. The trouble with this procedure is that the firm will incur transaction costs on five separate occasions. Secondly, a much higher rate of interest can be offered for longer term loans. It may still not be possible to obtain sufficient loanable funds of ten-year maturity, but there may be a market for five-year loans. This would result in the saving of three lots of transaction costs.

This is one aspect of the transmutation of claims, that is, borrowing money on a short-term basis and lending long-term.[1] In fact, the acceptance of funds for short periods does not necessarily imply that the funds will be withdrawn. Small savers are often not very sensitive to financial investment opportunities and tend not to switch their funds quickly from one institution to another. It is therefore quite possible for a short-term deposit to be left for a long period. Similarly, the loans made on a long-term basis may well be repaid before they become due. In the case of building societies, borrowers will usually not stay in the same house for the full term of the mortgage, and building societies report that loans are frequently repaid in much less time than twenty-five years. In any event, the high number of small investors ensures that withdrawals of savings are offset by the funds inflows provided by new depositors.

Volume transformation

This is a repackaging exercise that collects a number of small amounts from savers into a sufficiently large amount for investment purposes, that is, transmutation in relation to volume. In this process, the intermediaries can rely to a considerable extent on the assumption that the many small lenders will be unlikely simultaneously to withdraw their deposits, although the possibility of this happening cannot be discounted entirely.[2] If for some reason, there are an abnormally large number of withdrawals, such as for a major privatisation issue, the intermediary has to be operating on a large enough scale to absorb the withdrawals. This can be done easily only if there are loans maturing frequently. If the intermediary is small, the risk of a mass withdrawal can only be covered by keeping a large percentage of its funds in cash or other assets which can be quickly converted into cash.

Risk transformation

In terms of risk, lenders will have to be recompensed for the probability that the borrowers will default on the loan. If the funds are collected from small-scale savers in as large bundles as those individuals are able to offer, the savers will face the risk of losing their entire savings if the firm should be unable to repay its debt. The firm will have to pay very high interest rates on the loans to compensate for this, which may not be attractive to them. In this case, the firm may attempt to seek out less risk-averse, possibly wealthier, savers or to spread the risk over a larger number of lenders and minimise the size of the loans obtained from each investor. Heavy costs can be involved in either procedure, as already noted. The only alternative is for the firm to borrow money on a preferential basis, agreeing perhaps to protect the lenders from loss by offering specific security, such as a mortgage secured on some readily marketable asset of the firm, maybe land or buildings.

Spreading of risk by diversification would be impossible for most depositors, since a small-scale saver could lend to no more than a single firm. If that firm defaults then all the saver's investment is lost. A bank has the means of assessing the credit risk, and in any case, can rely on the fact that the proportion of bad loans will be small and offset by good ones, thereby offering the saver a risk-free investment opportunity. They are also able to diversify across a range of firms in different business sectors. Only those intermediaries who have specialist knowledge of a particular market sector have more limited portfolios, and these will offer higher expected returns to compensate for the increased risk.

Disintermediation

Before leaving this discussion of intermediation, we should comment briefly on a development known as disintermediation. This is the move away from the traditional central role of the banks in the intermediary process towards the other two groups, namely the investment banks and the investing institutions. This situation is referred to as *disintermediation of the banking system*.

This development has occurred because, historically, the deposit-taking institutions were able to do a number of things better than the investment banks and the non-bank intermediaries, but in some cases these advantages have now almost entirely ceased to exist. The reasons for this are as follows. In the past, non-banking institutions could use savings to create portfolios of securities that gave an equal or higher return at acceptable risk levels compared with the banks. Another is that the expansion of the savings institutions provided a secondary market in many assets where one did not previously exist, for example, that of mortgages. This ensured liquidity in these markets, although different from the liquidity available from short-term deposits in banks and building societies. Lastly, traditional lenders had special expertise in credit assessment covering a number of areas, including personal loans, small business and venture capital, which institutional investors do not.

However, the expansion of credit rating agencies[3] that categorise debt on the basis of the risk of the borrower gives confidence to lending decisions and reassures savers. Furthermore, the fact that some firms gained higher rating than the banks provided considerable encouragement for disintermediation to become popular. Thus although intermediation is still an important activity for many financial institutions, the banking sector has lost many of the inherent advantages it enjoyed in the past and now plays a less pivotal role.

3.5 Transactions costs

In the above discussion of financial intermediation, we frequently mentioned the costs of undertaking both saving and investment. It is crucial that costs should be as low as possible, to avoid disincentives or distortions influencing the behaviour of one or more of the market participants. At the same time, the service provided by the intermediary has a value and an associated price. Thus relative transactions costs are important.

Transactions costs will be greater the more there are divergencies between the requirements of borrowers and lenders with respect to term to maturity, loan size and risk associated with the loan. In the absence of special mechanisms, a firm which wants to raise, say, £1 million, might have to collect £100 loans from 10,000 different households, with all the attendant advertising, postage and other expenses, and including the opportunity cost of management time involved.

The alternative is for the firm to compete with other firms with similar needs for the funds of wealthy savers, thereby driving up the rates of interest which these wealthy individuals are able to charge. Competition within the financial sector from non-traditional institutions, and also from foreign entrants, has significantly lowered the transaction costs charged by British institutions, as will be discussed in later chapters.

3.6 Primary and secondary markets

In a market economy the existence of financial markets can greatly ease the process of exchanging loanable funds for financial claims. A firm that wants to borrow money can go to the market in the knowledge that those with funds to lend will be there. The process is made easier still if specialist traders are known to be actively participating in the markets, buying and selling financial claims on their own account, thereby smoothing over days on which trading is thin or when there is an excess of potential borrowers or lenders.

Further economies are achieved if agents or brokers can be employed to enter the market representing the customer to buy and sell securities. If the brokers provide investment advice and can be contacted directly or through financial intermediaries, so much the better. The existence of the market serves borrowers and lenders alike by reducing the search costs which each has to incur to get in touch with the other, and also maintains confidence in market prices.

Markets do not always have a physical location. A market for loanable funds might consist of nothing more than a list of known dealers who can be contacted by letter or telephone. The International Stock Exchange is the centre of the UK *securities market*. It has both a physical trading site which is used for a very small number of securities, and a highly developed system of trading which takes place in a number of locations via computer linkages. The *discount market* is another traditional financial market, but one which operates without a physical site at all.

This market operates by representatives of the discount houses maintaining close daily contact with the leading banks, either by telephone or personal visits, to determine where trading opportunities are.

Two types of financial markets exist for real and financial assets, and it is important to distinguish between them. A primary market for financial assets deals in new issues of all types of loanable funds. Transactions in primary markets result either in the creation or in the extinction of financial claims. The creation of a new loan causes the transfer of cash from a lender to a borrower in exchange for a financial claim on the latter. The claim is extinguished when the cash, usually interest and principal, has been repaid to the lender.

A secondary market is a market in old issues. Transactions in secondary markets do not create or extinguish financial claims. Cash does not pass between borrowers and lenders, but existing issues simply change hands. The borrower remains unaffected by the transaction while the lender transfers the right of repayment to another.

The main economic function of the secondary markets is to support the operations of the associated primary markets for new issues by providing liquidity to lenders. In the absence of a developed secondary market an individual saver might be very unwilling to lend out money for long periods of time, except at rates of interest too high to be attractive to borrowers. If the chances of making a sale when necessary are unacceptably low, no lender would commit funds. Therefore an active secondary market is essential for an active primary one. However, there is no guarantee that the lender will receive back in sale proceeds the full amount at the time they are sold, since markets fluctuate all the time, and prices are not constant.

Secondary markets also contribute to the efficiency of the primary market by providing pricing information. In the share market, for example, the current prices of traded securities significantly reduce the problem of setting a price on new issues with similar risk profiles, and information from the secondary market will also influence the attitude of potential participants in primary markets.

Figure 3.2 illustrates the connections between primary and secondary markets. Not all primary markets have secondary markets associated with them and some securities are issued for which there are no secondary markets, that is, the securities are not negotiable. Conversely, for every secondary market there must exist, or have existed, an associated primary market.

The distinction between primary and secondary markets is not unique to financial markets. The same is true in the markets for physical goods. There is both a market for new and for used cars. In the primary car market, newly manufactured cars are sold, and in the secondary market, often in a different location and involving another group of participants, used cars are bought and sold. On the other hand, a haircut is an example of a good, or in this case a service, bought in a primary market, but for which a secondary market does not exist.

It is possible for a physical good to be sold or a financial security to be issued in

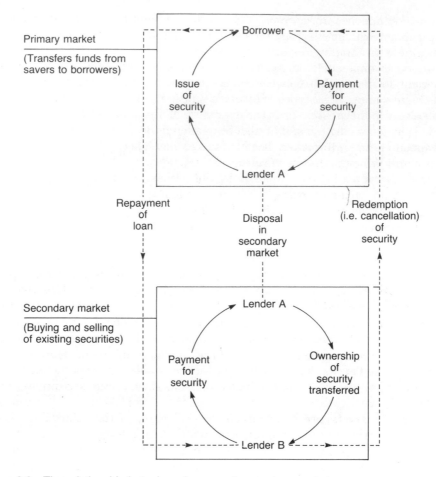

Figure 3.2   The relationship between primary and secondary markets.

a primary market which subsequently ceases to function, leaving the secondary market only. Examples are to be found in the markets for farm land and the paintings of old masters. The creation of new farm land is limited to countries still exploiting formerly unused land, whereas in the UK, there has been a substantial and continuing loss of farm land to other uses. In the case of the paintings of old masters, the primary market is by definition non-existent, although a few entrepreneurial artists may rectify the lack of primary markets by forgery!

A similar phenomenon exists in certain financial markets. A particular financial instrument may be in demand at some time, but not sustained. Thus the primary market dries up, although the goods continue to be traded in the secondary market. An example of this is the fashion for corporate bonds, which were popular in Britain in the 1970s but then lost their appeal, although old bond issues continued to be actively traded. The mismatch in activity levels of the primary and secondary markets for securities is not usually quite so marked, but it is considerable.

Another example is that of ECU denominated bonds where the market effectively disappeared during 1992/3 and then recovered. Trading in new issues of ordinary shares, for example, is variable in frequency and may ·be subject to distortionary pricing. But trading in existing corporate issues is very active, although the monetary value of money transactions is not always very great.

Some controversy surrounds the economic function of the secondary markets. The fact that there is active trading in these markets, sometimes in circumstances where the associated primary market appears to have disappeared, often leads financial commentators and others to conclude that the activities of these secondary markets are bringing about a misallocation of resources. But consider the choices open to savers who wish to invest. They can invest in the markets, either directly or through an intermediary.

The saver has the choice of either lending directly to a deficit unit via the primary markets or of purchasing an existing security in the secondary markets. If an existing security is purchased, the previous holder of that security will receive cash which can be used either to spend on consumption goods and services or reinvested in the financial markets. Only if the money is spent on imported goods, or in the acquisition of foreign assets are the proceeds lost to the economy.

Finally it is desirable that markets should operate in such a way that savings are directed to the most productive firms, or be allocatively efficient. This is attractive to individual lenders, as it leads to maximum return and minimum risk, the optimal trade-off facing the investor. If managers in financial institutions consistently place lenders' funds with borrowers yielding low returns or high default records, investors will either take their funds elsewhere, increase the interest compensation they require, or impose severe restrictions on the kinds of business in which they will invest.

Allocative efficiency may also be desirable from a social point of view and savings should flow to the most productive firms to benefit the economy as a whole. The problem gets more complicated when viewed from this angle because the definition of productivity from a social perspective may be different from that taken by lenders. Lenders may not care whether the firms to whom they lend are monopolists, pollute the atmosphere or engage in illegal activities, but other groups in society might. Clearly, it is possible for there to be conflict between the objectives of the individual decision-makers and the wishes of society.

This problem can even exist within a single group of investors. Pension funds, for example, invest money in order to provide pensions for their members but may find that some of their members demand that the funds are not invested overseas or in a competing firm in the same sector. Whilst these decisions may, if sufficiently widespread, affect the relative issue costs, it is not clear that the result should be interpreted as being allocatively inefficient. This idea that investors should have a strong view about the uses to which their funds are put is becoming increasingly important and is taken seriously by fund managers, and many financial institutions use ethical or environmental factors in their marketing.

In a monetary economy, the distinction between saving and investment is a real one. Savings can always be held in the form of cash and near-cash assets, such as precious metals. To lend is to forgo liquidity. In order to stimulate long-term lending it is necessary to provide the means by which lenders can restore liquidity without calling in their loans. This is the function of the secondary markets.

3.7 Desirable characteristics of markets

Whenever funds change hands as a result of voluntary exchanges, financial markets can be said to exist, but some markets function better than others. It is helpful to have criteria which can be used to evaluate the effectiveness of these markets.

To begin with primary markets, the most pressing need of users is that they should be able to do business with each other at low cost. If transactions costs, such as brokerage fees, are a significant proportion of the funds borrowed then the effective rate of interest paid on loans will be very high, reducing the demand for loanable funds. So one test of the economic value of a primary market is the average proportion of the borrowed funds consumed in transaction costs.

It is also beneficial to be confident about the existence of a healthy secondary market, and be sure that securities are truly negotiable. The main value here is in minimising the interest compensation sought by lenders. It follows that a primary market should operate in such a way that it minimises disruptions to the secondary markets. Suppose each new issue of loans caused dramatic falls in the prices of old issues, perhaps because each new issue more than marginally increased the total stock of a particular type of security. The effect of new issues might then be to decrease the price and undermine the value, and hence the liquidity, of old issues, in turn negatively affecting the primary market. Therefore, it is desirable that transactions in the secondary market should be much greater in value and volume than those in the primary one.

There are limits to the extent to which it is possible for markets to bring about the optimal allocation of funds. Mistakes occur because decisions are made with imperfect information, but the costs of gaining more information are greater than the benefits. The additional information may be known to transactors in the secondary market, and if so, the condition and prospects of borrowers will be monitored there.

To now consider secondary markets, it is important to remember that the purpose of a secondary market is to enable holders of securities to convert them into cash without undue loss. Therefore one desirable characteristic of this market is for it to be an active one. There are two criteria used to determine the level of activity:

The depth of the market This refers to how closely bunched the buy and sell orders for a security are around the price of the last sale. A 'sell order' is an instruction from the owner of a security to a broker to sell. In some cases, this order will be conditional on the security climbing above a specified price. A 'buy order' is an instruction to buy and again this may be conditional on the security price falling below a specified level. To illustrate this point:

Suppose the last trade occurred at £105 and there are ten buy orders between £103 and £104, and five sell orders between £106 and £107. The price cannot decline much below £105 before a buy order prevents it falling further; and it cannot rise very far before sell orders come into effect. Thus a deep market ensures that prices are not too volatile.

The breadth of the market A market is said to be broad when there is a large number of different types of investors buying and selling securities. A sufficient number of participants ensures the market is unlikely to be characterised by marked excesses of buys or sells, as investors will have various reasons for transacting and will form different expectations. A broad market should exhibit more price stability.

Price volatility is undesirable to the extent that it increases uncertainty about the eventual payoffs from holding securities. Risk-averse savers will tend to prefer to hold short-maturity instruments rather than rely on having to sell long-dated ones in a very volatile market. Thus the availability of deep, broad secondary markets helps to bring savers and lenders together. Nevertheless, there are limits to the possibilities of reducing price volatility, since any new information is bound to result in price movements.

Another important consideration is the efficiency of the market. Three aspects of efficiency can be identified: allocative efficiency, operational efficiency and information-processing efficiency. Allocative efficiency, or the use of funds by the most efficient firms, has already been discussed in respect of primary markets. Secondary markets are not directly involved in the transmission of funds from savers to borrowers, so it is not strictly appropriate to speak of the allocative efficiency of the secondary markets. Nevertheless, a secondary market can affect the allocative function of the primary market in two ways. First, it should ensure that operations of the primary market are not distorted, and secondly it can provide reliable and timely flows of information to lenders about the conditions and future prospects of borrowers.

Thus allocative efficiency in primary markets requires that secondary markets should be operationally and informationally efficient, two concepts which can now be defined. A market is operationally efficient when there is only a small difference between the net proceeds from selling a security and the total cost of buying the same security, that is, transactions costs are low. Financial intermediaries make a profit by the spread between the buying and the selling price, although details of the extent of the spread are not available to investors. At any particular moment, a dealer will quote a buy–sell spread and the more active the market, the lower the spread will be.

In addition, brokerage costs are incurred by all buyers and sellers of securities, and the brokerage costs of a purchase have to be added to the buy price in determining the total acquisition costs, and deducted from the sale price to get the net sale proceeds. The greater the difference between gross acquisition costs and net sale proceeds, the more expensive it is for lenders and borrowers to do business in the primary market, or for holders of old securities to restore liquidity without loss in the secondary market. Spread and buy-sell brokerage costs, taken as a proportion of price, provide another measure of the efficiency with which securities can be converted into cash.

The third type of market efficiency refers to the level of price information in the public domain, and the extent to which it reflects current knowledge about expected future income streams from traded securities. In a market which is fully informationally efficient all buyers and sellers must bargain on an equal footing. Some investors might be more informed than others, that is have insider knowledge, but they are unable to use this to gain an advantage over other investors because the prices of securities already fully reflect everything which is currently known.

By contrast, in a market which is informationally inefficient the informed investors can take advantage of the uninformed and gain abnormal profits. An example of market inefficiency would be where insiders knew that a particular company was about to announce the discovery of valuable mineral deposits when others did not. This individual could buy the securities of the firm in question from unsuspecting holders in the confident knowledge that the price would rise following the announcement. In an efficient market, information gets to the market and is absorbed into the price structure through the actions of all the participants in aggregate, ensuring that there is no monopoly of information.[4]

In active securities markets there will always be individuals searching for opportunities to make abnormal profits. Their operations can be relied upon to promote the informational efficiency of the market. However, if transaction costs are considerable then differences in prices can exist which cannot be traded away. Therefore informational efficiency depends on operational efficiency.

The characteristics required for well-functioning markets addressed in this section are essentially static in nature, and the operations of the primary and secondary markets are considered at a given point in time. In reality, markets are dynamic mechanisms which necessarily have to be flexible to adjust to changes in external circumstances, such as amendments to the tax system, the creation, alteration and dismantling of exchange control regulations, and alterations in patterns of savings and investment over time. They also have to adapt to changes prompted by events outside the domestic economy, such as the impact of international economic shocks, examples of which are the oil price rise in the mid-1970s, or defaults or rescheduling of debt by one or more countries. A financial system which is capable of adjusting to changes such as these, possibly by the introduction of new markets and institutions, without major disruptions to the savings transmission process, must be judged to be dynamically efficient, regardless of its level of static efficiency.

3.8 Risk, diversification, hedging and arbitrage

Financial institutions and markets are the products of uncertainty. In a certain world, there would be no need for a financial system as such. Money would be needed only as a unit of account, and then only for the present since the future would be known. It would not be required to serve as a means of payment nor as a store of value since there would be perfect certainty about all present and future transactions and opportunities. Transactions could take place on a credit or bookkeeping basis. Investment could occur without fear of loss, and saving would take account of the prices which are certain to prevail in the future. Length of life, circumstances and consumption requirements of the saver would be known. But uncertainty changes everything.

Financial institutions and markets provide the means with which individuals can try to cope with uncertainty about economic conditions. Risk cannot be avoided entirely as far as society is concerned, but it can be reduced or transferred from one individual to another.

Certain risks can be eliminated by sharing or by diversification. Investors can choose to divide their total funds into a number of firms rather than only one, or if the funds are insufficient to do this, they can be invested in a firm which itself has very diversified business interests. Alternatively, a financial intermediary, such as a unit trust, will collect the savings of many small-scale investors and put the funds into a diversified portfolio. A bank is another such institution providing diversification services, and so are pension funds and insurance companies. The financial system provides many and varied means of avoiding diversifiable risks.

However, not all elements of risk are diversifiable. Firms' profits vary due to the competence of their managers and the specific demands of the industry they are in. But in addition, the general level of economic activity varies with the business cycle. Therefore, to a certain extent, the profits of firms move together, and thus diversification will not reduce risk of this kind. Spreading investment across industries or foreign markets may reduce some uncertainty, but ultimately, the common movements in profits and share prices of firms are traceable to inter-dependencies between parts of the economy and between the economies of different countries. Indeed, nations with a limited number of productive sectors can be very drastically affected by a poor harvest or the collapse of raw material markets. In the extreme case, the failure of the international banking system could bring about the destruction of international trade. Thus risks can be shifted from one individual to another, but they cannot be removed entirely.

The financial system provides many opportunities for minimising risk, in particular by offering several types of security, and by the presence of forward contracts and insurance markets. We should give these brief consideration here, although later chapters discuss them more fully.

The issuance of different classes of securities. In addition to raising ordinary share capital, a firm can issue fixed interest-paying bonds, secured by a guarantee of pledged assets. The fixed interest charges and prior claims of the bondholders make the ordinary shares more risky. The effect is to shift virtually the whole of the risk of the business on to the equity holders. These ordinary shareholders, if they are rational, will demand higher expected returns, compared to the bondholders, as compensation for the extra risks carried.

The creation of forwards contracts

Although maybe not the most cost-efficient activity, financial or commodity forward contracts remove the risk of a particular transaction completely. If a debt is due in three months' time and is to be paid in $US, the holder of the debt can purchase a forward contract for the specified amount to hedge against changes in the dollar-sterling exchange rate during the period prior to payment. The date, price and amount are fixed when the contract is purchased. The disadvantage is that no profit can be made if interest rates change in favour of the holder of the debt, but equally no loss is incurred if rates change in favour of the creditor. Overall the hedging operation will eliminate the risk of exchange rate changes, at a price equal to the transactions costs, plus the loss of the opportunity to make excess profits if they arise.

The insurance market

There are limits to the possibilities of hedging and diversifying, limits which are themselves the products of uncertainty. Uncertainty which takes the form of asymmetry of information, that is where one party has more or different information than another, can result in market imperfections. This can occur because one agent may give the other false information, or is somewhat cavalier about possible losses, conditions which can both fall under the definition of moral hazard, or result in only those agents posing a particularly high risk seeking insurance cover, known as adverse selection.

For example, a risk-averse individual might want to insure against all risks of loss of property, maybe due to damage caused by fires, thefts or accident, but would be unable to find an insurer willing to write all the contracts involved. If an insurer covers all risks the insured has no incentive to take care, so the insurer will accept only part of the losses. Similarly, a company will find that there are limits to the amounts of capital it can raise in the form of bonds. Buyers of the bonds will be afraid that if the amount of debt is very high, the chances of getting their funds back diminish as the probability of bankruptcy increases. This is worse in times of economic recession, when the chance of bankruptcy is increasingly likely, and is exacerbated as managers with share holdings have little incentive to perform well, given shareholders are behind bondholders in the event of a business failure.

Finally, we should examine the effect of transaction costs on equilibrium prices. Transaction costs can limit the scope of the market. As transaction costs increase, the incentive to issue and to take up new securities, or to create new kinds of securities, diminishes. Transaction costs are themselves largely the products of uncertainty, for they arise in large measure from the need to seek out full information. Financial markets and institutions create information, but information costs money, in terms of search costs, analysis and interpretation and there are limits to the gains from further extension and elaboration of the financial system.

Therefore, transaction costs can impede the process of achieving a market price. Equilibrium is achieved when identical securities, that is, securities with the same risk and return profile, sell at the same price.[5] If two securities are identical in all respects, but are priced differently, it is reasonable to expect the demand to be higher for the cheaper one. Such excess demand would lead to sales of the more expensive one until the excess demand is reduced to zero and the markets are again in equilibrium. The process that ensures equilibrium is arbitrage. Prices are out of equilibrium when abnormal returns can be made from arbitrage profits. An example of this is as follows:

> Suppose there are two securities, A and B, both offering £10 annually in perpetuity, but A sells for £100 and B for £80. An investor could buy one unit of B and thereby acquire an annual income of £10, but could also sell one unit in A, thereby taking on the liability to pay an annual income of £10. The net annual cash flow would therefore be zero, yet the investor has paid out only £80 for B and received £100 for A. This has resulted in an immediate arbitrage profit of £20. This arbitrage profit would disappear, however, if the transaction costs involved in selling the unit of A and buying B exceeds the £20 difference in price between the two securities.

Thus transaction costs can cause a breakdown in the law of one price. The smaller the transaction costs the more effective are market mechanisms.

3.9 Summary

Financial markets exist for both those with excess funds and with a deficit of funds. The financial institutions help to make the markets accessible for both groups, which generally requires some transformation of funds. This they do in a number of ways. Markets work smoothly if primary and secondary trades can be undertaken with confidence if they are efficient. Efficiency requires flows of information, low costs and special markets to reduce the risk of the transaction.

Notes

1. Perhaps building societies provide the most striking example of this transmutation function, borrowing effectively on demand and lending to home buyers on as much as a twenty-five-year repayment basis.
2. Regulation does require a certain reserve level. This will be discussed in later chapters.
3. See Appendix B, Chapter 9 for more information on rating agencies.
4. Only informational efficiency demands intervention by the regulators. This is further discussed in Parts II and IV.
5. This is known as the *law of one price*. Another example is where the same security is offered on markets in different countries. We shall return to this in the later chapter on global trading mechanisms.

Further reading

Bain, A. D. (1992), *The Economics of the Financial System*, Blackwell. Chapters 1, 3 and 4 provide a rigorous account of the economic theory of financial systems. Some previous or concurrent economics course would be beneficial.

Cobham, D. (ed.) (1992), *Markets and Dealers: The Economics of the London financial markets*, Longman. Chapter 1 is an overview of the City of London and the markets that exist there.

Polakoff, M. E. and T. A. Durkin (eds) (1981), *Financial Institutions and Markets*, 2nd edn, Houghton Mifflin. This book is over 700 pages in length and provides excellent coverage of virtually every aspect of the American financial system. Chapters 1, 12, 31 and 32 deal with the theoretical aspects of institutions and markets.

Scott-Quinn, B. (1990), *Investment Banking: Theory and practice*, Euromoney Books. Rather advanced in general, but Chapter 2 clearly explains the nature of financial intermediation.

Questions

3.1 What is the distinction between a primary financial market and a secondary market? Is it possible to have a primary market without a secondary market? A secondary market without a primary market? Give examples.

3.2 Discuss what is required for a secondary market to function well.

3.3 What is the relationship, if any, between financial intermediation and economic growth?

3.4 Discuss the following statement:

Financial institutions provide means of minimising the costs of collecting information and of dealing in the financial markets. If these costs were the same for all, then there would be no need for financial institutions and a system of financial markets would suffice.

3.5 The cost to a firm of raising new finance can be broken down into two elements.
   (a) The interest charged (or profit expected) by the lender and issue costs, and
   (b) The net return to a lender consists of the interest charged to the borrower, less (i) any tax deducted from the interest and (ii) costs incurred in making the loan.
   Explain the ways in which economic forces can be expected to equalise:
   (a) The total costs of all sources of finance to a particular firm.
   (b) The net returns which a lender can expect to get from different investments with the same risk.

3.6 Explain the significance of *depth* and *breadth* of a market. Give examples of markets, both real and financial, which you think are likely to score poorly in terms of depth and breadth.

3.7 Explain the distinction between allocative efficiency and information-processing efficiency. Is it possible for the financial markets to be judged to be allocative efficient but not informational efficient, or vice versa?

3.8 How highly would you rate the market for home-purchase loans (mortgages) in the UK, in terms of allocative, operational and informational efficiency?

3.9 Suppose two individuals have inherited £1,000 each. One individual is very risk-averse, and the other is by nature a gambler. Outline some of the ways in which these two individuals might invest their money, and the ways their choices might differ. How different would your answers be if each inherited £100,000 rather than £1,000?

CHAPTER 4

The monetary system and the role of the central bank

4.1 Introduction

The purpose of this chapter is to consider some of the ways in which government monetary policy is implemented through the financial system. Since the Bank of England plays an important role in this, we shall begin by outlining the various responsibilities of the Bank and then go on to discuss the impact of a number of aspects of policy which have a direct effect on the financial sector.

4.2 The Bank of England

The Bank of England was founded in 1694, and has operated in its present form since it was nationalised in 1947. It is the central bank of the UK and therefore loosely equivalent to the Federal Reserve System in the US and the Bundesbank in Germany, although there are a number of differences between the central banks in practice.

The Bank for International Settlements (BIS) defines a central bank to be *the bank in any country to which has been entrusted the duty of regulating the volume of currency and credit in that country*. Other definitions are much wider and include the responsibility for undertaking the financial operations of government, and exerting influence over the behaviour of the financial institutions so as to support the economic policy of government.

Since the 1946 Bank of England Act, the Bank has had a subordinate status with respect to government, whereby HM Treasury formulates policy and the Bank controls the technical implementation of those policies. However, changes in this relationship are anticipated, and the increased independence of the Bank is currently under review. This is especially important in the context of the European Monetary Union, which we shall discuss in more detail in Chapter 6.

The Bank is divided into an Issue Department and a Banking Department, and for accounting purposes, has separate balance sheets to differentiate the two activities, in accordance with the Bank Charter Act of 1844. The government account, known as the Exchange Equalisation Account, holds the official reserves of gold; convertible currencies and special drawing rights from the International Monetary Fund are in a further account. Table 4.1 shows an example of weekly returns, although we are more interested in the composition of the two accounts rather than the volumes, which are fairly static.

The accounts of the Issue Department are very simple, with the only liability being notes in circulation with the public and within the Bank, and assets consisting of government guaranteed, and public and private sector securities.

The Banking Department acts as a banker to the government, to domestic banks, to overseas central banks and international organisations, a small number of other domestic institutions and a few private individuals, and all of these are represented in the accounts. Therefore liabilities are made up of deposits, the largest of which are public deposits, reflecting the balance held by central government. These include the accounts of the Exchequer, the National Loans Funds, the National Debt Commissioners and the Paymaster General, as well as taxes and other items. Bankers' deposits consist of operational deposits held mainly for clearing purposes and also cash ratio deposits required from institutions under the 1987 Banking Act. The majority of other liabilities are reserves held for foreign central banks.

Assets credited to the Banking Department are government guaranteed securities and Treasury bills, advances made to the discount market, loans to customers and support loans to deposit-taking institutions. These are adjusted for loss provision. Other securities, such as ordinary shares and bonds, and finally, physical assets, building and equipment are accounted for at market prices and all included items.

In its present form, the Bank carries out a wide range of activities, the most important of which are to act as banker to the government and the monetary sector; to be regulator of UK banks and act as prudential supervisor for depositors; and to implement and manage monetary policy. These activities are outlined below.

Banker to government and the monetary sector

From Table 4.1, we saw that the public liabilities in the Banking Department comprised the major government accounts. These are used for transactions between the public and private sectors, with funds flowing between the two to meet expenditures and receive taxes, for example. Other flows between these accounts can be induced by sale or purchase of government stock transactions with private sector investors. These are known as open market operations. The Bank, as manager of the national debt, plays a predominant role in the gilt-edged market. It is usually in the position of seeking to sell new debt in the short term but is also concerned with promoting efficient trading mechanisms, and to sustain the demand for government debt in the long term.

Table 4.1 Bank of England balance sheet, February 1994

£ millions

			Issue Department				Banking Department								
			Liabilities		Assets		Liabilities					Assets			
Year	Month	Day	Notes in circulation	Notes in Banking Department	Government securities	Other securities	Total	Public deposits	Special deposits	Bankers' deposits	Reserves and other accounts	Government securities	Advances and other accounts	Premises, equipment and other securities	Notes and coin
			ROWAEFA	ROWAEFB	ROWAEFC	ROWAEFD	ROWAEFE	ROWAEFF	ROWAEFG	ROWAEFH	FOWAEFI	ROWAEFJ	ROWAEFK	ROWAEFL	ROWAEFM
1994	Feb.	2	17,102	8	5,394	11,716	11,361	5,205	—	1,595	4,547	1,387	9,522	445	7
	:	9	17,078	12	5,307	11,783	9,859	2,478	—	1,509	5,858	1,372	8,029	446	12
	:	16	17,096	4	5,694	11,406	9,251	1,129	—	1,628	6,479	1,272	7,530	445	4
	:	23	17,104	6	5,270	11,840	9,423	2,038	—	1,549	5,822	1,419	7,535	463	6
	Mar.	2	17,206	4	5,578	11,632	8,257	1,067	—	1,564	5,611	1,006	6,783	464	4
	:	9	17,252	8	7,485	9,775	6,390	1,071	—	1,554	3,750	1,002	4,916	464	8
	:	16	17,246	4	8,937	8,313	5,995	1,094	—	1,457	3,430	1,004	4,368	620	3
	:	23	17,345	5	11,492	5,858	5,703	744	—	1,492	3,453	1,183	2,438	2,077	5
	:	30	18,031	9	12,724	5,316	6,808	1,149	—	1,447	4,198	1,234	2,482	3,083	9
	Apr.	6	18,076	4	15,301	2,779	6,136	883	—	1,604	3,634	1,044	2,179	2,909	4
	:	13	17,588	12	14,422	3,178	6,287	1,193	—	1,615	3,464	1,235	2,730	2,310	11
	:	20	17,484	6	14,779	2,711	6,508	1,155	—	1,680	3,659	1,167	2,704	2,631	6
	:	27	17,700	10	13,861	3,849	6,005	1,110	—	1,508	3,372	1,072	2,776	2,147	10
	May	4	17,958	12	14,034	3,936	5,618	669	—	1,803	3,131	1,012	3,438	1,156	12
	:	11	17,655	5	13,972	3,688	5,705	1,127	—	1,619	2,944	1,004	3,487	1,208	5
	:	18	17,622	8	15,923	1,707	5,435	1,046	—	1,501	2,873	1,164	1,969	2,293	8
	:	25	17,963	7	15,936	2,034	5,279	915	—	1,526	2,824	1,003	2,020	2,249	7
	Jun.	1	18,254	6	14,752	3,508	4,872	256	—	1,670	2,932	1,020	2,564	1,282	6
	:	8	17,890	10	15,828	2,072	5,782	1,135	—	1,508	3,124	1,031	2,185	2,556	10
	:	15	17,820	10	16,847	983	5,552	1,129	—	1,624	2,784	1,093	1,745	2,705	9
	:	22	17,810	10	16,715	1,104	5,305	865	—	1,561	2,865	1,022	2,224	2,049	10
	:	29	17,939	11	15,233	2,717	5,623	1,145	—	1,597	2,867	1,043	2,667	1,902	11

Source: Bank of England Quarterly Bulletin, August 1994.

The Bank is also banker to the banking sector as a whole. Again as we saw in the Banking Department balance sheets, the retail banks hold deposits of their own with the Bank. As a result of the clearing banks' operations, some banks will be in deficit and some in surplus at the end of each business day. These can be settled by short-term inter-bank loans to maintain the smooth running of the cheque-clearing process. Other occasions where the Bank may be required to extend credit to the retail banks are when there is an unexpected demand for liquidity. Banks can replenish their stock of currency from their own reserves held at the Bank, and internal transfers take place at the Bank between the Issuing and Banking Departments.

An extension of this process of providing short-term funds is available when the banking sector as a whole suffers a deficiency in liquidity. The Bank can restore the overall cash positions of the banks, but this takes place through the money markets, and not by borrowing from Bank reserves directly. This is often termed the 'lender of last resort' role. The Bank uses the discount houses to obtain cash for this purpose, and we shall examine the operation of these institutions in the next section. In a much more general respect, the Bank of England does intervene to support banks in the UK suffering liquidity difficulties. This is to maintain confidence in the financial system as a whole.

Supervision and regulation

The 1979 Banking Act requires the Bank to license all deposit-taking institutions, and to ensure regular disclosure of accounts. This was extended under the 1987 Banking Act, in which the Bank is made responsible for the supervision of all those institutions within the monetary sector. This takes the form of screening senior management, limiting individual shareholding and making the submission of misleading information a criminal offence. There are also restrictions concerning ownership of shares, mergers and takeovers, and a change in senior management personnel, details of which are notifiable to the Bank. An interesting point in this respect is the redefining of deposit-taking institutions, in anticipation of innovation in the financial sector, and restructuring of markets.

Because of the *lender of last resort* facility, the Bank undertakes prudential regulation of banks to minimise situations of moral hazard, that is, banks behaving in a more cavalier manner if they have a safety net. This is done on an individual bank basis and incorporates two fields of activity. The first is to investigate each institution before allowing it to become established, and to prohibit operations if illegal activities are proven. The second is concerned with the risk associated with each bank's activities, with particular attention centred on capital adequacy and liquidity. We shall return to regulation issues in Chapter 19.

Management of government policy

The Bank implements government policy, and is able to influence financial markets by the management of the negotiable securities which make up the national debt. As we shall see, public sector expenditure is usually in excess of taxation, and the deficit is funded in a number of ways. The most common is by issuing bonds at a variety of maturities from three months to perpetuity. The administration of these securities is carried out by the Bank. This includes keeping the register of bondholders, controlling the issue of new bonds and replacing those that have matured and arranging for debt redemptions and interest payments. The Bank has considerable influence in this respect, since the choice of debt in terms of maturity is reflected in the liquidity of the financial markets as a whole.[1]

The Bank can also exert influence on the level of short-term interest rates through its operations in the sterling discount markets. This involves the purchase or sale of government securities not simply to fund government expenditure, but to affect monetary policy through open market operations. For example, if the government wishes to tighten monetary conditions and increase interest rates, the Bank issues new government securities at a higher rate. Purchasers of these securities withdraw funds from the banking sector to pay the government. This causes bank deposits to fall, and along with them, their assets held at the Bank of England. To replenish these deposits at the Bank, the retail bank will call in loans and sell off other assets, including some holdings in government securities. As loans are recalled, deposits fall further still and the stock of money is reduced. Since this funding is in excess of that required for government expenditure, the overfunding has resulted in a shortage of liquidity. The sale of government securities previously issued will cause a fall in price, and thus a rise in the rate of interest. This then spreads throughout the economy. At the same time, as a result of this process, a higher proportion of government debt is held by the public and a lower proportion is met by monetary financing.

4.3 The creation of money and credit

While government does have some control over the money supply, currently exercised through the Bank of England as we saw in the previous section, other institutions within the monetary sector influence the creation of money in the system. In practice, the Bank of England controls the issue of money, in terms of notes and coin, although the process of governmental control of the stock of money is much less direct. All the operational definitions of money include assets other than notes and coin. In even the narrow definition given in Chapter 1, notes and coin form a small part of the total. Most money is created by the activity of commercial banks. Thus while it may be correct to say that the Bank of England influences and even tries to control money creation, a more detailed description of how banks, non-bank financial intermediaries, households and businesses, and the authorities interact is required to appreciate the entire process.

In Britain, the main component of the money supply is current account balances, called demand deposits or instant access accounts. Demand deposits qualify as money because they are accepted as the final settlement of a debt, and they arise in three ways. In the first a demand deposit is created when a customer deposits currency or a cheque. No money is created because the inflow already consists of money. The second method of creating a demand deposit is when a customer shifts money from a time deposit, or savings account, into an instant access account. In this situation, the supply of money increases because near-money has been turned into money. This source of monetary increase is likely to be of short duration and can easily be followed by reverse shifts in the opposite direction.

The third way in which banks increase demand deposits is by acquiring financial assets. Whenever a bank acquires a financial asset, by buying a security or making a loan, spending power is injected into the system. If a security is purchased, a cheque is issued by one institution which will usually be paid into a demand deposit in the same or another institution. If a loan is made, a demand deposit is created immediately. In either case, the total supply of money has increased, since the total stock of money has decreased as a result of the transaction.

Although the banks are largely responsible for the creation of money, their ability to expand demand deposits is not without limits. Their freedom of action is restricted by regulation. Government controls aside, considerations of prudent portfolio management set bounds to the possibilities of creating more and more money by buying securities or advancing loans to customers. The continued acquisition of financial assets becomes increasingly risky, since there is always the possibility of a large number of depositors wanting to withdraw their funds at the same time and the institution not having the cash to pay them. However, the larger the institution and the more varied its customers, the less likely is such an event to occur. Banks know from experience that it is prudent to keep a proportion of their assets in reserve, generally in the form of highly liquid assets, such as cash, near-cash assets liquidated on demand and deposits with the Bank of England. The reserve ratio defines the amount of money any bank can create, where the reserve levels are often determined by legal requirements. In the UK there have been no national reserve requirements since 1981, apart from a prudential requirement to maintain 0.45% of total liabilities in cash, which is called the cash ratio.

The process of money creation can best be appreciated by a simple example.

Suppose there are just two banks in the economy, A and B, both of which aim to keep 10% of deposits invested in the form of reserves with the balance in higher-yielding loans. A and B each have deposits of £100. A's deposits are invested in the desired proportions of £10 in reserves and £90 in loans, but B has £20 in reserves and only £80 in loans. B advances £10 of its reserves as loans. Loans and deposits will therefore initially rise by £10. But the customers who have received the loans will purchase goods by writing cheques on their account at B. Suppose for simplicity these funds are used to buy goods from A's customers and hence find their way into deposits in A. Cash has flowed into A's tills and its reserves now amount to £20. But

A only needs 10% of its deposits (now £110) in reserve, which is £11, so it makes further loans of £9. Suppose those find their way into B's tills. B now has excess reserves of £8.1.

The adjustment process continues, until the deposits of A and B together have increased from their initial aggregate level of £200 to £300, at which point no further bank portfolio revisions will be called for. Eventually, B's excess reserves of £10 will bring about a tenfold increase in demand deposits, or money. The money multiplier is the reciprocal of the banks' reserve ratio, here assumed to be 10% (i.e. $1/.10 = 10$), and inflows of funds to the banks enable them to create credit up to ten times the magnitude of the inflow.

Conversely, withdrawals of funds destroy credit. To continue our example:

If B had £10 shortfall of reserves, loans would be reduced and this would negatively affect the demand deposits of both banks. Equilibrium will be restored when the £200 initial joint deposits of the banks have fallen to £100.

Liquidity ratios determined for precautionary motives are based on experience and judgement and are under the control of the senior management of individual institutions. These are separate and additional to the capital adequacy requirement imposed by the supervisory authority. They are concerned with the stock of capital held by the bank in relation to the various kinds of risk associated with the bank, and are part of the process of preserving the stability of the financial system as a whole.

The usefulness of reserve asset regulations to the government can be seen in the simple two-bank economy example used previously. To continue:

We imposed a reserve ratio of 10% for each bank. Following a number of transactions, total deposits in the two banks increased to £300. Supposing the central bank is concerned about this increase in the money supply and therefore increases the reserve ratio from 10% to 12.5%. Reserves were 10% of deposits, that is £30, and they must now rise to 12.5%, requiring an additional £7.50. The banks will have to reduce loans to achieve this. As the money multiplier is now 8, the reciprocal of the 12.5% reserve ratio, these adjustments to bank portfolios will reduce demand deposits by eight times the original increase in required reserves: $£7.50 \times 8 = £60$

In other words, the central bank has reduced the money supply by £60, simply by increasing the reserve ratio.

We will return to the role of government in the money-creation process again later in the chapter, but first we should examine the effect of changes in the money supply on the financial institutions and markets. The commercial banks are immediately and obviously affected by changes in the money supply. As we have seen in the example, their everyday asset management decisions directly influence the money supply.

Conversely, inflows and outflows of bank funds, for whatever reason, stimulate asset portfolio revisions by the banks. A corollary of the banks' central role in the money creation process is that their operations are closely overseen and regulated by the central bank. Bank competitors, such as non-bank financial intermediaries, have taken a considerable amount of traditionally banking business in the personal sector, while not being subjected to the same level of regulation. The entry of foreign financial institutions has exacerbated this, although new opportunities for banks do exist.

Any monetary change affects all institutions in the financial system. For example, an increase in the money supply augments the stock of loanable funds thereby tending to put downward pressure on interest rates. A fall in interest rates on new loans and securities increases the attractiveness of existing securities and hence drives up the prices of bills and bonds. The increase in money balances might have some effects on the real economy as well, and these will in turn impinge on the financial system. Cash not invested earns no return so individuals can be assumed to limit their holdings to that required for immediate use. Substitution of cash into other assets, real as well as financial, and into consumable expenditures will occur as individuals attempt to make the best use of excess cash. This will put upward pressure on production and on prices. In turn, price inflation will reduce the attractiveness of money-denominated financial securities, thereby pushing down their prices and putting upward pressure on interest rates.

To the extent that there is any impact on production, or the relative prices of goods and services, share prices will react accordingly. The net effect of changes in the monetary sector is to send shocks through the financial system, particularly if the monetary changes are unanticipated. The effect of changes in the money stock on the real economy has important implications for government policy and hence for the financial system.

4.4 Introduction to monetary theory

Macroeconomic policy is divided into two parts. Fiscal policy is defined as the control of the size, form and timing of government expenditure and taxation. Monetary policy is concerned with the manipulation of financial variables, the supply of money, the flow of credit and interest rates and the control of inflation. Of course, these two aspects of policy are not independent, since the way government expenditures are undertaken has effects on the money supply and the sale and purchase of government securities can be used to direct monetary policy. We shall briefly address these issues before looking at the results of recent government policy.

The money supply

Differences in practice have reflected the change in emphasis on monetary compared with fiscal policy, and there has been controversy in the economics literature on the importance of the money supply for a long time. The Keynesians argue that changes in money stock have no effect on real income or output in either the short run or in the long run. Rather, they suggest that the demand for

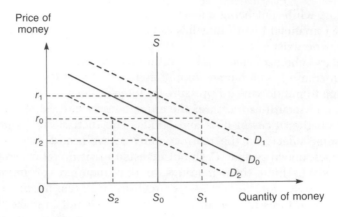

Figure 4.1 Monetary control.

money is very sensitive to changes in the yields on alternative financial assets and hence the demand for money is both unpredictable and unstable. Economic activity responds to variations in credit flows and rates of interest. As the demand for money is unstable there is no point in attempting to control its supply, for any variation will simply alter interest rates rather than the level of economic activity. Real investment is not very responsive to changes in interest rates, but depends on expected changes in output. To Keynesians, fiscal policy is the most effective instrument of economic management.

Conversely, the monetarists argue that the demand for money, and its velocity of circulation, is a stable and predictable function of permanent incomes, and thus is insensitive to the yields on alternative financial assets. It follows that if the demand for money is stable and not affected by changes in interest rates, any restriction in its supply will deprive people of liquidity and restrict their real expenditures. If the money stock is allowed to grow much faster than the rate of growth in economic activity, the result will be inflation and not the stimulation of economic growth. To monetarists, the central task of economic management is that of matching the supply of money with the demand for money, with the aim of controlling inflation.

One possible policy is to set monetary targets, although there are some difficulties in timing these announcements appropriately. Using monetary targets, it is possible to announce a precise set of objectives for each year of the policy, for example, monetary growth will be no more than 6% in the first year, and 5% thereafter. No such time path can be announced for interest rates. With an interest rate target, all the central bank can do is say they will remain high until inflation has been reduced, although this is not very specific. To show the effect of monetary targets, we should consider how the supply and demand for money, usually a broad money aggregate such as M4, is derived.

Figure 4.1 shows the supply and demand for money. Equilibrium in the money market is the rate of interest which equates supply and demand. If the Bank of England money supply target is S_0 and the demand for money is D_0, the Bank can either set the interest rate to be r_0, the market equilibrium rate, or it can control the quantity of money by only supplying S_0. It cannot control interest rates and the quantity of money at the same time, although both will produce the same outcome.

But the difficulty facing the Bank with respect to the control of the money stock is that the demand for money is not clear. Estimates of demand at different interest rates are derived using econometric models but, in reality, it is not certain where D_0 is for sure. In this case, having control over interest rates is not the same thing as controlling the money supply. For example, if the interest rate was set at r_0, but the demand for money was D_1 rather than D_0, the Bank would be required to supply money at S_1 rather than at S_0. On the other hand, if the bank controls the quantity of money, variations in the demand for money between D_1 and D_2 would mean that interest rates fluctuate between r_1 and r_2. Thus, while interest rate policy is aimed primarily at the supply of money, not surprisingly the demand for money will also be affected.

Perhaps one of the most crucial issues, as far as financial economists are concerned, is the question of the substitutability between the narrow definition of money and other financial assets. This arises as a direct consequence of the rapid growth of non-bank financial intermediaries. It can be argued that these intermediaries do not possess the money-creation capacity of banks but are merely money brokers. The deposits they obtain while competing with the banks eventually find their way back into the banks' tills. None the less, if non-bank deposits are sufficiently liquid that they can replace money to such an extent that personal sector expenditure is maintained in the face of tight monetary policy, then that policy could be made ineffectual. Conversely, if other financial assets are not good money substitutes then a monetary policy intended to control the supply of narrowly defined money can be expected to be efficient and have the desired controlling effect on aggregate spending.

The public sector borrowing requirement

One of the main concerns of monetary policy is to finance the public sector borrowing requirement (PSBR), which we referred to in Chapter 2 and in the earlier discussion of the role of the Bank of England. The public sector includes central government, local authorities and public corporations, although since privatisation many of this latter group have been transferred to the private sector. There are strong links within the public sector, with funds shifted from areas in surplus to those in deficit, and it is the overall position which is important. Table 4.2 shows the size of the public sector borrowing requirement, with contributions to it.

The public sector holds a number of tangible assets, such as buildings, plant and machinery, civil engineering works, etc. However, there are considerable

Table 4.2 Public sector borrowing requirement (£m), 1989–93

	Central government		Local authorities			General government borrowing requirement	Public corporations			Public sector borrowing requirement	PSBR excluding privatisation proceeds
		Of which: Own account (CGBR(O))		of which				of which			
	CGBR		LABR	from central government	other	GGBR	PCBR	from central government	other	PSBR	
	1	2	3	4	5	6	7	8	9	10	11
	ABEA	ABEB	ABEG	ABEC	AAZK	ABEH	ABEM	ABEI	AAZL	ABEN	ABII
Not seasonally adjusted											
1989	−5,134	−9,656	585	2,577	−1,992	−7,126	−223	1,945	−2,168	−9,294	−4,733
1990	−4,647	−1,109	3,903	762	3,141	−1,506	−4,910	−4,300	−610	−2,116	2,169
1991	7,706	6,588	1,878	1,230	648	8,354	−762	−112	−650	7,704	16,331
1992	29,192	33,708	−5,562	−5,818	256	29,448	746	1,302	−556	28,892	36,146
1993	45,674	46,171	−2,869	−1,540	−1,329	44,345	−260	1,043	−1,303	43,042	48,410
1989/90	−5,630	−5,369	1,321	2,262	−941	−6,571	−3,903	−2,523	−1,380	−7,951	−3,732
1990/91	−2,459	−2,916	3,451	1,472	1,979	−480	−987	−1,015	28	−452	4,893
1991/92	12,925	11,735	1,685	639	1,046	13,971	459	551	−92	13,879	21,802
1992/93	36,287	42,370	−5,843	−7,267	1,424	37,711	43	1,184	−1,141	36,570	44,754
1993/94	48,754	47,892	−2,789	−659	−2,130	46,624	779	1,521	−742	45,882	51,301
1991 Q2	6,673	6,522	269	−31	300	6,973	284	182	102	7,075	9,330
Q3	3,428	3,638	256	−340	596	4,024	−193	130	−323	3,701	5,128
Q4	116	−162	−5	268	−273	−157	−323	10	−333	−490	2,774
1992 Q1	2,708	1,737	1,165	742	423	3,131	691	229	462	3,593	4,570
Q2	10,709	10,467	52	−450	502	11,211	95	692	−597	10,614	12,429
Q3	9,448	9,096	−1,157	10	−1,167	8,281	−260	342	−602	7,679	10,800
Q4	6,327	12,408	−5,622	−6,120	498	6,825	220	39	181	7,006	8,347

1993 Q1	9,803	10,399	884	-707	1,591	11,394	-12	111	-123	11,271	13,178
Q2	12,775	13,022	-99	-868	769	13,544	446	621	-175	13,369	14,937
Q3	12,335	12,155	-1,218	125	-1,343	10,992	-171	55	-226	10,766	12,684
Q4	10,761	10,595	-2,436	-90	-2,346	8,415	-523	256	-779	7,636	7,611
1994 Q1	12,883	12,120	964	174	790	13,673	1,027	589	438	14,111	16,069
1992 Sep	4,498	4,387	-273	-56	-217	4,281	-102	167	-269	4,012	5,466
Oct	1,570	6,827	-5,529	5 393	-136	1,434	300	136	164	1,598	1,604
Nov	2,346	3,015	-575	-421	-154	2,192	-388	-248	-140	2,052	2,049
Dec	2,411	2,566	482	-306	788	3,199	308	151	157	3,356	4,694
1993 Jan	-3,210	-2,890	-555	-248	-307	-3,517	-298	-72	-226	-3,743	-3,743
Feb	5,712	5,918	-149	-237	88	5,800	-282	31	-313	5,487	5,898
Mar	7,301	7,371	1,588	-222	1,810	9,111	568	152	416	9,527	11,023
Apr	3,214	3,288	1,014	-362	1,376	4,590	359	288	71	4,661	6,022
May	5,295	5,340	-512	-246	-266	5,029	-68	201	-269	4,760	4,757
Jun	4,266	4,394	-601	-260	-341	3,925	155	132	23	3,948	4,158
Jul	1,489	1,132	40	177	-137	1,352	269	180	89	1,441	3,390
Aug	4,559	4,825	-852	-49	-803	3,756	-528	-217	-311	3,445	3,429
Sep	6,287	6,198	-406	-3	-403	5,884	88	92	-4	5,880	5,665
Oct	3,211	3,235	-569	-157	-412	2,799	-119	133	-252	2,547	2,518
Nov	4,527	4,367	-1,282	63	-1,345	3,182	-83	97	-180	3,002	2,997
Dec	3,023	2,993	-585	4	-589	2,434	-321	26	-347	2,087	2,096
1994 Jan	-788	-993	-384	228	-612	-1,400	-348	-23	-325	-1,725	-1,721
Feb	5,124	5,133	-528	-43	-485	4,639	-43	34	-77	4,562	5,284
Mar	8,547	7,980	1,878	-11	1,887	10,434	1,418	578	840	11,274	12,506
Apr	3,073	3,443	878	-270	1,148	4,221	-170	-100	-70	4,151	4,542

Sources: Bank of England, Central Statistical Office and HM Treasury.

financial assets and also liabilities, accounted for by the accumulation of past borrowing. Table 4.3 lists the financial assets and liabilities of central government which represent the current borrowing requirement.

Apart from the collection of tax, the PSBR can be financed in four ways: issuing notes and coins to the public; borrowing from the non-bank private sector (that is, selling gilts and bonds to the private sector); raising external finance (which is foreign currency borrowing and sales of gilts and bonds to non-residents); and borrowing from the domestic banking system. When the amount of gilt sales required has been estimated, the target for broad money growth can be set, and provision made by the Bank of England.

The rate of interest

We have referred to the rate of interest repeatedly during the discussion of monetary policy, but have said very little formally about it. The interest rate is the price of loanable funds, and there is considerable variety in rates depending on how risky the funds are. Not surprisingly, interest rates play a central role within the financial system. As a general rule, the higher the interest rate, the greater the supply of and the less the demand for loanable funds. The funds market is in equilibrium when supply and demand are equal, as was shown in Figure 4.1.

Interest rates are also the subject of some debate between Keynesians and the monetarists. Keynesians view money primarily as an asset rather than a medium of exchange and asset choice is the cost of forgoing liquidity. If cash is exchanged for bonds then the investor's ability to respond to favourable business opportunities is diminished. Hence interest is the price demanded by the market for sacrificing liquidity, and a reward for taking on risk. Therefore interest rate changes are very important to the success of policy and the transmission of monetary effects to the real sector.

To the monetarist, interest is the reward demanded for deferring consumption, and emphasis is placed on the medium of exchange function of money. Investment requires the forgoing of current consumption. Equilibrium is achieved when the rate at which each individual is willing to exchange consumption now for consumption later is equal to the market rate of interest, and when the market rate of interest is equal to the marginal rate of return available on business investment.

These competing viewpoints can be reconciled as follows. The rate of interest offered by a particular instrument can usefully be thought of as consisting of two components. The first part is the return offered on an appropriate riskless asset, that is, a reward for forgoing consumption. The second element is the reward for risk. Together, these form the basis of the differences in the rates of interest or yields on various financial instruments. In this case, the following three items should be noted:

- Term to maturity. In normal circumstances we would expect long-term liabilities to pay higher rates of interest than short-term ones, partly because of the lenders' preference for short-term securities, but also because of the risk to lenders of having to liquidate long-dated securities prior to maturity if they should unexpectedly need the cash. The risk is entailed because interest rates fluctuate and security holders could wish to sell at a time when the price is low.

- Risk proper, which can be thought of as variability in expected yields. In the case of a bond the interest rate and redemption value are usually fixed, so risk is simply the probability of default or exposure to future interest rate changes, again a function of the term to maturity. In the case of equities, any dividends and the final liquidation values are inherently uncertain.
- Transaction costs and taxes. The rates of interest charged to borrowers must cover transaction costs and taxes on interest earnings. We shall return to these characteristics of interest rates in Part II when we consider fixed income securities and other marketable instruments.

Inflation

The causes of inflation are numerous and varied, but for our purposes it is sufficient to recognise the distorting effect changes in price levels, or the expectation of such changes, can have on savings and investment decisions, and on asset values. Particularly, inflation affects the level of interest rates. Suppose, for example, an individual is only willing to save if a 2% real return is expected. If the expected rate of inflation in the coming year is 10%, the return on the planned investment must be at least 12% to be worthwhile. It should follow that changes in the market rate of interest reflect changes in expected inflation.

Measures of inflation are published in the form of indices, such as the retail price index (RPI). This is an indication of the change in overall purchasing power, although many more specific price indices are available for individual industries or regions. The index is used to adjust nominal prices to real, or market, prices.

4.5 The impact of government policy

Recent history shows a number of important changes in the approach to monetary policy, partly arising from political philosophy and also from a number of regulations and more recently, deregulations in the financial sector. These have all had a significant effect on the structure of the British economy.

During the 1950s and 1960s, macroeconomic policy was largely governed by Keynesian principles. Following the Second World War, the primary economic goal was to maintain employment, and the main constraint was the balance-of-payments in a period of fixed exchange rates. The major concerns were to avoid a serious balance-of-payments deficit, drawing away official reserves, and subsequent insufficient demand resulting in increased unemployment. The main

Table 4.3 Financing government borrowing (£m), 1989–93

Analysis by type of instrument

	Liabilities										Assets				
	Borrowing requirement	Notes and coin	Sterling Treasury bills	British government securities	National savings	Tax instruments	Net indebtedness to Bank of England Banking Department[1]	Northern Ireland central government debt[2]	Cost of exchange cover scheme on repayment of principal	Other public sector financing: central government	Government foreign currency debt	Other government overseas financing	Issue Dept. transactions in bills, etc. and indirect lending to other public sector[3]	Net change in official reserves	Deposits with banks
	ABEA	AACB	AACC	AACD	AACE	AACF	RRBT	AACH	AACI	AADP	AACL	AACM	ACMO	AIPA	AADM
1989	−5,134	1,245	2,936	−18,327	−1,547	150	370	−13	87	−97	1,256	−83	3,733	5,436	−284
1990	−4,647	78	2,149	−7,330	800	293	353	−2	−33	213	131	−73	−684	−74	−467
1991	7,706	207	−1,675	9,178	2,222	−24	−131	1	−34	206	1,706	−74	−1,585	−2,680	382
1992	29,192	1,397	−4,423	21,373	5,065	−448	−206	−34	−28	65	9,798	−99	−4,389	1,404	−278
1993	45,674	1,336	−1,250	51,853	2,971	−91	−6,725	−10	−46	1,123	−1,414	−94	−1,447	−701	232
1989/90	−5,360	771	5,733	−15,792	−1,720	268	443	−14	−20	436	880	−83	−1,580	5,064	−18
1990/91	−2,459	1,053	1,029	−2,955	1,387	149	−190	6	−28	−354	1,885	−73	−1,810	−2,349	−209
1991/92	12,925	−1,082	−1,683	11,997	3,129	22	36	−32	−18	−148	695	−74	1,279	−848	−357
1992/93	36,287	949	−4,374	28,079	4,353	−329	−787	6	−50	779	6,982	−100	−1,448	2,182	51
1993/94	48,754	2,932	−2,014	46,733	4,205	−252	283	−27	−43	—	−1,638	−93	—	−1,294	−115
1988 Q1	−2,017	−171	−1,009	1,688	803	−525	−341	−6	153	347	−131	—	−2,397	−653	225
Q2	61	−250	275	−1,453	390	−189	150	−2	21	−399	−18	—	2,196	−631	−29
Q3	−436	705	16	−1,569	385	−137	10	2	−6	451	−1	—	659	−995	42
Q4	−2,541	1,192	2,053	−3,698	−52	−146	319	—	20	51	−301	−73	−834	−482	−590

1989															
Q1	-4,203	-845	-1,884	-6,608	-101	-163	-108	-1	101	-132	385	—	4,275	501	376
Q2	1,953	226	2,647	-5,611	-120	76	282	-2	-38	1,237	-6	—	1,043	2,134	85
Q3	349	293	3,366	-4,340	-699	126	271	-8	-1	-368	339	—	1,062	356	-50
Q4	-3,233	1,571	-1,193	-1,768	-627	111	-75	-2	25	-834	538	-83	-2,647	2,445	-695
1990															
Q1	-4,699	-1,319	913	-4,073	-274	-45	-35	-2	-6	401	9	—	-1,038	129	642
Q2	4,255	581	2,779	-904	368	258	164	4	-1	439	-72	—	756	-76	-23
Q3	-557	21	1,258	-918	369	-27	-385	3	-9	-367	197	—	-286	-433	19
Q4	-3,646	795	-2,801	-1,435	337	107	609	1	-7	-260	-3	-73	-116	306	-1,105
1991															
Q1	-2,511	-344	-207	302	313	-189	-578	6	-1	-166	1,763	—	-2,164	-2,145	900
Q2	6,673	-77	2,671	2,536	581	25	448	-2	-12	129	—	—	1,273	-845	-56
Q3	3,428	-558	-2,018	4,158	739	122	-247	1	-11	-35	-54	—	1,382	136	-189
Q4	116	1,186	-2,121	2,182	589	17	246	-4	-10	278	-3	-74	-2,076	176	-273
1992															
Q1	2,708	-1,633	-215	3,121	1,220	-143	-411	-27	15	-520	752	—	700	-314	161
Q2	10,709	422	-1,125	10,221	1,542	-74	29	-2	-10	342	308	—	-716	-350	109
Q3	9,448	272	-1,795	2,561	1,200	-66	-1,367	-1	-16	436	11,413	—	-4,922	1,657	76
Q4	6,327	2,336	-1,288	5,470	1,103	-165	1,543	-4	-17	-193	-2,675	-99	549	391	-624
1993															
Q1	9,803	-2,081	-166	9,287	508	-24	-992	13	-7	194	-2,064	-1	3,641	464	490
Q2	12,775	473	-1,203	16,147	751	-67	588	-16	-16	-11	524	1	-3,396	-750	-243
Q3	12,335	351	-234	13,608	591	23	-2,326	-2	-5	508	254	—	-223	-541	340
Q4	10,761	2,593	353	12,271	1,121	-23	-3,995	-5	-18	432	-128	-94	-1,469	126	-355
1994															
Q1	12,883	-485	-930	4,707	1,742	-185	6,016	-4	-4	—	-2,288	—	—	-129	143

Notes:

Assets: increase -ve/ decrease +ve;
Liabilities: increase +ve/ decrease -ve.

1. From first quarter 1983 includes deposits by the National Loans Fund. Also includes sterling bank lending to central government.
2. Excludes borrowing from European Investment Bank.
3. Includes Issue department transactions in ECGD backed promissory notes and in shipbuilding credit promissory notes and government guaranteed stock (redemption). (£10 million in 1990 quarter one.)

Sources: Bank of England, Central Statistical Office and HM Treasury.

instrument was fiscal policy. If the balance of payments was negative, a reduction in government spending or an increase in taxation would return government reserves to a satisfactory level. These policies were reversed when the reserves were recovered.

At this time, monetary policy was concerned only with financing the government borrowing requirement. However, it should be remembered that exchange rates were fixed at this time, and there were a number of restrictive regulations in place. These included ceilings on lending by banks and other institutions and also on variability in interest rates. In line with other countries, credit controls were introduced to prevent flows of capital into and out of the country. The emphasis was not on the supply of money, but on the price and availability of credit.

Then in September 1971, credit controls in the UK were abolished, and policy relied on a reserve assets system. The aim of the reforms was to encourage competition between financial institutions, including the widening of the definition of which organisations were part of the monetary sector. The philosophy was that by encouraging competition the authorities could influence monetary aggregates through manipulating interest rates. The money supply was adopted as an indicator of monetary policy but was not made the primary instrument of policy. The new system was intended to be more market orientated, allowing the banks to compete on equal terms and relying on flexible interest rates to control the allocation of credit.

Monetary policy is intended to influence financial behaviour. However, the actual effects have not always been those intended. For instance, the reserve assets system did not provide an effective means of controlling the monetary base. The clearing banks began to seriously compete for business, and other institutions joined in, offering new products and services and creating high levels of debt to the private and commercial sector, all of which increase the supply of money. This continued since the discount houses could, in effect, create money by borrowing on a call basis from the banks and use the funds to acquire bills, certificates of deposit and other short-dated assets. The call money was treated by the authorities as a reserve asset and hence could provide the basis for further bank lending. Thus the banks and discount houses had the ability to create reserve assets at will. In 1972, the government intervened to slow the growth in the money supply, and even this took some time to have any significant effect.

Greater emphasis began to be placed on the money supply, and the practice of announcing money supply targets began in 1976. The monetary aggregates chosen as targets were usually either M0 or M1 (i.e. one of the narrowly defined monetary indicators) and the broader M3. But beginning from 1982, and more particularly from 1985, successful monetary policy was judged by the growth of various money and credit aggregates and by nominal income, along with the exchange rate, rather than money supply alone. Thus while tight monetary policy was the supposed policy instrument of choice, the growth rate of the money supply was not a true target.

The growth in non-bank intermediaries might well have complicated monetary policy in another way. Even if non-bank intermediaries are simply viewed as brokers rather than creators of money, there remains the possibility that the increased activity in non-bank intermediation escalated the velocity of circulation of money and hence weakened the link between aggregate expenditure and the money supply.

Another development during the 1980s was the publicising of public expenditure targets. This is consistent with supply side control, for the public sector borrowing requirement (PSBR) is a large component of the Bank's definition of money stock:

$$\text{Money stock} = \text{PSBR} + L + X - D \tag{4.1}$$

where L is sterling lending to UK private sectors, X is external and foreign currency flows to the private sector, and D is sales of public sector debt to the non-bank private sectors.

By restricting growth in the PSBR (a component purportedly directly under central control), growth in the money stock can be slowed. Growth of the PSBR increases the supply of money because the expansion of net governmental spending (i.e. excess of spending over tax receipts) finds its way into bank deposits, unless this increase in the PSBR is financed by increased sales of debt to non-bank private sectors. In this latter situation, the increase in bank deposits caused by the growth in the PSBR is exactly offset by a decline in deposits occasioned by private sector purchases of government debt.

An interesting aspect of the last decade was the temporary government sector surplus. It is very rare for the public sector to have a surplus of funds. However, during the late 1980s, the PSBR was replaced with a public sector debt repayment (PSDR). This is illustrated in Figure 4.2. Gilts were redeemed by the government rather than sold, although the money stock was still growing very fast. The major source of monetary growth during this time was bank and building society lending to the private sector, again in part a response to deregulation in the housing markets. This period is now known as the Lawson credit boom, named after the Chancellor of the Exchequer at that time.

For most of the 1980s, UK monetary policy was conducted on the basis of explicit monetary targets. This has now been abandoned in favour of a variety of economic indicators, and interest rates are the main instrument used to influence monetary growth. One of the reasons for the failure of monetary targets was the extent of innovation within the financial sector. For example, the competition between banks and building societies to provide retail services resulted in interest-bearing deposit accounts. Another reason was the fall in the rate of inflation during the mid-1980s which increased the private sector's willingness to hold financial assets. These both led to a fall in the circulation of money, not a situation conducive to the effective implementation of monetary targeting.

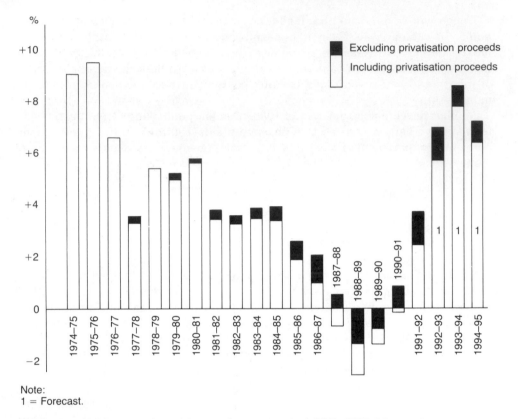

Note:
1 = Forecast.

Figure 4.2 Public sector borrowing requirement as % of GDP, 1974–94.

4.6 Summary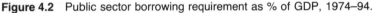

Macroeconomic factors influence the workings of the financial system in a variety of ways, with the Bank of England contributing a major part in implementing monetary policy. The Bank also acts as lender of last resort and provides prudential supervision to the financial sector. Of central importance to monetary policy is the way changes in the supply of money cause banks to change their asset portfolios, put pressure on interest rates and (if unexpected) alter expectations. Government attempts to influence the workings of the real economy by regulation and subsequent financial innovation can have unplanned effects on the financial markets and institutions.

Note

1. A description of the market for gilt-edged securities and the valuation of bonds in general is discussed in Chapter 9.

Further reading

Bain, A. D. (1992), *The Economics of the Financial System*, 2nd edn, Blackwell.

Bank of England Quarterly Bulletin (1993), *The Bank of England's Role in Prudential Supervision*, vol. 33, no. 2, pp. 260–4.

Buckle, M. and J. Thompson (1992), *The United Kingdom Financial System in Transition*, Manchester University Press. Chapter 3 has a detailed discussion of the Bank of England.

Struthers, J. and H. Speight (1986), *Money: Institutions, theory and policy*, Longman. Provides a very thorough treatment of monetary theory and practice in the UK, although some aspects of practice have inevitably been overtaken by more recent developments.

The *Bank of England Quarterly Bulletin* has numerous articles about the Bank's policies and recent economic and financial developments, as well as a statistical appendix.

Questions

4.1 Explain how banks are able to create money. What limits are there on the money-creation capacities of banks?

4.2 Explain the distinction between money and credit.

4.3 Discuss the ways in which an unanticipated increase in the money supply could be expected to affect the financial system.

4.4 Compare and contrast Keynesian and monetarist views on the effectiveness of trying to influence the level of economic activity by controlling the money supply.

4.5 What has been the main character of changes in methods of monetary control in the past two decades?

4.6 Discuss the following proposition:

Control of the money supply does not carry with it any implication about control of the PSBR. An increase in the PSBR can be contained within a given money stock by either increasing the sales of public sector debt to the non-bank private sectors, by a reduction in inflows of foreign currency or by a reduction in bank lending.

4.7 Explain why there are variations in the rates of interest offered on different financial assets. Does the existence of these rate variations necessarily imply that some assets will earn a higher return than others?

4.8 What is the distinction between the expected real rate of interest and the expected money rate of interest? Explain why the difference between the two rates need not necessarily be equal to the observed rate of inflation.

4.9 What is the difference between the national debt and the national deficit?

CHAPTER 5

The valuation of financial instruments

5.1 Introduction

In Chapter 4, we defined the rate of interest to be the price of loanable funds to the borrower and the opportunity cost of holding cash for the lender. In this way, savings and investment are balanced within the economy. The total cost charged for funds differs with maturity, liquidity, riskiness and the transactions costs incurred. Thus funds go to the highest bidders, after allowances are made for perceived differences in risk and the cost of lending.

This chapter shows how individual participants in the financial system can use information about interest rates and the prices of securities to make decisions about lending, borrowing and investing funds. We begin with the concept of the time value of money and its relationship to interest rates and then use this to develop a number of important financial relationships. The mathematics of compound interest are presented in the appendix at the end of the chapter.

5.2 Present and future value

The concept of the time value of money, or time-preference, is based on the idea of the interest rate as an opportunity cost. It states that the value of £1 today is greater than the value of £1 tomorrow. This follows from the fact that idle money can be invested in the financial markets to yield a positive rate of interest.

The ability of money to earn interest and increase in value over time is fundamental to the notion of delayed consumption. The same argument is used to rationalise the decision to borrow funds in order to invest now with the expectation of gains in the future. Interest is a direct cost to the investor, and the borrower carefully considers whether the returns earned from the investment are likely to exceed the interest cost incurred. Similarly, if the decision is whether to borrow funds to enhance current consumption, the borrower compares the benefits to current consumption against the loss of consumption in the future. In both cases, £1 now is obtained only at the cost of more than £1 in the future. Therefore the cost of funds is the market borrowing rate of interest.

In the case of savers, there are no direct interest costs incurred in lending, but the loss of available funds may result in a lost opportunity to benefit from an alternative investment opportunity should one arise. Funds used for one purpose are not available for use in another, maybe more attractive, investment. This cost of holding cash to finance present transactions, or investing in a project in the real economy, is the market lending rate of interest.

The time value of money can be equal to the rate of interest for borrowing or for lending, depending on the time preference of the participants. Either the borrowing rate must be greater than or equal to the lending rate or borrowing must be rationed. If this were not so, it would be possible to borrow and lend without limit and amass a fortune in the process. In fact, borrowing is rationed by price, that is, the higher the level of borrowing, the higher the perceived risk of default, and thus the higher the cost of funds.

Since there is a price-based restriction on borrowing, investment beyond a certain point is not feasible. Where borrowing is rationed, the time value of money is no longer equal to the borrowing rate but to the rate of return on the most attractive investment forgone through lack of funds. For example:

> Suppose an individual has £100 savings and three investment projects, A, B and C, each requiring £50 outlay and offering the prospect of 15%, 20% and 10% annual rates of return, respectively. The logical decision would be to invest in projects A and B but to reject C. The time value of money invested in A and B is the 10% rate of return offered by the rejected project C, for if an extra £50 had been available then 10% is the annual rate of return which would have been earned on the incremental investment. If the 10% yield on the marginal project C is less than the lending rate then the opportunity cost of funds is equal to the lending rate. The cost of investing in A and B is not now the forgone opportunity of investing in C, as this is no longer the highest-earning alternative, but is the loss of returns from lending.

We have identified two possible measures of the time value of money. The first is the market rate of interest, and this measure can be divided into two subordinate market measures, the borrowing rate and the lending rate. The second measure is applicable only in conditions of strict capital rationing and defines the time value of money as the return on the most attractive investment opportunity passed over because of lack of funds. Circumstances will dictate which of the two monetary measures is appropriate to a particular decision problem.

These monetary measures of the time value of money are suitable for use in making decisions about what business investment opportunities will give the highest return in the future, and help to differentiate between the benefits of borrowing or using another means of raising capital, maybe by issuing new shares, to finance new investment. Similar measures are appropriate in decisions about how much an individual should consume now rather than in the future, which is the basis of the saving decision. This is essentially a function of each individual's time-preference. An individual who places a high time value on money, has a high personal rate of time-preference and will want considerably more than £1 of extra consumption tomorrow to warrant giving up £1 today.

On the other hand, another individual who is maybe more risk-averse, and wishes to provide for the future, will have a low personal rate of time-preference. In contrast with market rates, personal rates are unobservable and unique to each individual. Market rates do enter into the consumption-saving decisions of individuals because of the impact on borrowing and lending. Indeed, the market rate of interest can be viewed as a weighted average of the personal rate of individuals.

The connection between market and personal rates of time-preference is as follows. Assume a simple world where all future events are known with certainty, where there is only one market rate of interest, and where all individuals can borrow or lend freely at this rate. Suppose individual X's personal rate of time-preference is less than the market. This means that X is more willing than people in general to trade current consumption for future consumption, and would benefit by reducing current consumption by lending at interest. However, a certain level of liquidity must be maintained and X's personal rate of time-preference will increase. The optimal position will be reached when X's personal rate is equal to the market rate. Given that personal rates are unobservable, it seems likely that the consumption-saving decisions of individuals will be taken more on the basis of subjective trade-offs than on the results of financial calculations. Nevertheless, in principle, consumption-saving decisions involve the use of the time value-of-money concept in exactly the same way as do business decisions.

The concept of personal time-preference rates can be extended from the individual to society as a whole. In the same way as there is a trade-off between current and future consumption for a particular individual, so one can think of there being a social rate of time-preference. This is expressed through the political institutions of the country, and is reflected by the level of importance given to investment in physical infrastructure for industry and health care, education and training for the population.

Clearly the choice of an appropriate measure of the time value of money can be a complex one and must depend on the individual situation. The only general principle is that the measure employed should reflect the cost of applying funds to the particular purpose under consideration. Costs are either the cash outlays on interest to be incurred, the costs of an alternative project, or the opportunity cost of not investing at all. In this chapter we will concentrate on the conventional business problems of valuing financial instruments, investments and financing options.

In a certain world with perfect capital markets, such as those outlined in Chapter 3, firms and individuals alike would be able to borrow and lend at the same risk-free rate of interest. However, in reality, uncertainty and market imperfections can result in many market rates of interest operating simultaneously. In markets dominated by risk-averse investors, interest rates will contain a risk component, which will vary from one financial instrument to another, depending on the perceived degree of that risk. Transaction costs can also cause borrowing and lending rates to diverge.

The valuation of specific financial instruments is presented in Chapters 8, 9 and 10, but the general rule on the appraisal of alternative projects is as follows. For a financial valuation exercise, two sets of data are required. The first is directly relevant to the project, and consists of estimates of the additional cash inflows and outflows which are expected to occur if the project is undertaken. For example, if the project consists of a decision to purchase a government bond, there will be an immediate outlay equal to the purchase price of the bond, followed by inflows of interest coupons at half-yearly intervals.

If it is expected to be held to maturity, the repayment of principal will also be included, which is known as the contractual redemption value of the bond. However, if it is to be sold prior to redemption, the anticipated market value on resale will be included. The second data item required is an estimate of the time value of money.

Assuming these data are available, they can be used to measure the value of the investment. We shall begin with a single period. Assume you are owed £1,000 by a firm with scarce liquid resources at present. They are willing and able to settle up now, but have offered to pay you an additional £100 if settlement is deferred for one year. Assuming you are fully confident of the firm's ability to meet its obligations next year, should you take the £1,000 now or £1,100 in twelve months' time?

The first issue is, what could you do with £1,000 extra right now? One option is to deposit it in a bank at an annual interest rate of, say, 8%. Therefore, one way to decide whether to defer settlement would be to calculate the return on this investment. This is done as follows:

$$£1,000 \ (1.08) = £1,080$$

Since this sum is less than the sum offered, you should agree to defer settlement. You will be £20 richer in a year's time, by the amount of the net terminal value (NTV), which is the value of an investment's cash flows compounded to a focal date at the end of the project.

Another way of approaching the problem would be to try to find an investment, P, which would give a return of exactly £1,100 in one year's time:

$$P(1.08) = £1,100$$

Solving for P gives

$$P = (1100)/(1.08)$$
$$= £1,018.52$$

P is the present value (PV) of the future sum £1,100. As the value of the investment P is greater than the value of the deferred payment project, the net present value (NPV) is:

$$£1,018.52 - £1,000 = 118.52$$

This is the value of an investment's cash flows, discounted to a focal date at the beginning of the project. In this case, the number is positive and therefore the deferred payment will give a higher return in the future. Therefore we can state the simple, although very important rule. If the net present value of a project is positive, funds invested in this way result in a higher future return than if they were invested in a risk-free bank deposit.

Another method of evaluation is to calculate the internal rate of return (IRR). This is the rate of interest which will ensure a return of £1,100 from an investment of £1,000 one year later:

$$£1,000(1 + IRR) = £1,100$$
$$IRR = 0.10 \text{ or } 10\%$$

The internal rate of return can be compared with the market opportunity rate of 8% forgone. As the IRR of 10% is the greater, it is worthwhile deferring settlement.

In this simple example, the three measures give the same signal to the decision-maker, and the choice of which to use here is immaterial. Each measure has a slightly different meaning. NTV indicates the impact of the investment on wealth at a future date; NPV can be thought of as the impact on present wealth; and the IRR is a rate of return which can be compared with the time value of money.

5.3 Compound interest

The previous section considered a single period investment, but many projects have a much longer life. In order to extend our analysis to cope with multi-period investment problems it is necessary to have some understanding of the economic logic of compound interest.

Returning to our simple credit example, what if the offer is to pay £1,100 in two years' time? Is it now a good investment? To compute the net terminal value, the initial sum must be invested for two years. If it has been deposited in the bank at 8%, after one year it has grown to £1,080, and if this new amount is invested for a further year it will be worth:

$$NTV = 1100 - 1080(1.08)$$

This could be expressed more concisely as:

$$NTV = 1000 - 1000(1.08)^2$$
$$= -£66.4$$

But as this is a negative value, final wealth will be diminished, and deferment for two years should not be accepted.

To find the net present value we solve for P in the following expression and subtract the initial £1,000 investment:

$$P(1.08)^2 = 1100$$
$$P = (1100)/(1.08)^2$$
$$= £943.07$$

so net present value $= 943.07 - 1000 = -£56.93$, again a negative number, confirming that initial wealth is diminished, and should be rejected.

Finally, the internal rate of return can be found from either the net present value or the net terminal value formulations. Using the latter:

$$1000(1 + IRR)^2 = 1100$$
$$= 0.0488 \text{ or } 4.88\%$$

Again, this confirms the decision that this project returns a lower level than the cost of capital, i.e. 4.88% is less than 8%, and deferment will leave us worse off. Thus all three methods are consistent, and lead to the same decision.

The extension to problems involving multiple cash flows is now a simple matter. If the cash flow at time t, denoted by C_t, is negative, that is $C_t < 0$ then a payment is expected, and if $C_t > 0$ a receipt is anticipated. In order to carry out a valuation exercise all these cash flows must be converted into equivalent values at a common date. The date selected could be the present, in which case all flows are expressed in present values, or it could be the date at the end of the project where all flows are converted into a terminal value. Or indeed it could be any other date.

Figure 5.1 shows the mapping of a series of cash flows into present values and into terminal values. When each cash flow has been converted to the equivalent value at the given date, they can be added together to give a net present value figure.

Consider another simple example. A bond pays interest of £100 at the end of each year. The bond is to be redeemed at the end of two years for £1,000. The current market price is £950. An alternative investment would pay an annual rate of return of 12%. Is the bond a good investment?

The most natural focal date is the present. This requires replacing each cash flow by its present value. Figure 5.2 illustrates this. Using a present value approach, the first interest coupon of £100 is discounted back for one year, and the second plus the redemption is discounted for two years:

$$NPV = C_0 + C_1/(1 + i)^1 + C_2/(1 + i)^2$$
$$= -950 + 100/(1.12)^1 + (100 + 1000)/(1.12)^2$$
$$= -950 + 100(0.8928) + (1100)(0.7972)$$
$$= -950 + 966.20 = £16.20$$

The present value of the cash inflows from the bond is £966.20, which is greater than the current price of £950, so it appears to be a good investment.

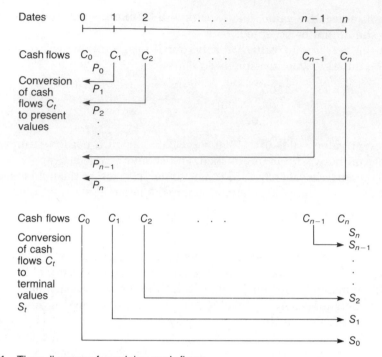

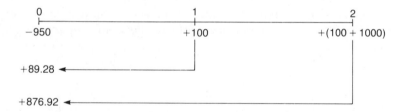

Figure 5.1 Time diagrams for valuing cash flows.

Figure 5.2 Bond example.

The internal rate of return is found by setting NPV=0 and solving for the unknown interest rate i, by trial and error:

$$\text{NPV} = C_0 + \frac{C_1}{(1+i)^1} + \frac{C_2}{(1+i)^2} = 0$$

$$= -950 + \frac{100}{(1+i)^2} + \frac{100+1000}{(1+i)^2} = 0$$

$$i = 0.13 \text{ or } 13\% \text{ approximately}$$

The internal rate of return of 13% is greater than the time value of money, 12%, so purchase is indicated.

If the bond has twenty years to run, the twenty coupons on £100 have to be converted to twenty separate present values, each of which will be different. Fortunately, the tedious arithmetic is avoided if the annual payments are the same, that is when $C_1 = C_2 = C_3 \ldots = C_{20}$, by using a simple annuity formula, given by equation (5A.7) in the appendix. Applied to the present problem, we have

$$PV = 100a_{\overline{20}|.12} + 1000(1.12)^{-20}$$

The value of the annuity factor $a_{20,.12}$ can either be obtained from financial tables, as can all the discount factors used in these examples,[1] or be computed directly:

$$PV = (100)(7.4694) + (1000)(0.1037)$$
$$= 746.94 + 103.70 = £850.64$$

and is considerably less than the current market price of £950. The twenty-year bond is a very poor investment.

A similar labour-saving annuity formula is available for the computation of terminal values. Using equation (5A.8), the terminal value of the stream of twenty coupons, plus the redemption proceeds, is:

$$TV = 100a_{\overline{20}|.12} + 1000$$
$$= 100(72.0524) + 1000$$
$$= 7205.24 + 1000$$
$$= £8,205.24$$

The current market price of the bond has a terminal value of 950 $(1.12)^{20} = £9,163.98$, so the net terminal value is negative:

$$NTV = 8205.24 - 950(1.12)^{20}$$
$$= 8205.24 - 9163.98 = -£958.74$$

The annuity formulae can also save a lot of calculations when trying to estimate the internal rate of return of a long cash flow series. If the present value of the cash inflows is equal to the current market price:

$$100a_{\overline{20}|.i} + \frac{1000}{(1+i)^{20}} = 950$$

Substituting of a number of values of i, and solving for where NPV = 0, gives a result of $i = 0.106$ or 10.6%, which is near enough to £950 to be a useful approximation. This result states that the internal rate of return is lower than the alternative cost of funds. So again, not a good investment.

This section has examined ways of evaluating an investment using net present values and the internal rate of return. However, since the internal rate of return can be found by setting NPV=0, it is clear that these two concepts are closely

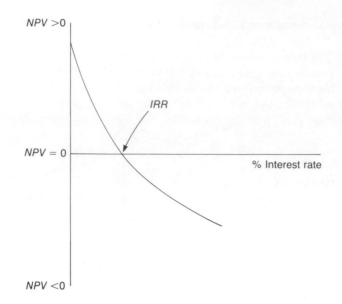

Figure 5.3 An investment's net present value and internal rate of return.

related. This relationship is illustrated in Figure 5.3, where it can be seen that when the internal rate of return is greater than the discount rate, i, the net present value of the investment is positive. Conversely, when the internal rate of return is less than i, the net present value is negative.

However, a number of theoretical difficulties exist in calculating the internal rate of return in multi-period problems, which makes the net present value method generally preferred. One is simply the difficulty in computation. If the project continues for more than two periods, it becomes a very complex calculation and is usually approached by trial and error and iteration, as above. Secondly, the reinvestment rate is assumed to be constant for every period. And thirdly, if there are more than two changes in the sign on the cash flows, that is, if there is additional outlay during the period of the investment giving a negative cash flow figure or a negative return in some periods (that is, a net loss rather than a net profit), there are multiple solutions to the internal rate of return calculation. In the light of these difficulties with the internal rate of return, the net present value calculation is the method of choice.

5.4 Effective rates of interest

The logic of compound interest is not always strictly adhered to in practice, and consequently it is possible to reach inconsistent results. In particular, nominal rates of interest are commonly quoted in the financial markets. The use of nominal rates can make comparisons between investment and financing options very difficult.

Assume two mutually exclusive investments, A and B, each of which will cost £100 to acquire and will generate an income of £10 per year. The only difference between the two is that the income from A is received at the end of each year whereas that from B comes in two equal six-monthly instalments. The interest rate reported in the financial press is the same for both and is arrived at by dividing the annual income by the investment outlay = 10/100 = 10% p.a. An interest figure which takes no account of the frequency of payment during the year is known as a nominal rate; so that 10% quoted is a nominal rate.

However, A and B are not equally attractive. Each year, part of the income of B is received sooner than A's, and referring back to the discussion of present and future value, we know that £1 today is worth more than £1 in the future. To quote the nominal rate is therefore misleading. To correct this, we need another rate of return concept which can be used in comparing alternatives, that is, an effective rate of return.

Consider how £1 invested in B would grow. Every half-year an interest payment of 5% is paid. Thus, after six months the investment would have increased to £1.05. If the interest of £0.05 is reinvested to earn 5%, by the end of the year, the investment will have grown to

$$(1.05)^2 = £1.1025$$

Hence the total amount of interest will be £0.1025 during the year, which is an annual rate of 10.25%. Now a proper comparison between A and B can be made using their effective rates of interest of 10% and 10.25%, respectively.

A third investment, C, also paying interest of £10 annually, but at quarterly intervals, can be treated in the same way. The quarterly rate of interest offered on C is 10/4 = 2.5%. £1 invested at 2.5% per quarter would grow to

$$(1.025)^4 = £1.103813$$

by the year-end. This has an effective yield of 10.38% p.a.

The effective rate increases with greater frequency of compounding. In the limit, where interest is paid continuously, the effective annual rate would become

$$e^{0.10} - 1 = 0.1052 \text{ or } 10.52\%$$

See equation (5A.15).

Many countries, including Britain, have introduced laws which require money lenders and consumer credit organisations to be truthful about the real cost of funds, and disclose the effective rate of interest charged on loans. This is known as the annual percentage rate (APR). But in other areas of finance nominal rates are still widely quoted.

Another distinction to be made is between nominal interest and simple interest. A nominal interest rate is calculated as if all interest were paid or charged at the end of each year, as discussed above. In effect, compounding is assumed to occur once a year. On the other hand, simple interest is computed only on the principal, and interest is not charged on past interest charges, and there is no compounding.

Whether interest is charged on a simple or compound basis can make some difference even during the course of one year, as we have seen in our previous example. Money invested at simple interest grows a constant amount each year, whereas investments compounded grow exponentially. For example, £1 invested at 10% increases as follows:

$$\text{year} = 0 \quad 1 \quad 2 \quad 3 \quad 4 \quad \ldots 20$$
$$\text{simple interest} = 1.00 \ 1.10 \ 1.20 \ 1.30 \ 1.40 \ \ldots 3.00$$
$$\text{compound interest} = 1.00 \ 1.10 \ 1.21 \ 1.33 \ 1.46 \ \ldots 6.73$$

Over short periods the differences are small, but they increase dramatically for longer maturities.

5.5 Non-constant rates of interest

We have assumed throughout this chapter that the time value of money is constant from period to period. This need not be so in theory and is clearly not in practice. We have already noted that interest rates vary from instrument to instrument since securities vary in the term to maturity. A one-year bond might offer a different rate of interest than, say, a two-year one, and this will be discussed further in Chapter 10. It is sufficient for present purposes to note the implications of interest rates varying through time.

Assume we are trying to estimate the present worth of an investment offering £100 in each of the next two years. The interest rate of borrowing for one year is quoted as 10%. If the loan is required for a second year, the cost is 14.03%. Information can be gained from this. First, we have to discount the second year's receipts back to year one at 14.03%:

$$\frac{100}{1.1403} = £87.696$$

and then add the result to the first year's receipts. Secondly, we discount this sum back to the present at 10%,

$$\frac{100.000 + 87.696}{1.10} = £170.63$$

This procedure is equivalent to discounting the flows back at the rates appropriate to each period:

$$PV = \frac{100}{1.10} + \frac{100}{(1.10)(1.1403)} = £170.63$$

The year-one rate of 10% is known. It is the one-year spot rate[2] and can be found by looking at the yield on one-year bonds. But the year-two rate of 14.03% is more difficult, since it is the future spot rate. One way is to find the spot rate on a two-year zero-coupon bond and compare this with the one-year spot rate, as follows.[3]

Assume the yield, in terms of the internal rate of return, on a two-year bond is $(1.12)^2 = £1.2544$ in two years' time. A £1 investment in a one-year bond, will grow to £1.10 after one year. In order to be indifferent between investing (a) in a two-year bond, and (b) in successive one-year bonds, the one-year rate in year two must be 14.03%:

$$(1.10)(1.1403) = 1.2544$$

Thus 14.03% is the forward rate which is implicit in the two-year spot rate of 12%.

A corollary of this relationship between spot rates and implied future rates is that 10% could have been used as the discount rate for the first cash receipt and 12% for the second in the example above, with exactly the same result:

$$PV = \frac{100}{1.10} + \frac{100}{(1.12)^2} = £170.63$$

The two cash receipts of £100 are treated here as distinct claims and are priced, or discounted, quite separately.

5.6 The effects of inflation

In our discussion of present and future value, the implicit assumption was that there was no change in overall price levels, and therefore purchasing power was constant over the life of the investment. Clearly this is untrue, inflation does occur and has a marked impact on the financial system. Therefore we should consider how to take account of this in present value calculations, for example, if projects with different time horizons are being compared.

Inflation affects all cash flows and the expectation of changing price levels increases the difficulty of forecasting future income streams and outflows when valuing an investment in the real sector. However, inflation also affects interest rates, and thus the decisions of savers and investors. Savers can be expected to try to hedge against the effects of inflation. Consider the individual who is only willing to save if the gain to delayed consumption is 2%. If expected inflation is 10%, the investment will have to return 12% in order to be 2% better off in a year's time. In a well-functioning market, interest rates should incorporate the market's anticipated inflation correctly. To the extent that the expectation of price changes the propensities to save and to borrow, then the real rate, in this case 2%, will change as well.

Using i for interest rate, and Δp for the anticipated change in prices, we can adjust the nominal (or money) interest rate by the expected inflation rate to give a market (or real) interest rate as follows:

$$1 + i_{\text{nominal}} = (1 + i_{\text{market}})(1 + \Delta p)$$

Therefore for accuracy and consistency, discount nominal cash flows at the nominal interest rate, and real cash flows at the real interest rate. If anticipated price changes are expected to affect all cash flows, and the interest rate by the same amount, there will be no difference in the outcome. But this is sometimes not the case, and so a comparison is worth computing. Example:

If the market rate of interest is 5% and expected inflation is 3%, nominal interest rates are:

$$i_{\text{nominal}} = (1 + 0.05)(1 + 0.03) - 1 = 0.0815 = 8.15\%$$

5.7 Valuation and pricing

It is interesting to contemplate a state of affairs in which the investment, financing and perhaps even savings decisions of individuals and firms can be represented in terms of the logic of compound interest. Individuals increase their savings from current income if the prospective yields on investments exceed their personal rates of time-preference. They compute the present values of alternative investment opportunities and choose those which are greater than or equal to the purchase price, and they sell investments where the present value is less than the purchase price.

Firms compute the net present value of potential investment projects and select those which are greater than zero, sometimes raising additional finance where necessary to do this. If there were general agreement about the pattern of future cash flows from different securities, then market prices would fall into line with those present values estimated by the market participants. More realistically, there may often be considerable disagreement about expected returns in the future, and hence the perceived value of investments varies, and with it, the demand for them.

The PV formula (equation 5A.4) provides insight into the market-pricing process. A share or a bond can be thought of as an entitlement to a series of future n cash payments, $C_0, C_1 C_2, \ldots C_n$, each of which has a price of its own $P_0, P_1 P_2, \ldots P_n$, respectively. The price of the complete security, the present value, must be equal to the sum of the prices of the constituent cash flows:

$$PV = P_0 + P_1 + P_2 + \ldots + P_n$$

If this equation does not hold, there are arbitrage profits to be made by selling overpriced securities and buying underpriced ones. The price P_t of the component cash flow C_t, is calculated by discounting at the market rate of return i:

$$P_t - \frac{C_t}{(1+i)^t}$$

The discounting factor $(1+i)^{-t}$ can be thought of as the price at time t_0 of £1 at time t_1. For example, with $i = 15\%$ and $t = 5$, the current price of a dividend or interest coupon of £1 in 5 years' time is £0.497. A payment of £1 at $t = 6$ will have a current price of £0.432.

It is worth noting that short-term money instruments are sometimes valued by an equivalent, although slightly different, procedure. The present value is computed by deducting, or discounting, a proportion d of the final proceeds S:

$$P = S - dS = S(1-d)$$

in the case of a twelve-month bill. In contrast, the present value calculation uses the market rate i:

$$P = \frac{S}{(1+i)^1}$$

There is a direct relationship between i and d, shown in equation (5A.12). It makes no difference which method is applied, as long as it is applied consistently. In practice, the discounting is done on a simple rather than compound basis:

$$P = S(1-nd)$$

For example, a three-month £1,000 bill will be discounted at 12% per annum on a simple basis to

$$P = 1000(1 - (0.25)\,(0.12)) = £970$$

5.8 Summary

This chapter has discussed the methods used to analyse and value financial assets. In explaining the time value of money, alternative methods have been shown to be consistent. Thus if two investment opportunities are compared by discounting the cash flows back to one common date, the same order of preference will be revealed if evaluation takes the form of compounding forward the cash flows to a terminal common date. The existence of different levels of interest rates were briefly examined, including rates that change over time, rates that are computed at frequent intervals and rates affected by expected changes in purchasing power. These techniques will be used with respect to specific securities in later chapters.

Notes

1. Financial tables are printed on pages 344–51, and it would be a valuable exercise to work through the examples in this chapter using these tables to find the value of the discounting factor. Note that Table 1 lists the single period value and Table 2 provides the annuity factor, which is a cumulative value.
2. The rate of interest to maturity currently offered on a particular class of bond or bill.
3. Zero-coupon bonds are needed for this calculation to avoid reinvestment complications. These are bonds where no annual interest is paid, but which are heavily discounted.

Further reading

Brealey, R. A. and S. C. Myers (1991), *Principles of Corporate Finance*, 4th edn, McGraw-Hill. Contains a very thorough treatment of financial decision-making, with extensive coverage of economic and computational aspects and numerous problem sets.

Bromwich, M. (1977), *The Economics of Capital Budgeting*, Penguin. An excellent and highly readable explanation of the economic principles of investment. The mathematics are treated lightly and there are few numerical examples and no problem sets. The first five chapters deal with basic principles, the remaining chapters being concerned with the problems of business investment and financial management.

Questions

5.1 Assume that you are given the choice between £100 now and £100 one year from now. Which would you choose? Explain. Assume that you could invest money at 10% p.a. How large would the amount one year from now have to be for you to be indifferent between the two choices?

5.2 The time value of money is 5% p.a. Compute the present value of £100:

(a) received one year from now
(b) received at the end of five years
(c) received at the end of twenty years.

Compute these values again using twenty years from now as the focal (i.e. valuation) date.

5.3 Assuming a 10% rate of interest, compute the present value of a series of five payments of £100 a year.

(a) the first to commence in one year's time
(b) to commence immediately.

5.4 Estimate the present market value of a ten-year bond which has a face and maturity value of £1,000 and pays interest annually at 3%. The first interest payment is one year from now. The current market yield on bonds of this type is 12%.

5.5 You are owed £1,000 by A. A wants to ease the strain of repayment by spreading it out over four years in equal instalments – the first now and the remainder at yearly intervals. If money is worth 15% to you, what should be the amount of each payment?

5.6 In the text it is shown that when the time value of money is 12% a £1,000 two-year bond paying interest at 10% has a present value of £966.20, whereas a twenty-year 10% £1,000 bond is worth only £850.64. This seems contradictory, when the second bond offers eighteen more interest coupons than the first. Explain.

5.7 You approach a money lender for a loan. The weekly interest charge is 1/2%, i.e. 26% per year. If interest is charged as stated, what is the effective annual rate?

5.8 You are planning to buy a house and need a mortgage of £20,000. The mortgage is to be of the conventional twenty-year repayment type, repayments to be made in equal monthly instalments commencing in one month's time. A building society states that it will charge interest at 16% p.a. whereas your bank quotes a rate of 1.25% per month, i.e. an effective rate of 16.0755% p.a. But on further enquiry you discover that they compute repayments differently. The bank computes the monthly repayment using the monthly interest rate of 1.25%. The building society calculates an annual repayment figure on the assumption that repayment occurs at the end of each year and then divides this figure by twelve to arrive at the monthly charge. Calculate the payments required by each and explain why they are different.

5.9 A £10,000 ten-year bond pays interest twice-yearly at 10% nominal. Its current market price is £7,055. Find by trial and error the effective rate of return currently yielded by the bond.

5.10 A £100,000 bill maturing in nine months' time is discounted at 16% p.a. simple.

What is the bill's current market price?

What is the implied (a) simple and (b) compound rate of interest on the bill?

5.11 Assume year-to-year interest rates for years one to three are 10%, 11% and 12% respectively. What should be the yields on no-coupon bonds maturing in (a) one, (b) two and (c) three years' time?

Appendix
The mathematics of
compound interest

Let i be the compound rate of interest per period, P be the principal (i.e. amount of money at the beginning) and S be the amount of the sum invested. After one period the investment P will have grown by the addition of interest iP to

$$S = P + iP$$
$$= P(1 + i)$$

If the increased sum $P(1 + i)$ is left to earn interest for yet another period, the amount will grow by the addition of interest on both the principal and the interest already earned:

$$S = P(1 + i) + iP(1 + i)$$
$$= P(1 + i)^2$$

After n periods the amount will have grown to

$$S = P(1 + i)^n \qquad (5A.1)$$

Now, suppose we already know the final amount S to be received n periods hence and want to know what it is worth now. Clearly the present value of S is the principal P which could be invested now such that it will grow to S after n periods. To find P, all we have to do is solve (5A.l) for P:

$$P = \frac{S}{(1 + i)^n} \qquad (5A.2)$$

These results can be generalised without difficulty to deal with more complicated patterns of cash flows. Suppose an investment offers the prospect of cash receipts of amounts $C_0, C_1, C_2, \ldots, C_n$, occurring at the end of periods $0,1,2, \ldots, n$, respectively. Each receipt can be invested at compound interest up to the end of period n by separately applying equation (5A.l):

$$S^t = C_t(1 + i)^{n-t}, t = 0,1, \ldots, n$$

The terminal value TV of the investment at n is obtained by adding together the amounts of the separate cash flows:

$$TV = S_0 + S_1 + \ldots + S_n$$
$$= C_0(1+i)^n + C_1(1+i)^{n-1} + \ldots + C_n$$

$$TV = \sum_{t=0}^{n} C_t(1+i)^{n-t} \tag{5A.3}$$

Present values can be obtained by application of (5A.2) to each cash flow in turn:

$$P_t = \frac{C_t}{(1+i)^t}, \, t = 0, 1, \ldots, n$$

The present value (PV) of the series is obtained by application of the fundamental Additivity Principle of finance, i.e. by adding together the present values of the separate elements:

$$PV = P_0 + P_1 + \ldots + P_n$$

$$= C_0 + \frac{C}{(1+i)} + \ldots + \frac{C_n}{(1+i)^n}$$

$$PV = \sum_{t=0}^{n} C_t(1+i)^{-t} \tag{5A.4}$$

Simpler versions of equations (5A.3) and (5A.4) can be developed when the cash flows take the form of an *annuity*, i.e. when all the cash flows are of equal sign and amount (or grow or decline in a mathematically regular fashion). For our purposes it is sufficient to concentrate on *ordinary annuities*. An ordinary annuity is a series of n equal and equally spaced payments starting at the end of the first period:

$$C_0 = 0 \text{ and } C_1 = C_2 = \ldots = C_n = C$$

The PV of an ordinary annuity can be written as

$$PV = \frac{C}{(1+i)} + \frac{C}{(1+i)^2} + \ldots + \frac{C}{(1+i)^n}$$

$$= C\left[\frac{1}{(1+i)} + \frac{1}{(1+i)^2} + \ldots + \frac{1}{(1+i)^n}\right]$$

Following traditional actuarial practice, we put $v = (1+i)^{-1}$ and write out the geometric progression in square brackets in more compact form:

$$an,i = v + v^2 + \ldots + v^{n-1} + v^n \tag{5A.5}$$

Multiplying the left-hand side of (5A.5) by $(1+i)$ corresponds to dividing by v. Thus $an, i(1+i) = 1 + \ldots + v^{n-1}$ and subtracting (5A.5) from the result yields

$$a_{\overline{n}|i}(1+i) - a_{\overline{n}|i} = 1 - v^n$$

so

$$a_{\overline{n}|i} = \frac{(1-v^n)}{i} \tag{5A.6}$$

The PV of an ordinary annuity can therefore be reduced to a simple formula:

$$PV = Ca_{\overline{n}|i}$$

$$= C\left[\frac{1-V^n}{i}\right] \tag{5A.7}$$

The TV of an ordinary annuity can be obtained by multiplying (5A.7) by $(1+i)^n$

$$TV = Ca_{\overline{n}|i}(1+i)^n$$
$$= Cs_{\overline{n}|i} \tag{5A.8}$$

where

$$s_{\overline{n}|i} = \frac{(1+i)^n - 1}{i} \tag{5A.9}$$

The annuity formula most commonly employed in investment work is (5A.7). Relevant formulae for other annuities can be derived straightforwardly from (5A.7) and (5A.9) and are therefore not developed here.

For some financial instruments interest is charged not at a specified rate i on the principal (or present value) P but as a proportion d of the final amount S. Suppose the instrument has only one period to go before maturity. Its present value with one period to run is P and during the period the instrument increases in value by the amount of discount dS:

$$P + dS = S$$
$$P = S(1-d) \tag{5A.10}$$

In order to find the value of the instrument two periods before maturity it is only necessary to apply the discount rate d to the value one period later, given by (5A.10):

$$P + dS(1 - d) = S(1 - d) = p = S(1 - d)^2$$

More generally, for an instrument with n periods to run to maturity the present value is

$$P = S(1 - d)^n \tag{5A.11}$$

The relationships between d and i can be obtained by comparing the two present value formulas, (5A.2) and (5A.11). Setting them equal and solving yields an expression for i in terms of d,

$$i = \frac{d}{(1 - d)} \tag{5A.12}$$

and another for d,

$$d = \frac{i}{(1 + i)} \tag{5A.13}$$

Obviously, $d < i$ because d is computed on the final value S and i is on the present value P where $P < S$.

This brief review of the mathematics of compound interest is concluded with an examination of the implications of variations in the frequency of compounding. Interest on a bond is usually payable semi-annually; for many types of loans it is charged monthly. Interest rates are almost invariably quoted on an annual basis, even when interest is charged more (or less) frequently than once a year. In many financial markets the annual rate quoted is a *nominal* one, meaning one which simply takes the total amount of interest paid during the year as a proportion of the amount invested, with no account being taken of the returns which could be gained from reinvesting interim interest payments. Proper comparison of instruments with different payments frequencies requires the use of effective annual interest rates.

Suppose interest is added at equal intervals m times per year. (If $m = 2$, interest is added twice yearly; if $m = 4$, interest is on a quarterly basis, and so on.) We denote the nominal rate of interest by r. The *effective rate of interest* is therefore given as the amount of interest which would accumulate during twelve months on a compound basis when interest at the rate r/m is added m times and reinvested:

$$i = [1 + (r/m)]^m - 1 \tag{5A.14}$$

The payoff on a security offering interest at the rate of $100i\%$ once at the end of the year will be the same as that on another in which interest is added m times during the year at the rate of $100(r/m)\%$ on each occasion.

For a given nominal rate r, the result of increasing the frequency of compounding is to produce a larger effective rate i. In the limit with m approaching infinity, compounding becomes continuous and (5A.14) becomes

$$i = \lim_{m \to \infty} [1\,(r/m)]^m - 1$$

$$= e^r - 1 \tag{5A.15}$$

where $e = 2.718$ is the base for natural logarithms, and a constant.

The PV and TV formulae for an ordinary annuity, (5A.7) and (5A.8), can be changed to deal with the case where payments are made continuously rather than at the end of each year and are presented below without proof:

$$PV = C \left[\frac{1 - e^{-n}}{r} \right] \tag{5A.16}$$

$$TV = C \left[\frac{e^n - 1}{r} \right] \tag{5A.17}$$

CHAPTER 6

International macroeconomic policy

6.1 Introduction

There are a number of ways in which the economy of the UK is linked to the financial markets in other countries. This chapter considers the position of the UK within Europe, and continues with some comments about the wider implications of an international financial system. We also include a discussion of exchange rates, which is one instrument of monetary control excluded from the previous chapter, and in particular, the effect on the ability of the UK to implement monetary policy while operating within an international financial environment.

To address the position of the UK as part of the European community, two broad topics need to be considered. One is the increased competition in all aspects of business which has resulted from more open markets for a wide range of goods and services, including those in the financial sector. This originated with the passing of the Single European Act in 1987, most of which became effective in 1992. The other is the effect of economic and monetary union on the member states of the European Community. Thus, whereas the first is about increased competitiveness in the marketplace, the second implies a more fundamental change in the relationship between the member states and raises questions about the control of national economic and monetary policy.

However, before these two issues are discussed, we should put the current international exchange rate systems into perspective by briefly considering recent history, since the present European Monetary System is the latest in a long series of possible arrangements in an international financial system which appears to be permanently in a state of evolution.

6.2 International financial systems: a historical perspective

When exchange rates between countries are flexible, they are freely determined through the mechanism of supply and demand, whereas when they are fixed, they are managed by governments through the authority of their central bank. During the twentieth century, systems of both flexible and fixed exchange rates have existed, although with various methods of adjustment in the latter.

Systems of linked exchange rates set to a common standard are not new. This adjustment mechanism between currencies is known as the *price-specie*[1] model and has been centred around either a precious metal, such as gold or silver, or more recently, tied to a major currency like the US dollar. Until 1914, the world was on a gold standard but this was brought to an end by the First World War. After the war there followed a period of flexible exchange rates, during which many countries suffered from hyperinflation. The gold standard was readopted in 1926 but not very successfully as many national economies were, at that time, in a severe depression and there was little chance of any formal reorganisation of the international financial system in such an environment. The onset of the Second World War did nothing to improve this situation.

But in 1944, at the meeting at Bretton Woods, a new system to replace the failed gold standard was agreed, in the hope that it would prevent another breakdown of the international financial order. The *Bretton Woods Agreement* reintroduced a worldwide standard tied to the US dollar. The system was required to maintain control of exchange rates so that member countries were not allowed to change their rates to gain individual competitive advantage. In addition, a reserve base for deficit countries would be organised, and the International Monetary Fund (IMF) was established to collect and allocate these funds.

Many of the features in the Articles of Agreement signed in 1944 were commendable and can be recognised in the articles of subsequent systems. The main items agreed were intended to:

- Promote international monetary cooperation.
- Facilitate the growth of trade.
- Promote exchange rate stability.
- Establish a system of multilateral payments.
- Create a reserve base.

The reserves were contributed on a quota system, based on the national income and world trading activity of the individual members. Associated with the quotas, *Special Drawing Rights* (SDRs) could be used to meet payment imbalances and provide a net addition to the stock of reserves within the system. Exchange rates were set at parity with the price of gold, expressed in US dollars. Rates had to be maintained within 1% of the official parities, and intervention by central banks occurred if they exceeded that, with revisions if necessary. At the same time, a proposal for a new, single unit of currency was suggested by the British delegate at Bretton Woods, Lord Keynes, but was rejected.

The system worked well for a number of years, but began to fall apart in the 1960s. In 1971 this agreement was replaced with the *Smithsonian Agreement*. This allowed a wider band around parity, which became known as the snake, and with some countries in the European Economic Community maintaining closer parities with each other, which became known as the snake in the tunnel. This European fixed exchange rate system was later revised to become the European Monetary System (EMS) in 1979.

6.3 The European Monetary System

The motivation for the European Monetary System was similar to that of Bretton Woods. It was to provide a zone of monetary stability in Europe by stabilising exchange rates and maintaining control over inflation. It was hoped the new system would be an improvement upon Bretton Woods in three ways:

- A symmetric responsibility to maintain exchange rates within the parity bands.
- Free capital mobility.
- The minimisation of destabilising revisions or realignments.

Major additions to the system were the form of the structure of the currency parities, which became the Exchange Rate Mechanism and the eventual adoption of a single currency, the European Currency Unit (ECU), whereas a reserve facility to a European central institution is similar to the contribution of SDRs to the International Monetary Fund. These features are now examined a little more fully.

The Exchange Rate Mechanism

The system of parities is more complex than the previous one. Rather than all currencies tied independently to a single standard, the member states who are still included are in a parity grid, known as the Exchange Rate Mechanism (ERM). This is constructed in the form of a matrix with all currencies set at a central parity with each other, and an upper and lower limit on either side. Thus all elements in the matrix consist of three rates, the high, low and central parities, as illustrated in Table 6.1.

Therefore the ERM is a system of exchange rates fixed within the community, but floating with respect to other non-union currencies. An important aspect of this matrix system is that if a currency moves outside its permitted range, the central banks of both countries involved have a mutual obligation to intervene to return the parity to its position. This means that not only weak currencies, but also strong ones, are required to assist the return to parity, hence the symmetry of responsibility rather than the onus being wholly on the weaker one as in previous systems.

Early warning systems prompt intervention before the limits are reached, in the form of the divergence indicator. This is based on the change in value of the individual currency in terms of the ECU. This indicator was introduced to reduce the need for destabilising realignments, although these are possible, with agreements with other member states.

The UK joined the ERM in October 1990, but in spite of being in a small group

Table 6.1 The parity grid of the exchange rate mechanism

		BFc/LFc 100	Dkr 100	FrFc 100	DM 100	I£1	Lit 1,000	Fl 100	Pis 100	£1
Belgium/Luxembourg:	S	—	553.000	628.970	2,109.50	56.5115	28.1930	1,872.15	33.6930	64.6050
	C	—	540.723	614.977	2,062.55	55.2545	27.5661	1,830.54	31.7316	60.8451
BFc/LFc	B	—	528.700	601.295	2,016.55	54.0250	26.9530	1,789.85	29.8850	57.3035
Denmark:	S	18.9143	—	116.320	390.160	10.4511	5.21400	346.240	6.23100	11.9479
	C	18.4938	—	113.732	381.443	10.2186	5.09803	338.537	5.86837	11.2526
DKr	B	18.0831	—	111.200	373.000	9.9913	4.98500	331.020	5.52600	10.5976
France:	S	16.6310	89.9250	—	343.050	9.18900	4.58450	304.440	5.47850	10.50550
	C	16.2608	87.9257	—	335.386	8.98480	4.48247	297.661	5.15981	9.89389
FrFc	B	15.8990	85.9700	—	327.920	8.78500	4.38300	291.040	4.85950	9.31800
Germany:	S	4.95900	26.8100	30.4950	—	2.74000	1.36700	90.7700	1.63300	3.13200
	C	4.84837	26.2162	29.8164	—	2.67894	1.33651	88.7526	1.53847	2.95000
DM	B	4.74000	25.6300	29.1500	—	2.61900	1.30650	86.7800	1.44900	2.77800
Ireland:	S	1.85100	10.00870	11.3830	38.1825	—	0.510246	33.8868	0.609772	1.16920
	C	1.80981	9.78604	11.1299	37.3281	—	0.498895	33.1293	0.574281	1.10118
£	B	1.76950	9.56830	10.8825	36.4964	—	0.487799	32.3939	0.540858	1.03710

Italy: Lit	S 3,710.20	20,062.0	22,817.0	76,540.0	2,050.03	—	67,912.0	1,222.30	2,343.62
	C 3,627.64	19,615.4	22,309.1	74,821.7	2,004.43	—	66,405.3	1,151.11	2,207.25
	B 3,546.90	19,179.0	21,813.0	73,157.0	1,959.84	—	64,928.0	1,084.10	2,078.79
Netherlands: Fl	S 5.58700	30.2100	34.3600	115.2350	3.08700	1.54000	—	1.84050	3.52950
	C 5.46286	29.5389	33.5953	112.6730	3.01848	1.50590	—	1.73345	3.32389
	B 5.34150	28.8825	32.8475	110.1675	2.95100	1.47250	—	1.63250	3.13050
Spain: Pis	S 334.619	1,809.40	2,057.80	6,901.70	184.892	92.2400	6,125.30	—	203.600
	C 315.143	1,704.05	1,938.06	6,500.00	174.131	86.8726	5,768.83	—	191.750
	B 296.802	1,604.90	1,825.30	6,121.70	163.997	81.8200	5,433.10	—	180.590
United Kingdom: £	S 1.74510	9.43610	10.7320	35.9970	0.964240	0.481050	31.9450	0.553740	—
	C 1.64352	8.88687	10.1073	33.8984	0.908116	0.453053	30.0853	0.521514	—
	B 1.54790	8.36970	9.5190	31.9280	0.855260	0.426690	28.3340	0.491160	—

Notes:

These are the parity rates from 8 October 1990.

S = Exchange rate at which the central bank of the country in the left-hand column will sell the currency identified in the row at the top of the table.

C = Bilateral central rate.

B = Exchange rate at which the central bank of the country in the left-hand column will buy the currency identified in the row at the top of the table.

Source: Bank of England Quarterly Bulletin, November 1990.

of countries with wider limits around central parity than the rest, was unable to
maintain the required parity, and was suspended from the Exchange Rate
Mechanism on Black Wednesday, 16 September 1992.

The single currency

Although rejected at Bretton Woods almost fifty years ago, the unit of single
currency is now part of the current European Monetary System. The European
Currency Unit, the ECU, is based on a combination of the currencies of the
member states, weighted by individual countries' gross domestic product and
their strength in international trade. The ECU was originally intended for
transactions between governments, but is used more widely than that, with
corporations issuing debt, the UK government issuing Treasury bills, and some
futures and options all denominated in ECUs. General use by individuals as part
of their daily financial transactions is part of the final stage of European Union.

Very short-term financing facility

Another feature originally established at Bretton Woods is the member states'
contribution of reserves. Similar to the system of SDRs, states in the European
Union make contributions to the European Monetary Cooperation Fund, receiving
ECUs in exchange. Further funds can be borrowed by central banks to be used if
intervention is necessary to return a currency to its required range in the fixed
parity system. This is known as the very short-term financing facility, and
provides automatic credit for up to three months.

6.4 European Economic and Monetary Union

At its completion, European Monetary Union would allow the possible convergence of national monetary policies to a single European system of exchange rates
with the determination of monetary policy through a European Central Bank. In
preparation for this, the European Monetary Institute has been established to
strengthen cooperation between the central banks and coordinate policy.

The EMS works best if the member states have convergent economic growth
patterns, and more importantly, controlled inflation. From its inception, the
countries who were most successful at managing inflation within the limits
imposed by the ERM benefited from less volatility in their exchange rates,
providing a stable environment for the real sector to plan long-term investment
and remain competitive. Many member states were able to use the constraining
external influence of the fixed exchange rates to converge on a common path,
typically dictated by Germany, and were then able to benefit from sharing this low
inflation. Under these conditions, the disadvantage of having to sacrifice monetary

independence is outweighed by the help gained from the discipline of being aligned with a low-inflation economy.

Full monetary union in Europe as set out in the December 1991 *Maastricht Treaty* is still to be achieved, although original plans were for this to occur before the end of this century. Included in this is the introduction of a single currency to replace all existing national currencies. Along with this, a European Central Bank will be responsible for European monetary policy, that is, setting European money supply and setting European interest rates. But before this can take place, convergence criteria relating to inflation, interest and exchange rates as well as national debt and public sector borrowing requirements have to be met and national central banks must become independent of government. Whether this is possible is still not clear, and the original schedule has already been set back.

It is proposed that the European Central Bank is established as an independent institution, with a council of governors consisting of the governors of the national central banks. The implementation of policy decisions taken by the European Central Bank will be the responsibility of the national central banking authorities within their own country. Nevertheless, since the control would be at the European level rather than at national level, it is essential that the national central banks are independent of their national governments, an issue we will return to later.

6.5 International aspects of the law of one price

Having outlined a system of monetary union, we should consider the difficulties in implementation, many of which are founded in the relationship between economic conditions and exchange rates. To understand this, we should consider the basic theory of exchange rate determination.

Two factors affect changes in exchange rates over the long run, interest rates and inflation. Both are important and we should consider them briefly.

Purchasing power parity

This relationship is commonly known as the law of one price, and essentially states that a good should have the same value in two countries, only differing in the currency in which that value is expressed. If this were not so, there would be an advantage to be gained from purchasing the good in one country and selling it in another, assuming free trade and no transactions costs. This trade would continue until prices adjust and there is equality between the prices in the two countries. Such an adjustment is based on the arbitrage rationale explained in Chapter 3.

Example:

Suppose that the exchange rate between the UK and the US is £1:$1.50. Now suppose that the price of a beer in London is £1 and in New York it is $1.50. If this were representative of the average good or service, we could say that purchasing power parity holds since the relative prices are 1.5/1, which is equal to the exchange rate. But supposing inflation in the UK pushes the price of a beer to £1.10. Now the ratio of the prices is 1.5/1.1. This is equivalent to an exchange rate of £1:$1.36. Sterling is now weaker relative to the dollar, because of the UK inflation.

Interest rate parity

If purchasing power parity applies in the goods market, interest rate parity is a parallel situation in the securities market. Therefore we can say that funds are simply another good, and the law of one price can explain interest parity too, since interest rates are the cost of borrowing. If interest parity holds, funds invested in one country will earn the same as in another. If interest rates are different, investors will move their funds abroad and earn a higher amount. This process will continue until the costs of borrowing are the same, again assuming no barriers to the movement of funds and no transactions costs.

Extending the example used above:

> Suppose that the exchange rate between the UK and the US is again £1:$1.50. Now suppose £1 is invested in the UK at 10% per annum; at the end of the year it will be worth £1.1. But if £1 can be invested in the US at 12% per annum, it will be worth £1.12. Expressed in dollars, this is $1.34. The exchange rate is now £1:$1.34, and the higher interest rate in the US has strengthened the dollar against sterling.

Of course, in both these situations there are transactions costs, including the costs of currency exchange, search costs to gain information on relative prices, different tax advantages to investment, and in some cases, barriers to movement of funds and other goods across national borders. Because of this, the previous analysis based on a basket of goods rather than a single item is often more appropriate.

6.6 The UK in the European Monetary Union

The implications of the two parity conditions above are made clear when we consider the effects on the UK of the European Monetary Union.

We have already explained the relationship between currencies in the Exchange Rate Mechanism, including the structure of the parity grid. Given the inflexibility of this system, the ability of the UK to conduct monetary policy through exchange rates is very limited if sterling were to rejoin the system.

In particular, in the light of the law of one price outlined above, it is clear that neither the manipulation of interest rates nor control over the money supply is available, since both of these would have an effect on the exchange rate. Indeed, within the fixed parity stage of the ERM and with a single currency, it is necessary for interest rates to be equal in each member state. Consequently, it would be impossible for independent states to be able to control their domestic policy, and monetary policy will be set at a European level, by agreement of the council of governors. Full monetary union implies economic convergence, and as long as there are structural differences between economies complete monetary union will not be achieved.

6.7 The single market for financial services

However, while monetary union is still uncertain, the European market for financial services is already established. The idea of a common market in Europe was first proposed in the *Treaty of Rome* in 1957, but progress was slow, and it was not until the 1985 publication of the European Commission White Paper on Completing the Internal Market that the plan began to be implemented.

The original purpose of the single European market was to benefit both suppliers and consumers by lowering the costs of trade. This included the removal of non-tariff barriers and the introduction of the free movement of capital. The expectation was that the increased competitiveness would allow institutions to benefit from economies of scale and improve the efficiency of firms operating within the community. Investors would gain from decreased costs and increased access to additional services. In this way the countries in Europe could become more competitive in world markets and achieve higher economic growth than they could independently.

The single market for financial services has raised a number of issues in terms of the regulation of entry and the conduct of operations, and of the supervision of institutions within the financial sector. Restrictions on capital movements had already been eliminated by the UK – it was the first country in the community to remove restrictions on flows of capital – but some member states continued until 1992 when they were required to comply with the directive on capital movements. This established the right for anyone to open a bank account anywhere in the Community, to obtain a loan from any bank or building society, take out insurance in any country or invest through an institution of their choice.

Within the single market for financial services, the European Union has adopted directives covering banking and the securities business. These are the *Second Banking Directive* and the *Investment Services Directive*, and they apply to banks and other financial institutions, providing a common framework for the regulation of investment firms as well as the securities activities of banks. All financial firms are also subject to the *Capital Adequacy Directive*, which covers many aspects of their business including various types of risk and settlement.

One component of the Second Directive deals with the right of entry to markets, that is, the right to operate a business in any member state, and this is now established in the financial sector. Any product or service offered in one member state can be offered in all of the others, provided the suppliers comply with the host country regulations. This means that, for example, anyone wishing to operate a bank in the UK has to apply for a licence from the Bank of England, whether they are a UK resident or from another state in the European Union. Then, having acquired a licence for one member state, they can operate equally in any other.

Another aspect of the Second Directive is concerned with home country control and reciprocity. This requires that supervision of non-UK financial institutions in the UK is the responsibility of the home regulatory authority rather than that of the host country, although efforts have been made to harmonise regulations, particularly prudential requirements.

This directive also implies that institutions are able to offer the same range of services in the host country as they do in their home country. Consequently, if the home country rules are more liberal than those of the host, institutions can offer certain services in the host country that domestic rivals are prohibited from selling. This situation has resulted in speeding up deregulation in some countries, as they seek to avoid giving their national operators a competitive disadvantage.

These directives have had some effect on the markets within the UK financial system, especially for mortgages and insurance. In addition there has been considerable restructuring in the sector as a whole, such as mergers and acquisitions, frequently involving organisations across borders. In some cases this has been from outside the European Community, as foreign-owned institutions have acquired access to the UK markets and used this method as a route to the other member states with maybe harsher entry requirements. Other mergers have been internal to the UK in an attempt to defend against acquisition by foreign companies, particularly within the building society sector.

6.8 International financial markets

Extending the discussion to the global financial markets, there are two issues to mention briefly in this section. The first is concerned with the effect of the economic climate in other countries on the UK and the second with the interaction of international capital markets.

It has been noted for a long time that there is a significant effect on all countries of world economic cycles of boom and recession, particularly on countries whose economies are largely built on trade, such as the UK. Economic conditions are rarely contained nationally, and world recessions have followed especially when economically dominant countries perform poorly. Examples of this are the downturn in industrial production and high unemployment in Germany following unification in 1989 and the US recession of the early 1990s, from which, hopefully, economies are now recovering.

The other international effect is a result of increased global integration in capital markets. Capital is moved around the world in the form of goods traded in the real sector and funds between borrowers and investors in the monetary sector. However, the availability of more technology to access information and easier trading, along with less regulation, has increased the flow of funds between markets throughout the world. As was shown by the 1987 crash, it is impossible to contain a price fall in securities in one financial centre, as global trading transmits this to other markets.

One difficulty arising from this phenomenon is the inability of central banks and monetary authorities to control liquidity nationally. As global markets become more accessible, and the international capital markets become separated from the underlying international trade in goods and services, the flow of investment funds may become influenced by competition from different financial centres as they try to capture trade. Subsequently, pressure from the financial institutions as they develop increasing numbers of new financial products may cause the flow of investment capital to diverge from the patterns of real sector trade. We shall see in later chapters that in some markets securities are more tradable than in others, and settlement systems are not equally operationally efficient.

6.9 Summary

The UK has always been involved in international trade in physical goods, and is now also a central part of the increasingly global financial markets. Membership of the European Union has already created changes in the structure of the financial sector with respect to competitiveness within the single market.

The ability to control inflation and achieve stable exchange rates is required before the UK can re-enter the ERM, and to participate fully in the European Monetary Union. If this does take place, aspects of monetary control will be determined in conjunction with other member states. This will require the Bank of England to be considerably more independent from the Treasury than is currently the position, a topic we shall return to in the concluding chapter.

Note

1. *Specie* simply means precious metal.

Further reading

For information on the activities of the European Investment Bank and other EEC institutions, *European Economy* is a useful quarterly publication of the Commission of the European Communities.

Begg, D. (1994), *Economics*, McGraw-Hill. Part 5: *The World Economy* outlines the international system and European financial integration.

Blake, D. (1993), *A Short Course of Economics*, McGraw-Hill. Chapter 12 gives a detailed account of the British withdrawal from the Exchange Rate Mechanism in September 1992, and the conditions of the Maastricht Agreement.

Buckle, M. and J. Thompson (1992), *The United Kingdom Financial System in Transition*, Manchester University Press. Chapter 15 is particularly good on the European Union, and the implications for the market in financial services.

Levi, M. (1990), *International Finance*, 2nd edn. McGraw-Hill. Chapters 6 and 7 explain parity conditions and the Addendum gives an outline of systems of exchange rates, both historically and the current European model.

For those interested in the history of international finance, the price-specie model was explained by David Hume in 1752 in:

Hume, D. (1752), *Of the Balance of Trade*, in *Of Money, Political Discourses*, reprinted in Richard Cooper, *International Finance*, Penguin, 1969.

More on European directives related to the financial sector, and a survey of practitioners on the same topic in:

Dale, R. (1994) 'Regulating investment business in the single market', pp. 333–40, and Thomson, G. and M. Taylor, 'The developing single market in financial services', *Bank of England Quarterly Bulletin*, November, pp.341–6.

Questions

6.1 Compare the main features of the Bretton Woods Agreement and the European System.

6.2 What is the *law of one price*?

6.3 Discuss the following statement:

After monetary union, one country will not be able to change its competitiveness against other countries in the union. This can result in economic disaster.

6.4 Two countries, the US and the UK, produce one good, cotton. Suppose that the price of cotton per kilo in the US is $3.40 and in the UK is £2.26, using purchasing power parity, what is the $:£ spot rate of exchange?

Analysis of UK financial markets

Introduction to Part II

Securities are issued to allow those with a financial deficit, whether they are companies, governments, local authorities or international organisations, to access capital to fund their activities. Part II outlines the main groups of securities traded, their issuing, pricing and trading mechanisms as well as the institutional arrangements to ensure that markets function efficiently.

One way of classifying the different financial markets is in terms of the liquidity of the assets traded. The conventional division is between the money markets, where the more liquid financial instruments are traded, and the securities' markets, which handle the issuance and trading of debt and equity instruments. All markets have undergone considerable reform during the past decade and the UK is facing competition in securities trading from new financial centres. These markets are described in this section, as are the increasingly important markets for derivatives and eurocurrency securities.

CHAPTER 7

The structure of securities markets

7.1 Introduction

In Part I we defined some of the principal characteristics of financial markets and institutions, identifying criteria for the evaluation of their efficiency. In the UK, the markets for securities have developed over many years, expanding and adapting to external conditions in the domestic and international environment. Within the market for financial securities there is a wide range of trading and institutional arrangements. In this chapter, we first consider types of trading mechanisms and the organisational structure of the major markets. We then examine how pricing information is disseminated and the extent to which this contributes to market efficiency.

7.2 Trading mechanisms

The analysis of market structures is concerned with the mechanisms by which orders are collected and prices are determined. There are two basic approaches to this: a call or batch market, or a continuous market. These function in the following ways:

Call markets Call markets are where trading occurs as a discrete event, such as an auction. Written buy and sell orders accumulate over a period and then the market is *called*. At this time, prices are set by an auctioneer, who either uses the information from the submitted quotes directly, or presents a starting price from these quotes which is then adjusted by traders' verbal interventions.

Continuous markets Alternatively, continuous markets take place at any time that buy and sell orders coincide. These can be either matching or dealer markets. Matching markets are *order-driven* which simply means finding a buy and sell order with matching prices, whereas dealer markets are *quote-driven* and require a dealer to negotiate an acceptable price with a trader. The UK and

113

US security markets have operated continuous trading for some time, and many European exchanges are now moving from batch systems to continuous markets.

Two important considerations in the choice of system are cost and efficiency. Batch trading is considerably cheaper, particularly with respect to the technology required to disseminate information and to enact the trade. However, continuous information implies much greater efficiency with respect to pricing, and once the technology is in place, it can handle large volumes of transactions at low unit costs.

7.3 Types of securities traded

Securities are defined as financial instruments that can be traded. We have referred extensively to assets as financial claims on future outcomes, but not all assets can be directly exchanged. For example, a current account in a bank or building society cannot be sold, neither can a National Savings certificate, but both are financial assets owned by the account holder. The only way to dispose of these assets is to cancel them, or close out the account. However, assets such as equity or bonds can be sold between third parties without involving the original issuers, and therefore are defined as securities. Furthermore, a decision to purchase equity is generally a matter of exchanging ownership of that security with the current shareholder, rather than waiting until the company wishes to increase the number of shares outstanding by issuing additional ones.

The best-known long-term security traded in the capital markets is the ordinary share. This is truly long term, in fact, usually it is irredeemable, and offers the investor a variable cash income in the form of dividends in addition to the possibility of a capital gain or loss when it is sold.

Another long-term security is the corporate or government bond. In this case, the security will usually be issued only for a specified time and will therefore be traded on the securities market for a predetermined period, that is, until maturity. But in this case, the traditional division between the capital markets for long-term securities and the money markets for short-term securities becomes less distinct, since as the maturity date approaches, the bond will tend to behave more like a short-term money market instrument. However, the distinguishing feature of securities being exchanged through trading, still applies.

In addition to equity and bonds, there are also a number of securities which largely depend for their value on either the present or expected future price of another security. These include warrants, futures, options and convertibles and are described as being contingent claims, or derivatives, since they derive their value from an underlying security.[1] They fulfil an important role in making the markets more 'complete', and allow investors to adjust the price-volatility risk of their portfolios, by buying or selling contingent securities. This concept of completeness by maintaining liquidity in the market contributes towards efficiency. If the market is illiquid, and thus incomplete, investors would find it impossible to protect themselves against foreseeable events.

Of the securities mentioned above, ordinary shares, bonds, warrants and convertibles are all issued first by debtor institutions (e.g. companies) and are subsequently traded on the secondary market by transferring ownership from one investor to another. However, derivatives such as options and futures are securities which are effectively issued by an investor directly onto the secondary market.[2]

7.4 The markets for long-term securities

Securities traded in the long-term markets have a maturity of at least one year, more often five years, and sometimes are irredeemable (equity) or perpetual (bonds). In the UK, the major trading institution for these securities is the London Stock Exchange, regardless of the fact that physically the trading takes place in dealing-rooms all over the country.

The Stock Exchange was formally established in 1773, although a market for securities has existed in London since the end of the seventeenth century. At its foundation, the London Stock Exchange was one of a number of exchanges throughout Britain and only became a single, integrated market in 1973. Its present form results from a merger with the International Securities Regulatory Organisation, the representative body for international bond dealers in London, in 1986, when it became the London International Stock Exchange.

The trading systems and overall organisational structure of the London markets have evolved over two centuries, as a series of new financial instruments and markets have developed in response to the increased demand for innovative investment opportunities. The most recent major changes occurred in 1986, in a set of reforms known as Big Bang. Prior to this, three main features had been in place since the early part of this century. These were: the single capacity trading system; a fee structure for brokers defined on a minimum commission basis; and the restriction of membership to the exchange to private partnerships only, although this was revised to some extent in 1971. These features became the focus of the reforms, and to understand the motivation for the changes, we should briefly describe the significance of these practices, and the problems which became associated with them.

Single capacity trading This required that the market intermediaries were separated into two distinct groups according to their function. One group were the brokers who acted on behalf of their clients, buying and selling securities at the most favourable prices. The other group were the dealers, or jobbers, who quoted bid and offer prices to the brokers on the particular securities they were prepared to deal in on their own account. Thus dealers, acting as principals, traded with brokers, while brokers were agents for their customers. This system was established to provide a guarantee of the integrity of the intermediaries.

But the growth of the institutional investors caused difficulties with this structure, as they began to trade in very large blocks of shares. In single capacity markets the jobber is required to take a position, that is actually hold the security before trading with the brokers. The size of the block trades puts extreme pressure on the capital resources of the jobbers. Many jobbing firms withdrew from the market, leaving only a small number to set prices, and resulting in an increasingly shallow and thus non-competitive market.

Minimum commission This was a cartel type of arrangement favouring the brokers, whereby minimum commissions were fixed for all trades irrespective of size. A fee structure which is based on a fixed percentage of the transaction was especially unattractive to the investment institutions, who expected to be able to benefit from economies of scale, while brokers' earnings were protected as long as investors were not able to negotiate a lower transactions price. This led to non-price competition where brokers attempted to capture the business of lucrative institutional investors by offers of research services and hospitality, which was open to corruption and abuse.

Membership restrictions Membership of the Stock Exchange, that is, the ownership of brokers and jobbers, was restricted to personal partnerships. This was later extended and ownership by corporate members was allowed by outsiders, although no single shareholder could hold more than 10% of the capital of a single firm. The consequence was that firms were very small, especially by international standards, with low capitalisation and therefore the inability to compete on prices in a number of deals, a problem again compounded by the continued existence of the single capacity structure.

The pressure for reform of the system came from two directions. First, the Exchange was clearly not operating in a competitive environment. The barrier to entry in terms of membership, and the minimum commission rule setting the price level for trading were both obstacles to a fair and competitive market. Secondly, the UK government abolished exchange controls in 1979, allowing the free movement of capital throughout the international financial markets. Foreign capital markets were particularly attractive to the institutional investors who were beginning to trade so extensively that they had to search for a more cost-effective trading environment. They found this outside the UK. Given they were not able to obtain reduced dealing costs on what were very sizeable transactions if they traded in London, they looked to other exchanges, such as New York.

Deregulation was creating an increasingly competitive market between international exchanges, and improved computer technology, used both for the transmission of information and for trading itself, made the London firms appear very inefficient and expensive. It was also becoming very easy to trade UK securities outside the UK, notably in New York in the form of American depository receipts (ADRs), enhanced by the US market-makers' aggressive selling techniques and skilful investment advisory services. As a consequence, a significant share of domestic security business began to take place abroad.

The Stock Exchange was investigated by the Office of Fair Trading, and in 1979, referred to the Restrictive Trade Practices Court. However, the government pre-empted any action on the part of the Court and an agreement between the Secretary of State for Industry and Trade and the Chairman of the Stock Exchange reached an Accord in July 1983. This agreement resulted in a number of changes which have revolutionised the institutions of the London Stock Exchange. The three major reforms were:

- The introduction of dual capacity, and the abolition of single capacity trading.
- The abolition of minimum commissions.
- The admission of domestic and foreign corporate members to the Stock Exchange.

The three facets of the changes are interrelated. For example, since the abolition of minimum commissions, few firms could function purely as brokers or purely as market-makers. They have been forced by the need to seek out alternative sources of income to undertake a variety of responsibilities, and to resort to dual capacity trading. Likewise, the huge capital resources needed to fulfil both these roles have made the entry of firms with huge capital resources, such as UK and foreign retail banks, imperative. These are now members of the Exchange, some as individuals and some as financial conglomerates like Barclays de Zoete Wedd. Thus membership now comprises a number of financial firms which under the old regime were excluded. An indication of the change in the membership structure of the exchange is given in Table 7.1.

In the case of the equity market, the introduction of dual capacity trading has resulted in a single form of institution known as a broker/dealer, who is able to operate as a principal or as an agent for a third party, be it an individual or an organisation. There are subgroups registered to act purely as market-makers or as dealers. In any particular bargain, a broker/dealer who is not a market-maker, or a market-maker who is not a broker/dealer, can both act as an agent as long as the price is as good as that available from other agents in the market.

An additional new intermediary, the inter-dealer broker, has facilitated intra-market dealings. As well as trading between market-makers or between market-makers and broker/dealers acting as principals, this new category of trader acts as a principal on both sides of the transaction. Confidentiality is maintained by the offers and bids being quoted anonymously. This improves the liquidity of the market and increases the resources of the individual market-makers.

Trading was affected in the corporate and government bond markets in much the same way. Domestic corporate bonds are registered securities, and are listed on the London Stock Exchange, as are government bonds. Government (gilt-edged[3]) bond markets moved from single to dual capacity and gilt-edged market-makers (GEMMs) were created with a role similar to that of broker/dealer. GEMMs are obliged to provide continuous quote-driven markets, and to deal in all government issues, although they may choose also to deal in other sterling fixed interest securities and derivatives, but not in equity. Inter-dealer brokers are also

Table 7.1 Stock Exchange membership, 1940–91

	Brokers		Jobbers	
	Firms	Principals	Firms	Principals
1940	426	1,630	278	na
1950	364	1,743	187	791
1955	329	1,791	135	632
1960	305	1,886	100	545
1965	270	1,893	60	417
1970	192	1,810	31	273
1975	284	2,129	21	231
1980	240	2,104	19	203
1984	209	2,034	17	183
1986	207	2,189	18	247
	Firms		Members	
1987	357		5,433	
1989	389		5,114	
1991	413		5,192	

Source: ISE, *Quality of Markets Quarterly Review*, April 1991.

also active in the gilts market, although separate from those in other markets, and are an important part of the large inter-market share of the total gilt business.

Although gilt-edged bond trading takes place through the London Stock Exchange along with other securities, close links with the Bank of England are maintained, particularly in the supervision of traders, who have to report their positions – i.e. what their security holdings are – to the Bank at the close of each trading day. The size of transaction and the risk exposure are determined on an individual basis between the GEMM and the Bank, and the GEMMs have access to direct borrowing facilities.

7.5 Market organisation

The 1986 Financial Services Act identified the London Stock Exchange as a Recognised Investment Exchange. As such, it is the largest market for raising equity in Europe. But along with exchanges in Paris and Frankfurt, it is not one single market, but is a combination of a market for fully listed companies and those on the unlisted securities market (USM), although the latter is not expected to continue. An additional, so-called Third Market, was also

Table 7.2 London Stock Exchange markets

	Full listing	Unlisted Stock Market
Trading	At least 5 years	At least 3 years
Yearly turnover	No lower limit Sponsors usually expect more than £10m	No lower limit
Yearly pre-tax profit	No lower limit Sponsors usually expect more than £1m	No lower limit
Market capitalisation	£700,000 equity Sponsors usually expect over £10m	No lower limit
Latest audit prior to flotation	Six months	Nine months
Percentage of shares in public hands	At least 25%	At least 10%
Information to shareholders on substantial capital changes – disposals and acquisitions	Where 15% or more of assets, profits or equity involved	Where 25% or more of assets, profits or equity involved
Advertising and Publicity		
Placings and introductions	Formal notice in one national daily paper and listing details in Extel Statistical Services	Formal notice in one national daily paper plus circulation of prospectus via Extel
Offers for sale	Listing details in two national daily papers and circulated in Extel	Formal notice in one national daily paper

Source: ISE, *Quality of Markets Quarterly Review*, Winter 1989.

established earlier, but in 1991 merged with the USM in the interests of harmonisation with other European Union member states.

The differences between the listed and unlisted markets are reflected in the required levels of disclosure of company information, the amount of capital raised by public issue and the costs involved. Table 7.2 illustrates these distinctions. The introduction of new levels of listing, and the decision to conform with other European Union countries, was done to ease the access to the capital markets for a larger number of companies, particularly the smaller or more recently established ones, and was certainly cheaper.

The USM was established to operate on the same principles as the main listed market but imposed less stringent regulations on companies wishing to have their shares traded. As can be seen from the table, whilst the listed market requires at least 25% of a company's shares to be offered in the primary issue before the shares can be listed, the USM required only 10%. However, no new quotations are to be allowed from the beginning of 1995.

Since the emphasis in establishing the USM was to encourage small companies to have their shares traded prior to graduating to a full listing, it is not surprising that these companies are relatively young and therefore tend to be more risky. The risk may have also been increased by the lower level of corporate financial disclosure demanded. But there has been some concern about the level of efficiency in a market which is insufficiently active, which is why the USM may not survive long into 1995.

Finally, since 1970, a series of somewhat fragmented markets have existed where securities are traded *over the counter*, operating through a computerised network but where the availability of pricing information is far from perfect. Securities traded in this way are very illiquid and risky. The number of companies trading on the OTC is small, although with the demise of the Third Market and probably the USM, it is a cheaper alternative to a full listing, and is now being taken very seriously by the regulators to give investors more confidence. This market is expected to gain significance when the USM ceases to exist formally. Secondary market transactions in eurobonds frequently take place in OTC markets, partly for historical reasons, but also because of their non-standard nature.

7.6 Efficiency of the Stock Exchange

In Chapter 3 we introduced the concept of efficiency as an important feature of financial markets. This is now expanded to describe different types of efficiency, including how the securities markets can influence the use of funds available to companies, how well prices reflect the value of securities and how well the practical operations of the markets are carried out.

Allocative efficiency

Secondary markets do not strictly allocate funds to firms. New capital is made available in the primary markets, and for any one company, new issues are generally few and far between. But in order to make even infrequent use of the primary market, a firm must continue to be listed on the secondary market, and to do this it must provide financial information about past performance. Using this information, potential investors will decide whether to advance more capital to fund the company for future projects.

In this respect, Stock Exchange regulations go some considerable way beyond the accounting disclosures to shareholders required under the various Companies Acts. More to the point, these disclosures are widely disseminated and are frequently the subject of public comment and specialist interpretation in the financial press.

Investment analysts will be continuously monitoring the performance and financial results of companies and will also directly question the senior managers of some of them. In many cases, meetings are held regularly at which the chairmen or managing directors from a number of firms discuss their individual company's performance, and can receive comments from analysts directly.

Another way in which the secondary markets can influence the use of resources is by relaying information back to company management. Many investment firms employ a number of analysts whose job it is to appraise the performance of a group of companies in each sector. By carrying out this research, the analysts will often find out a great deal about managerial effectiveness. These results are then circulated in published reports, and frequently can substantially influence the share price. Thus movements in the share price signal the industry's view of company performance. In some cases, companies may react to a sustained fall in their share price by appointing new management or changing their managerial policies to forestall criticism by their shareholders.

Although influential to a certain extent, monitoring of this kind cannot always serve to correct inadequate managerial performance. A more striking effect can come from a takeover bid. Takeovers occur for a variety of reasons. A company may wish to establish stronger control of a product market by taking over a competitor, and with it their market share. Or a company may wish to diversify by acquiring an existing business in an emerging market. Typically a bid may come after some informal approach by the directors of one company to another, or if the target is thought to be performing below its potential, a surprise offer may be made.

The offer will sometimes be announced publicly, and circulated to all shareholders. Invariably the offer will be at a higher price per share than the currently quoted price. The rationale for the acquisition is that the predator company expects to be able to achieve higher profits than the existing management. The claim is usually disputed by the existing management who may similarly circulate forecasts of improved profits to their shareholders, urging them not to accept the alternative offer. Ultimately, the takeover or the threat of takeover, should improve performance, resulting in an efficient use of funds. Thus the secondary markets ensure that the funds allocated in the primary markets are directed to those companies considered to be performing well.

Allocative efficiency is difficult to assess, although a great deal of research has been directed at the effects of the threat of takeover on managerial performance.

Informational efficiency

From the discussion above, it is clearly important to consider the efficiency with which prices in the market fully reflect all available *relevant* information, and the quoted share price is the single most unambiguous signal available to market participants. But the notion of informational efficiency depends very much on what is understood to be relevant information.

Three levels of efficiency, which together are known as the efficient market hypothesis, have been defined as follows:

1. *Weak-form efficiency.* No investor can earn excess returns by developing trading rules based on historical prices, that is, the information in past prices is not useful or relevant in earning excess returns.
2. *Semistrong-form efficiency.* No investor can earn excess returns from trading rules based on any publicly available information, where public information consists in company annual reports, investment advice or the financial press.
3. *Strong-form efficiency.* No investor can earn excess returns using any information, whether available publicly or privately.

This means that if it is considered that capital markets are semistrong-form efficient, which is the generally accepted view, prices will not change following new information published in an annual report, as the price already reflects the current performance of that company. The information value of share prices has been the topic of numerous research papers, using prices from the American and British securities markets. In both countries, small anomalies have been found, but broadly they have indicated that the markets react very quickly to information as it becomes available.

The concept of efficiency sometimes appears to be implausible, but this is usually based on distortions resulting from single huge profits or losses from a particular investment. But whilst it is true that an individual investor may from time to time be in a position to benefit from specialist knowledge of a firm's prospects, the case for efficient markets depends on the behaviour of share prices in aggregate. Although there are over two thousand companies registered in the UK with ordinary shares listed on the Stock Exchange, fewer than forty of these account for nearly 45% of the value of the total.

Because of the impact of particularly large companies trading on the Exchange, any remarks on efficiency must take into account the possibility of mispricing of companies such as J. Sainsbury, Beecham, Marks & Spencer, ICI or Barclays Bank. However, these are precisely the companies that will be closely followed by investment analysts, and which in many ways, reflect the performance of the market as a whole. The accuracy of information signalled by share prices depends on the activity of the analysts and more crucially, on the institutional investors, each of whom will be trying to outperform their competitors. The effects of the volume of trading carried out by these investors will be discussed in a later chapter, as will the role they play in the allocation of capital to industry.

Smaller companies present a different set of issues. Some individuals may be more informed about the future prospects of a smaller, newer company than analysts covering several industrial sectors. But this does not necessarily imply that markets for small firms are priced inefficiently. First, the interpretation of future profitability has to be made within the framework of a firm's own market environment. It is not enough for investors to know that the profits of a company are going to rise. They must also know something about that rise, relative to others in the sector. Secondly, individual investors believing that a small company is mispriced may find that their advantage is very short-lived as share prices adjust very quickly on trading even modest numbers of shares. Thus observed mispricing does not necessarily result in large profits from trading in smaller companies.

Having suggested that theory and evidence indicate the UK Stock Exchange is by and large informationally efficient, we would not wish to leave the impression that this inference is undisputed. Many analysts and managers of institutional funds argue that some sectors are less efficient than others, or that the market overemphasises short-term considerations. In the case of property companies, for example, the assets of the firms are usually regularly and independently valued, yet the value of the shares held in these companies can be as much as 20 or 30% less than the reported values of their underlying property assets. These discounts can fluctuate considerably from one month to the next and can vary dramatically between apparently similar companies, often reflecting the state of the economy as a whole, rather than the prospects for a particular firm. If the sector were informationally efficient one might expect the two valuations to be consistent. Although there are a number of factors which might go some way to explaining some of the differences, some discrepancies still persist.

Operational efficiency

The application of the concept of operational efficiency to the Stock Exchange is only possible given many of the preconditions for efficiency noted in Chapter 3 are present. There are, for example, many buyers and sellers, at least for the major companies listed, and the transaction costs are relatively low, although this still represents some difficulties with respect to the costs of trading in London compared with the international competition.

It is easy to trade in shares, even with quite small amounts of capital, and transactions by private clients account for a large proportion of the business of Stock Exchange firms. However, these transactions are costly to administrate, and commissions can now reflect this following the earlier reforms.

The informational efficiency discussed above, requires that prices convey all information about the company. But operationally, this information has to be disseminated. Informal channels convey a lot of information, but technology now makes prices available to a large number of market participants. Gaining a reputation as being a source of timely and accurate information will give the broker a competitive advantage, and advice on potential bargains will hopefully lead to commissioned business. There are therefore considerable incentives for the analyst to find information that will cause a revision in investors' expectations and to disseminate this information as quickly as possible.

The extent of operational efficiency is largely dependent on technology to provide prices, both spot quotes and completed bargains, as well as final settlement following the transfer of ownership. These issues will be discussed in the following sections.

7.7 Price information systems

Technology allows fast transmission of pricing information. The Stock Exchange automatic quotation (SEAQ) system operates through a central computer in which price quotes, market size and transactions are reported by market-makers as bargains are completed. This information is conveyed by TOPIC, the Stock Exchange videotext information service to subscribers in dealing-rooms located in financial institutions and elsewhere. As part of the SEAQ screen-based information, the best bid and offer prices are highlighted in a yellow strip, and other information such as the previous day's closing price, cumulative trading volume and recent prices of transactions in that security. Updates of price information are required to take place within specific times for all securities, with frequently traded, or large trades to be reported within a given time limit.

7.8 Settlement systems

Settlement of accounts following securities transactions has been something of an anachronism in London for a long time, although this is about to change. The account system has worked in two-week periods, and all settlement takes place on a single day, six working days after the end of the account period. This obviously is a benefit for the buyer and a cost to the seller, but the real difficulty is the opportunities it gives for speculation during the account settlement period. Under this system, it is quite possible to buy and sell the same security during an account period, without the buyer being liable for any payment.

Other systems have been proposed, such as a five-day rolling settlement, but the transfer of ownership in London is still a paper-based facility, with share certificates passing to buyers from sellers. Only the institutional investors are allowed to settle all of their day's transactions by the transfer of a single amount, under the institutional net settlement (INS) system.

The *TAURUS* system was expected to solve both the settlement and transfer of ownership requirements, but failed, largely because of the increasing costs of development. A new system is now being developed to modernise equity settlement, and plans for this have been set out in a report to the Governor of the Bank of England.

This system of electronic book-entry settlement, *CREST*, is now being developed and is expected to be in place by 1995. In preparation for this, changes in the settlement procedure have already taken place. From July 1994, the London Stock Exchange moved to a system of rolling settlement, ten business days after trades take place (T+10); this will be followed by a T+5 rolling settlement in early 1995. This will require operational changes, as this is a very short period of time to transfer ownership, especially for retail investors. Current practice will have to be improved with respect to the time it takes for institutional investors to pass instructions to their custodian banks, and for the registration of security ownership, particularly for investors who trade frequently. Smoothing out these difficulties will be a prerequisite to a successful settlement system.

7.9 The measurement of market performance

For many years, the performance of equities on the International Stock Exchange had been measured in terms of either the FT Actuaries or FT-30 indices. These were indices constructed from the prices of a number of financial assets. However, when the derivative markets were developed, and many of the contracts were to be based on equities, neither of these seemed to be appropriate for an index which had to be constantly updated. Therefore, the *Financial Times* Stock Exchange 100 index was created in 1984. Since this involved only 100 securities, it is small enough to be updated regularly and yet reflects the actual movement in a sufficiently large number of active securities. The FT-SE 100 is an index comprising the largest listed UK companies, weighted by market capitalisation. It is based at 1000 and recalculated continuously during market trading hours. More specific indices are constructed for specialised sets of securities, such as industrial sectors or the Hoare Govett Smaller Companies index. Examples of many of these are shown in Table 7.3.

Other indices from major international markets are also reported in the financial press, such as the Dow Jones and Standard & Poors 500 (S&P500) from New York, the Nikkei Index from Tokyo and many others. Table 7.4 shows the international indices regularly reported.

7.10 Summary

The Stock Exchange is the major market for securities in the UK. It has undergone major changes during recent years, the most drastic being the series of reforms in 1986, commonly known as Big Bang. In this chapter we have tried to provide a motivation for those changes, and to illustrate the nature of modern securities trading. We have also used the concepts of efficiency to examine the operations of the securities markets and the impact of technology on trading and settlement procedures.

Notes

1. These are discussed in Chapter 12.

The structure of securities markets

Table 7.3 Performance measures: FT-SE 100 and industrial sector indices

	Aug 16	Day's chge%	Aug 15	Aug 12	Aug 11	Year ago	Div. yield%	Earn. yield%	P/E ratio	Xd adj. ytd	Total return
FT-SE 100	3,147.3	+0.2	3,142.2	3,142.3	3,138.2	3,025.0	4.00	6.79	17.36	86.62	1,184.84
FT-SE Mid 250	3,715.1	-0.1	3,719.2	3,728.8	3,726.6	3,465.9	3.32	5.59	21.50	84.58	1,377.84
FT-SE Mid 250 ex Inv Trusts	3,717.9	-0.1	3,723.0	3,736.5	3,731.5	3,474.0	3.47	6.05	20.01	87.75	1,375.55
FT-SE-A 350	1,590.2	+0.1	1,588.7	1,589.7	1,587.9	1,518.2	3.84	6.51	18.18	42.02	1,224.63
FT-SE SmallCap	1,877.64	-0.1	1,879.00	1,877.40	1,876.11	1,731.17	3.01	4.16	31.48	36.25	1,450.70
FT-SE SmallCap ex Inv Trusts	1,844.69	-0.1	1,846.99	1,845.96	1,843.54	1,718.34	3.18	4.59	29.07	37.20	1,428.78
FT-SE-A ALL-SHARE	1,578.30	+0.1	1,576.94	1,577.78	1,576.04	1,503.20	3.78	6.34	18.75	40.92	1,236.29
FT-SE Actuaries All-Share											
10 MINERAL EXTRACTION(18)	2,723.80	—	2,723.66	2,715.11	2,711.54	2,268.80	3.33	4.30	29.25	54.71	1,085.29
12 Extractive Industries(4)	3,956.32	—	3,954.52	3,955.08	3,955.83	3,224.00	3.22	5.09	24.61	54.24	1,079.66
15 Oil, Integrated(3)	2,669.32	+0.1	2,667.37	2,655.18	2,647.89	2,207.50	3.45	4.43	28.13	59.99	1,087.04
16 Oil Exploration & Prod(11)	1,967.09	-0.8	1,982.06	1,989.79	2,008.68	1,796.20	2.46	1.24	80.00	20.34	1,127.86
20 GEN MANUFACTURERS(264)	2,039.34	—	2,039.11	2,043.12	2,052.02	1,911.70	3.72	4.60	26.67	48.57	1,032.86
21 Building & Construction(32)	1,166.67	-0.4	1,171.31	1,179.86	1,192.62	1,147.10	3.31	4.54	28.38	21.23	906.73
22 Building Matls & Merchs(31)	1,988.00	-0.2	1,992.61	1,994.49	2,002.58	1,815.00	3.70	4.03	31.22	45.76	930.84
23 Chemicals(22)	2,514.48	-0.1	2,518.09	2,515.61	2,504.38	2,209.30	3.69	4.03	31.39	72.17	1,112.39
24 Diversified Industrials(16)	2,045.67	+0.1	2,043.02	2,052.83	2,062.70	2,006.50	4.44	4.59	26.75	54.88	1,036.94
25 Electronic & Elect Equip(35)	1,979.98	+1.0	1,960.06	1,948.17	1,962.29	2,109.60	3.78	6.31	18.97	55.02	967.10
26 Engineering(70)	1,929.52	+0.1	1,927.48	1,935.66	1,952.25	1,711.20	2.95	4.57	26.02	39.09	1,098.93
27 Engineering, Vehicles(12)	2,422.58	-1.8	2,467.89	2,469.48	2,479.05	2,002.30	4.33	2.40	59.40	42.17	1,159.43
28 Printing, Paper & Pckg(26)	2,867.73	+0.2	2,863.15	2,871.21	2,882.96	2,415.60	2.94	5.01	23.48	52.47	1,121.46
29 Textiles & Apparel(20)	1,705.53	-0.1	1,708.09	1,709.29	1,697.57	1,869.30	3.88	6.18	19.79	39.54	960.05
30 CONSUMER GOODS(97)	2,822.19	+0.6	2,806.26	2,795.65	2,766.36	2,745.40	4.12	7.16	16.21	83.21	966.95
31 Breweries(17)	2,309.15	+0.1	2,305.78	2,282.89	2,259.09	2,034.00	4.09	7.44	16.33	60.23	1,034.05
32 Spirits, Wines & Ciders(10)	2,890.59	+0.6	2,873.33	2,863.04	2,828.94	2,941.40	3.83	6.64	17.44	89.92	969.00
33 Food Manufacturers(23)	2,394.73	+0.6	2,380.08	2,371.56	2,319.23	2,321.10	4.00	7.38	15.73	71.03	1,004.26
34 Household Goods(13)	2,586.82	+0.1	2,583.20	2,569.88	2,506.54	2,321.30	3.40	7.12	16.74	52.15	922.12
36 Health Care(21)	1,714.06	—	1,714.55	1,702.22	1,703.65	1,736.50	2.91	2.95	69.58	32.89	989.18
37 Pharmaceuticals(12)	3,127.11	+0.8	3,103.09	3,085.20	3,075.18	2,895.40	3.99	6.99	16.49	70.05	982.15
38 Tobacco(1)	3,565.36	+0.5	3,548.58	3,586.33	3,548.58	4,054.50	6.09	9.64	11.14	217.07	813.29
40 SERVICES(220)	1,999.88	+0.2	1,996.05	1,995.98	1,995.29	1,903.20	3.09	6.03	20.00	40.11	978.03
41 Distributors(31)	2,750.10	—	2,750.77	2,748.59	2,747.06	2,718.30	3.29	6.37	18.54	61.44	948.83
42 Leisure & Hotels(24)	2,127.10	+0.5	2,116.30	2,118.04	2,115.54	1,939.70	3.45	4.54	25.74	48.31	1,046.85
43 Media(38)	2,916.86	+0.3	2,908.10	2,923.58	2,939.20	2,486.80	2.35	5.18	22.48	53.51	1,009.35
44 Retailers, Food(17)	1,781.90	+0.5	1,772.69	1,771.19	1,770.79	1,953.50	3.59	9.01	13.71	45.10	1,062.81
45 Retailers, General(45)	1,716.00	+0.1	1,715.03	1,709.38	1,709.27	1,626.90	3.04	6.32	19.71	33.47	912.95
48 Support Services(40)	1,600.10	—	1,600.16	1,601.50	1,591.92	1,612.70	2.54	5.94	19.87	25.51	968.78
49 Transport(16)	2,435.33	-0.1	2,437.57	2,435.02	2,429.18	2,237.40	3.44	4.92	23.65	41.78	949.05
51 Other Services & Business(9)	1,264.86	-0.7	1,273.47	1,282.91	1,227.55	1,281.00	3.88	2.41	70.65	20.78	1,082.33

60 UTILITIES(36)	2,371.25	+0.4	2,362.69	2,370.91	2,364.13	2,295.00	4.44	7.94	15.34	73.42	913.40
62 Electricity(17)	2,462.05	+0.1	2,459.57	2,476.29	2,452.15	1,909.50	3.72	10.00	11.95	83.46	1,023.87
64 Gas Distribution(2)	1,914.91	+1.3	1,889.54	1,914.29	1,901.50	2,157.50	6.26	—	—	66.79	875.13
66 Telecommunications(4)	1,989.09	—	1,988.70	1,983.43	1,991.22	2,107.30	4.15	7.92	15.38	50.22	848.23
68 Water(13)	1,854.42	+1.1	1,834.40	1,842.83	1,837.60	1,844.40	5.24	12.73	8.57	69.35	927.01
69 NON-FINANCIALS(635)	1,716.79	+0.2	1,712.72	1,712.49	1,709.19	1,617.67	3.73	6.04	19.92	42.80	1,207.80
70 FINANCIALS(104)	2,148.41	-0.7	2,164.55	2,174.67	2,180.46	2,188.30	4.45	9.02	12.72	72.48	848.35
72 Banks(10)	2,722.95	-1.2	2,756.07	2,769.16	2,775.38	2,678.20	4.42	9.68	11.71	101.62	814.47
73 Insurance(17)	1,225.82	-0.3	1,229.41	1,241.15	1,245.75	1,496.20	5.41	12.24	9.11	43.25	834.02
74 Life Assurance(6)	2,375.83	-0.4	2,385.40	2,387.94	2,392.72	2,511.30	5.23	7.65	16.05	82.97	901.93
75 Merchant Banks(6)	3,008.58	+0.1	3,004.18	2,989.34	2,998.03	2,945.80	3.35	11.00	10.59	76.42	905.08
77 Other Financial(24)	1,966.03	—	1,965.27	1,961.47	1,961.03	1,760.60	3.54	8.01	14.85	45.22	1,044.54
79 Property(41)	1,556.70	-0.2	1,559.98	1,572.68	1,580.28	1,566.80	3.87	3.97	31.50	36.91	887.72
80 INVESTMENT TRUSTS(123)	2,867.05	+0.1	2,862.79	2,857.78	2,862.75	2,601.80	2.10	1.82	55.70	44.49	961.20
89 FT-SE-A ALL-SHARE(862)	1,578.30	+0.1	1,576.94	1,577.78	1,576.04	1,503.20	3.78	6.34	18.75	40.92	1,236.29

Hourly movements

	Open	9.00	10.00	11.00	12.00	13.00	14.00	15.00	16.10	High/day	Low.day
FT-SE 100	3,139.1	3,145.8	3,145.5	3,147.1	3,149.5	3,148.5	3,143.1	3,148.3	3,148.7	3,151.6	3,138.7
FT-SE Mid 250	3,716.2	3,718.3	3,714.8	3,718.1	3,717.7	3,716.8	3,715.4	3,716.3	3,716.0	3,718.3	3,714.3
FT-SE-A 350	1,587.2	1,590.0	1,539.5	1,590.5	1,591.4	1,590.9	1,588.7	1,590.8	1,590.9	1,592.1	1,587.0

Time of FT-SE 100 Day's high: 3.16 p.m. Day's low: 8.36 a.m. FT-SE 100 1994 High: 3,520.3(2/2) Low: 2,876.6 (24/6).

FT-SE Actuaries 350 Industry baskets

	Open	9.00	10.00	11.00	12.00	13.00	14.00	15.00	16.10	Close	Previous	Change
Bldg & Cnstrn	1,121.1	1,120.5	1,120.2	1,119.9	1,117.8	1,117.5	1,115.5	1,115.5	1,116.2	1,116.4	1,121.9	-5.5
Pharmaceuticals	3,080.7	3,087.6	3,085.8	3,089.7	3,096.4	3,092.6	3,086.6	3,085.0	3,102.8	3,104.1	3,080.4	+23.7
Water	1,823.7	1,827.3	1,824.9	1,839.0	1,850.0	1,851.6	1,855.1	1,855.4	1,854.0	1,853.8	1,833.5	+20.3
Banks	2,768.5	2,774.9	2,765.7	2,765.6	2,772.5	2,772.7	2,759.7	2,763.6	2,763.6	2,756.8	2,790.6	-33.8

Source: Financial Times, 17 August 1994.

Table 7.4 International market indices

Exchange	8/31/94 Close	NET CHG	PCT CHG
Tokyo Nikkei 225 Average	20,628.53	+36.41	+0.18
Tokyo Nikkei 300 Index	299.25	+1.09	+0.37
Tokyo Topix Index	1,640.39	+3.02	+0.18
London FT 30-share	2,535	−4.9	−0.19
London 100-share	3,251.3	+1.7	+0.05
London Gold Mines	254.1	+3.3	+1.32
Frankfurt DAX	2,212.85	+2.00	+0.09
Zurich Swiss Market	2,654.6	+9.9	+0.38
Paris CAC 40	2,069.08	−8.71	+0.42
Milan MIBtel Index	10,985	−25	−0.23
Amsterdam ANP-CBS General	281.9	0	0.00
Stockholm Affarsvarlden	1,452.5	+1.1	+0.08
Brussels Bel-20 Index	1,481.53	+2.53	+0.17
Australia All Ordinaries	2,122.1	+5.6	+0.26
Hong Kong Hang Seng	9,929.39	+242.83	+2.51
Singapore Straits Times	2,312.7	+13.19	+0.57
Taiwan DJ Equity Mkt	165.92	+0.82	+0.50
Johannesburg J'burg Gold	2,288	−9	−0.39
Madrid General Index	312.02	−1.16	−0.37
Mexico I.P.C.	2,702.73	−30.11	−1.10
Toronto 300 Composite	4,349.5	+15.79	+0.36
Euro, Aust, Far East MSCI-p	1,087.8	+2.0	+0.18

Notes:
p = Preliminary
na = Not available
Source: The Wall Street Journal, 1 September 1994.

2. It is important to distinguish option contracts which are derivative securities, from the share options given by companies to selected employees, for example, directors of a company. Share options are the right to buy shares from the company at a specific price, and are often part of a remuneration package. These share options, if exercised, result in an increase in the total marketable stock of shares. Options contracts do not.
3. This term is used for all UK government securities and is derived from the original stock certificates which actually had a gilt edge.

Further reading

Byland, T. (1990), *Understanding Finance with the Financial Times*, Harrap.
Cobham, D. (1992) (ed.), *Markets and Dealers: The economics of the London financial markets*, Longman.

Rutterford, J. (1992) (ed.), *Handbook of UK Corporate Finance*, Butterworth.
Rutterford, J. (1993) *Introduction to Stock Exchange Investment*, 2nd edn, Macmillan.

Details of the CREST system for settlement can be found in: *The Bank of England Quarterly Bulletin*, various issues in 1994.

Details on current market operational arrangements are in: Cobham, D. (1992), *Markets and Dealers*, Longman, Chapter 2.

The following two articles provide insights into the difficulty of making comparisons between the USM and other securities markets:
Chan, L. G. and R. C. Stapleton (1982), 'Performance in USM, a preliminary analysis', *Investment Analyst*, no. 65, July, pp. 1–13.
Roden, D. H. (1983), 'The measurement of performance in the USM', *Investment Analyst*, no. 68, April, pp. 22–4.

Questions

7.1 Discuss the rationale behind the Big Bang reforms.

7.2 Do you think that financial journalists should be able to trade in securities about which they are writing? What safeguards or restraints would you propose?

7.3 *Asset stripping* is a term used to describe the taking over of a firm and the selling of its fixed assets to realise cash. Discuss the contribution to allocational efficiency arising from this type of activity.

7.4 In estimating the return obtained from holding a share for a day, the capital gain can be taken to be the difference between the buying and selling price. Would this correspond to the bid-offer spread quoted by the dealer? How would these prices relate to the share prices published in newspapers such as the *Financial Times*?

CHAPTER 8

The equity market

8.1 Introduction

This chapter is concerned with the description of securities traded on the equity markets and issuing procedures of ordinary shares in UK firms which account for most of the transactions, by number, on the London Stock Exchange. We shall also look at two approaches to security valuation, technical and fundamental analysis, and at the investor groups participating in this market.

8.2 Characteristics of traded shares

Given a public company is owned by its shareholders, these individuals have a right to claim a share of any profits earned by that company. However profitability may be anticipated, but is not guaranteed, and investors should be aware that in holding ordinary shares, the income received in the form of dividends may fall and even disappear if the company becomes unprofitable. Furthermore, even if the company is profitable, the management may decide to retain earnings to ensure sufficient funds are available to maintain an investment programme that will benefit shareholders in the longer term. In this case, future earnings resulting from the investment are substituted for dividend payments now.

From this, it will be recognised that shareholders will need to consider the likelihood of dividends rising or falling before they buy shares in a company. If forecasts show a large and sustained increase in dividends, the price of the shares may rise in response to the increased demand. If expectations of future dividends are revised downwards, the price of the share may be similarly affected. The implication is that prices of shares will fluctuate in response to expectations of future dividends and underlying profitability.

Despite the diversity of information that investors might find useful in forming expectations, it is evident that some benchmarks would generally be looked for. One is an indication of expected share price movements. The financial press publish information each day about a large number of shares traded on the International Stock Exchange. As an indication of the fluctuations in share prices, the high and low for the year are also quoted.

The dividend is important and useful information, and therefore the dividend yield is published as well. Dividends are usually paid semi-annually on a net-of-tax basis. The first payment, which is called the interim dividend, is fixed by the directors of the company, and will usually be less than the final dividend, which has to be agreed by the shareholders. Hence, in dividing the grossed-up dividend (i.e. the sum of the net-of-tax dividend and the tax deducted) by the current share price, a simple interest basis is implicit in the calculation. Furthermore, because the fluctuations in share prices will usually cause the reported dividend yield to change substantially over time, no adjustment is made for the accrued dividend effect.

The usefulness of the dividend yield is limited because it does not take into account changes in the dividends that have yet to be announced. Dividend yields for similar companies pursuing identical dividend policies, can still differ markedly because the dividends may be announced and paid at different times of the year. The published yields take this problem into account to a limited extent by indicating changes in, say, interim dividends or using published forecasts where appropriate. Professional investment analysts will usually prefer to make an explicit forecast of the dividends that will be paid over the following twelve months, thus making the analogy between dividends and the return on other investments, such as bonds, easier to compare.

As a complement to the dividend yield, the earnings yield or its reciprocal, the price earnings (P/E) ratio, is also commonly reported. This is particularly relevant if earnings are retained, and information on earnings is more important than on dividends. Therefore the shares of two companies, with different dividend policies but similar investment programmes, might be expected to trade at similar earnings yields but with different dividend yields.

The earnings yield is calculated by dividing the profits after tax by the number of shares, and expressing the result as a percentage of the current share price. Adjustments are often made for such factors as the effect of dividend policy on the company's tax liability, the impact of overseas tax, and so on.

The interpretation of the earnings yield is difficult for the same reasons noted when interpreting dividend yields. If calculated on a historical earnings basis, two companies may differ in reporting dates and the reported earnings will refer to different periods. The earnings yield will be low (and the P/E ratio correspondingly high) if shareholders expect future earnings to increase steadily over a number of years. This characteristic is considered further in the next section, which deals with the ways in which shares may be valued.

Sometimes attached to the sale of equity is a warrant. This is an instrument which entitles the holder to buy an ordinary share at a specified price. In many ways a warrant and an option are similar, since both allow the holder to purchase equity if they wish to, and is thus a contingent claim on an underlying asset.[1] If a portfolio consists of a warrant and a fixed interest bond it should effectively provide the same return as that obtained from a convertible bond (which can be changed into equity). The portfolio will increase in value as the price of the company's ordinary shares rises, whilst the payment of interest on the bond provides income in the form of cash before conversion.

In the case of convertible bonds and warrants, the financial structure of the issuing company will be affected by the investors' decision to exercise their rights. Convertible bonds will involve the company replacing debt financing by equity, while warrants can imply the issue of additional equity.

8.3 Share issues

The issue of ordinary shares for cash results in two related outcomes. The first and most obvious is the receipt of cash by the issuer company, while the second is that the new shareholders become part-owners of the company. In looking at the issuing process, these two outcomes may dictate the particular method of issue chosen.

The most common situation is for an existing public company with shares already listed on the Stock Exchange wishing to raise additional funds, perhaps for new investment projects or, more frequently, to replace some of its existing finance, perhaps debt which has matured. In this case, existing shareholders may wish to increase their ownership by purchasing additional shares. In particular, institutional investors may be more willing to increase their shareholding in a small or medium-sized company through participating in a rights issue than by purchasing in the open market and precipitating a price rise. Furthermore, Stock Exchange regulations normally require companies with shares already quoted on the Stock Exchange to offer additional shares first to existing shareholders or to have the approval of shareholders in offering the shares to other investors.

A rights issue is initiated by sending a prospectus with details of the offer, including the purpose of the issue and the number of shares for sale, to each of the existing shareholders. These new shares will generally be offered to the shareholders at a discount to the market price of shares currently trading. If taken up, shares from the rights issue can be sold straightaway in the market, potentially at a profit. Alternatively, the shareholder may sell the rights separately without actually buying the shares offered. In this case, the price of the rights will approximately equal the discount, and the new investor will pay the same in aggregate as if the shares were bought on the market directly.

Rights issues are of major importance to companies raising new finance, and there are a number of examples drawn from the banking sector, as shown in Table 8.1. The pricing of a rights issue does not affect the wealth of those existing shareholders who exercise their rights. This is somewhat surprising, and is clearer with a simple illustration. Example:

Table 8.1 Rights issues in the UK banking sector (£m)

Bank	Date	Amount	% of market value
Barclays	March 1985	507	25
	April 1987	210	6
	April 1988	921	26
Midland	July 1983	155	21
	July 1987	700	46
	Nov 1987	400	24
Nat West	July 1984	236	31
	May 1986	714	23
	Sept 1986	121	3
Royal Bank of Scotland	April 1984	42	20
	Jan 1985	121	26
	April 1985	81	21

Source: Financial Times, various issues.

Consider a company with issued capital of one million ordinary shares, and a quoted market price of 100p per share. The total value of the equity will be £1 million. If the company wishes to raise an additional £200,000 it can do this by offering one million shares at 20p each or half a million shares at 40p each. In either case, the company will acquire £200,000 which will be added to the value of its total equity.

But the price of each share after the rights issue has been made will depend on the number of shares issued. In one case, there will be a total of two million shares, making the price of each share 60p (1.2/2 million), whereas in the other the price will be 80p per share (1.2/1.5 million).

Assuming the first case, shareholders exercising their rights will spend 20p for each new share, equal to the number originally held. After the issue, they will hold twice as many shares, each worth 60p. Their total shareholding will therefore be worth 120p multiplied by the number of shares originally owned. But in acquiring this extra holding they have spent 20p multiplied by the number of shares owned before the issue. Therefore the net value of their portfolio is 100p multiplied by their original investment which is exactly the same as the original value. This is true in the second case also, and the value of the portfolio will remain unchanged (see Table 8.2).

This analysis is too simplistic to explain the changes in share prices before and after a company proceeds with a rights issue. In practice, the announcement of a rights issue may signal a profitable opportunity which may cause investors to bid up the price of the traded shares. On the other hand, during the interval between the announcement of the offer and the acceptance day, the market may move for a variety of reasons not directly connected with the issuing firms. If a fall in price

Table 8.2 Example of a rights issue

Pre-issue			Issue				Post-issue	
(1) Number of shares	(2) Market price	(3) = (1) × (2) Market capitalisation	(4) Number of shares offered	(5) Price	(6) Value	(7) = (6) + (3) Total value	(8) = (1) + (4) Number of shares	(9) = (7) ÷ (8) Market price
(A) 1m	100p	£1m	1m (1 for 1)	20p	£0.2m	£1.2m	2m	60p
(B) 1m	100p	£1m	0.5 (1 for 2)	40p	£0.2m	£1.2m	1.5m	80p

Case (A) Owner of 1 share (value 100p) will spend 20p and (after issue) will hold a portfolio of 2 shares, each worth 60p = 120p, therefore no change in shareholder's wealth.

Case (B) Owner of 2 shares (value 200p) will spend 40p and (after issue) will hold a portfolio of 3 shares each worth 80p = 240p, therefore no change in shareholder's wealth.

does occur, shareholders are unlikely to take advantage of the offer to buy additional shares, particularly if the price is now below the rights offer price. Because there is some risk of this happening, the discount has to be sufficiently large to allow for some price movement downwards, but not too large as to signal a lack of confidence on the part of the issuing company.

Generally, the issuer will arrange for the financial institutions to underwrite the issue. The underwriting institutions, which will usually include the major institutional investors, frequently agree to buy the issue if existing shareholders fail to accept the offer. This is insurance against a low take-up of the issue, and for this the underwriters receive a commission. Given the costs of underwriting, it may be cheaper to set the issue price low enough to foreclose the chance of the issue failing.

The majority of share issues are carried out by either an *offer for sale* at a fixed price or *sale by tender*. An offer for sale by fixed price is arranged by an intermediary, generally a merchant bank or stockbroker. The issuing house will take ownership of the shares and advertise them for sale at a fixed price in the financial press. An accompanying prospectus will contain a considerable amount of information about the history of the company and its present financial position as well as some estimates or forecasts of its future profitability. The information supplied is largely determined by the Stock Exchange rules which specify the conditions under which new issues can be traded on the Exchange.[2]

If the offer price is fixed too high, there will obviously be insufficient applications and the issuing house will be left with the excess shares. They will transfer this risk to underwriters, but again, a fee will be paid. If the offer price is fixed too low, there will be an excess demand for shares, and an equitable method of allocating the shares among applicants has to be devised, for example, a ballot. Since there are advantages in trying to achieve a widely distributed share ownership, the issuing institution may discriminate in the allocation of shares in favour of individual investors.

For an issue which arouses a great deal of interest from individual investors, the institutions try to overcome the bias against institutional applications by submitting multiple applications, each for small numbers of shares. It is therefore not unusual to hear of sackfuls of applications arriving on the closing date. The privatisation programmes in the 1980s provide many examples of this, where there were numerous applications both from private investors and the investing intermediaries.

If an issue is heavily oversubscribed the price of the shares when initially traded on the open market will be considerably higher than the offer price. The possibility of a price increase following an offer for sale consequently encourages investors to apply for shares, intending to sell them after issue. Thus trading in the primary market is arranged so as to ensure an active secondary market. This practice is known as 'stagging'. Table 8.3 gives a list of new issues, showing the various degrees of stagging and the extent of price recovery.

Setting the offer price for new issues is considerably more difficult than setting

Table 8.3 New equity issues – London Stock Exchange

Issue price p	Amt paid up	Mkt cap (£m)	1994 High	Low	Stock	Close price p
—	F.P.	1.74	66	62	Abtrust Nw C Wts	66
—	F.P.	26.7	100	98	Aromascan	99
—	F.P.	21.4	89	83	Baillie G Shn Wrts	85
100	F.P.	19.4	102	100	Beacon Inv Tst	102
—	F.P.	1.71	45	43	Do. Warrants	45
18	F.P.	5.18	31	21	Carnell	28
165	F.P.	77.2	173	165	Chamberlain Ph.	173
120	F.P.	11.8	133	118	Copyright Prom.	118
—	F.P.	26.0	58	52	Emrg Mkts Country	52
—	F.P.	3.40	36	26	Do. Warrants	34
—	F.P.	6.90	71	69	Freeport	70
—	F.P.	32.2	94	91	INVESCO Jpn Disc	92
—	F.P.	3.43	50	42	Do. Warrants	49
—	F.P.	59.2	285	238	Ideal Hardware	280
—	F.P.	—	77	63	JF FI Japan Wrts	70
3	F.P.	1.87	3½	3	John Mansfield	3½
—	F.P.	16.7	40	35	Magnum Power	40
100	F.P.	67.2	98	94	Old Mutual SA	96
—	F.P.	6.02	45	43	Do. Warrants	43
23	F.P.	10.6	31	29	Orbis	29
90	F.P.	15.8	95	90	Panther	90
—	F.P.	0.60	17	5½	Do. Warrants	17
—	F.P.	1.26	40	39	Petroceltic	40
150	F.P.	178.8	162	157	Pillar Property Inv	158
—	F.P.	122.5	98	91	Schroder Japan G	98
—	F.P.	13.0	52	42	Do. Warrants	52
—	F.P.	4.32	44	37	Suter Wrts 99/04	37
100	F.P.	3.66	102	97	Tr Euro Gth Ptg	101
272	F.P.	1,822.4	315½	280	3i	313½
—	F.P.	2.48	35	29	Tops Ests Wrts	31
—	F.P.	55.4	49	34	VideoLogic	40½
140	F.P.	67.1	180	148	Yates Bros Wine	173

Source: Financial Times, 17 August 1994.

the price of a rights issue, since the demand comes from investors in general, rather than those already in some sympathy with the company. During periods of share price instability, this is exacerbated, and in conjunction with the reluctance of the underwriters to be left holding unwanted shares, highlights the problems with this method of issue.

The mid-1980s was a time of highly volatile prices. One new issue wrongly priced at that time was Superdrug Stores. Example:

A new issue of ordinary shares was announced in February 1983 of 8.8 million at 175p, but the offer was oversubscribed 95 times! At the end of the first day of trading the share price had risen to 270p, an increase of 54%. This was not due to a volatile market but to stagging, and the excessive discount is demonstrated by the evidence that 60% of the shares were traded on the first day. Prices opened at 295p and reached a maximum of 300p. Two months later the share price had fallen slightly to 263p, while during that period the *Financial Times* All Share Index had risen by 10%.

Another example of an issue which suffered because of changes in the market between the announcement and offer date was BP, where the October 1987 crash occurred in time to make the issue a disaster.

Other issues which have aroused criticism of the fixed price method were the sale on behalf of the government of shares in Amersham International and in Associated British Ports. In both cases, the issues were heavily oversubscribed and the share prices at the end of the first day of trading were between 20% and 35% higher than their offer prices. Many of the early privatisations in the 1980s were oversubscribed twenty- or thirtyfold.

The other method of share issue, sale by tender, does not attract the same criticism, although this is considerably less popular with the market. Investors have to specify the price and quantity of shares they require at application. The issuing house will then rank the applications in order of price and allocate all the available shares to those offers greater than or equal to the lowest acceptable price, known as the striking price. Some indication of the minimum acceptable price will be given in the prospectus and if insufficient tenders are made, the surplus shares will be sold to the underwriting institutions at the striking price.

Critics of this method question the efficiency of these markets because in practice, prices in the period following the issue are often very flat. The argument is made that offers by tender fail to attract sufficient interest from professional traders. This results in the issue price being lower than the price that could be set if the shares were sold by offer at a fixed price and then were subject to market pressure. A counter-argument is that this method truly determines the view of the market, and the institutions are given the opportunity to participate if they wish.

Another example of a failure share issue in the 1980s is Britoil plc. This was an equity issue by tender, in November 1982. The issue was undertaken not to raise new funds, but solely to change the ownership of the equity. Partly because of a number of events that occurred in the interval between arranging the sale and the day on which applications were finally accepted, the minimum acceptable price was too high and there were insufficient applications, and the underwriting institutions had to buy most of the shares on issue. When the share was subsequently traded on the Stock Exchange, the price was almost 20% less than the minimum tender price. A further anomaly was the case of the British Airways privatisation, where tenders were received, but rather than deciding on a striking price, the shares were sold at whatever the offer price was. The result was that investors paid different amounts for the same security.

Three other methods of issuing shares which should be mentioned are placing, introduction and capitalisation issues. Of these, only placing generally represents the raising of additional finance for the company on whose behalf the shares are issued. It is mainly associated with corporate debt but can also be used for small equity issues when the issue cost of a full offer for sale would be relatively high.

Placement issues can be either private or public. Private companies in the UK are forbidden by law from advertising and selling securities to the general public, but they can sell to professional investment firms, or to those with knowledge of the company, that is, employees or existing shareholders. These securities are very illiquid, and only if the company expects to gain an exchange listing in the future are the bulk of final investors interested in them. However, the fact that the issue has occurred at all and an investment firm has confidence in the company, is a strong signal of their potential profitability.

In a public placement, the issuing institution will sell shares to a number of institutional and individual investors as well as providing stockbrokers with a supply in order to facilitate the market-making process. The Stock Exchange regulates such placings, requiring that at least 25% of the shares are offered to market-makers, allowing a wider group to gain access to a proportion of the shares. They also require that information about the issue is published. These requirements differentiate it from a private placement, and improve the liquidity of the issue to a certain extent.

An introduction is usually the method of choice for foreign registered companies wishing to have their shares listed on the UK Stock Exchange. Introductions do not necessarily involve new shares but shares will be sold to brokers for market-making purposes.[3] In some cases, an introduction will be made for a company with a number of existing shareholders who may then sell part or all of their holdings. In both instances, the issue has the effect of changing the composition of the shareholdings, even if only marginally.

Finally, capitalisation issues create more shares but without any cash passing to the company from this issue. The procedure creates shares by transforming some part of the profits retained from the operations of previous years, and is essentially a change in accounting only. The balance sheet entries for retained earnings will fall by the nominal value of the shares created which will appear in the balance sheet as an increase in the issued capital of the company. Consequently, the company will distribute these additional shares to its shareholders in proportion to the number of shares held.

The effect of capitalisation issues is that more shares are owned, and presumably traded. The total value of the company is nominally unchanged, so the price of the shares should adjust accordingly, that is, if the number of shares is doubled, the price of each share should halve. In practice, this does not often occur, mainly because of the signalling effect observed with rights issues noted earlier, but may be done to save cash and reduce tax liability, and can be in lieu of a dividend.

Table 8.4 New equity issues in the UK, by method of issue, 1985–9

Method	Amount raised	Number of issues
Offers for sale	5,855	94
Tenders	361	11
Placings	725	120
Privatisations	16,661	15
Total	23,602	240

Source: Bank of England Quarterly Bulletin, May 1990.

Capitalisation issues seem to be made during a period in which the company is making superior profits, and after the issue the company may expect to increase the total amount of dividends paid to shareholders. Obviously, if a company doubles the number of shares and maintains the dividend payment per share, the shareholders will receive double the amount of cash anticipated. If they believe that the company will be able to maintain this increased dividend in subsequent years, the share price will reflect these increased expectations and may consequently fall very little, stay the same or even increase.

The reason for capitalisation issues is to bring the company's accumulated reserves into line with the issued capital. Suggestions are that high-priced shares are unpopular with individual investors. Alternatively, capitalisation issues may be used to avoid some restriction on income or dividend payouts. In the US this is called a stock split. The two are essentially the same, but with small differences in the form of the new issue: for example, in the UK a capitalisation issue nominated as 4:1 would leave the shareholder with five times the number of original shares, whereas in the US a stock split of 4:1 would leave the shareholder with four times the number of original shares.

The method of choice relating to new issues is largely influenced by the amount of funds to be raised, as well as the relative costs involved in the issue of equity, as well as the costs of alternative funding, such as syndicated loans. The cost varies considerably across the range of procedures discussed above. As can be seen from Table 8.4, for the latter part of the 1980s, the most common method was placing, but offers for sale were almost equally popular for large issues. These have become less popular during the past few years, and the last tender issue was in 1986.

A survey undertaken by the Bank of England showed that placing is the cheapest method for fairly small amounts, and has been common practice on the unlisted securities market. Costs associated with offers for sale were approximately 11% of the total raised, whereas placings cost nearly 18% of the value of the issue for amounts less than £3 million and only 4.7% for amounts over £10 million. Clearly, considerable economies of scale exist in raising funds in the securities markets.

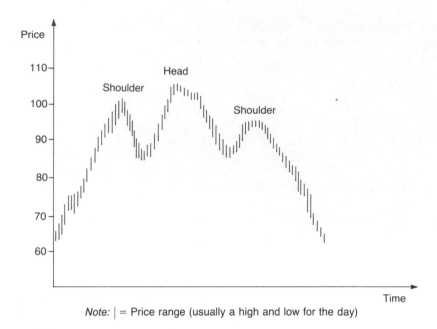

Note: | = Price range (usually a high and low for the day)

Figure 8.1   Head and shoulders chart.

8.4 Share valuation

There are two approaches to share valuation. One uses past patterns of prices and mechanical trading rules and is known as technical analysis. The second is based on many different aspects of information known about the firm, especially stressing the importance of earnings and P/E ratios. This is called fundamental analysis. We shall now consider both of these.

Technical analysis

As stated in the introduction to this section, technical analysis relies on trading decisions based on past patterns of prices. Analysts draw graphs of prices and try to identify trends in the past which may be replicated in the future. This reliance on charting historical data to enable them to recognise patterns has resulted in these analysts being labelled *chartists*. Some of the common shapes are known as head and shoulders and triangles, and the first of these is illustrated in Figure 8.1. Notice that it is trends in price changes rather than absolute values.

In reality there are considerable problems with this method. Identifying patterns *ex post* is clearly a simple task, but forecasting when they will recur is not. An extension of this approach to markets generally, for example identifying changes

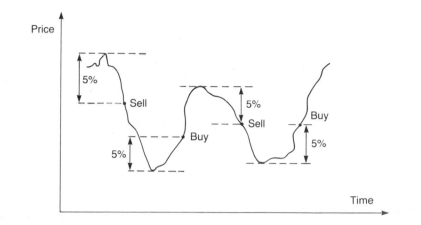

Figure 8.2 Example of a 5% filter rule.

in the market index, confirms the existence of business cycles, while *ex ante* the turning-points in the trend remain hard to predict.

A further aspect of technical analysis is the use of mechanical trading rules which are set to capture the trends in the pattern of price changes before the market adjusts. This requires a filter rule to activate trading which is sufficiently small to pick up the trend early, but large enough that only true changes are identified. An example of a filter rule is shown in Figure 8.2.

Criticism of this technique is based on the higher levels of risk given the portfolio models aimed on diversification are ignored, a topic discussed later in this chapter, and the high transactions costs resulting from frequent trades. But in addition, the notion of a successful trading strategy based on past evidence is contrary to the efficient market hypothesis outlined in Chapter 7. There it was claimed that the weak form of efficiency required that no investor can earn excess returns by developing trading rules based on historical prices, as information in past prices is not useful or relevant in earning excess returns.

However, despite this contradictory evidence, technical analysts still use both of these methods in the securities markets and in foreign currency dealing. This may be prompted by the lack of sufficient or reliable data for fundamental analysis or simply a failure to be convinced by the academic argument for efficient markets.

Fundamental analysis

Fundamental analysts do examine past performance, but within the context of an industry specialist and with a knowledge of the activity of the firm as a whole. However, it should not be assumed that fundamental analysis precludes the use of formal mathematical models. For example, the method of generating models of P/E ratios and share valuation uses discounting techniques. In this section, we will use discounting models in conjunction with the dividend component of earnings, as well as other measures of performance.

The valuation of a share is assumed to depend on the receipt of future dividends and the price of the share when sold. Therefore the value of a share at time t_0 will be

$$P_0 = D_1(1+r)^{-1} + D_2(1+r)^{-2} + D_3(1+r)^{-3}$$
$$+ \ldots + D_n(1+r)^{-n} + P_n(1+r)^{-n} \tag{8.1}$$

where D_t = annual dividend, r = the appropriate discount rate, and n = number of years between the current period and the date at which the share is sold. It is assumed that the share is being valued twelve months before the total dividend is paid. That is, the first dividend is received at the end of the first period and therefore needs to be discounted to the present.

By making certain assumptions, simple formulae can be derived. The simplest assumption is that dividends are constant over all periods. In this case, the valuation can be expressed in terms of the annuity formula, introduced in Chapter 5.

$$P_0 = D_1 a_{\overline{n}|} r + P_T(1+r)^{-n} \tag{8.2}$$

Furthermore, since equities are perpetual – that is, they are transferred from one owner to another, but continue to exist unless formally withdrawn – the dividend flows are perpetual, and the valuation will simplify to

$$P_0 = \frac{D_1}{r} \tag{8.3}$$

A more interesting case is a model which assumes some systematic growth in dividends over time. Suppose dividends are expected to grow annually at a rate of $g\%$. The general form is

$$P_0 = D_1(1+r)^{-1} + D_1(1+g)(1+r)^{-2}$$
$$+ \ldots + D_1(1+g)^{n-1}(1+r)^{-n} + P_n(1+r)^{-n} \tag{8.4}$$

If n is very large then the last term, $P_n(1+r)^{-n}$, will be very small, and become insignificant. Then the valuation can be expressed in the form[4]

$$P_0 = D_1(1+r)^{-1}[1 + (1+g)(1+r)^{-1} + (1+g^2)(1+r)^{-1}$$
$$+ \ldots (1+g^{n-1})(1+r)^{-1}] \tag{8.5}$$

In this example we are assuming that n is indefinitely large so x^{n-1} can be ignored as long as x is less than 1. This is equivalent to imposing the condition that the dividend growth rate is less than the discount rate.

Thus we can substitute $(1+g)(1+r)^{-1}$ for x to produce

$$P_0 = \frac{D_1}{r-g} \tag{8.6}$$

This growth formula is an oversimplified but useful model which can be used as a basis for comparing firms which differ in dividend policy but which are expected to have comparable profitability. The assumptions are: (i) constant dividend growth rate, g; (ii) constant interest rate, r; (iii) g is less than r; and (iv) either the share is held for an indefinitely large period or sold to another investor with the same expectations, hence being valued as a perpetuity.

Equation (8.6) can be rewritten in the form

$$r = \frac{D_1}{P_0} + g \tag{8.7}$$

which clearly separates out the yield from the capital growth effect.

There have been numerous variations on this type of model. The growth rate may be assumed to fall or rise over time or a high rate of growth may be fixed for a specified number of years, before decreasing. More realistically, a company may be slow to pay dividends during an initial period of establishment, and then begin to distribute earnings after a number of years.

The difficulty with all dividend discounting models is that there are usually too many unobserved values to be included. Consequently the valuation can be based on estimates which embody very arbitrary assumptions. For example, in using a model that requires the specification of a number of periods of superior growth, it is unlikely that all potential profitable investment opportunities for future years will be known. In view of these difficulties, the models are rarely used in practice, other than to compare the performance of similar companies which may reflect very different expectations. Further discussion of discounting approaches is deferred to Appendix A to this chapter.

The method most often used by professional analysts to value shares is by fundamental analysis of the companies and their management. This does involve judgement in choosing which information is most useful, and there is a wide variation in the factors considered by different analysts. However, it is still possible to examine the general techniques of share valuation using the fundamental approach.

The main emphasis in analysing a company's previous performance is to assess how successful the managers of the company have been in operating and developing the company. The task of forecasting the future profitability of the company involves forecasting the trading conditions for a number of years ahead, and assessing the skill with which the management will handle the problems that are likely to arise. Fundamental analysis, therefore, emphasises the competence of the management. Given an assessment of the management and of the future economic environment (the competitive structure of the industry, the economic and political changes, etc.), analysts will then form estimates of the future profits that each firm can subsequently expect. The term *earnings quality* is sometimes used to describe the behaviour of a company's profits through time, and profits which increase at a reasonably predictable rate with no unpleasant surprises are considered by analysts to be of high quality.

Fundamental analysis derives a share valuation from multiplying the forecasted profits per share by a forecasted P/E ratio.

$$\text{Fundamental price} = \frac{P}{E} \times \hat{E}$$

where P/E is the price/earnings ratio, and E the forecasted earnings per share.

The ratio is chosen by reference to the capitalisation rate used by the market for the shares of other similar companies, and is frequently used as an estimate of potential earnings. Thus if profits are expected to grow faster than others, the P/E ratio will be adjusted upwards, whereas if profits are expected to be more variable or less certain, the P/E ratio will be lower. Since even the P/E ratios of firms within the same industry can vary widely, the selection of the appropriate number can be crucial to the share valuation. Investors have to take into account not only their own estimates of the future profitability of the company, but also the views of other investors which will be reflected in the share price after the profits are reported.

The popularity of this ratio in fundamental analysis has prompted the derivation of more formal methods of arriving at P/E-based valuations. In a simple model, the P/E ratios of different companies, together with indicators of financial performance and profitability will be used in a statistical analysis. The aim of such exercises is to find a number of variables that will explain the behaviour of P/E ratios sufficiently well for forecasting purposes. Statistical models have also been used to forecast the share prices directly, although there are problems at both a practical and theoretical level. In practical terms, the useful variables that explain share prices in one period are not the same as those which are useful in another period. In fact it may be difficult to identify any variables which are consistently useful.

8.5 Share price behaviour

Although we have commented on the lack of information about the method of valuation actually employed by analysts, we do know that profits are of prime importance. We can observe that the share price is particularly volatile around the date at which the profits of the respective company are announced. We also note that in reporting changes in share prices, there are sometimes comments which refer to the market's reaction to 'disappointing' profits or to forecasts of profits expected to be announced in the near future.

The market's reaction to earnings announcements is a topic which has considerable relevance to the assessment of market efficiency. In a highly efficient market, the release of the profits figures should not have any predictable effect on the share price. On the day of the announcement the market price should rise or fall with equal probability. In the event of a rise, commentators will say the market was pleased with the unexpectedly good results, whereas if there is a fall, there will be references to the market's disappointment. But the market is reacting to informed expectations within the industry. Market efficiency, as outlined in Chapter 7, implies that expected earnings should on average be equal to the actual announcement with errors equally likely in either direction.

A good deal of research has been done on the reaction of share prices to the release of specific announcements. Usually the studies have tracked the behaviour of share prices before and after the announcement. After controlling for other sources of disturbance, the overwhelming evidence suggests that the market reacts to important news prior to a formal announcement. For example, with companies reporting high profits, the share price will increase before the announcement, as investors trade on the basis of their expectations. Another area of research is the movement in share price following an event such as a takeover bid. The initial response may be very short-lived and prices return to their pre-event level very quickly.

This discussion of share price reactions raises the related issue of the behaviour of share prices over time. We have suggested that prices are more variable around the time at which announcements are made. What may not be so obvious is that prices will usually be variable over time. If investors are continuously monitoring the news, a large proportion of the reported events may be interpreted to have implications for share prices. For example, a change in government policy may imply heavier taxes on consumers with a drop in consumer expenditure. But less consumer expenditure means less income for retailing and consumer good manufacturing. Investment analysts would thus examine the sensitivity of company profits to the changes in tax, perhaps recommending investors to sell those companies most seriously affected. The consequent effect is that share prices for specific companies might fall as market forces interact, but many macroeconomic policy implications will affect the market as a whole.

Since many news items are of potential significance share prices are observed to change almost continuously. In fact, many policy decisions taken by management are interpreted as a signal to the market, for example, a change in dividend policy or the level of gearing within the firm. Most research studies of share prices have found that over time they move in what seem to be 'random walks' and it is now recognised that this randomness in share price behaviour is one indication that the market is operating efficiently.

8.6 Portfolio models

Approaches to the analysis of stock markets have developed in a number of ways since the 1960s and 1970s. This is partly due to advances in finance theory, but also because of the influence of the institutional investors and their domination of the capital markets. Given these institutions are managing huge funds involving many different kinds of investment instruments, and that they are doing so on behalf of various groups of clients with a range of expectations and risk profiles, the performance of the portfolio is of considerably more importance than the performance of a single security.

For institutional investors, with large portfolios containing perhaps hundreds of different shares, a change in the return of one asset is unlikely to affect the return on the whole portfolio. However, when the market as a whole becomes more optimistic, and investors revise their expectations of profits and dividends upwards, most shares in the market may rise in response to the more confident environment. In this case, an investment intermediary should achieve a satisfactory return during such a period if they are fully involved in the market rather than selecting a few companies which are expected to perform particularly well. At other times, a single industrial sector may do poorly, but if the portfolio is well diversified, the overall outcome will be relatively unaffected.

The acceptance that diversification is of crucial importance in determining portfolio performance has had the effect of concentrating investors' attention on distinguishing market effects from individual firm effects, since risk from the former cannot be reduced by diversification while the latter can. Therefore the forecasting of future dividends from a single company is not as important as analysing the relationship between the elements of the portfolio and between the portfolio and the market in aggregate.

The really important question is whether the share price and dividends of a single share change more or less than the market, where market performance is measured by an index consisting of all available assets. For example, if the market index rises by 10%, does the single share price also move by 10%, or by more or by less? This is solved by statistical techniques to compute the degree of covariability between the individual share prices and the market index. The approach used is derived directly from the capital asset pricing model, which allows the investor to construct portfolios that behave in a way that is systematically related to the changes in the market as a whole. This is developed in more detail in Appendix B at the end of this chapter.

Individual risk preference can be reflected in the construction of the optimal portfolio. Risk-averse investors will aim for a portfolio which is more stable than the market index; risk-lovers can construct a portfolio which is more volatile than the market; and risk-neutral investors can construct a portfolio which matches the market index. An example of these portfolios is index funds that are often used by institutional investors involved in managing pension funds. Indexed funds aim to achieve an average performance and to yield a return that never differs much from the return that would be earned from the market as a whole.

The related concept of a market model (also discussed in Appendix B to this chapter) is developed from these elementary ideas of the importance of portfolio diversification and relative price changes with respect to the market overall. At this stage we only wish to point out that portfolio theory and other related models have been rigorously developed from a statistical and mathematical approach, and readers wishing to further their interest in portfolio modelling are referred to the texts included in the further reading listed at the end of this chapter.

8.7 Share clientele and the effects of block trading

There are a number of issues resulting from the presence of different groups of investors in the equity market. This is partly due to the varying trading patterns and investment objectives found among any group of heterogeneous investors but also because of the size of the trades undertaken by the investing institutions. A further debate about the investment behaviour philosophy of the large funds and their contribution to the funding of industry as a whole, is delayed until Chapter 18.

First addressing the clientele effect, we stated that individual investors, or institutions acting on their behalf, have different risk profiles, but other factors may influence the investment decision. Two related issues that are particularly important are their time-preferences and their tax liabilities.

In the market for ordinary shares, profits earned by capital gains are more leniently treated for tax purposes compared to the receipt of income in the form of dividends. Thus, personal investors paying high marginal rates of income tax might be expected to prefer low dividend-paying shares if proportionately high capital gains are expected. Other investors in a lower tax band may prefer income in the form of dividends, rather than a capital gain some time in the future. Correspondingly, institutional investors such as pension funds who are exempt from both capital gains and income tax, might prefer the shares of companies paying relatively high dividends. Although there are arguments in favour of this type of portfolio clientele effect, the inherent variability of share prices precludes wholesale commitment to a tax-based investment policy. Generally the arguments in favour of diversification outweigh those based on tax clientele.

Another effect arises from the choice of companies in which to invest. Private retail investors tend to invest in both large and small companies, sometimes motivated by a wish to take advantage of a special interest or their own experience, or to support local companies or those with household names for quality consumer goods. Conversely, institutional investors buy large quantities of shares and will tend to concentrate on mature, *blue chip* companies because the shares may be traded more frequently, and thus are priced more efficiently. Since individual investors tend not to revise their portfolios as often as institutional investors, the shares of smaller companies may not be traded as regularly as those of large companies. This has led to suggestions that the shares of small companies are less efficiently priced than those of larger companies, or that there is a two-tier market consisting of large companies with shares traded by institutions in the first tier and small companies with shares held mainly by individuals in the second tier. To the extent that these tiers exist, it is reasonable to refer to a clientele effect for ordinary shares.

However, while the institutions tend to hold shares of large companies they also are apt to favour particular industry sectors. Ownership concentration by one client group can lead to biased investment strategies, allowing companies in the currently fashionable sectors to grow at the expense of others. This has resulted in some companies transferring their Stock Exchange listing from their original industrial classification to a more currently attractive one.

Finally, a number of questions are raised about how the market reacts to blocks of shares suddenly becoming available. During the typical day for an actively traded security on a major stock exchange, thousands of shares will be traded, usually in bundles of around one hundred. If this is a new issue, it can be dealt with by the issuing institution. But in the secondary markets, a block of shares may disrupt the market for the individual security, or the market as a whole. For example, if the price falls following a sale, is this a liquidity effect or an information effect? If it is due to a loss of liquidity in the market, we may expect prices to recover quickly, whereas if it is a response to new information, the change will be reflecting this and be permanent. The basis of the problem is that there is no sure way for outsiders to know whether a block sale is motivated by portfolio rebalancing by an insurance company or pension fund, or a response to adverse information gained by the considerable research teams within these investing institutions.

8.8 Summary

Shares can be issued on the markets in a number of ways, with the initial price set to clear the market, and ensure an active secondary market. Valuation of equity can be done for a single share using technical or fundamental analysis, although increasingly portfolio analysis is the most common approach. The impact of large holdings by institutional investors may have an effect on the efficiency of market-pricing mechanisms.

Notes

1. Because of their contingent claim characteristic, many texts include warrants in the section on derivatives.
2. See the information required for listing in Chapter 7.
3. Shares in foreign companies may of course be traded on the Stock Exchange directly. There may also be investors in London who own and are trading in foreign securities who may be instrumental in supplying shares to the market.
4. The first n term inside the parentheses is a recognised geometric progression of the form

$$[1 + x + x^2 + \ldots x^{n-1}]$$

and the solution

$$\frac{1 - x^n}{1 - x}$$

Further reading

Elton, E. J. and M. J. Gruber (1991), *Modern Portfolio Theory and Investment Analysis*, 4th edn, Wiley.
Foley, B. J. (1991), *Capital Markets*, Macmillan.
Rutterford, J. (1993), *Introduction to Stock Exchange Investment*, 2nd edn, Macmillan. This provides an excellent introduction to investment principles with a clear discussion of modern portfolio theory.
Sharpe, W. F. (1982), *Investments*, 2nd edn, Prentice Hall.

Problems

8.1 A shareholder is holding 1,000 shares (price 200p) when the company unexpectedly announces a rights issue (at 140p) on the basis of one new share for every existing five shares held. What would you expect the market price of the shares to be after the rights issue? For how much could the rights of the shareholder be sold?

8.2 An investor is analysing a share, currently priced at 55p. The dividend (of 4p) is payable within the next few days. The following dividend is forecast to be 5p, and thereafter it is expected that dividends will grow by 10% a year. What return will be earned on the share if it is bought now and held indefinitely?

8.3 All companies in the same sector are expected to yield the same return to shareholders, and the dividends on Beemrup (Printing) are expected to grow at 5% per year. What growth rate of dividends is expected on (a) English Print, (b) McDonalds (Printing) using the following information?

	Price	Forecast dividends (p) 12 months' time
Beemrup	128	4
English Print	35	1
McDonalds	180	8

8.4 Using the information in 8.3, calculate the share prices of the three companies:
(a) in twelve months' time
(b) immediately after the dividends have been paid.

8.5 The dividends and profits of a bio-technological company have been growing steadily at 22% per year over the life of the firm. If a shareholder expects to earn 20% from the investment, value the share if dividends are currently 50p. Comment on your calculations.

8.6 The price of shares in Fluidonics is 500p and the P/E ratio is forecast to be 20 (for the next reported earnings at the end of the current year). Fluidonics have regularly paid out 30% of their profits in dividends, but unexpectedly announce that they are changing their dividend policy. In future their pay-out ratio will be 50%. The share price falls to 192p. Estimate the return expected from holding the shares and the expected return on investment. (Assume both are constant.) Refer to Appendix A.

Appendix A
Discounted earnings
models

In this chapter, we have briefly described the simple dividend growth model

$$P_0 = \frac{D_1}{r - g} \qquad (8A.1)$$

where D_1 = the estimated dividend, payable at the end of the current year; r = the discount rate, and $100g\%$ = the percentage annual growth in dividends. In this appendix we look at a valuation model based on dividend policy and earnings per share.

The model owes its derivation to the observation that firms *tend* to pay out dividends as a stable proportion of their profits, taking one year with another. Thus if profits per share are E_1, dividends paid may be written $(1 - b)E_1$, where b is the proportion retained in the business for reinvestment. Earnings per share are assumed to be net of depreciation, interest and tax and are assumed to be maintainable at this level in perpetuity. It follows that the firm will, after the end of year, be able to maintain its profits of E in perpetuity but also will be able to earn *additional* profits from its reinvested funds.

If the firm is assumed to earn $100R\%$ from the reinvested profits, the profits will be:

in the second year: $E_1 + RbE_1$, or $E_1(1 + Rb)$
in the third year: $E_1 + RbE_1 + Rb(E_1 + RbE_1)$
or $E_1 (1 + Rb)^2$

and so on. Thus the earnings in the nth year will be given by

$$E_1(1 + Rb)^{n-1}$$

of which $(1 - b)$ will be paid out in dividends. The present value of the dividends will be given by

$$P_0 = \frac{(1 - b)E_1}{(1 + r)} \left[1 + \frac{1 + Rb}{1 + r} + \left(\frac{1 + Rb}{1 + r} \right)^2 + \ldots + \left(\frac{1 + Rb}{1 + r} \right)^{n-1} \right] \qquad (8A.2)$$

151

The terms in the square brackets again have the same form as

$$[1 + x + x_2 + \ldots + x^{n-1}] \tag{8A.3}$$

which we have already identified in the chapter as a geometric progression with sum equal to $(1 - x^n) / (1 - x)$. As n becomes very large, the nth term becomes insignificantly small as long as x is less than 1. In this case, the same condition requires Rb to be less than r.

Thus

$$P_0 = \frac{(1-b)E_1}{(1+r)} \left[1 - \left(\frac{1}{\frac{1+Rb}{1+r}} \right) \right] \tag{8A.4}$$

which can be expressed as

$$P_0 = \frac{(1-b)E_1}{i - Rb} \tag{8A.5}$$

It will be noted if $g = Rb$, this expression reduces to (8A.1), since $(1-b)E_1$ is by definition the same value as D_1. Thus Rb can be interpreted as the growth rate of dividends (or earnings, since earnings are a constant multiple of dividends) or alternatively as the product of the proportion of earnings retained times the (marginal) return on investment.

From this discussion it will be recognised that

$$E_1 = E_0(1 + Rb)$$

so

$$\frac{P_0}{E_0} = \frac{(1-b)(1+Rb)}{r - Rb} \tag{8A.6}$$

This expression provides a basis for evaluating the P/E ratio based on historic (current) earnings. Reverting to equation (8A.5) for ease of discussion, it will be expected that for a higher value of R (the return earned by the firm on its reinvested funds), the greater the P/E ratio. Similarly, the greater the value of Rb (the growth rate), the higher will be the P/E ratio. Caution should be taken, however, in accepting these tentative inferences, because the variables are not independent. At higher estimated growth rates, for example, investors might employ a higher discount rate to allow for increased risk. Thus the P/E ratio might fall if both r and Rb increased.

Similarly, a company which retained most of its profits (b approaches 1) would tend to be assessed as a risky company because of the higher growth rates implied. Finally, we should re-emphasise that the model requires a constant earnings growth rate, a constant return on reinvested earnings, a constant proportion of retained earnings and a constant discount rate. It will be recognised therefore that the model is illuminating in its general form rather than useful for prediction.

Appendix B
Market models

In our discussion on portfolio-based approaches to share evaluation, we referred to the construction of portfolios which behaved systematically in relation to the market as a whole. The purpose of this appendix is to explain briefly one method of analysing portfolios using this approach, and to apply this to security pricing.

The assumption is made that since shares seem to be influenced by market sentiment, the returns on shares are *linearly related* to a market index:

$$R_{jt} = \alpha_j + \beta_j R_{mt} + e_{jt} \tag{8A.7}$$

where
R_{jt} = the rate of return on share j in time t
R_{mt} = the rate of return on the market index in time t
α_j, β_j = constants over time for share j
e_{jt} = error term

In combining two shares, j and k, equally in a portfolio, we would expect the portfolio to earn a return that would consist of $0.5\,R_{jt}$ and $0.5\,R_{kt}$. It would follow from (8A.7) that the portfolio return would be given by

$$R_{pt} = 0.5(\alpha_j + \beta_j R_{mt} + e_{jt}) + 0.5(\alpha_k + \beta_k R_{mt} + e_{kt}) \tag{8A.8}$$

Since the αs and βs are constant, we can rewrite this as

$$R_{pt} = 0.5(\alpha_j + \alpha_k) + 0.5(\beta_j + \beta_k)R_{mt} + 0.5(e_{jt} + e_{kt})$$

or letting $\bar{\alpha}$ = the average of α_j and α_k, and $\bar{\beta}$ = the average of β_j and β_k

$$R_{pt} = \bar{\alpha} + \bar{\beta}R_{mt} + 0.5(e_{jt} + e_{kt}) \tag{8A.9}$$

In considering this expression for the portfolio return, the variability or uncertainty depends on the behaviour of $e_{jt} + e_{kt}$. If, for example, the companies j and k are in the same industry, then it is quite possible that in any period, if e_{jt} is positive, e_{kt} will also be positive. On the other hand, if j and k were in different industries, e_{jt} might equally be positive or negative for any observed e_{kt}. In the latter case, the average variation in e_{jt} and e_{kt} would tend to be less than the average variation in e_{jt} alone.

In increasing the size of the portfolio by adding more shares, the total influence of the error terms would become less and less important and the relationship would become more and more like the following:

$$R_{pt} = \bar{\alpha}_p + \bar{\beta}_p R_{mt} \tag{8A.10}$$

An advantage of the market model is its simplicity. In (8A.10), we can see that the portfolio returns depend on only the two constants ($\bar{\alpha}_p$ and $\bar{\beta}_p$) and the return from the market index. Further, the values of the constants can be estimated, using linear regression.

The importance of the relationship is if a portfolio is constructed with many shares (in different industries) with, say, high values of the constant β_j, the portfolio will tend to magnify movements in the market index. Professional investors would call this an aggressive portfolio, and would consider that it represents a high-risk investment strategy. In other words, the value of β_p, being the average of all the individual β_js, will determine the risk of the portfolio.

This has become widely recognised in the security markets. A share j with a high β_j is described as having a high *beta* factor. Portfolios can be evaluated by reference to the beta factor and the values of the beta factor for most shares regularly traded on the Stock Exchange are available from published sources, such as the London Business Risk Management Service. Finally, the analyst evaluating individual shares can concentrate on assessing the α_j value (or *alpha*) for each company. Unlike the beta factor, the alpha is difficult to estimate and will require close study of the characteristics of the individual firm and its management.

Capital asset pricing model

The linear relationship presented in the market model above can be applied to asset pricing. However, this requires three important assumptions:

1. The market for securities operates with no distorting effects, i.e. there are no transactions costs or taxes, investors are rational and there is perfect information.
2. All investors have the same expectations about security returns for a given period, and face the same investment opportunities in the form of a diversified market portfolio, denoted R_m.
3. Unlimited risk-free funds (represented by a Treasury bill) are available for borrowing and lending, denoted R_f.

Then let investors choose a portfolio which is a combination of risk-free assets and risky assets from the market portfolio. The return on this portfolio is the weighted average of the return on these two types of assets.

Let x be the proportion of risky assets, R_m, and $(1-x)$ the proportion of risk-free assets, R_f. The expected return on the portfolio is

$$E(R_p) = R_f(1-x) + xE(R_m)$$

This can be rearranged as follows

$$E(R_p) = R_f + x(E(R_m) - R_f) \tag{8A.11}$$

The risk of this portfolio can be measured by its variance, where the variance of a sum is:

$$\text{Var}(R_p) = \text{Var}(R_f)(1-x)^2 + x^2\,\text{Var}(R_m) + 2(x(1-x)\,\text{Cov}(R_f, R_m))$$

The variance of $R_f = 0$, since by definition, it is a risk-free asset, and so the variance of the returns on the portfolio is

$$\text{Var}(R_p) = x^2\,\text{Var}(R_m)$$

solving for x in terms of standard deviations

$$x = \frac{SD_p}{SD_m} \tag{8A.12}$$

Substituting x into (8A.11) gives

$$E(R_p) = R_f + (E(R_m) - R_f)\left(\frac{SD_p}{SD_m}\right) \tag{8A.13}$$

This is known as the *capital market line*, and states that the expected return of a portfolio, risk-adjusted, is a linear combination of a risk-free asset and the market portfolio.

Finally, consider the expected returns of a single security in terms of its risk, using (8A.13). The market model (8A.7) was derived on the assumption that share prices are *linearly related* to a market index. This relationship is called the *security market line*, and can be stated

$$E(R_j) = R_f + (E(R_m) - R_f)\left(\frac{\text{Cov}_{jm}}{\text{Var}_m}\right) \tag{8A.14}$$

If security j is risk-free, then $E(R_j) = R_f$, since $\text{Cov}_{jm} = 0$. However, if security j is risky, then $E(R_j)$ will be greater than R_f by the amount of some premium determined by $(\text{Cov}_{jm}/\text{Var}_m)$, that is, the covariance of the risky asset with the market portfolio.

But $\text{Cov}_{jm}/\,\text{Var}_m = \beta_j$, and can be substituted into (8A.14)

$$E(R_j) = R_f + (E(R_m) - R_f)\beta_j \tag{8A.15}$$

which is the most common form of the capital asset pricing model.

CHAPTER 9

The bond market

9.1 Introduction

In this chapter we examine fixed income securities. Traditionally, debt has been a low-risk investment compared with equity, but when interest rates are volatile, this is no longer true. We begin by describing the market for bonds and what determines the price of a bond, particularly the effects of interest rate changes. We then consider how bonds are issued and who issues them, before going on to discuss credit assessment, and the standardised techniques which have evolved to perform this task. More detail about the theory of the behaviour of interest rates and details of credit ratings are given in the appendices.

9.2 Characteristics of traded bonds

Debt markets have been established in London for several centuries. The government, in particular, has raised funds by issuing fixed income securities on organised markets since the seventeenth century, mostly to finance numerous wars. Nowadays the government still issues debt to fund national expenditure, but so too do companies undertaking new and ongoing investment programmes as well as foreign governments and various international agencies requiring further funding.

In the UK, the market in government securities was very active until a few years ago. However, as shown in Chapter 4, the Conservative government reduced public sector expenditure during the 1980s and for three years from 1988 to 1990, ran a fiscal surplus, although many foreign governments were in the opposite situation. An example is the US federal deficit which ran on average $150 billion annually, throughout the 1980s. Fortunately for the London market, the removal of exchange controls in 1979 allowed both government and corporate borrowers to issue sterling debt on the London Stock Exchange. Table 9.1 shows the

Table 9.1 The market for sterling bonds, September 1991 (£m)

	Number of securities	Nominal value	Market value
UK Government bonds			
Short-term (0–7 years)	39	53,950.7	55,524.4
Medium-term (7–15 years)	29	38,437.3	40,612.0
Long-term (over 15 years)	13	16,346.5	16,301.9
Undated	9	3,213.4	1,148.3
Index linked	13	12,851.7	16,555.5
Total	103	124,799.6	130,142.1
UK local authorities and public corporations	108	362.9	290.2
Overseas public sector	166	4,242.1	4,074.3
Company securities			
UK	800	13,068.9	13,980.4
Foreign	25	134.7	384.3
Total	825	13,203.6	14,274.7
Sterling eurobonds			
UK	362	34,635.5	33,688.6
Foreign	236	9,679.6	10,046.5
Total	598	44,315.1	43,735.1

Note: Securities listed on the USM and non-sterling denominated bonds omitted.
Source: Stock Exchange Quarterly, July–September 1991.

distribution of sterling debt issuers on the International Stock Exchange in September 1991.

Debt instruments suffer a decline in demand when interest rates are highly volatile, hence bonds are high risk. During the 1970s and early 1980s when interest rates were very high, bond prices were low[1] and therefore not very attractive to investors. However, more recently interest rates have been lower, and this market has recovered such that a growing number of companies are seeking to raise funds through fixed income securities. This increase in corporate issues, and a return to a budget deficit from 1991, has prompted a recovery in the bond market.

The aspect of bonds which differentiates them from other loans is their negotiability. Bonds can be transferred between owners in a secondary market, and in the UK, trading in bonds takes place alongside equities, through the International Stock Exchange. Of the total securities listed, more than 50% are bonds, and another 15% are preference shares.[2] Thus fixed income issues dominate the total securities traded.

The problems of assessing the risk associated with fixed income securities will be discussed in the later sections on valuation and on credit rating. Risk does affect investment decisions in the bond market differently from that of other securities, since there is the possibility of default and formal bankruptcy on behalf of the issuer, either following a failure to meet regular interest payments or to repay the principal at maturity. On the other hand, loan stockholders and ordinary creditors will be repaid after debenture holders but before ordinary shareholders. Furthermore, many companies issue more than one debt security, and if this is the case, the priority of payment between each bond will be made known at the time of issue, and is called the seniority of the debt.

Maturity, tax and coupon

Bonds vary in maturity, some up to thirty years. Most are medium term, in the seven-to-ten-year range. The life of the bond determines the number of years for which the interest is paid, although bonds are rarely held by one investor for the whole period. The longer the maturity the higher the expected return, and also the more volatile the price. The relationship between maturity and the market yield is known as the yield curve. The relationship between the expected return and the term of a bond is known as the term structure of interest rates. We will return to both of these concepts later.

Table 9.2 is an extract of the information on bonds listed in the *Financial Times*. This example shows gilt-edged securities, although details of numerous UK and foreign bonds are published daily. There are five categories: shorts (bonds with less than five years to redemption), mediums (five to fifteen years), longs (over fifteen years), undated and index-linked bonds.

As noted above, securities are classified as short if they are likely to be redeemed within five years. Within this category, there is a range of securities which differ in their maturity and in their coupon, that is the rate of interest paid. In 1994, the terms ranged from a Treasury 9.5% bond redeemable in 1999 and an Exchequer 13.25% bond redeemable in 1996.

The coupon, or interest payment, differs for two reasons. First, the market rates of interest change so that the government may at one time be able to borrow at 8% and another at 12%, and bonds may be redeemed to take advantage of these fluctuations. Secondly, there are tax implications whereby the profit made by buying and selling a bond at a higher price (the capital gain) may be liable for tax at a different rate than the rate charged on income received in the form of interest. In the case of government securities, there is no tax paid on any capital gains made if the stock is held for more than one year, whilst income received by government bond investors by way of interest payments is liable to income tax only for some investors. Charities, for example, may not be liable for tax.

A complicating issue in looking at shorts is that the price quoted in the financial pages of newspapers does not indicate the effective cost of the bond to an investor. Using an example from Table 9.2:

> For an investor buying Exchequer 13.25%, 1996 at £109.56, the price would be increased to include the part of the interest which had built up between the last interest payment and the date on which the stock is paid for. All gilts payments are divided into two and paid every six months, so if we assume interest is paid on 25 August and 25 February, the investor who bought the stock for settlement on 1 November would have to pay £109.56 and a further $68/365^3$ of £13.3 or £112.03 in total.

Correspondingly, when the stock is quoted ex dividend the buyer effectively pays less than the quoted price because the seller has to refund the amount of interest that accrues between purchase and the next payment of interest. For gilts with longer than five years to maturity the price quoted is inclusive of this accrued interest.

The effects of these UK conventions can be seen during the period in which the stocks become quoted ex dividend, from the following hypothetical example:

| | | Date ex | Quoted prices | |
	Interest paid	dividend	14 April	16 April
Short gilt 12%	22 May, 22 Nov.	15 April	100	100
Long gilt 12%	22 May, 22 Nov.	15 April	104.73	98.85

Continuing the example in the case of the short gilt:

> Here the buyer on the 14 April will have to pay an additional £4.73 to the seller, representing accrued interest from the previous interest payment (144 days have elapsed since the previous interest payment on 22 November). In the case of the long gilt the price includes the accrued interest. On 16 April, the buyer of the short gilt is credited with 35/365 of the coupon (payment is made on the day after the transaction and there are 35 days between 16 April and 22 May). Taking these adjustments into account, the prices of the stocks can be seen to coincide as far as the buyer and seller are concerned, even though the quoted prices differ.

Undated stocks are different, but although no date is fixed for their redemption typically the government can redeem them at three months' notice. These issues typically offer low interest payments of between £2.50 and £4.00 per £100 nominal value. Needless to say, these bonds are worth far less than their nominal values, and as interest rates rise and fall over time their prices fluctuate.

It has already been noted that the tax regulations are complex in their effect, and professional tax and investment consultants can substantially improve the

Table 9.2 Government bond prices and yield

Notes	Yield		Price £	+ or −	1994	
	Int	Red			High	Low
'Shorts' (Lives up to five years)						
Treas 9pc 1994‡‡	8.92	5.46	$100\frac{7}{8}$	—	$103\frac{13}{32}$	$100\frac{7}{8}$
12pc 1995	11.69	5.74	$102\frac{5}{8}$	$-\frac{1}{16}$	$107\frac{9}{32}$	$102\frac{5}{8}$
Exch 3pc Gas 90–95	3.05	5.37	$98\frac{5}{16}$	$+\frac{1}{32}$	$98\frac{9}{16}$	$97\frac{3}{4}$
10¼pc 1995	9.92	6.42	$103\frac{3}{8}$	$-\frac{1}{32}$	$107\frac{25}{32}$	$103\frac{3}{8}$
Treas 12¾pc 1995‡‡	11.92	6.81	$106\frac{15}{16}$	$-\frac{1}{16}$	$113\frac{5}{8}$	$106\frac{15}{16}$
14pc 1996	12.80	7.00	$109\frac{3}{8}$	$-\frac{1}{32}$	$117\frac{3}{16}$	$109\frac{3}{8}$
15¼pc 1996‡‡	13.54	7.27	$112\frac{5}{8}$	$-\frac{1}{32}$	$121\frac{15}{16}$	$112\frac{5}{8}$
Exch 13¼pc 1996‡‡	12.09	7.31	$109\frac{9}{16}$	$-\frac{1}{32}$	$117\frac{25}{32}$	$109\frac{9}{16}$
Conversion 10pc 1996	9.55	7.63	$104\frac{11}{16}$	$-\frac{1}{16}$	$112\frac{7}{32}$	$104\frac{21}{32}$
Treas Cnv 7pc 1997‡‡	7.13	7.70	$98\frac{5}{32}$xd	$+\frac{1}{8}$	$100\frac{5}{8}$	$97\frac{13}{16}$
Treas 13¼pc 1997‡‡	11.85	7.79	$111\frac{13}{16}$	—	$121\frac{11}{16}$	$111\frac{23}{32}$
Exch 10½pc 1997	9.93	7.88	$105\frac{25}{32}$xd	—	$114\frac{7}{32}$	$105\frac{23}{32}$
Treas 8¾pc 1997‡‡	8.60	8.07	$101\frac{25}{32}$xd	—	$110\frac{7}{16}$	$101\frac{21}{32}$
Exch 15pc 1997	12.63	8.18	$118\frac{23}{32}$	—	$131\frac{19}{32}$	$118\frac{9}{16}$
9¾pc 1998	9.36	8.30	$104\frac{1}{8}$	$+\frac{1}{16}$	$114\frac{21}{32}$	$104\frac{1}{32}$
Treas 7¼pc 1998‡‡	7.49	8.27	$96\frac{25}{32}$	$+\frac{1}{8}$	$106\frac{7}{32}$	$96\frac{9}{16}$
Treas 6¾pc 1995–98‡‡	7.10	8.28	$95\frac{3}{32}$	$+\frac{3}{32}$	102	$94\frac{27}{32}$
14pc '98–1	11.94	8.51	$117\frac{1}{4}$	$+\frac{1}{8}$	$131\frac{7}{32}$	$116\frac{31}{32}$
Treas 15½pc '98‡‡	12.46	8.37	$124\frac{3}{8}$	$+\frac{7}{32}$	$140\frac{3}{16}$	$124\frac{1}{16}$
Exch 12pc 1998	10.71	8.53	$112\frac{1}{32}$	$+\frac{5}{32}$	$125\frac{31}{32}$	$111\frac{3}{4}$
Treas 9½pc 1999‡‡	9.17	8.48	$103\frac{9}{16}$	$+\frac{3}{16}$	$116\frac{5}{32}$	$103\frac{9}{32}$
Five to fifteen years						
Exch 12¼pc 1999	10.80	8.64	$113\frac{13}{32}$	$+\frac{5}{32}$	$128\frac{7}{32}$	$113\frac{7}{32}$
Treas 10½pc 1999	9.78	8.57	$107\frac{5}{16}$	$+\frac{9}{32}$	$121\frac{5}{16}$	$106\frac{7}{8}$
Treas 6pc 1999‡‡	6.63	8.36	$90\frac{15}{32}$xd	$+\frac{7}{32}$	$101\frac{21}{32}$	$89\frac{25}{32}$
Conversion 10¼pc 1999	9.62	8.65	$106\frac{1}{2}$	$+\frac{1}{4}$	$121\frac{13}{32}$	$105\frac{7}{8}$
Treas Fltg Rate '99	—	—	$99\frac{25}{32}$xd	—	$100\frac{3}{32}$	$99\frac{25}{32}$
9pc 2000‡‡	8.85	8.60	$101\frac{23}{32}$xd	$+\frac{9}{32}$	$116\frac{3}{16}$	$101\frac{1}{8}$
Treas 13pc 2000	10.92	8.78	$119\frac{1}{16}$	$+\frac{9}{32}$	$136\frac{25}{32}$	$118\frac{3}{32}$
10pc 2001	9.45	8.78	$105\frac{27}{32}$xd	$+\frac{9}{32}$	$122\frac{1}{16}$	$104\frac{9}{16}$
7pc '01 ‡‡	7.66	8.59	$91\frac{13}{32}$	$+\frac{5}{16}$	$106\frac{5}{16}$	$90\frac{3}{32}$
7pc '01 A	7.67	8.61	$91\frac{5}{16}$	$+\frac{3}{8}$	$101\frac{7}{32}$	$89\frac{29}{32}$
9¾pc 2002	9.26	8.79	$105\frac{5}{16}$xd	$+\frac{7}{16}$	$123\frac{9}{32}$	$103\frac{5}{8}$
8pc 2003‡‡	8.37	8.68	$95\frac{5}{8}$	$+\frac{11}{32}$	$113\frac{15}{32}$	$94\frac{1}{32}$
10pc 2003	9.31	8.79	$107\frac{3}{8}$xd	$+\frac{15}{32}$	$127\frac{1}{16}$	$105\frac{15}{32}$
Treas 11½pc 2001–4	10.24	9.06	$112\frac{1}{4}$xd	$+\frac{13}{32}$	$129\frac{17}{32}$	$110\frac{7}{8}$
Funding 3½pc '99–4	4.83	7.44	$72\frac{1}{2}$	$+\frac{1}{16}$	$86\frac{5}{32}$	$71\frac{1}{16}$
Conversion 9½pc 2004	9.06	8.74	$104\frac{7}{8}$	$+\frac{15}{32}$	$125\frac{3}{16}$	103
Treas 6¾pc 2004‡‡	7.70	8.57	$87\frac{5}{8}$	$+\frac{3}{8}$	$105\frac{1}{8}$	$85\frac{25}{32}$

Table 9.2—*contd.*

Notes	Yield Int	Yield Red	Price £	+ or −	1994 High	1994 Low
Conv 9½pc 2005	9.02	8.69	105⅜	+½	125½	103⅜
Treas 12½pc 2003–5	10.32	9.06	121³/₃₂	+⁷/₁₆	143⁷/₁₆	119¹/₃₂
7¾pc 2006‡‡	8.31	8.64	93⁵/₁₆xd	+½	112¹⁷/₃₂	91½
8pc 2002–6‡‡	8.45	8.71	94⅝	+⁹/₁₆	111⅝	93¹/₁₆
Treas 11¾pc 2003–7	10.18	9.06	115¹⁵/₃₂	+½	136¹/₃₂	113⅝
Treas 8½pc 2007‡‡	8.60	8.63	98²⁷/₃₂	+¹⁹/₃₂	119⁹/₃₂	96¹⁵/₁₆
13½pc '04–8	10.55	9.06	128	+⁷/₁₆	151⁹/₁₆	125¾
Treas 9pc 2008‡‡	8.73	8.60	103⅛	+²¹/₃₂	124¹¹/₁₆	101

Over fifteen years

Notes	Yield Int	Yield Red	Price £	+ or −	1994 High	1994 Low
Treas 8pc 2009	8.43	8.60	94⅞	+⁹/₁₆	115⁹/₁₆	93
Treas 6¼pc 2010	7.75	8.45	80⅝	+¹⁷/₃₂	98³/₃₂	78⁹/₁₆
Conv 9pc Ln 2011‡‡	8.68	8.57	103²³/₃₂	+²³/₃₂	126¹¹/₁₆	101¹/₃₂
Treas 9pc 2012‡‡	8.66	8.55	103¹⁵/₁₆	+²¹/₃₂	127⅝	101³/₁₆
Treas 5½pc 2008–12‡‡	7.45	8.32	73¹³/₁₆xd	+¹³/₁₆	93⅞	72¹/₁₆
Treas 8pc 2013‡‡	8.41	8.51	95⅛	+²¹/₃₂	117²³/₃₂	92⁵/₁₆
7¾pc 2012–15‡‡	8.37	8.48	92⁹/₁₆	+⅜	114¾	91¹/₁₆
Treas 8¾pc 2017‡‡	8.52	8.48	102²¹/₃₂xd	+²³/₃₂	128¾	99²³/₃₂
Exch 12pc '13–'17	9.20	8.71	130¹³/₃₂	+²⁷/₃₂	159½	127⅛

Undated

Notes	Yield Int	Yield Red	Price £	+ or −	1994 High	1994 Low
Consols 4pc	8.77	—	45⅝	+⅝	59¾	44¹⁵/₃₂
War Loan 3½pc‡‡	8.54	—	41	+⁷/₃₂	54¹³/₃₂	39¹³/₁₆
Conv 3½pc '61 Aft.	6.16	—	56¹³/₁₆	−¼	71	55¾
Treas 3pc '66 Aft.	8.89	—	33¾	−2³/₁₆	44⅝	33⅝
Consols 2½pc	8.70	—	28¾	−¹/₁₆	38½	28⁵/₁₆
Treas 2½pc	8.73	—	28⅝	+³/₁₆	37⅝	27¹³/₃₂

Notes	Yield (1)	Yield (2)	Price £	+ or −	1994 High	1994 Low
Index-linked (b)						
2pc '96 (67.9)	2.89	4.04	199½xd	+¹/₁₆	203⅝	197²⁷/₃₂
4⅝pc '98‡‡ (135.6)	2.92	3.65	107⁷/₁₆	+¹/₁₆	113⁹/₃₂	106³/₁₆
2½pc '01 (78.3)	3.44	3.83	165⅜	+¹/₁₆	176⅞	163½
2½pc '03 (78.8)	3.54	3.85	161⁵/₁₆	+¹/₁₆	173⅝	159⁵/₁₆
4⅜pc '04‡‡ (135.6)	3.54	3.83	108¾	+¹/₁₆	118⅜	107⅛
2pc '06 (69.5)	3.58	3.81	168	+⅛	184¹⁷/₃₂	165⁹/₁₆
2½pc '09 (78.8)	3.64	3.84	152⁵/₁₆	+⅛	168⁷/₁₆	149⅛
2½pc '11 (74.6)	3.67	3.85	157⁷/₁₆xd	+³/₁₆	175⅝	154⅛
2½pc '13 (89.2)	3.68	3.85	129²¹/₃₂xd	+⁷/₃₂	146⅛	126⅜

Table 9.2—*contd.*

Notes		Yield				1994	
		Int	Red	Price £	+ or −	High	Low
2½pc '16	(81.6)	3.71	3.86	138$\frac{1}{16}$	+$\frac{3}{16}$	157$\frac{5}{32}$	134$\frac{3}{8}$
2½pc '20	(83.0)	3.74	3.87	132$\frac{5}{16}$	+$\frac{3}{16}$	152$\frac{21}{32}$	128½
2½pc '24‡‡	(97.7)	3.72	3.84	110$\frac{3}{16}$	+$\frac{3}{16}$	129$\frac{1}{16}$	106$\frac{3}{8}$
4⅛pc '30‡‡	(135.1)	3.75	3.88	109$\frac{5}{16}$	+$\frac{3}{16}$	128$\frac{11}{16}$	105$\frac{7}{8}$

Notes: Prospective real redemption rate on projected inflation of (1) 10% and (2) 5%. (b) Figures in parentheses show RPI base for indexing (i.e. 8 months prior to issue) and have been adjusted to reflect rebasing of RPI to 100 in January 1987. Conversion factor 3.945. RPI for November 1993: 141.6 and for June 1994: 144.7.

‡‡ Tax-free to non-residents on application.
xd Ex dividend.
Closing mid-prices are shown in pounds.

Source: Financial Times, 17 August 1994.

performance of a gilt portfolio by careful investment transactions. Furthermore, for gilts, commission charged by stockbrokers is considerably lower than for other securities. In the circumstances, it is not surprising that the volume of trading in government stocks is very large.

Over the last few years, for example, the value of transactions in government bonds has been about five times larger than the value of ordinary shares traded, even though the number of transactions in gilts has been less than a quarter of the number of transactions in equities. This difference clearly reflects the tendency of investors to trade large blocks of government bonds in order to make small per unit gains from relative changes in prices and tax liability.

The interest paid on government bonds has historically been fixed in money terms, although some types of bonds described in the next section, in particular indexed bonds, are variable. In the case of fixed interest bonds, the interest payment is expressed as a percentage of the nominal price of the stock, which in the UK is £100. Therefore a 12% bond will pay £6 semi-annually. This payment is the coupon. In fact, with the exception of those who purchase bonds through the National Savings Register, investors receive a direct payment of less than this as interest is paid after tax, assuming the standard rate of tax, and adjustments are made by the holder. As can be seen in Table 9.2, some are denoted as tax exemptions to non-UK residents, which makes these bonds attractive to overseas investors.

Types of bonds

The important characteristics of a bond are the issuer, the maturity and the coupon. However, within these parameters, a variety of bonds exist, including the following:

Straight bond. This is the simplest type. It has a fixed coupon ensuring annual interest income, and a fixed maturity date at which the whole amount of the issue is payable. These are sometimes called vanilla, or bullet loans, as they are uncomplicated and progress straight from issue to maturity without deviation.

Convertible bonds. These are fixed income securities, issued at a lower interest rate than non-convertible bonds, which can be converted into equity, either of the issuing company or of some other. The conversion price is known at issue, but since the market price of the equity changes, the holder may or may not wish to convert at any point during the life of the bond. For the issuer, this represents deferred equity, and ranks above equity but is subordinate to other debt in terms of seniority.

Zero coupon bond. As the name implies, this is issued without a coupon. Thus they pay no interest but are sold at a deep discount to their face value and with the expectation of a capital gain when the bond matures. For the issuer who wishes to fund an investment which will not make a positive return for some time, this is attractive, while to the investor, there may be a tax advantage.

Perpetual or irredeemable bonds. Also as the name implies, these bonds have no maturity. Some old government stock was issued in this way. Only if interest rates were to fall below the value of the coupon will the issue be redeemed.

Warrants. Warrants were discussed with respect to equity in Chapter 8. They are options which can be sold along with a bond, as they can with equity. They are detachable from the bond and are tradable separately. It gives the holder the right to purchase a further bond at a predetermined price.

Index-linked bonds. These are structured so that their value at maturity tracks a specified index, such as a corporate issue linked to the FT-SE 100, or a government bond linked to the retail price index.

Strips. The range of available bonds is increased further still by stripping off some features and selling these separately, or by denoting the interest payment and the principal in different currencies. These are called strips and dual currency bonds, respectively.

Call provisions. Finally, call provisions are an important characteristic of some bonds. This means that the debt can be called in, or bought back, by the issuer, prior to maturity. From the issuer's point of view, it may be important to call the bond and reissue at a lower coupon if market changes are sufficiently great to make this a viable course of action, bearing in mind the cost of such financial restructuring. The initial period of such a bond's maturity is protected, generally up to several years. This is a valuable option for both issuer and holder, and a call feature will give a callable bond a higher coupon than a non-callable one.

9.3 Bond issues

For many years, sterling bonds have been issued by the UK government, British companies and local authorities, although this last group have dwindled almost to nothing in the wake of the Conservative government's policy of centralised public sector borrowing and the privatisation of the utility companies. Foreign issuers include companies, public authorities and various overseas institutions such as the European Investment Bank, the African Development Bank or the Province of Nova Scotia, all of whom for one reason or another have decided to issue bonds in London.

The issuing procedure for government debt is quite different from that for private corporate and foreign debt. Gilt-edged securities are bonds issued by the British government, and unlike other debt instruments, they are not secured against assets. All issues, and redemptions, are carried out by the Bank of England on behalf of the government, with new issues made in the following three ways:

By tender. An offer of sale of newly created stock by tender is used for large amounts, generally not less than £1 billion. Bids are submitted, and taken up by all those at or above the specific minimum price. All bids are accepted at a common price. An example of a Bank of England tender is shown in Table 9.3.

By auction. This method is relatively new in the UK, with the first in May 1987, although it has been used for US government securities for some time.

Table 9.3 Example of Bank of England tender

UK Government 5.25% ECU Treasury Bill
Result of tender 19 July 1994

The tender is oversubscribed.
ECU 500m of notes on offer allocated in full.
Details are as follows.
3-year notes allocated 21 Jan 1994 for delivery 21 Jan 1997:

Amount of notes on offer	ECU	500m
Amount applied for		2,102
Amount allocated		500
Lowest yield accepted		6.94
Highest yield accepted		6.97
Average yield on notes allocated		6.9576
Pro rata % of highest yield accepted		10.47

Coupon set at 5.25% on the basis of the result of the last auction of notes of this maturity on 18 Jan 1994.

Tenders that were accepted when made at yield below the highest accepted yield have been allocated in full at yield bid.

Again used for newly created stock issues of greater than £1 billion, bids are requested, but the minimum price is not specified, and the stock is sold to the highest bidder. Following the auction, the Bank publishes details of the average, the highest and the lowest yield on accepted bids.

Direct sale. The last method involves the Bank taking stock on in its own right, and then selling this over a period of time in daily dealing with GEMMs. This is very flexible and can be used for large and small amounts. Table 9.4 shows details of some government issues, and the methods used.

Settlement of trades in gilt-edged securities takes place using a computerised system developed in the 1980s, jointly by the Bank of England and the London Stock Exchange. The system provides a same-day transfer between member firms and investors through accounts held at the Central Gilts Office (CGO), with payment guaranteed by a number of settlement banks. The use of the CGO has decreased settlement costs for members, lowered the number of paper-based transfers and eliminated the credit risk involved in delivering stock against a promise of payment. By the end of 1991, 70% of outstanding gilt-edged securities was managed in this way.

Companies may issue bonds either in the form of loan stock or debentures. Both types of bond involve the appointment of a trustee who checks that the borrowing company is carrying out the terms of the contract. In the case of debentures, the loan is secured by specific assets such as land or buildings which can be confiscated by the receiver and sold to the debt holder in the event of bankruptcy.

New issues by UK or foreign borrowers are made in very similar ways to equity. In many cases, a placing is preferred as it is the least expensive method. As with new equity issues, pricing is not especially simple. If the price is too high, the bonds will not sell, if too low, the company has less funds than they could have.

The most important indication of the expected return is the gross redemption yield and this can be used to compare alternative investment on an equivalent basis. It follows from this that the issue should be designed to give the highest gross redemption yield possible. Yields are compared at the margin in basis points, that is in one hundredth of a per cent, and will have to take account of the risk of the specific issue.

9.4 Bond valuation

The nominal, or face, value of a bond in the UK is £100, and $1,000 in the US, but in neither case is this the market value. Coupon rates are of considerable importance in valuation, but again are not the only factor. Equality of coupon does not mean that the bonds will have the same prices, although they do have an important effect. For example, if one bond pays £6 each half-year and another of the same maturity pays only £2, other things being equal, they are unlikely to

Table 9.4 Examples of government debt issues, 1991

Stock	Amount (£m)	Date issued	Method of issue	Price at issue	Details of payment	Yield at issue[1]	Yield when fully sold[2]	Date when fully sold
9% Conversion 2011 'B'	1,500	28 Nov	Auction	93.5	Part paid[3]	9.75	9.75	28 Nov '91
10% Conversion 1996	200	29 Nov	To Bank	100.2813	In full	9.92	9.86	5 Dec '91
10% Treasury 2001	200	29 Nov	To Bank	100.5625	In full	9.89	9.86	4 Dec '91
9½ Conversion 2005	100	29 Nov	To Bank	97.6875	In full	9.81	9.81	2 Dec '91
8½ Treasury 2007 'A'	1,000	13 Dec	To Bank	93.25	Part paid[4]	9.33	9.28	9 Jan '92

Notes:

1. Gross redemption yield per cent.
2. With 33.5 payable at issue and the remainder on 18 December 1991.
3. With 33.5 payable at issue and the remainder on 18 December 1991.
4. With 20 payable at issue, 40 on 13 January 1992 and the remainder on 14 February 1992.

Source: Bank of England Quarterly Bulletin, 1992.

trade at the same price. Furthermore, tax implications can influence the market valuation of a bond.

These complications apart, there are two statistics which are calculated for all bonds, the running, or interest, yield and the redemption yield, both of which are published in the financial press. The interest yield is calculated by dividing the coupon amount by the bond price, net of accrued interest. The interest yield indicates, rather imprecisely, the relative importance of the coupon payments in the return but no account is taken of the delay before the interest payments are received. From an investor's point of view, receiving the payments in two or more instalments will increase the value of the bond because the cash receipts are accelerated compared with annual payments. The calculation of the interest yield will depend on whether or not the bond is issued as a short-term debt. If it is a short bond, the interest yield is given simply by dividing the annual coupon by the quoted, or clean, price of the bond.

For longer term bonds, the price must first be adjusted to remove the effect of the accrued interest. Thus if interest on a 12% ten-year bond is paid on 10 May and 10 November, the adjustment for 15 July will be 66/365 of the annual interest payment. The interest yield (y) will then be given by

$$y = \frac{12}{P - (66/365)12}$$

where P is the quoted price of the bond.

The redemption yield indicates the return earned from the investment if the bond is held until redemption. It includes both the return from receiving interest and the capital gain or loss on redemption. Although redemption yields are normally calculated by ignoring the effect of taxation, analysts often estimate the net of tax redemption yield from the point of view of a particular investor. As can be seen from Table 9.2, there have been considerable differences between the interest and redemption yields. For example, in the case of the short-term Exchequer 15%, 1997, the gross (i.e. pre-tax) interest yield is 12.63%, whilst the gross redemption yield is 8.18%. The interest yield shows the importance of the high coupon compared with current rates of interest (at time of writing about 5%), while the redemption yield indicates the capital loss if held to maturity, that is, the difference between the current price (£118.72) and the maturity value (£100) in the course of the bond's remaining life.

The calculation of these yields can best be explained from an investor's viewpoint. We will start by considering a very simple example of a bond, on which interest is paid every six months and on which the interest has been paid the day before the investor pays for the bond. In this way we will defer some of the complications such as accrued interest. Let us assume the investor is considering a bond which pays £6.00 per half year and will be redeemed in two years' time. The value of this bond will be given by

$$P_t = 6a_{\overline{4}|}i + 100(1 + i)^{-4}$$

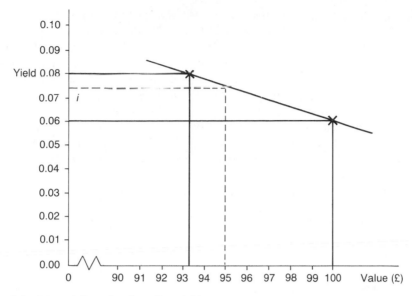

Figure 9.1 Interpolation of redemption yield.

where i is the investor's opportunity cost of capital per half-year. If i is given, there is no difficulty in estimating P_t. But supposing the bond is quoted on the International Stock Exchange at £95. What is the interest rate that will be earned if the bond is held until it is redeemed? This has the same difficulties in calculation as the internal rate of return. Trial and errors, interpolation and more conveniently, technology is the solution.

To illustrate by an example

Rate	Value
0.06	100.00
i?	95.00 (the quoted price)
0.08	93.37

From these calculations we can estimate i by the following expression

$$(i - 0.06)(0.08 - 0.06)^{-1} = (95 - 100)(93.37 - 100)^{-1}$$

Therefore $i = 0.07508$, or approximately 7.5%. We can represent this calculation in the form of a diagram, see Figure 9.1.

To check the approximation, the estimated yield should be substituted in the valuation formula,

$$P_t = 6a_{\overline{4}|}\ 0.075 + 100(1 + 1.075)^{-4} = 94.976\%$$

which approximates very closely to the market price of £95. In this example, the interest yield would be taken as 12/95 or 12.63% and the redemption yield would be 7.5% per half-year or an effective annual rate $(1.075)^2 - 1 = 15.56\%$ or 15% nominal. In practice, the redemption yields are usually quoted in nominal terms.

In general, the redemption yield will be calculated on dates which do not coincide with interest payments, and the calculation has to be adjusted to reflect the accrued interest and the delay in the time before the next interest payment is due. This is shown in more detail in the appendix to this chapter.

To calculate the redemption yield for an investor paying tax at 25% on interest income, the conventional method is to deduct from the interest received the rate of tax and to treat the tax as being payable at the same time as the interest is due. In this example, this would reduce the £6 to £4.5 and the redemption yield would then be calculated using the method shown.

Although the redemption yield is widely quoted, it is not an altogether satisfactory indicator. It shows the highest rate of interest that could be paid by the investor on a loan to finance the investment without making a loss. It can be also thought of as the average return on the investment if all intermediate cash flows are reinvested at the same rate throughout the life of the investment. It is in this latter aspect that the weakness of the redemption yield can be seen because, as Table 9.2 shows, the redemption yield of bonds that differ only in maturity can be markedly different.

For example, the Treasury 12%, 1995 stock has a redemption yield of 5.74% whilst the Exchequer 12%, 1998 stock has a redemption yield of 8.53%. The redemption yield can be thought of as a kind of average of the rates of interest over the remaining life of the bond. Thus the differences might at first suggest that the bond with the highest redemption yield would be the most profitable investment. However, as we shall show later, this interpretation is too simple.

As the preceding discussion may have suggested, some differences in redemption yields arise from the effect of tax, but some residual part stems from the inherent weakness of the redemption yield as an indicator of the investment return. The distortionary effects of tax can be clearly seen in Table 9.2 by comparing the redemption yields on Treasury 13%, 2000 and Funding 3.5%, 1999–2004. The redemption yield on the first is 8.78% compared with 7.44% on the second. The 3.5% stock was attractive to investors paying tax at high marginal rates, and their attention caused the price to rise with a consequent fall in the redemption yield, because they could realise their income in capital gains subject to lower tax rates.

Despite these shortcomings, redemption yields remain popular, if not very subtle indicators, which are widely referred to in commentaries on the behaviour of bond prices over time. They are also used to indicate market sentiment regarding bonds of different maturities, an issue we will examine now.

9.5 Term structure of interest rates

In the previous section we showed that different tax rates on capital gains and interest income distorted the prices of bonds. One way to analyse the effect of maturity on the redemption yield, while minimising this distortion, would be to limit the analysis to bonds on which returns would be earned only from a change in the price, that is, bonds for which the coupon is zero. In addition, we will assume in this section that all returns are based on annual compounding.

Assume an investor examined a series of bonds and found that one bond was redeemable in one year's time with a redemption yield of 10%, and another was to be redeemed in two years' time with a redemption yield of 12%. Under what circumstances would the two-year bond be a better investment?

For this, we need additional information, in particular, the investor's time-preference and attitude to risk. Let us assume the answers to these question are that the period of the investment is two years, and the objective is to maximise returns over the period. But this is still insufficient to make the decision. The investor still has to decide whether to buy two one-year bonds or one two-year bond. If the first is chosen, the investor buys a one-year bond, then in one year's time the bond will be redeemed and cash will be available for investment in another bond that will mature at the end of the second year. If the second, only one investment is required.

As an example, using the hypothetical rates above:

> If the investment is £1,000 and the return is 10%, £1,100 will be available for reinvestment in the second year. If the return in one year's time is 15%, the second investment will be worth £1,265 (£1,100 × 1.15). Alternatively, the investment could be for two years, and the return would be £1,254 (£1,000 × 1.12²).

Some rates will make the first option more profitable and others the second. One rate of return will leave the investor indifferent between the two. When this occurs, the term structure is unbiased, a situation known as the unbiased expectations hypothesis. Clearly, knowledge of the future interest rate is crucial to making this decision.

This example can be extended to include a large number of investors all considering the same problem. If we observe market prices when all investors have made their decisions, we may assume that the effect of their actions reflects the view of the market. Therefore, if we observe two-year bonds trading to give a redemption yield of 12% and one-year bonds at 10%, then on average investors expect that rates of interest in the second year will be 14%. Crude empiricism would imply that a redemption yield of 10% on a one-year bond and 12% on a two-year bond indicates an expected one-year rate of about 14% in one year's time.

This can now be generalised. From a series of redemption yields, one can derive a series of short-term expected or implied interest rates linking bonds of different maturities. These are the forward rates discussed in Chapter 4.

The implied single period forward rate for year n is given by

$$F_n = (1 + i_n)^n \{(1 + i_{n-1})^{n-1}\}^{-1} - 1$$

where i_n = the redemption yield on an n-year bond.

In the example above, $n = 2$, $i_2 = 0.12$ and $i_1 = 0.10$, so

$$F_2 = (1 + 0.12)^2 (1 + 0.10)^{-1} - 1 = 0.1404 = 14\%$$

In other words, the investor buying one-year bonds would expect to receive an average of 12% annually, 10% per cent in the first year and an implied rate of 14% in the second. This illustrates the comment made earlier in the chapter that a redemption yield represented a type of average return over the life of the bond.

It would be possible to derive a series of implied forward rates if we had redemption yields for a number of bonds that differed only in maturity. Suppose, for example, that we observed redemption yields as follows:

Maturity	1 yr	2 yr	3 yr	4 yr	5 yr	6 yr	7 yr	8 yr
Redemption	10	12	13	13.73	13.78	13.48	13	12.6

The implied forward rate for the second year has already been shown to be 14%. Likewise, the forward rate of the third year can be calculated by

$$F_3 = (1 + 0.13)^3 \{(1 + 0.12)^2\}^{-1} - 1 = 0.15 = 15\%$$

Clearly, the expected returns will be the same regardless of the specific bonds in which funds are invested. This calculation can be confirmed by estimating the position if we invest in three one-year bonds. Final wealth would be

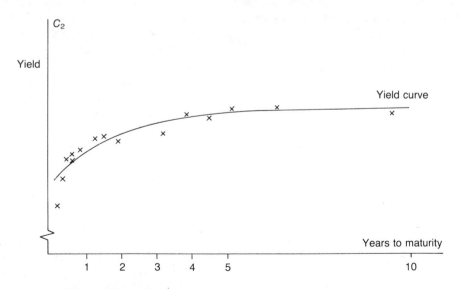

Figure 9.2 The yield curve and term structure of interest rates.

(1.10)(1.14)(1.15) = 1.44, whereas the final wealth from the three-year bond would be $(1.13)^3 = 1.44$. Final wealth is constant regardless of the maturity of the bonds, and therefore the returns are the same.

By similar calculations, the complete set of one-year forward rates is found to be 10%, 14%, 15%, 16%, 14%, 12%, 10% and 10% respectively.

Notice the relationship between the forward rates and the redemption yields. If the forward rate is above the redemption yield, the redemption yield will be rising, and if the forward rate is below the redemption yield, the redemption yield will be falling as maturity increases. Equally, if the redemption yields rise with increasing maturity, the short-term forward rates are above today's short-term rate.

Observers of the bond market might infer that the market expectation is that short-term rates will rise in the future. This interpretation was made on the basis of some restrictive assumptions about the behaviour of investors. Nevertheless, it helps us to understand why, for example, redemption yields of long maturities do not fluctuate as much as shorter term yields. Referring to the series of forward rates above, suppose investors revised their beliefs about the one-year forward rate in the eighth year to 20% from 10%. Because the redemption yield for an eight-year bond is the same as the yield on a seven-year bond, followed by the implied one-year forward rate, it follows that

$$(1 + i_8)^8 = (1 + 0.13)^7 (1 + 0.20)$$

$$\text{or } i_8 = 0.1385$$

The redemption yield on the eight-year bond would therefore be 13.85% rather than the 12.6% shown above. The redemption yield has changed by less than 2%, compared with the difference of 10% in the forward rates. For longer terms, the redemption yields will change even less significantly, and so it is common to find that if the series of redemption yields are graphed against the maturity, the resulting curve becomes flat as the maturity increases over about ten or fifteen years. This curve is known as the yield curve, and is illustrated in Figure 9.2.

In the shorter term, the shape of the yield curve can change sharply. During the last fifty years or so, the 'normal' shape of the yield curve has been upward sloping over the one-to-ten-year maturity range and almost flat thereafter for some periods. But many other shapes have been observed. For a short while, the curve was upward sloping for maturity under four years and almost flat thereafter, while at other times it sloped upwards for maturities less than six years, and downwards for greater maturities. Whatever the shape, the redemption yield curve will be determined by present and expected future interest rates.

Figure 9.3 illustrates some common shapes to the yield curve. From the figure, the inverted curve, (A), is where yields on long bonds are below those on short bonds. Curve (B) shows the curve initially to rise between short- and medium-term bonds but then to fall over long-term issues. And finally, curve (C) is almost flat, where there is little difference between long and short maturities.

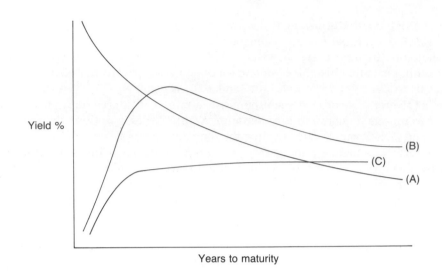

Figure 9.3 Alternative yield curves.

9.6 Hypotheses on the behaviour of interest rates

We referred above to the behaviour of the yield curve as the expectations hypothesis of the term structure of interest rates. The principal shortcoming of the expectations hypothesis is that the forward rates derived from the redemption yields often do not bear a close relationship to the short-term rates subsequently observed in the market. In the example, this is equivalent to finding that the short-term rates for the second, third and fourth years turn out to be, say, 10%, 9% and 8% instead of the implied forward rates of 14%, 15% and 16% respectively. But this finding is, by itself, insufficient evidence that the expectations hypothesis is invalid. There are several reasons, including the tax bias arising from the coupon effect, that preclude easy answers. Also, major changes in global economic conditions can occur which may not have been foreseen. Nevertheless, the evidence is sufficiently ambiguous to encourage the discussion of other possible interpretations of the yield curve. In particular, researchers have remarked upon and tried to explain the common upward-sloping pattern of the yield curve.

These other explanations usually involve an assumption that the market is segmented in some way. One way this could arise is if some institutions decided, as a matter of policy, that they would invest only in short-term bonds. This kind of restraint seems to operate to some degree in practice. When the Bank of England publishes a graph of its version of the yield curve, it explicitly divides the curve into two parts.

Just as there may be investors who are restricted to the short term, so there are other investors who may concentrate on long-term bonds. The effect of the segmentation is that the assumptions and expectations of one set of investors may be inconsistent with the other. Put simply, the long-term investors may be expecting the short-term rate to rise while the short-term investors may expect it to fall.

If there are restrictions on the dealing between different segments of the market, there is no particular reason why the assumptions should ever be consistent between long-term investors and short-term ones. Thus the persistent upward slope of the yield curve may simply represent the competition among buyers of bonds to hold short-term instruments. This competitive pressure, unless satisfied by borrowers, would make itself evident through a consequent rise in the price of short bonds and the associated fall in yield. Since borrowers may be reluctant to substitute short- for long-term instruments, the pattern of the yield curve could be derived from the segmentation hypothesis.

Another possible reason for the upward-sloping yield curve is risk aversion on the part of the investors. In these circumstances, investors will want additional reward for investing in long-term securities and will therefore demand a greater yield. Their preference for liquidity dictates that if this is forgone, they will demand a higher yield on long-term securities than on short. This explanation for short-term bonds having a lower redemption yield to long-term bonds is known as the liquidity preference hypothesis.

9.7 Bond clientele

In the same way as groups of investors chose a particular investment strategy in equity holdings, a clientele effect can be identified in the markets for fixed income securities. It has already been suggested that some investors may limit their bond purchases to specific maturity ranges. In this section we consider the effect of maturity and tax liability on bond investment.

We have seen that the effect of tax alone can make the analysis of bond investment a complicated and technical problem. But the principle is simple enough. Many investors pay different rates of tax on their income and capital gains and the actual rates vary between different groups of investors. The effect is to encourage investors to look for particular combinations of income that will maximise their return net of tax.

Since pension funds and charities do not pay tax on their investment income, we would expect their investment policy to take this tax advantage into account. However, there are other factors that also influence investment policy. For example, pension funds and life assurance companies both have very long-term liabilities and, in order to reduce their risks, will try to match their long-term liabilities with long-term assets. These could be long-term fixed interest stock, and especially gilts.

Table 9.5 shows how the market is dominated by the investing institutions, with pension funds and insurance companies holding over 50% of government

The bond market

Table 9.5 Market share in gilts (% of market value), 1991

Banking sector	2.9
Building societies	2.5
Insurance companies and pension funds	52.7
Investment and unit trusts	0.7
Private individuals	9.2
Foreign central banks	5.6
Other foreign holders	6.4
Bank of England	12.9
Miscellaneous	7.1
Total	100

Source: Bank of England Quarterly Bulletin, November 1991.

stock. Other investors in gilt-edged securities are private individuals, some foreign central banks and about 13% is included in portfolios held by the government and the Bank of England.

Individual investors have alternative investment opportunities using non-marketable securities such as National Savings certificates and premium bonds, so their involvement in the marketable securities markets is less than one might expect from a consideration of the tax and term implications of marketable debt.

Clearly, some idea of the clientele effect can be gained from a consideration of the relative weights that various types of investors hold in the different maturities of government securities shown in Table 9.5. However, this is still a rather general picture. For example, the insurance activities divide into short- and long-term business, and we have aggregated the gilt holders together, and not differentiated by maturity. For general insurance companies carrying out business such as household and motor insurance, funds may be available for investment for up to three or four years, and therefore the insurance companies tend to invest these funds more heavily in short-term government securities. Banks are clearly biased towards the short-term market whilst the investment and unit trusts, who are investing on behalf of their individual share or unit holders, are apparently reproducing the type of investment that individual investors are making on their own account.

9.8 Credit rating

Assessing the risks of corporate bonds is a complicated process, and it is not surprising that professional investors and investment advisers have tried to find ways of simplifying the problem. In the United States, where bonds are a more important source of corporate finance than in Britain there are a number of specialist firms which produce *ratings* of bond issues, and details of these are in the appendix to this chapter. By far the most popular of these rating services are Moody's, Standard & Poor's and Fitch & Co, although in London, Dun and Bradstreet have now entered the market.

There are two features which determine the rating of the company and the issue. The company is rated according to its size, the relative amount of debt it uses for financing its operations and the proportion of its profits required to pay interest. Other, more qualitative measures are also taken into account, although companies vary as to the weight put on different factors. For example, Moody's places emphasis on the issuer's total debt burden and the cash flow position, while Standard & Poor's take the issuer's economic environment into account. This can result in two different ratings.

The issue is rated according to the security, its seniority in the event of default, and the borrowing limits which are fixed for other issues which might subsequently be made. An important aspect of bond rating is that it relates to individual issues and not the company issuing the debt, and therefore a company may have several bond issues outstanding with different ratings attached to them. This allows a company to raise funds for a higher risk project while also renewing their usual debt levels when these issues reach maturity. Furthermore, a correct interpretation of the rating is crucial. Credit ratings do not reflect the market price, expected return or the quality of the investment, nor the personal risk preferences of the investor. It is simply an assessment of the default risk on a specific issue.

There is as yet no universally recognised rating service and there are difficulties in estimating the risks of international bonds, a factor we shall return to in Chapter 12. The US agencies have begun to turn their attention to non-US bond markets, and both Moody's and Standard & Poor's rank some bonds by the type of issuer, which in the case of official bond issues includes an assessment of the political stability of the government.

The costs of acquiring a rating from one of the recognised agencies are substantial, but it is becoming increasingly important as many of the institutional investors seek to include high-grade securities in their portfolios. In particular, the large US funds are restricted from trading in securities which have not been rated, and this is proving a powerful incentive for issuers wishing to attract the large investors.

9.9 Summary

A number of fixed income instruments are offered on the London securities markets, for a range of maturities and at different coupon rates. The market is dominated by gilt-edged securities, although a number of foreign issuers also offer debt to investors. Valuation is determined by expectations about interest rate movements, and a number of hypotheses attempt to explain these. The creditworthiness of fixed income securities is important, and assessment is increasingly formalised, particularly in the global bond markets.

Notes

1. We shall explain the inverse relationship between bond prices and interest rates in the next section.
2. Preference shares are equity which behaves like debt. We will return to these below.
3. There are sixty-eight days between 25 August and 1 November.

Further reading

Goff, T. G. (1980), *Theory and Practice of Investment*, 3rd edn, Heinemann. Chapters 3, 9 and 10 provide some institutional-based discussion of the tax effects of bond investment. The book is aimed at bankers taking the investment paper in the Institute of Bankers examination and tends to be light on arithmetical calculations.

Rutterford, J. (1993), *Introduction to Stock Exchange Investments*, 2nd edn, Macmillan. This provides a clear introduction to bond calculations with a UK emphasis. The book contains a very useful explanation of the indexed gilts and their valuations.

Scott-Quinn, B. (1990), '*Investment banking: Theory and practice*', Euromoney Books.

The Bank of England Quarterly Bulletin also contains illustrations of the yield curve for government stocks in its Financial Review. The method of fitting the yield curve was first described in the December 1972 and September 1973 issues but has since been modified several times.

Questions

9.1 It is sometimes suggested that the term structure of interest rates is directly related to the state of the economy. In recessions, for example, the yield curve may be steeply sloping if the recession is expected to be temporary. What shape would you associate with:
   (a) economic recovery
   (b) the peak of an economic boom?

9.2 What difference might you expect if an accurate and widely accepted bond rating service were to be established in the international bond markets? Consider, in particular, the effects on:
   (a) the rates of interest payable
   (b) the behaviour of bond prices.

9.3 Explain the relative bond holdings shown in Table 9.5. In what other ways do *individuals* borrow or lend money at fixed rates of interest? Do you think the personal sector tends in aggregate to lend/borrow for short/long periods of time?

9.4 Compare the benefits and risks of investing in:
   (a) short-term
   (b) long-term
   (c) indexed gilt-edged securities.

Problems

9.5 An investor is considering (on 1 November 1994) applying for a ten-year government bond for which £20 is paid immediately, a further £40 on 1 January 1995, and a balance of £36 on 1 March 1995. What price will the bond have to trade for on 2 March 1995 if the investor is to earn a return of 12% on this investment?

9.6 The following are redemption yields for bonds maturing in 1, 2, 3, 4 and 5 years respectively: 8%, 8.5%, 9.33%, 11.9% and 11.7%. Estimate the implied one-year forward rates. Comment on your results and suggest an appropriate investment policy to profit from any market anomalies.

9.7 Estimate the gross redemption yield as at 5 March for a 13% corporate bond which will be redeemed in the following year on 4 September with interest payments made on 4 March and 4 September. The price on the 5 March was £94. Estimate the redemption yield for an investor subject to a 30% capital gains tax and income tax at 65%.

9.8 When was interest last paid on Exchequer 10.5%, 1997 if the price on 5 December was £99 and the running yield was 10.95%?

9.9 A 5% convertible bond is quoted at 90 (ex div). The conversion terms provide for £100 nominal to be converted into fifty ordinary shares in two years' time. What will be the redemption yield on the convertible if the expected share price at the date of conversion is 300p? (Assume annual payments of interest.)

Appendix A
Calculation of redemption yields

In this chapter we simplified the calculation by assuming away the need to adjust the accrued interest. In general, there will usually be accrued interest which is either included in the price (for long-dated stock) or will require an adjustment to the quoted price (as in the case for shorts). The following example illustrates the method.

Consider an investor who wishes to buy, on 27 January 1993, 14% Exchequer Stock, priced at £103.25 and with interest payments due on 22 May and 22 November, redemption due 22 May 1994.

To estimate the redemption yield we carry out the following steps:

1. Adjust the price to include the effect of accrued interest. In this case the adjusted price will be

$$P_0 = 103.25 + \left(\frac{\text{Days between 22/11/82 and 28/1/83}}{365} \right) 14$$

$P_0 = £105.82$

2. Take as the first date, that on which interest is payable and specify the valuation of the remaining cash flows in half-yearly periods.

In the example, the interest is next payable on the 22 May 1993. The valuation at that time will be

$$V_1 = 7 + \frac{7}{1+i} + \frac{7}{(1+i)^2} + \frac{100}{(1+i)^2}$$

In general terms this would be expressed as

$$V_1 = 0.5c(1 + a_{\overline{n}|}i) + 100(1+i)^{-n}$$

where C = coupon, and n = the number of periods (usually six-monthly periods) between the next interest payment date and redemption.

180

3. Discount the valuation expressed in step (2) to the appropriate date.

$$V_0 = \frac{V_1}{(1 + i)^t}$$

where t = the number of days between 'tomorrow' and the next interest payment date divided by the number of days between interest payment dates. In the example $t = 114/181$ or 0.630

$$V_0 = \left[7(1 + a_{\overline{2}|} i) + \frac{100}{(1 + i)^2} \right] \frac{1}{(1 + i)} \, 0.63$$

4. Equate this valuation to the adjusted price P_0, interpolate and find i.

$P_0 = 105.82$ and $V_0 = 105.825$ using 0.05624

5. The annual (nominal) redemption yield is then $200i\%$. Thus in this example, the redemption yield is 11.248%.

Appendix B
Credit ratings

Standard & Poor's credit ratings on long-term debt are as follows:

AAA   Highest quality debt, indicating an extremely strong capacity to pay interest and repay principal.

AA   High quality debt, indicating a very strong capacity to pay interest and repay principal. This differs from the highest rated issues only to a small degree.

A   Good quality debt, indicating a strong capacity to pay interest and repay principal. Somewhat more susceptible to the adverse effects of changes in circumstances and economic conditions than higher rated debt.

BBB   This debt is regarded as having an adequate capacity to pay interest and repay principal, but certain protective elements may be lacking in the event of adverse economic conditions, leading to a weakened capacity for payment.

Debt rated BB, CCC, CC and C is regarded as having predominantly speculative characteristics, with respect to capacity to pay interest and repay principal, with BB the least speculative and C the highest. Although such debt is likely to have some quality protective characteristics, these are outweighed by large uncertainties or major exposure to adverse conditions. Some non-investment-grade debts are known as *junk-bonds*. Debt rated D is in default.

For short-term securities, such as commercial paper, the ratings are:

A   Highest rating, regarded as having the greatest capacity for timely payment. These are sub-divided into 1, 2 and 3.

A/1   The degree of safety regarding timely payment is either overwhelming or very strong. Those issues possessing overwhelming safety characteristics denoted A+ rating.

A/2   Capacity for timely payment is strong, but their relative degree of safety is not as high as for those designated A/1.

A/3   Capacity for timely payment is satisfactory. They are more vulnerable to the adverse effects of changes in circumstances than higher rated denominations.

B   Capacity for timely payment is adequate. Capacity may be damaged by changing or short-term adversities.

C   Capacity for timely payment on these short-term debt obligations doubtful.

D   The issue is in default or expected to be in default at maturity.

CHAPTER 10

The derivatives markets

10.1 Introduction

Standard financial markets provide a means of exchanging ownership of securities. This provides investors with the confidence that a degree of liquidity is maintained, and access to the listed securities is ensured. However, there are three ways in which trading in these markets can be carried out, and investors can choose between them.

The first is to buy a traded asset (maybe a security or some currency) now or later, in the spot market where current prices prevail. Most of the chapters in this section have dealt with transactions of this sort, that is, where market prices are current and commodities are paid for and delivered now, rather than at some future date. The second way is to acquire a claim on an asset in the form of a two-way commitment, fixed now but occurring at a later date, known as a forward or futures contract, or a one-way commitment fixed now but exercisable later, which is an option contract. Finally, the third is to agree to exchange its cash flows for another asset, called a swap.

The securities arising from the second and third choices are the subject of this chapter. We shall examine how these markets have developed, the trading mechanisms for each, and how they are valued. We shall also consider how they can be used in risk management, both by investors and in the real sector.

10.2 Characteristics of derivative instruments

In Chapter 7, we introduced the concept of a security which is itself based on a contingent claim on another underlying asset. These are known as derivative securities, because their value is derived from the underlying asset with which it is associated.

The most simple of the derivative securities is a forward contract. This is an agreement to buy or sell an asset at a future date. The quantity, price and delivery date are known at the outset, and the contract is set between the issuer of the contract and the purchaser directly. A futures contract is another important derivative security which has many of the same characteristics as a forward contract, but the organisational structure of the market and the pricing of the contracts are very different.

A third group of derivatives to be considered are options. Options have been traded on an organised exchange since 1973, and are now traded on many exchanges with contracts written on equity, stock indices, foreign currency, debt, commodities and futures contracts. These contracts are known as either American or European options, although these labels are nothing to do with the origin of the holder, or the market on which they traded. It is simply that an American option can be exercised before the maturity date, known as the expiry date, while a European option can only be exercised on the expiry date.

Finally, we shall examine the market for swaps. A swap is a private agreement between two parties to exchange cash flows at prearranged times in the future. Their terms are determined by a formula and the amount of cash involved is contingent on the value of an underlying security, hence their derivative nature. For example, for an interest rate swap, the underlying asset may be the LIBOR rate. In other cases it can be the price of a commodity.

Separate markets have developed in which trading takes place in instruments derived from the underlying commodity or security. Sometimes the entities underlying derivative securities are the prices of traded assets.[1] Examples of these are equity options, where the security's value is contingent on the price of the equity. Other derivative securities are linked to movements in the Stock Exchange Index or even the weather, while the value of financial derivative securities can depend on interest rates or exchange rates. Some of the earliest derivatives were developed along with the market for physical commodities, although in London the exchanges trading commodity-based derivatives are separate from those based on other assets. However, the structures and valuation of the contracts are common to all derivatives, regardless of the underlying assets.

The market in derivatives has developed as a response to uncertainty about prices. The crucial factor operating in these markets is that they provide a means of separating out this price volatility. This allows purchasers of the underlying asset, whether it is the end user of a commodity or an investor managing a portfolio, to make decisions which reflect their personal risk preference. Thus, a producer importing raw materials, such as coffee, grain or cotton, will be exposed to price changes resulting from exchange rate fluctuations. This purchaser may be risk-averse and willing to hedge by passing the risk on to a counter-party. On the other hand, the counter-party may consider this to be exactly the feature they find attractive, and are willing to take on the risk as a speculative investment. So for a premium, these markets allow hedgers to avoid risk by transferring it to speculators who seek it. Of course, this transfer of risk is possible in many markets, including spot markets, but the derivatives markets are particularly efficient in this respect, since the transactions costs are generally low.

We should now consider the more important derivatives in some detail.

10.3 Forward contracts

Forward markets grew out of uncertainty about prices in the future. The earliest forward contracts were written on commodities to hedge against changes in price between the date of order and the date of delivery. This could be due to a poor harvest resulting in a reduced supply of agricultural produce and a subsequent price rise. Or, as was particularly important in the UK which was so dependent on the import of goods from abroad, the failure to deliver merchandise at a time when travel was both dangerous and very slow.

Examples of forward contracts can be found in the eighteenth century, when traders on the Liverpool Cotton Exchange would come to an agreement over the price for a quantity of raw cotton being transported from the US. If the cargo arrived and complied with the prior agreements the deal would be concluded. Later, when relative currency rates were volatile, the uncertainty of the price of future imports became important, and futures contracts removed much of the risk of input prices in industrial and manufacturing sectors.

Although forward contracts are now much more varied and complex, the use of these markets to reduce risk from price changes is still valid. Particularly in the case of forward contracts more than other derivatives, there remains the characteristic of a contract agreed between the two parties. Of the two participants in a forward contract, one agrees to buy the underlying asset in the future, and one agrees to sell the asset at the same time, thus taking a long position and a short position respectively. Because of this, there is generally no secondary market since they are essentially customised contracts.

Market mechanism

There is no formal trading market for forward contracts. Arrangements are made directly with the supplier, or in the case of financial contracts, with a bank. An intermediary would be involved purely on a brokerage basis. Because all contracts are inflexible, they are a very illiquid instrument, which cannot be cancelled without mutual agreement.

Forward contracts are settled entirely at maturity. This raises another negative aspect of forwards, since apart from the lack of a secondary market, and hence the illiquidity, there is the risk of default, with the purchaser failing to meet the obligation specified. The chances of this occurring are higher if the spot price has moved away from the forward price, resulting in a loss to one of the two participants. In practice, the financial institution, in most cases a bank, may require investors entering into a forward contract to deposit some funds initially to act as a guarantee. These funds earn interest and will be a small proportion of the total value of the contract.

Valuation

The price specified in the contract is known as the delivery price. The forward price is defined to be that delivery price which would make the value of the contract zero. Thus at the date the contract is agreed the forward price and the delivery price are equal. During the life of the contract, the forward price may change in either direction, although the delivery price is constant.

The main determinant underlying the value of a forward contract is the market price of the asset. Given the contract is valued at zero on the opening date, if the price rises, the value of the long position rises and of the short position falls. If the price of the asset falls, the opposite will be true. For example, consider the spot and forward quotes on the £/$US exchange rates on 16 August 1994 which are:

Spot price (bid/offer)	(mid-point)	1 month	3 months	1 year
1.5397/1.5405	(1.5401)	1.5396	1.5378	1.5263

The spot price is the mid-value of the bid and offer quotes, for immediate delivery, ignoring commissions and other transactions costs. The one-month forward is again the mid-value of the bid and offer quotes for delivery in one month's time.

Thus if a US company has a debt due in one month's time, for a known fixed amount of £1,000,000, it can choose to enter into a long forward contract to buy that amount of pounds sterling on that date for $1,536,600. In the same way, a US company expecting to receive £1,000,000 in one month's time can enter into a short forward contract to sell £1,000,000 in one month's time for $1,536,600. In both of these cases, they have hedged against the risk of foreign exchange changes. However, in neither case can they take advantage of any currency changes, as they are locked into the forward price.

But this same contract can be used for speculation. An investor anticipating a decrease in value of the $US against sterling can speculate by taking a long position in a forward contract on sterling. Supposing the spot rate after three months is, say, $1.6000. Then this investor will be able to purchase sterling for $1.5378 when they are worth $1.6000, making a profit of $0.0622 per pound.

In general terms, the value at maturity of a long position in a forward contract per unit of underlying asset is

$$S_T - K$$

where K is the delivery price and S_T is the future spot price at the termination of the contract. In the same way, the terminal value of a short position is

$$K - S_T$$

Since it costs nothing to enter into the contract, the value on maturity is equal to the investor's gain or loss.

For a speculator, the advantage of entering into a forward contract over purchasing funds in the spot market is the increased gearing it provides. Apart from the small deposit referred to above, the final payment is delayed for the life of the contract, whereas purchases in the spot market have to be met in full at the time of purchase.

10.4 Futures contracts

The concept of a specified quantity at a fixed price, for delivery at a future date, holds for futures contracts as it does in the forward market. However, the quantities are standard and contracts are only offered for delivery at certain dates, most often during the months of March, June, September and December. Therefore the terms of the contract are not negotiable between buyer and seller.

The obvious advantage of standard packages such as these is that a secondary market can exist, and contracts can be exchanged through the usual transaction mechanisms. Also, unlike forward contracts, delivery is not due on a specific date, but within a defined interval. In the case of contracts on commodities, this is dictated by the party holding the short position, whereas financial futures are less flexible.

The example in the previous section on forward contracts used the spot and forward exchange rates as the basis for hedging and speculation. But not every risky asset has a forward market, for instance gilt-edged securities do not. We saw from Chapter 9 that the price of gilts and other fixed interest securities fluctuates inversely with interest rates, and if these are volatile, there is interest rate risk. Therefore, if an investor wishes to take advantage of favourable yields but recognises this may increase interest rate exposure, the financial futures markets provide an opportunity to hedge against possible loss. A futures contract can offset any loss in value from the gilts. However, this can rarely result in a perfect hedge, due to the inflexibility of the futures contracts, but the closer the match, the lower the risk from changes in the value of the underlying asset.

Very few futures contracts are actually delivered. The holder of the contract closes out their position in the vast majority of cases prior to maturity by entering into an offsetting contract with the same delivery month as the original contract. This is quite different from forward contracts, where delivery almost always takes place.

Market mechanism

The original exchange-traded futures were in contracts for agricultural products, and markets for these securities have existed in Amsterdam since the seventeenth century. The current system of futures markets has developed from the American system of the nineteenth century, where commodity futures were traded using a clearing house system of settlement. New York and Chicago are still the leading centres of futures trading. The early financial futures contracts were introduced in foreign exchange by the Chicago Mercantile Exchange in 1972 and in bonds by the Chicago Board of Trade in 1976.

Four classes of futures contracts are traded in London: short-term and long-term interest rate contracts, currency contracts and a stock index contract, although new ones are introduced if there is considered to be a sufficiently strong market demand for them. Examples of the specifications of some of these are shown in the appendix to this chapter.

The ownership of futures contracts is held by anonymous third parties, so there is no method of assessing the credit risk involved and thus the probability of default on the contract. Therefore a clearing house system is in place which guarantees that all contracts will be fulfilled. This is done by a daily series of payments made throughout the duration of the contract, known as 'marking to market'. The broker will demand a deposit from the investor which represents a proportion of the total value of the contract. This is called the initial margin and is put into a margin account. On each subsequent trading day, any change in the price of the underlying asset is noted, where the smallest price change permitted by the exchange on a particular futures contract is called the tick size of the contract. These changes vary depending on the contract, but commonly are 1 basis point of 1%, or 0.01% of the value of the contract.

When price changes occur, the investor will be requested to contribute more, a margin call, or is able to withdraw any balance in the margin account depending on the direction of the price change. If this maintenance is not honoured, the contract is closed out, or sold. The implication of this system is that the risk of default is very low, as regular payments ensure that at maturity very small amounts remain outstanding. But this does mean that the pattern of cash flows is very different from a forward contract, when all is paid at the end.

The exchange clearing house requires brokers to settle daily in the same way as the brokers' clients contribute to their margin accounts. This system of regular interim payments effectively minimises risk to the clearing house which is normally the risk-bearing counter-party to all transactions. The absence of risk, and the presence of low transactions costs, ensures a highly liquid secondary market. In some cases a contract can be open on an exchange in one country and closed on an exchange in another country, such is the high quality of the futures markets.

Valuation

Prices, exclusive of commission, are determined by supply and demand. The futures price is the market's expectation of what the spot price will be on the delivery date of the particular contract. Therefore there is a close relationship between spot and futures prices, particularly as the delivery date becomes due.

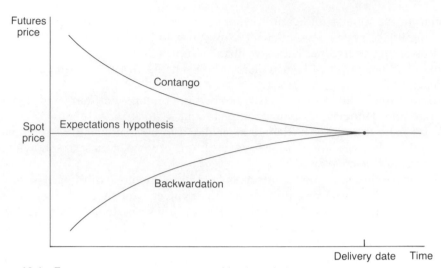

Figure 10.1 Futures contracts – contango and backwardation.

On the delivery date itself, the settlement price is determined by the spot price, but prior to this the futures price could be above or below the spot. The difference is known as the basis, where

$$\text{Basis} = \text{Futures} - \text{Spot price}$$

If the futures price is greater than the spot it is called contango. In this case, the futures price tends to fall over time towards the spot, equalling the spot price on delivery day. If the spot price is greater than the futures price it is called backwardation. Then the futures price tends to rise over time to equal the spot price on the delivery day. So in either case, the basis is zero at delivery.

The direction of the change in price tends to hold for cycles of contracts with different delivery dates. If the spot price is expected to be stable over the life of the contract, a contract with a positive basis will lead to a continued positive basis, although this will be lower in nearby delivery dates than in far-off delivery dates. This is a normal contango. Conversely, normal backwardation is the result of a negative basis, where nearer maturing contracts have higher futures prices than far-off maturing contracts. These are shown in Figure 10.1.

10.5 Options contracts

Options are similar to futures in that certain aspects of the contract are fixed. The amount, the price and the maturity are known, but the difference is the holder of an option can exercise it or not, depending on the price or value of the underlying security on expiry day. These securities are particularly valuable if prices are

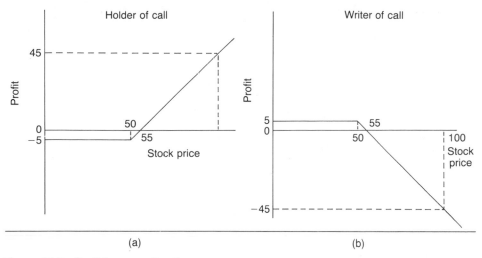

Figure 10.2 Profit from a call option.

likely to change, especially if this is expected to be more in one direction than the other. Thus investors can take advantage of an expected price increase while also protecting themselves against a price fall, and vice versa.

There are two main types of options, calls and puts, with the opportunity to buy or sell both. The holder of a call option has the right to buy a fixed amount of the underlying asset on which the call is written either before or at the expiry date, for a fixed price. Similarly, the holder of a put option has the right to sell a fixed amount of the underlying asset on which the put is written either before or at the expiry date, for a fixed price. In both cases, the option contract is only exercised if it is expedient for the holder to do so, and if not, is discarded. However, there is an unconditional obligation on the part of the writer to meet the call or put.

At any time during the life of the option, if the current market price (spot price) is equal to the exercise price, the option is 'at-the-money'. If the spot price is less than the exercise price, the option is 'out-of-the-money', and if greater than the exercise price, the option is 'in-the-money'.

The following example illustrates this.

First consider a call option, as in Figure 10.2. Suppose the call is purchased for 5p with an exercise price 50p. 10.2 (a) shows the position of the purchaser of the call. At maturity, if the share price is below 50p, it would not pay to exercise the call, as shares can be bought on the open market for less than the exercise price. If the share price is above 50p, it would pay to exercise the call and gain by the difference between the market price and the exercise price. At a price of 45p, the holder of the call benefits by being able to purchase the share at 50p and sell at 54p, although the original price of the option at 5p means there is an overall loss. Only when the price is 55p or greater, is there net profit, and in theory, this could be unlimited.

The position of the writer of the call is shown in 10.2 (b), and is the mirror image of

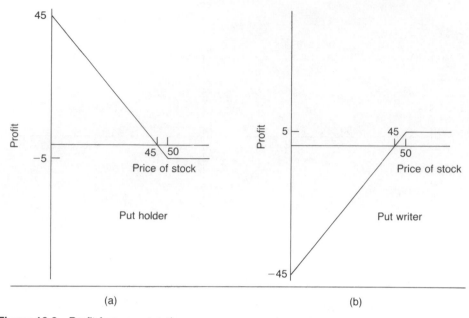

Figure 10.3 Profit from a put option.

the purchaser. If the share price is below 50p, the writer makes 5p from the purchaser. For a price between 50p and 55p, there is a partial loss in having to provide the stock at a price lower than the market price, and above 55p, the call writer faces a net loss.

A put option can be analysed in the same way, as shown in Figure 10.3. Continuing our example, 10.3 (a) shows that for a price greater than 50p, the owner of the put would prefer to sell shares in the market rather than to the writer of the put, since the exercise value is zero. For prices between 45p and 50p, the owner of the put would prefer to exercise the option rather than selling the shares on the open market. But the owner of the put loses money, since the price of the option is greater than the gains from selling the share at a higher price. At prices below 45p, the owner makes a net profit as the amount gained from the sale of the share is greater than the cost of the put. 10.3 (b) indicates that for prices greater than 45p, the writer of the put makes a profit, and for prices below 45p, there is a net loss.

Having examined simple call and put options, we can now consider some of the numerous combinations available on the market. Many fanciful terms describe such combinations, where there is a common exercise price and expiry date. For example, a call and a put combination is a straddle, two puts and a call is a strip, while two calls and a put is a strap. We can compare the possible profit available to the holder and the writer of a straddle with the diagrammatic approach used above.

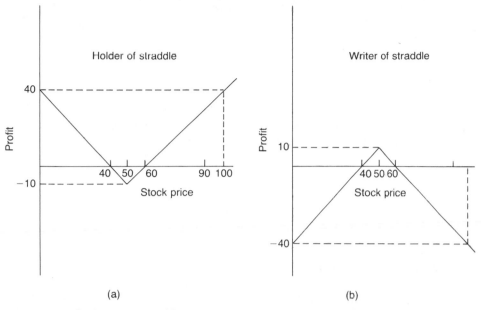

Figure 10.4 Profit from a straddle.

The reasons for writing and for holding a straddle arise from different expectations of price movements. Figure 10.4(a) shows that the straddle is held if the price of the underlying security is expected to move considerably, in fact more than the market generally anticipates, although the direction of the change is uncertain. On the other hand, Figure 10.4(b) shows that the straddle is written by an investor who expects the price to move very little, and certainly less than that anticipated by the market as a whole.

Finally, we should consider combining an option contract, either a put or call, with the underlying security. If the security is held at the same time as a contingent claim on that security, it gives the investor two assets whose price is expected to move together. One combination is to write a call and hold the security, known as a covered call. Suppose the exercise price is 50p, as is the price of the security, and the cost of the call is 5p. Figure 10.5 shows the three possible outcomes. An investor writing a covered call raises the return to the investment in cases where it is low while forgoing a high return if this should occur. Therefore this is a risk-reducing hedging position.

The notion of investors acquiring the right to buy or sell contingent on the price of another security has been raised above, in Chapter 9. Convertible bonds have this characteristic, although the right to purchase equity is available only in conjunction with the ownership of the bond itself. This represents a combination of a bond and a call option, although in this case, the bond has to be given up if the option to purchase the equity is exercised. This makes a convertible bond a

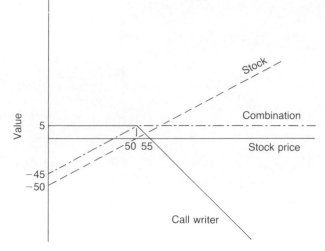

Figure 10.5 Profit from a covered call.

special case of an option/security combination, where the exercise price is not fixed but changes as the price of the bond changes.

Market mechanism

The London Traded Options Market (LTOM) dealing in UK equity stock options and index options was established in 1978 as one of the markets within the International Stock Exchange. Trading initially took place on the floor of the London Stock Exchange building, and continued long after other trading business had moved to individual dealing-rooms.

Traded options are subject to minimum units, and each contract is normally set at 1000 shares. Therefore options are quoted in number of contracts. If this seems as though each trade involves a lot of shares, this probably reflects the preference in London for low-priced shares. In the US, the normal contract involves 100 shares, reflecting a preference for heavily priced shares.

Financial options have always been traded at LIFFE since these contracts were introduced in 1986. However, in 1992 the LTOM merged with LIFFE, resulting in the London International Financial Futures and Options Exchange (still called LIFFE) becoming the centre for both traded and financial options as well as futures. We will return to this in more detail later in this chapter.

Valuation

Traded options allow the holder to exercise the contract at the expiry date if they wish, or they can sell it before this date. These options are written on actively traded securities including the FT-SE 100 share index.

Traded options buy a specified number of ordinary shares in a company at a specified price, and the conversion is usually constrained either to specified dates or to a period. In the case of traded options, the period will initially be confined to three, six or nine months.

A price is paid for the protection offered by this type of contract, and this is known as the option premium. It is derived from two sources, intrinsic value and time value, which can be considered separately. The intrinsic value is the possible gain due to a favourable movement in the price of the underlying security. The time value reflects the possibility that if there is sufficient time to expiry, the price may move favourably. This can be stated

Option premium = Intrinsic value + Time value

Thus for a call option which is *at-the-money* or *out-of-the-money*, the intrinsic value is zero, and there is only time value. For a call option which is *in-the-money*, the intrinsic value is

Intrinsic value = Share price − Exercise price

Prices are listed daily, for call and put options, for a number of expiry dates, along with the price of the underlying security. For example, a call option (expiring in three months) in Marks & Spencer shares might be quoted at 34p for an exercise price of 180p when the ordinary shares were listed at 200p. An investor buying the option would hope that the ordinary shares would rise in price. If shortly before the option expires, the share price has increased to, say, 220p, the investor can exercise the option by paying an additional 180p. The ordinary share has been acquired for an effective price of 214p (180+34) and can immediately realise a 6p profit by selling the ordinary shares for 220p.

In practice, option holders can realise their profits by selling the option in the traded option market, and mostly they do. Since there will always be the alternative method of exercising the option, prices of options will tend to converge to their *fundamental* price. In the above example, we would expect the call option to sell shortly before expiry at about 40p and thus the investor can realise the 6p gain either by selling the option on the market or by exercising it as described above. The investor has therefore geared up the 10% gain in the underlying share (220-200)/200 to more than 17% gain in the option (40-34)/34. However, if at expiry of the option, the share price has fallen below the exercise price, the option will be worthless and therefore discarded. The gearing effect of the option will therefore magnify the effect of share price movements both upwards and downwards.

In a simple form, the valuation of call options can be carried out by discounting the expected value of the option on maturity, thus:

$$C_t = (S_T - E) (1 + i)^{-q} \tag{10.1}$$

where

C_t = the value of the option at time t
S_t = the value of the underlying share at t
T = expiry date (for European options is the exercise date)
E = exercise price
i = the discount rate
$q = (T - t)/365$ time to expiry date

The problem arises from the difficulty of estimating the share price S_T at the exercise date. If we assume that no dividends are paid on the share and that it appreciates at an effective rate of $100i\%$ per year, we can rewrite 10.1 as

$$C_t = S_t - E(1 + i)^{-q} \tag{10.2}$$

Although this formula avoids the problem of estimating a future share price, it still requires the choice of a discount rate that must reflect the risk of the share being below the exercise price at expiration of the option. Fortunately this difficulty can be overcome.

If the investor buys a put option at the same time as a call option, the risk of the share price falling has been covered, so eliminating the risk of the portfolio. With such a portfolio, the discount rate will reflect only the cost of idle funds, or the risk-free rate of interest. Thus the value of the call option will be given by:

$$C_t = P_t + S_t - E(1 + i)^{-q} \tag{10.3}$$

where P_t is the price of a put option at time t (or provision against a price fall) and i is the risk-free rate of interest. This is known as the Put-Call Parity Theorem, and provides a useful check on the call option price if there are put options traded in the market. However, to show whether both put and call options are over- or under-priced, more complicated models are required.

There are various ways in which the option pricing models have been adapted, but among the more important are the allowance for dividend payments, the variation in interest rates and adjustments for share price behaviour. Some texts which show more details of option pricing models are listed at the end of the chapter.

10.6 The market for financial futures and options

When the London International Financial Futures Exchange (LIFFE) was established in 1982, it was the first financial futures market in Europe. Since merging with the London Traded Options Market (LTOM) it is the most comprehensive financial futures and options exchange in the world, with the exception of the United States. The appendix to this chapter gives details of some of the London contracts, including the size, the tick size, trading times, the months for which the contract is quoted and the form of delivery on maturity.

The London International Financial Futures and Options Exchange was opened on 23 March 1992 at Cannon Bridge, and operates with a single administration and common exchange systems and clearing arrangements. Since the merger, research and development expenditures directed into new products, as well as general operating costs have been reduced due to economies of scale and scope, with increases in operational efficiency.

Members of the International Stock Exchange are entitled to carry out a number of activities in LIFFE including broking, market-making and clearing. Some market-makers act on their own account, and some on behalf of clients, increasing the number of participants and enhancing liquidity. Members represent a wide selection of the financial services industry, including banks, stock exchange firms, commodity brokers, discount houses as well as individual traders, several of whom are from overseas.

Trading takes place in pits on the floor of the Exchange, each of which is dedicated to a type of contract during specific trading times. Contracts are bought and sold, with bargains made through open outcry, with all bids known to all traders. When traders have negotiated a price, and this has been confirmed by their clients, the contract is then valid. Prices are displayed on TOPIC (see pricing information system in Chapter 7), and bargains are registered through the Clearing House. Outstanding contracts are known as open interest.

For the majority of contracts strict rules forbid out-of-hours or off-floor trading. However, in 1989 an Automated Pit Trading (APT) system was introduced which simulated open outcry on a screen after the Exchange floor had closed. Specific contracts are traded exclusively on this system, and international market traders in time zones other than London and with restricted access to the trading floor can hedge their positions during the European trading day. Possibly future technology will be used for processing, clearing and maybe to ensure market dealings comply with regulations.

LIFFE uses an independent clearing house for settlement, the London Clearing House, which registers, clears and guarantees all trades generated in the pits or by the APT. It is owned by six major UK clearing banks and provides clearing facilities to a number of UK and foreign exchanges. All LIFFE's members must satisfy strict standards as regards their ownership, managerial control and tangible net worth and each firm's conduct and capital adequacy is monitored. Supervision of the market is the responsibility of LIFFE's Board of Management, although the Securities and Futures Authority is accountable for the selection of participating firms.

10.7 Swaps

Swaps are a more recent addition to the financial markets than the contingent claims discussed so far. The swaps markets has been in existence since the early 1980s, and the introduction of standardised contracts and dealing mechanisms through the International Swap Dealers Association has lowered the transactions costs and made operations more accessible to users.

Currency and interest rates swaps are the most common types in the market. A currency swap transfers the obligation for payment in one currency to another party who, in turn, undertakes an obligation for payment in another currency. The difference between the two types of swaps is that an interest rate swap only involves the exchange of interest payments, while the principal remains the obligation of the initial borrower. Therefore the riskiness of the loan is still associated with the writer of the debt, and not transferred.

Swaps are conducted through an intermediary, usually a market-maker, or a bank, who accepts the default risk, and earns a fee from both participants dependent on the level of that risk. Swap prices are negotiated by auction, usually conducted on the telephone, and are very much under the control of the market-maker.

The London swap market suffered from some controversy in the early 1990s, when the Law Lords decided in 1991 that local authorities were not allowed to enter swap agreements. This resulted in all outstanding contracts held in the local authority sector being cancelled, causing considerable losses to market-makers, and raised questions about other non-corporate swap activity, for example banks, building societies and pension funds. However, innovation in the development of products for 'financial engineering' continues to be practised as part of a strategic approach to hedging risk in a number of corporations and other institutions.

10.8 Index futures and options

Finally, we should briefly discuss contracts which do not derive their value from underlying securities, but from an index of security prices. It is useful for an investor wishing to hedge against movements in an index rather than individual securities.

One example is the FT-SE 100 index option traded on LIFFE. This option can be exercised by a cash payment equal to the intrinsic value of the option, although there is very active trading during the life of the contract. Another example is the FT-SE 100 futures contract, also traded on LIFFE. The futures contract is also settled by cash transfers from gainer to loser, and like any futures contract this has to be settled at expiry date, although this also is traded until maturity. One interesting aspect of this is the close correlation between the value of the futures contract and the underlying index. This is strengthened by the chance for arbitrage trading between the market for actual securities and the market for futures, known as index arbitrage, a process which has received some criticism from commentators claiming this leads to market instability.

10.9 Summary

Forward markets have existed for centuries, and are used to hedge against uncertainty, although trading in securities which derive their value from an underlying asset has increased in terms of both volume and variety. Predominant among these are futures and options contracts, but swaps and other innovative instruments are constructed in a process of financial engineering.

Note

1. It is important to remember that although derivatives are often written on corporate securities, they are not issued by individuals or institutions and therefore there is no effect on the financial structure of the company if the option is exercised.

Further reading

Blake, D. (1990), *Financial Market Analysis*, McGraw-Hill, Chapters 8 and 9.

Elton, E. and M. Gruber (1991), *Modern Portfolio Theory and Investment Analysis*, 4th edn, Wiley.

Foley, B. (1992), *Capital Markets*, Macmillan. Chapter 5 has a detailed discussion of the derivatives markets, including the controversy related to index arbitrage.

Hull, J. (1989), *Options, Futures, and other Derivative Securities*, Prentice Hall International, Chapters 1, 2, 5 and 6.

Scott-Quinn, B. (1990), *Investment Banking: Theory and Practice*, Euromoney Books.

Questions

10.1 Use the Financial Times to find the terms of a number of call and put options. Plot their payoffs at maturity on a diagram, as in Figures 10.2 and 10.3.

10.2 Shares in P & O were quoted at the beginning of February 1993 at 121p. Call options were available (exercise price = 100p), expiring at the end of February, May and August at 22p, 25p and 26p, respectively. If the expected return on both the shares and options is assumed to be constant over the whole period, which option is the best investment? (Ignore the effect of dividends.)

10.3 If the call options (exercise price = 90p, expiration end October) of Courtaulds are priced at 8p, and the share price is quoted at 88p at the beginning of May, what would be the value of the corresponding put option if the risk free rate was 12% per year? (Ignore the effects of dividends.)

10.4 Define the following derivatives:
  i A currency swap
  ii An interest rate swap
  How are they used?

10.5 What are the main differences between futures and forward contracts?

10.6 Comment on the following statement by a company executive:
  Last year we had a substantial income in dollars, which we hedged by selling dollars forward. Subsequently the dollar appreciated and our decision to sell forward cost us a lot of money. In future we should stop hedging our currency exposure.

Appendix
LIFFE derivative contracts

Commodity	Size	Tick size	Months	Hours	Delivery
Futures					
FTSE 100 index	£25 × index	£12.50	nearest 3 and Mar Jun Sep Dec	9.05–16.05	Cash
Eurodollars	$1,000,000	$25.00	nearest 3 and Mar Jun Sep Dec	8.30–16.00	Cash
3-month sterling	£500,000	£12.50	Mar Jun Sep Dec	8.20–16.02	Cash
Short gilt	£100,000	£15.625	Mar Jun Sep Dec	9.05–16.20	Physical
Medium gilt	£50,000	£15.625	Mar Jun Sep Dec	8.55–16.10	Physical
Long gilt	£50,000	£15.625	Mar Jun Sep Dec	9.00–16.15	Physical
US T-bonds	$100,000	$31.25	Mar Jun Sep Dec	8.15–16.10	Physical
Japanese T-bonds	¥100m	¥10,000	Mar Jun Sep Dec	8.10–16.05	Cash
German bonds	DM250,000	DM25	Mar Jun Sep Dec	8.10–16.00	Physical
British pounds	£25,000	$2.50	Mar Jun Sep Dec	8.32–16.02	Physical
Deutschmarks	DM125,000	$12.50	Mar Jun Sep Dec	8.34–16.04	Physical
$/Deutschmarks	$50,000	DM5.00	Mar Jun Sep Dec	8.34–16.04	Physical
Japanese yen	¥12.5m	$12.50	Mar Jun Sep Dec	8.30–16.00	Physical
Swiss francs	Sfr 125,000	$12.50	Mar Jun Sep Dec	8.36–16.06	Physical
Options					
FTSE-100	£25 × index		nearest 3 and Mar Jun Sep Dec	9.07–16.05	Futures
Long gilt	£50,000		Mar Jun Sep Dec	9.02–16.15	Futures
US T-bonds	$100,000		Mar Jun Sep Dec	8.17–16.10	Futures
Eurodollars	$1,000,000		nearest 3 and Mar Jun Sep Dec	8.32–16.00	Futures
3-month sterling	£500,000		Mar Jun Sep Dec	8.22–16.02	Futures
British pounds	£25,000		nearest 3 and Mar Jun Sep Dec	8.34–16.02	Physical
$/Deutschmarks	$50,000/DM		nearest 3 and Mar Jun Sep Dec	8.36–16.04	Physical
FTSE 100 index	£10 × index		nearest 4 months	9.05–15.40	Cash
Long gilts	£50,000		Feb May Aug Nov	9.05–15.40	Physical

Commodity	Size	Tick size	Months	Hours	Delivery
Short gilts	£50,000		Feb May Aug Nov	9.05–15.40	Physical
$/Sterling	$12,500		2 nearest and Mar Jun Sep Dec	9.00–15.40	Physical
$/Deutschmarks	DM62,500		2 nearest and Mar Jun Sep Dec	9.00–15.40	Physical
UK equity options	1,000 shares		up to 9 months out	9.05–15.40	Physical
French equity options	100 shares		Feb May Aug Nov	9.35–16.05 9.05–16.05	Physical
Restricted life options	1,000 shares		2-, 4-, 6-month expiry series		Physical

Options are also listed on the following equities:

Abbey National
Allied-Lyons
Amstrad
Argyll
ASDA
SmithKline Beech
BAA
Barclays Bank
Bass
BAT
Blue Circle
Boots
BP
British Aerospace
British Airways
British Gas
British Steel
British Telecom
BTR
Cable & Wireless
Cadbury Schweppes
Commercial Union
Courtaulds
Dixons

Eastern Electric
Fisons
Forte
GEC
Glaxo
Grand Metropolitan
Guinness
Hanson
Hillsdown
HSBC
ICI
Kingfisher
Ladbroke
Land Securities
Lasmo
Lonrho
Lucas
Marks & Spencer
National Power
NatWest Bank
P&O
Pilkington
Prudential
RTZ

Redland
Reuters
Rolls-Royce
Royal Insurance
Sainsbury
Scottish Power
Sears
Shell
Storehouse
Tarmac
Tesco
Thames Water
Thorn EMI
Tomkins
Trafalgar
TSB
Unilever
United Biscuits
Vodaphone
Wellcome
Williams
Zenaca

CHAPTER 11

The money markets

11.1 Introduction

The short-term markets for finance are characterised by large size, quick speed of reaction and low transaction costs. They are based mainly on telephone contact between dealers, with the markets invariably operating on verbal agreements for deals which usually individually account for millions of pounds. The markets are less formally established than the longer term capital markets but have more than compensated for their informality by their vigorous expansion.

In discussing the operations of the markets and the instruments which are traded, we have first to consider the ways in which profits are reported in buying and selling short-term *money*. We shall then examine the traditional discount market, and a number of other short-term sterling money markets which have developed along with this, known collectively as the parallel markets. Finally, we shall outline the characteristics of the London foreign exchange market.

11.2 Principles of bill discounting

In Chapter 5, we discussed the principles of simple and compound interest and showed how they could be used to compare the payment of money at different times. In the short-term money markets the life of a loan or security is usually less than one year, so perhaps it is not surprising that the comparisons are conventionally made using simple interest and the related concept of simple discount.

To illustrate the relationship between the two concepts, take the example of a bank loan that is taken out at the beginning of the year for £880 with the promise to repay, at the end of the year, the sum of £1,000. This transaction can be analysed from the lender's point of view as promising a return at the beginning of the year of (1000–880)/880 or an interest rate of just over 13.6% on the bank's initial 'investment' of £880. Alternatively, we describe the difference between

1000 and 880 as the discount and estimate the discount rate to be (1000–880)/1000 or 12% of the maturity value.

Another example will show how the discount rate is estimated if the loan is taken out for less than one year:

> A firm is owed £5,000 by a commercial customer and is faced with an immediate need for cash. It offers to accept £4,900 if payment is made immediately rather than at the end of the month. Calculate the interest and discount rates implicit in this offer.

In this example, the firm is effectively borrowing £4,900 for one month, and paying interest on the loan. In simple interest terms, the present value is given by

$$P = \frac{5000}{(1 + r/12)}$$

where r is the annual rate of interest. But the present value is known to be £4,900 so we can write

$$4900 = \frac{5000}{(1 + r/12)}$$

and solve for r to find

$$r = 0.245 \text{ or } 24.5\% \text{ p.a.}$$

The discount is the £100 difference between the initial payment and the final amount. The discount rate is found by dividing the discount by the sum owed and then annualising the result. In simple interest and discount terms, the annualising is achieved by multiplying the discount by 12 and the discount is obtained if payment is brought forward 1 month. Thus,

$$d = \frac{100}{(5000/12)}$$

$$d = 0.24 \text{ or } 24\% \text{ p.a.}$$

We can generalise these examples by letting $P =$ the initial value, $5 =$ the maturity value and $n =$ the time, in years, between the payments or receipts. The interest rate r is given by

$$r = \frac{(S - P)}{Pn} \text{ p.a.} \tag{11.1}$$

Whilst the discount rate is given by

$$d = \frac{(S - P)}{Sn} \text{ p.a.} \tag{11.2}$$

Alternatively we can express the present value of the loan either in terms of the interest rate or the discount rate by rearranging the above expressions:

$$P = \frac{S}{1 + rn} \tag{11.3}$$

$$P = S(1 - dn) \tag{11.4}$$

Finally we can equate these values to express the discount rate in terms of the interest rate,

$$d = \frac{r}{1 + rn} \tag{11.5}$$

The usefulness of these expressions can be seen by examining the *Bank of England Quarterly Bulletin* which presents yield statistics on various short-term investments. Supposing, for example, Treasury bills are reported to have been sold at an average discount rate of, say, 10% p.a. whilst local authorities' three-month loans may be reported as yielding an interest rate of 10.875%. It is not easy to see which is the most profitable investment since they are reported in different units. But by using expression (11.5) we can calculate that the discount rate equivalent to the local authority loan of 10.875% is

$$d = 0.10875/(1 + 0.10875 \times 0.25) = 0.1059$$

Comparing this discount rate of 10.59% with the 10% from the Treasury bills reveals that the local authority bills are yielding a discount of about 1/2% above the Treasury bills.

Usually the prices quoted in the bill markets will be in terms of the discount. Thus a £100,000 Treasury bill may be bought at a 10% discount rate to mature in 91 days' time. Using equation (11.4), the buying price will be

$$P = 100,000(1 - 0.1 \times 91/365) = £97,506.80$$

An investor will buy the bill for £97,506.80 and in 91 days' time can collect £100,000 on maturity to earn the 10% discount rate. The market price will rise from £97,506.80 to £100,000 as maturity draws nearer. Suppose, however, that the interest rate falls sometime during the life of the bill. The price of this bill will tend to rise faster than the market had anticipated. Perhaps the investor will want to sell the bill after 50 days have passed to realise the unanticipated profit. The market may be quoting a discount rate of 8%. To calculate the price of the bill, the investor can again use equation (11.4) thus

$$P = 100,000(1 - 0.08 \times 41/365) = £99,101.40$$

The realised return on this investment can now be calculated using expression (11.1) thus

$$r = (99,101.4 - 97,506.8)/(97,506.8 \times 50/365)$$
$$= 0.1194 \text{ or } 11.94\% \text{ p.a.}$$

In other words the seller has earned a profit equivalent to a simple interest return of 11.94% p.a.

The buyer of the bill who plans to hold the bill until it matures in 41 days' time will earn interest of $100,000 - 99,101.4$ or £898.60, which will represent a return of

$$= (100,000 - 99,101.4)/(99,101.4 \times 41/365)$$
$$= 0.08072 \text{ or } 8.07\% \text{ p.a.}$$

We can check this calculation by converting this interest rate back into a discount rate by (11.5). Thus

$$d = 0.08072/(1 + 0.08072 \times 41/365) = 0.08$$

which accords with the discount rate used to price the bill in the same market. Note that in calculating these rates we have used the convention of a 365-day year. In many markets, especially in Europe, a 360-day year is assumed. Having looked at the simple ways in which the short-term investments can be analysed, we pass on to the markets and their operations.

11.3 Characteristics of the sterling money market

The money markets are essentially wholesale markets and have developed as a smoothing mechanism between the trading of longer term instruments. It would be very difficult to coordinate flows of cash between buyers and sellers, but since the opportunity cost of holding idle liquidity is high, the short-term markets provide a convenient investment opportunity.

Transactions are usually for amounts in excess of £0.5 million, with a large number of participants and low transactions costs. The size of the market owes much to the development of eurocurrency trading and the liberalisation of domestic banking regulation during the 1970s. In addition, the range of short-term contracts traded at LIFFE has increased liquidity in the market.

Table 11.1 gives an indication of the volume of current sterling trade. Although listed separately, the markets shown in Table 11.1 are closely linked, often involving the same institutions. We shall examine them in the following sections.

11.4 The discount market

The oldest of the money markets is the traditional discount market, and is important for two reasons. The first was introduced in Chapter 4, where we

The money markets

Table 11.1 The London sterling money markets, December 1993 (£bn)

i	Traditional discount markets	10.091
ii	The local authority market	1.681
iii	The inter-bank market	68.531
iv	Certificate of deposit market	53.053
v	Finance houses deposit market	4.154

Notes:
i   Total borrowed funds by discount houses, Table 4.2D.
ii   Total stock of temporary money, Table 1.3B.
iii   Total sterling time deposits in UK banks, Table 4.2C.
iv   CDs issued by banks and building societies, Tables 4.2C and 4.3A.
v   Total short-term funds from non-bank credit institutions, Table 5.2B.

Source: Financial Statistics, June 1993.

discussed the ways in which the Bank of England manages the government's financing by raising money from selling government bonds and short-term Treasury bills. The daily open market operations are used to even out the flows of cash between the Bank and the retail banks or to implement interest rate policy. The retail banks use the discount market to even out the flows of funds from themselves and their deposits at the Bank through the discount houses.[1]

The effect of payments of funds passing between central government and the retail banks is to increase or decrease the banks' balances with the Bank. The volume of funds may be very large and variable and difficult to forecast. The discount houses would face considerable instability if the Bank did not intervene to smooth these cash flows, and any interventions are generally directly with the discount houses. This can involve buying or selling Treasury or other eligible bank bills or making loans.

Discount houses have sought to extend the range of investments in which they have traded. Among the various securities which can be classified as being traded in the discount market are local authority bills and government bonds of up to five years from maturity. Local authority bills are traded in the market and classified by the Bank of England on the same basis as Treasury bills.

In reporting its transactions on the money market, the Bank will usually refer to assistance given in both the morning and afternoon. The distinction is made for two reasons. First, the morning operations are based on preliminary estimates made by the Bank of the shortage of funds in the money market. During the day these preliminary estimates will be adjusted and reflected in the afternoon dealings, and by tradition the banks do not withdraw funds from the discount houses after mid-day. Secondly, the morning operations are confined only to help the market cope with funds shortage, whereas in the afternoon the Bank may also offer more bills to the discount houses, and in this case, to the commercial banks, if the market has an excessive supply of cash.

The daily report may therefore appear as follows:

The Bank gave assistance in the morning of £71 million, comprising purchases of £7m of Treasury bills in band 1 and, in band 2, £64m of eligible bank bills. All purchases were made at 11% (discount rate p.a.). The afternoon help was made up of bill purchases all at 11% of £205m, comprising £22m of Treasury bills, £23m of local authority bills, £40m of eligible bank bills in band 1; and in band 2, £1m of local authority bills, £104m of eligible bank bills and £15m of Treasury bills.[2]

Such reports on the Bank of England's day-to-day operations in the money markets are available on electronic screen-based services such as Reuters and published daily in the *Financial Times* report on the money markets. The Bank may choose to make loans rather than participate in the bills market to highlight a position, or give a signal about monetary policy.

An example is taken from the *Financial Times* in September 1990 when there was debate over the UK joining the ERM with a subsequent reduction in interest rates predicted. The report stated:

The Bank of England indicated its concern about lower interest rates by refusing to operate in the bill market. The authorities did not offer to buy bills, but underlined the present interest rate structure by lending money to the discount houses for seven days at the clearing bank base lending rate of 15 per cent.[3]

The other role of the discount market is to act as a buffer between the Bank and other commercial banks. The discount houses borrow money for very short periods and effectively lend to the Bank of England by buying Treasury bills. The Treasury bills issued by the Bank are usually for three-month terms, at weekly intervals. At any time, the discount houses can hold a portfolio comprising Treasury bills of various maturities, financed largely by overnight or other short-term loans from the commercial banks. Should the banks fail to renew their loans, the discount houses are allowed to sell any unfunded Treasury bills back to the Bank of England, or to borrow cash from the Bank if it were thought that the cash shortage is temporary.

By this operation, the Bank can smoothly increase interest rates, first by causing the commercial banks to suffer a shortage of cash and then reinforcing this shortage by helping the discount houses to cope with the induced lack of funds only at higher rates of interest. To ensure that this policy will work, the Bank relies on the agreement by the discount houses to buy any Treasury bills not taken up by other investors. Thus the Bank can always, if necessary, issue more Treasury bills than could be funded by commercial loans from the banks if it wished to force the discount houses into the position of asking for help. The discount houses also operate to make a market in Treasury bills, they underwrite Treasury bill tender and borrow and lend gilt-edged stock through the money-brokers. Because of this close relationship with the Bank, they are the subject of prudential supervision by the Bank.

This position of the discount houses between the Bank and the retail banks is unique to the UK financial system, and although it has been the subject of review in the past, there has never been any serious criticism of it and so it continues today.

The discount markets do not only deal with government instruments. The bill of exchange is a traditional method by which industrial and commercial firms obtained their short-term finance, especially those concerned in international trade. There are, in practice, two ways in which similar documents can originate. The conventional bank bill is created, known as drawn, by a creditor company on a debtor, maybe that debtor has bought goods from the company, and the liability is accepted by a bank or discount house which will guarantee to pay for goods being supplied by the creditor. Acceptance credits, on the other hand, are drawn by the debtor company and are accepted by a bank or discount house which will guarantee to pay the amount owing if the debtor defaults.

Bank bills can be further classified as eligible or ineligible. Eligible bills are those which have been accepted by banks such as the Midland, Chase Manhattan or Deutsche Bank and thereby become eligible for purchase by the Bank of England. Ineligible bills will be perceived to be either less secure or less marketable than their eligible counterparts.

Eligible bills can be sold to the Bank of England by the discount houses to improve their liquidity and when they find their other sources of finance are inadequate. In effect, eligibility depends on an eligible bank accepting the bill. In the past, the list of eligible banks was limited but the number increased dramatically in August 1981 to over 100 when the Bank of England announced changes in its method of carrying out monetary policy through control of the money market.

Currently, the Bank may announce that it will buy or sell bills daily. In some cases, the Bank will announce that it will buy bills which will be resold at a later date, or may only lend money to the discount houses. In order to let the market influence or even determine the pattern of interest rates, the Bank will frequently only operate in bills which are due to mature in the very near future. In the classification adopted by the Bank explained in note 2 at the end of the chapter, the Bank usually confines its dealings to bands 1 and 2.

The Bank also takes account of the risk and maturity of bills in fixing the terms under which the discount houses operate. Because of the nature of their business financing, discount houses are inherently risky. They borrow on a very short-term basis and lend over a longer term, all on a small capital base. Typically, the discount houses borrow and lend up to thirty times their own capital. Much of their funds is provided by the recognised banks, all of which place a specified proportion of their assets with the discount markets.

The discount houses' solvency in volatile markets depends on the Bank of England's role as lender of last resort, and it is this which helps ensure that the discount market responds quickly following information from the authorities. In setting restrictions on the extent to which the discount houses can enlarge their assets by borrowing, the Bank classifies their assets by category. Thus, eligible bills with a life of less than three months come within the least risky category, whilst ineligible bills with a life of between three months and a year come within the second category. In the third and most risky category as far as the bills of exchange are concerned, are some ineligible bills with over a year to run and trade bills, which are bills of exchange neither drawn on nor accepted by a bank, with a life of over six months.

The involvement of discount houses in government bonds began in the 1930s, during which period there had been a decline in the number of bills of exchange due to the world recession. The houses still hold short-term government bonds, especially when they believe that interest rates are likely to fall because as interest rates fall, so the price of the bonds will rise and profits will be made from the capital gain. The success and/or failure of the discount houses' forecasts on interest rates, as demonstrated in their gilt portfolio, has been one of the major influences on the performance of each discount house over recent years.

Short-term government bonds are also traded by other institutions such as banks and building societies. Dealers operate in a wide range of money markets ranging from the traditional discount market to the foreign exchange and other sterling deposit markets. It is not surprising that the markets in which short-term investments are so frequently trading should themselves respond quickly to external events.

11.5 The parallel markets

Operating alongside the discount market are the parallel money sterling markets. Of these, the most important constituent markets trade in inter-bank deposits, certificates of deposit and local authority deposits.

The sterling inter-bank market, as its name suggests, concerns the borrowing or lending of sterling funds between banks. Deposits are of a minimum size of £500,000 and are usually made on a short-term basis with the majority of deposits being made for maturities of less than three months. The operations carried out by the Bank of England in the discount market will usually affect the rates negotiated in the inter-bank market. For example, if the Bank injects more cash into the discount market, discount houses may find that they no longer require cash from clearing banks which in turn will place cash on the inter-bank market. If the amount is sufficiently large, the market rates of interest will fall.

Operations on the inter-bank market involve a large number of banks and commercial lenders and can at times result in highly volatile rates. For lesser-known banks, the volatility is exacerbated since their names may not be acceptable to some market participants or, if they are acceptable, only in limited amounts. All participants operate on a system of limits in which they will restrict the amount of money lent to any other bank, with limits imposed on smaller banks more restrictive than those imposed on commercial banks. In addition to the system of limits, rates quoted will also depend on the status of the bank bidding for funds.

Sterling certificates of deposit are basically negotiable receipts issued by the banks acknowledging that a specified sum of money has been deposited and will be repaid at a fixed rate of interest on a specified date. From the depositors' point of view, the issue of a negotiable certificate enables them to realise their cash if required before maturity, since the secondary market for these instruments means they will be sold at a rate that will take into account the earning capacity of the money on deposit. Depositors will pay a small price for this liquidity but the value of the facility does depend on how active this secondary market is, and the opportunity cost of funds in available alternative markets.

From the issuing bank's view, certificates of deposit represent an additional and slightly cheaper method of acquiring funds for a fixed term at fixed interest rates. In ensuring a strong secondary market, the discount houses have played an active role in promoting their use, and they provide useful additions to the banks' portfolios.

Unlike the bills traded in the traditional market, certificates of deposit are not issued at a discount but are instead issued for a minimum period of three months at face value, normally in amounts starting from £50,000, with interest payable on maturity. As with other short-term markets, the rates of interest quoted are calculated on a simple interest basis, unless they have a maturity of greater than one year. Thus a three-month (91-day) certificate bought at 12% would be expected to pay $(12 \times 91)/365 = 2.992\%$ interest on maturity.

A further complication exists if the maturity is greater than one year. In this case, the interest payable is still calculated on a simple interest basis. Estimating the return is therefore a slightly complex task if trading is carried out in the secondary market. For example, if a £1 million certificate issued for two years at 14% was sold after six months for a quoted yield of 12%, the price would be calculated in the following way. The interest would be £140,000 payable at the end of the first and second years. At the end of the first year the value would be

$$P_1 = £1m(1 + i)^{-1} + £0.14m(1 + i)^{-1} + £0.14m$$

where i = the market yield, in this case 0.12, and six months earlier

$$P_{0.5} = P_1(1 + it)^{-1} \text{ where } t = 182/365$$

Thus

$$P_{0.5} = \{1.14/1.12 + 0.14\}\{1 + 182/365 \times 0.12\}^{-1}$$
$$\text{Price} = £1.0925m$$

Although certificates of deposit can be issued for terms of one, two, three or more years, the secondary market for such long-term securities is very much thinner than that for shorter maturities. In response to this market constraint, issuing banks and depositors sometimes agree on roll-over terms whereby, for example, a six-month certificate will automatically be replaced by another at the time of maturity at a specified rate. In this case, the issuing house can rely on having the use of the money deposited for twelve months while the depositor will have the liquidity derived from receiving two certificates, one of six months' duration, maturing in six months' time, the second also of six months' duration, running from six months to twelve months ahead.

In this example, the issuing bank has agreed on a forward rate for the second six-month period. In principle, it is straightforward to compare the cost of a six-month certificate with a six-month roll-over, with the cost of a twelve-month one. In practice, the comparison depends on the rate of interest which will prevail in six months' time and professional judgement will be required in allowing for the small, but possibly significant, variations. The development of the trading in forward instruments of this kind was encouraged by the growth in financial futures trading.

The remaining parallel sterling market which will be briefly mentioned here is that for local authority short-term finance. Bills issued by local authorities and traded in the discount market are small in relation to the general deposits business carried out for periods varying from overnight to several years. These deposits are not traded in a secondary market, and only come within the area of parallel money markets because lenders are likely to consider the rates offered in the local authority market as an alternative to the inter-bank market.

As in the other markets, the technical aspects of the trading lead to anomalies from which traders can profit. One such opportunity is the activity known as round-tripping. If the market rates are appropriate, a commercial firm may typically create an acceptance credit which will immediately be accepted by a bank and sold for cash. The company then places the cash in the inter-bank market at a marginally higher rate. Similar round trips can be made by companies which have previously arranged with banks the right to overdraw their accounts.

Usually these overdraft facilities will be charged at a rate of interest that will be linked to the current short-term rates. But it is possible that, for a large reputable company, the overdraft rate is below the rate currently quoted for certificates of deposit or trade bills. Thus the company can borrow from the bank by using the overdraft facility and buy short-term money market securities with the funds borrowed. As with other money market arbitrages, large sums of money have to be traded in order to make small profits, particularly after the transactions costs. Such operations contribute to the informational efficiency of the market in transmitting changes in one market to other associated markets.

The scale of arbitrage deals is difficult to estimate. More importantly, the existence of arbitrage activity cannot be assessed from the published reports of the rates ruling in the respective markets. In *Financial Statistics*, for example, inter-bank sterling market rates may be reported 11–11.125% overnight and 10.90625% three months, with three-month sterling certificates at 11.0625%. But the inter-bank rates are, for the overnight rate, the range of the lowest bid and highest offer rates over the day. By contrast, the certificate of deposit rate is the mean of the lowest bid and highest offer rate at 10.30 a.m. In practice, rates for overnight money on the inter-bank market can be very volatile and crucially depend on the help given by the Bank of England in the discount market.

Besides the inter-market arbitrage trading, which essentially consists of simultaneously trading in more than one market, arbitrage can occur over time, as the forward market also operates in inter-bank deposits. Complicated arbitrage activity can involve both certificates of deposit, inter-bank forward deposits or foreign exchange transactions. Technically, the market refers to forward transactions, that is, ones involving delivery of securities at a later date, as occurring in the *forward-forward* market. Again, these transactions have been greatly facilitated by the establishment of a market in which standard contracts are traded, and the development of a financial futures market is of considerable interest to arbitrageurs.

11.6 The foreign currency markets

The UK foreign exchange market is situated in London and all the financial institutions carrying out transactions in foreign currency deal through it. The most common form of contract is spot currency negotiations with forward contracts accounting for the majority of the remainder. The most popular currency traded is the US dollar.

Historically, the favoured currency for international reserves was sterling, and so London developed as the centre for foreign exchange dealing. This has continued to be the case, and London has the highest average turnover of all financial centres, even though the US dollar is now the dominant currency.

The market is a continuous dealers' market, with market-makers, brokers, the Bank of England and individual companies and institutions, and with trading carried out by screen in private dealing-rooms. The market-makers are mostly the banks who buy and sell continuously, while brokers trade as agents on behalf of their principals. The Bank of England acts anonymously, with intervention carried out by a broker. Customers generally are companies who need currency for their business activities, since firms wishing to trade in currency derivatives will do so through LIFFE directly.

The international money markets came into existence for a number of reasons, the main one being the desire of international investors and multinational corporations to find ways around controls on international capital movements imposed by domestic governments – in particular the US government – and to circumvent various restrictions on the issuance of securities. The international markets for short-term financial instruments possess similar characteristics to the domestic money markets. Generally, the international money markets are concerned with trading in eurocurrency, which is included in Chapter 12.

The existence of the euro-money markets has had an enormous impact on the efficiency of currency and domestic money markets. The introduction of markets in which interests in future euro-certificates of deposit can be traded in both the US and the UK further enhances the opportunity for the arbitrageur. The international markets are essentially unregulated markets. Parameters such as maturity are important to distinguish between contracts, but regulation of the markets as a whole is much less rigorous than in other segments of the financial markets, probably a necessary situation as much of the trading is across national frontiers.

11.7 Summary

The short-term money markets are strictly wholesale markets in which large amounts of money are traded on small margins of profit. Operations are carried out by discount houses acting as intermediary between the central bank and the commercial banks. Since they involve only professional market participants, details of their operations are more difficult to ascertain. None the less, the pricing of assets within the markets can be analysed by referring to the general principles of discounting introduced in this and earlier chapters. The foreign exchange market is very important to London as a financial centre, trading in many currencies but predominantly the US dollar and eurocurrency.

Notes

1. This is explained in Chapter 14.
2. The bands refer to the outstanding maturity of the bill. Band 1 is 1–14 days; band 2 is 15–33 days; band 3 is 34–63 days and band 4 is 64–91 days.
3. This example is taken from Buckle and Thompson, see further reading.

Further reading

The Bank of England Quarterly Bulletin publishes regular commentaries on the operation of the money market and almost every issue of the *Bulletin* has some comment of interest.

Buckle, M. and J. L. Thompson (1992), *The United Kingdom Financial System in Transition*, Manchester University Press. Chapters 10 and 11 include an excellent coverage of money markets and foreign exchange trading.

The *Financial Times* 'money market report' gives details of the Bank of England's intervention in the markets daily.

Shaw, E. R. (1981), *The London Money Market*, 3rd edn, Heinemann. This book covers in considerable detail the operation of the London money markets, including the parallel and eurodollar markets.

Questions

11.1 Briefly describe the functions of discount houses. If they did not exist, how do you think the task of controlling the supply of money would be affected?

11.2 Explain how the Bank of England can affect the short-term rates of interest:
   (a) by buying or selling Treasury bills.
   (b) by buying and selling commercial bills

11.3 What risks are faced by the discount houses? How do these risks differ from those faced by any other financial institution borrowing and lending in different markets (e.g. banks or building societies)?

11.4 Discuss the advantages and disadvantages to:
   (a) the borrower
   (b) the lender
   of a loan made for a long period of time at a rate of interest that fluctuates in response to changes in the short-term rate of interest (LIBOR).

11.5 Briefly define the parallel markets.

Problems

11.6 If the market (simple) rate of interest is 9%, estimate the value:
   (a) today
   (b) six months from today
   (c) one year from today, of £1,000 due in three months' time.

11.7 Which of the following investments offers the higher rate of return:
   (a) 91-day bill at 12% discount rate
   (b) 91-day CD at 12 3/8% interest rate
   (c) 365-day bill at 12% discount rate
   (d) 365-day CD at 12 3/8% interest rate?

11.8 An investor buys a one-year 10% $CD which he sells after 180 days. What will be the return on the transaction if interest rates have remained unchanged over the intervening period? (Assume an initial investment of $10,000.) What would be the price of the CD at the time he or she sold if interest rates had unexpectedly fallen to 9.5%?

CHAPTER 12

Eurosecurity markets

12.1 Introduction

This chapter centres on securities which are denominated in eurocurrency. The eurosecurity markets involve many of the financial instruments we have already discussed, but with the added complexity of being denominated in various currencies. They are issued by nationals from many different countries, and transacted in markets throughout the world. These three features, the currency, the issuer and the residence of the financial intermediary managing the transaction, distinguish one eurosecurity from another.

12.2 Definitions

The eurocurrency markets, of which the eurodollar market is the largest part, were established when currencies became convertible at the end of the Second World War, and trading in the first truly international securities began. The 'euro' prefix occurred almost by accident and is somewhat confusing since it does not imply any European characteristics. Nowadays, eurosecurity business is transacted in all the major financial centres, although London does have a major share.

A number of definitions are needed to make the discussion of these markets clearer. To begin with eurodollars: these are bank instruments, consisting of a dollar credit or deposit managed by a bank not resident in the US. The implications of this are that the eurodollar is not subject to the supervision and regulation by the central banking authorities of that country, nor to the domestic interest rate structure, although it remains within the US banking system and is managed in the same way as all bank funds.

Neither the residence of the original lender nor the final borrower is relevant to the labelling of a eurocurrency transaction, as it is simply the location of the intermediary which is important. Thus, for example, if a US citizen lends funds to a US bank in London, which then uses these funds to make a loan to a company in the United States, these transactions would be undertaken using eurocurrency. Conversely, if the loan had gone through the US bank's office in New York, it would constitute a series of domestic dollar transactions.[1]

On the other hand, dollar eurobonds are securities, and are dollar-denominated bonds issued outside the United States. Eurobond issues can be made by US companies through US wholesale banks located offshore in locations such as Bermuda, Cayman, the Isle of Man, the Channel Islands and many others.[2] The feature of these is that they are not subject to the regulation of the US Securities and Exchange Commission.

Finally, a foreign bond is a security issued by a borrower in a domestic capital market other than their own, and normally denominated in the normal currency of the market. Therefore a German company issuing a sterling-denominated security in London, is creating a foreign bond, in this case called a Bulldog bond. Additional named foreign bonds are Yankee (dollar-denominated in New York) and Samurai (yen-denominated in Tokyo), as well as a number of others.

Two features distinguish eurobonds from foreign bonds. One is the composition of the underwriting securing the issue and the regulatory jurisdiction under which they operate. Eurobonds are underwritten by a group of international institutions and are not subject to the rules of the issuing bodies of any country, whereas foreign bonds are underwritten by domestic intermediaries complying with national rulings. The second is the coupon rate. Eurobond rates can behave quite differently from domestic rates, whereas foreign bond coupons are very similar to other domestic bonds.

12.3 The euromarkets

It appears to be commonly accepted that the development of the eurodollar market, and then eurocurrency markets generally, is a consequence of the need for Eastern European governments to purchase Western goods following the Second World War. These goods had to be paid for in US dollars and during the interval until the transaction took place, they had to be deposited in a secure financial institution. However, the US banks were not acceptable to Central and Eastern Europeans during the period of the cold war, since foreign assets could be frozen if relations deteriorated too badly. These dollar deposits were therefore safer in Paris and in London, out of reach of the US authorities.

A less intriguing corollary was the existence of the interest rate ceiling, known as Regulation Q, imposed on deposit-taking institutions at that time by the US Federal Reserve Board. Banks in London and Paris were not subject to this restriction, presenting the opportunity to earn higher interest rates. Furthermore, off-shore banks had a number of tax advantages, allowing them to operate at lower costs which they passed on to their customers through a lower deposit/lending interest rate spread.

Since the 1950s, the eurocurrency markets have grown rapidly, and London's

Table 12.1 International bond issues ($bn)

	Eurobonds	Foreign bonds	Total
1975	9.9	12.1	22
1980	25.6	11.3	36.9
1985	137.2	27.3	164.5
1988	183.7	43.1	226.8
1989	223.7	39	262.7
1990	212.4	50.8	263.2

Source: Bank of England ICMS database.

share in particular. The markets consolidated, the relatively deregulated environment allowed the introduction of innovative securities and the UK continued to be a channel of intermediation for international capital flows. This was helped by the fact that a system of distribution of primary issues and secondary trading had become established, but also the benefits from the ability to invest in a less regulated environment were clearly attractive.

The short-term money markets, as discussed in Chapter 11, include several eurocurrency transactions, particularly euro-certificates of deposit and euro-commercial paper.[3] In the medium term, euro medium-term notes are issued and this market has grown rapidly, with increases from $20 billion to $60 billion over the two years from 1991 to 1993. These are normally of two to five years maturity and the UK building societies are particularly prominent issuing institutions. Issue size is usually between $2 and $10 million, but they sometimes range from $50 to $250 million, and increasingly resemble eurobonds.

Eurobonds issues have increased dramatically, and there has also been growth in foreign bonds, particularly those denominated in Swiss francs. Table 12.1 indicates the levels of both of these covering a fifteen-year period. Because of the volume of eurobonds issues, and the fact that this market is predominantly London based, we will examine these in slightly more detail.

12.4 The eurobond market

Bonds issued on the eurobond market are similar to those of sterling bonds, but added complexity results from the number of currencies involved. Deregulation in a number of countries, particularly the relaxation of exchange controls, has widened the range of currencies in which eurobonds are issued from eleven in 1980 to twenty-one in 1990.

A range of instruments are available on the market, and new and innovative financial techniques continually become available. The most common type of eurobond issued is the straight fixed rate bond with bullet repayment, which has

Table 12.2 Eurobond issues by type, 1980–90

Year	Fixed rate	No. of issues	Floating rate	No. of issues	Convertibles	No. of issues
1980	12,223	179	4,128	63	2,475	68
1981	16,761	248	7,040	94	2,623	70
1982	34,962	455	11,602	98	1,298	35
1983	30,833	408	14,960	80	1,798	37
1984	43,448	563	31,680	187	4,160	49
1985	73,201	970	54,755	272	4,637	68
1986	125,955	1,298	47,512	228	6,413	76
1987	109,911	1,082	11,043	83	14,068	129
1988	150,686	1,350	19,280	108	5,793	47
1989	184,577	1,385	22,290	137	5,249	39
1990 (1st quarter)	53,841	424	13,761	62	2,010	17

Source: Bank of England Quarterly Bulletin, November 1991.

many of the features of its domestic equivalent, described in Chapter 9. A major difference, however, is that these bonds are bearer-denominated, whereas domestic bonds are registered to a specific holder. Thus they are essentially anonymous. They pay interest free of tax, with the payment not reported to the Inland Revenue Service, and are usually unsecured, although they offer a negative pledge, which means that no further debt can be issued which is more senior to the bond in question.

Floating rate notes differ from the straight eurobond in having a variable coupon set in relation to a reference rate, such as LIBOR. This is especially attractive to banks, partly for reasons of asset matching, and to large sovereign issuers. Equity warrant bonds, similar to the domestic convertible bond, offer warrants giving the right, but not the obligation, to buy the issuer's equity at some price and date in the future. Also as with domestic bonds, these features can be sold separately. Asset-backed bonds are secured against more illiquid loans, and offer financial institutions a means of removing assets from their balance sheets and reducing capital requirements. Some perpetual bonds and variable rate notes are also available. Table 12.2 illustrates the number of bonds issued by type, although this list is by no means inclusive.

Data such as that in Table 12.2 are useful in examining the rate of increase and comparing relative changes. However, it is also useful to try to explain the anomalies. Apart from the overall growth rates, 1985 and 1987 are particularly interesting. In 1985, floating rate notes reached their highest point as interest rates were rising. However, when rates began to fall, straight bonds became more popular due to the inverse relationship between the coupon and market interest

Table 12.3 Differences between domestic and eurobond markets

	Domestic market	Eurobond market
Instrument	Normally registered	Normally bearer but option to be registered
Security/covenants	Often secured or with detailed restrictive covenants	Usually unsecured but carrying a negative pledge
Tax	Coupon paid net of UK income tax	Coupon paid gross
Interest	Semi-annual payments	Normally annual
Issuing houses	UK merchant banks and stockbrokers	UK and overseas banks/securities houses
Listing	London	Usually London or Luxembourg
Placing	Placed at a fixed price on a specific day	Placed over a period and at varying prices
Secondary market	London Stock Exchange day after issue	Over-the-counter trading by issuing banks
Investors	Mainly domestic	Domestic and overseas

Source: Bank of England Quarterly Bulletin, p. 63, February 1988.

rate returning an expected capital gain. In 1987, the demand for convertibles was at its height, as equity prices rose, prior to the world stock market crash.

A number of characteristics are common to both domestic and eurobonds. However there are differences, some of which are outlined in Table 12.3.

The primary market

As in all aspects of the financial sector, part of the role of the market is to bring together buyers and sellers. There are a number of barriers to this in domestic markets, and most of the transactions costs incurred result from overcoming these difficulties. In the international finance markets there are additional problems. The source of funds from various currency areas fluctuates as relative exchange rates change, and individual economies respond to monetary policy decisions at a national level. Differences in risk and time-preference affect investors and changes in regulation as well as restructuring in the corporate sector affect issuers. Those managing eurobond business within the financial institutions must be aware of these issues in trying to match borrowers and lenders.

While some variety continues in the issuing group, there has always been a predominance of banks, industrial companies and international organisations. The certain requirement is that they should have high credit rating or are a recognised name. Data on borrowers by sector are given in Table 12.4.

Supranational institutions such as the International Bank for Reconstruction

Table 12.4 Eurobond borrowers by sector

Year	Industrial companies	Banks	Supranationals	Other financial	Public sector
1975	9.2	1.3	4.5	1.7	5.3
1980	13.8	5.0	6.6	3.6	7.9
1985	58.0	40.7	18.8	22.6	24.4
1988	91.7	50.8	20.5	28.4	35.4
1989	119.1	55.7	23.1	36.0	28.8
1990	92.9	63.0	30.3	42.9	34.1

Source: Bank of England ICMS database.

Table 12.5 Eurobond borrowers by country of origin

Year	US	Japan	UK	Canada	France	Germany	Other	LDC	Supranationals
1975	0.5	1.7	0.6	4.6	2.3	0.3	7.2	0.3	4.5
1980	5.1	3.8	1.7	3.2	3.2	0.1	14.2	0.5	6.6
1985	40.7	20.0	14.4	9.5	11.8	2.9	44.4	2.0	18.8
1988	17.1	50.8	26.8	12.9	16.2	11.8	69.0	1.7	20.5
1989	15.9	97.7	24.7	13.3	13.4	9.7	62.4	1.3	23.1
1990	21.9	58.0	23.4	13.1	20.4	7.8	87.5	0.7	30.3

Source: Bank of England ICMS database.

and Development, the European Investment Bank as well as the regional development banks have been consistently important participants in the international bond market. The larger supranational organisations have become significant issuers of large liquid bonds which, together with a few top-quality sovereign issuers, act as benchmarks in the eurobond market. Also included are banks and industrial companies from a number of countries. Details of borrowers by country are given in Table 12.5.

The issuing process requires detailed preparatory work on an individual level, including drafting the prospectus, determining the credit rating, assessing the coupon, setting the issue price, and organising underwriting and placing. It is entirely a wholesale operation, with a complex fee structure, varying with the detail of the issue, the size, the maturity and the name and reputation of the issuer. The yield is determined by a number of factors, including the credit status of the issuer, the maturity of the bond, the size of the issue, the type of instrument offered, the currency of issue and general market conditions.

The secondary market

Most secondary market transactions take place in over-the-counter trading, that is, not on a recognised exchange, although most eurobonds are listed on the London or Luxembourg Stock Exchanges.[4] This is partly historical, and due to the bearer registration of the issue. Settlement takes place through either CEDEL or EUROCLEAR, organisations which maintain book entry transfers of ownership. Turnover is generally high, reaching $6,262 billion in 1990 from a level of $240 billion in 1980.

Trading is carried out by intermediaries acting as reporting dealers, who make markets in securities for customers. These dealers have access to price information through the inter-dealer brokers, and make their own quotes known on screens, confirmed by telephone. There is a lack of liquidity in the secondary markets for small issues, and turnover is mainly in the large issues. Because of this, many international issues are privately placed. Some improvements in the market structures, for example the settlement and trading mechanisms, have encouraged more participation, but eurobonds issued in some currencies are still more liquid than those denominated in others.

12.5 The international money markets

The short-term markets have close parallels with the domestic operations. The eurodollar certificate of deposit is similar to its domestic UK and US counterparts. They are usually issued in 1 million units and vary in maturity from three months to five years. They are issued by US and other banks, clearing banks and branches of banks located in a number of countries including Canada, Britain and Japan. In some cases, small banks buy certificates of deposit from other banks on the understanding that they will not be traded. The effect of this agreement is that the liquidity of the small bank will appear from the balance sheet of the bank to be more liquid than it truly is. During times in which borrowing rates fluctuate considerably, the appearance of liquidity may substantially affect the credit rating of the small banks. A second effect of this type of agreement is that the secondary market for eurodollar certificates of deposit may lack breadth in proportion to the volume of those outstanding in domestic markets.

In pricing eurodollar certificates of deposit, calculations should take into account the convention that interest is accrued in a 360-day year. Thus, a 10% dollar certificate issued for 180 days would pay interest of 5% on the par value, whereas a domestic sterling certificate would pay interest of $10 \times 180/365 = 4.93\%$ on par. In analysing arbitrage operations between domestic and eurocurrency money markets, it is important to note this difference in convention.

Parallel to the euro-certificate of deposit market is the inter-bank euromarket in which a bank will trade deposits for fixed terms at rates inversely related to the bank's size and status. The rate charged may be fixed relative to LIBOR (London

Table 12.6 Eurocurrency interest rates

Aug 16	Short term	7 days' notice	One month	Three months	Six months	One year
Belgian Franc	$5\frac{1}{8}$–5	$5\frac{1}{4}$–$5\frac{1}{8}$	$5\frac{11}{16}$–$5\frac{9}{16}$	6–$5\frac{7}{8}$	$6\frac{3}{16}$–$6\frac{1}{16}$	$6\frac{3}{8}$–$6\frac{1}{4}$
Danish Krone	$5\frac{1}{2}$–5	$6\frac{3}{4}$–$6\frac{1}{4}$	7–$6\frac{1}{2}$	7–$6\frac{1}{2}$	7–$6\frac{1}{2}$	$7\frac{1}{2}$–7
D-Mark	$4\frac{7}{8}$–$4\frac{3}{4}$	$4\frac{15}{16}$–$4\frac{13}{16}$	$4\frac{15}{16}$–$4\frac{13}{16}$	5–$4\frac{7}{8}$	$5\frac{1}{16}$–$4\frac{15}{16}$	$5\frac{5}{16}$–$5\frac{3}{16}$
Dutch Guilder	$4\frac{15}{16}$–$4\frac{13}{16}$	$5\frac{1}{2}$–$5\frac{3}{8}$	$4\frac{15}{16}$–$4\frac{13}{16}$	5–$4\frac{7}{8}$	$5\frac{3}{16}$–$5\frac{1}{16}$	$5\frac{7}{16}$–$5\frac{5}{16}$
French Franc	$5\frac{7}{16}$–$5\frac{5}{16}$	5–$4\frac{7}{8}$	$5\frac{5}{8}$–$5\frac{1}{2}$	$5\frac{3}{4}$–$5\frac{5}{8}$	$6\frac{1}{16}$–$5\frac{15}{16}$	$6\frac{3}{8}$–$6\frac{1}{4}$
Portuguese Esc.	$12\frac{1}{8}$–$11\frac{7}{8}$	$11\frac{5}{8}$–$11\frac{1}{8}$	$12\frac{13}{16}$–$11\frac{3}{4}$	$12\frac{15}{16}$–$11\frac{15}{16}$	$12\frac{15}{16}$–$11\frac{15}{16}$	$12\frac{7}{8}$–$11\frac{7}{8}$
Spanish Peseta	$7\frac{7}{8}$–$7\frac{11}{16}$	$7\frac{7}{8}$–$7\frac{11}{16}$	$7\frac{15}{16}$–$7\frac{11}{16}$	$8\frac{1}{16}$–$7\frac{7}{8}$	$8\frac{3}{8}$–$8\frac{3}{16}$	$8\frac{11}{16}$–$8\frac{1}{2}$
Sterling	$5\frac{1}{8}$–$4\frac{7}{8}$	5–$4\frac{7}{8}$	$5\frac{1}{8}$–$5\frac{1}{16}$	$5\frac{5}{8}$–$5\frac{9}{16}$	$6\frac{1}{8}$–6	$6\frac{15}{16}$–$6\frac{13}{16}$
Swiss Franc	$3\frac{7}{8}$–$3\frac{5}{8}$	$4\frac{1}{8}$–$3\frac{7}{8}$	$4\frac{1}{4}$–$4\frac{1}{8}$	$4\frac{7}{16}$–$4\frac{5}{16}$	$4\frac{5}{8}$–$4\frac{1}{2}$	$4\frac{3}{4}$–$4\frac{5}{8}$
Can. Dollar	5–$4\frac{3}{4}$	$5\frac{1}{8}$–$4\frac{7}{8}$	$5\frac{3}{8}$–$5\frac{1}{4}$	$5\frac{3}{4}$–$5\frac{5}{8}$	$6\frac{5}{16}$–$6\frac{3}{16}$	$5\frac{7}{8}$–$5\frac{3}{4}$
US Dollar	$4\frac{1}{2}$–$4\frac{3}{8}$	$4\frac{9}{16}$–$4\frac{7}{16}$	$4\frac{3}{4}$–$4\frac{5}{8}$	5–$4\frac{7}{8}$	$5\frac{3}{8}$–$5\frac{1}{4}$	$5\frac{7}{8}$–$5\frac{3}{4}$
Italian Lira	9–$7\frac{1}{2}$	$9\frac{3}{8}$–$9\frac{1}{4}$	$9\frac{11}{16}$–$9\frac{9}{16}$	$9\frac{15}{16}$–$9\frac{13}{16}$	$10\frac{9}{16}$–$10\frac{1}{16}$	$10\frac{7}{8}$–$10\frac{3}{4}$
Yen	$2\frac{1}{8}$–$2\frac{1}{16}$	$2\frac{3}{16}$–$2\frac{1}{8}$	$2\frac{3}{16}$–$2\frac{1}{8}$	$2\frac{5}{16}$–$2\frac{1}{4}$	$2\frac{3}{8}$–$2\frac{5}{16}$	$2\frac{21}{32}$–$2\frac{19}{32}$
Asian \$Sing	$3\frac{7}{8}$–$3\frac{3}{4}$	$3\frac{7}{8}$–$3\frac{3}{4}$	$4\frac{7}{16}$–$4\frac{5}{16}$	$4\frac{3}{4}$–$4\frac{5}{8}$	$5\frac{3}{16}$–$5\frac{1}{16}$	$5\frac{13}{16}$–$5\frac{11}{16}$

Note: Short-term rates are call for the US Dollar and Yen; others: two days' notice.

Source: Financial Times, 17 August 1994.

Interbank Offer Rate) with large banks paying rates below LIBOR and lending their borrowed funds to smaller banks at a profit.

Alternatively the rate may be fixed in absolute terms. Smaller banks may also pass the funds on to other international banks, or may lend to corporate customers paying a margin over LIBOR. Reports of the inter-bank activity (and in fact of most other euromarket lending) will usually refer to LIBOR, which is simply the arithmetic mean of the rates on £10 million three-month deposits offered at 11 a.m. to the London Clearing Banks by the reference banks (typically National Westminster Bank, Bank of Tokyo, Deutsche Bank, Banque Nationale de Paris and Morgan Guaranty Trust).

Since almost all of the short- to medium-term loans in the eurocurrency market are determined on the basis of floating or pre-specified rates (in relation to LIBOR), a widely accepted and reported rate has obvious market advantages. Rates for maturities from overnight to one year for all the major eurocurrencies are published daily in the *Financial Times* (see Table 12.6).

The interpretation of this table requires some explanation, since it represents another change in the reporting convention. Unlike published foreign exchange quotations, the offer rate is given first, for example, short-term sterling rates quoted are 5.125–4.875. The reason is to make the quotes comparable to Treasury bills which are sold on a discount basis. Treasury bills are sold at a price below par and are redeemed at par. The discount is the amount of interest paid. The more cheaply the bill is sold, the higher the effective interest rate. This method is carried over to inter-bank deposits. This change is only a matter of presentation, and is to ensure consistency.

12.6 Euroequity markets

The section on eurobonds made it clear that the procedure for issuing eurobonds and distributing them developed as a market in its own right. Each eurobond issue is unique, and although sharing many of the features of domestic bonds, it has quite distinctive features. Equity, on the other hand, results in a residual ownership interest in the company, and therefore any security based on equity must be closely related to those of the domestic market, since all shareholders must be treated equally. The relationship between the shareholder and the company is defined by company law and in the UK is set out in the companies articles of association, with comparable charters in other countries.

Consequently, whereas eurobonds were specifically designed for international transfers of funds, equity markets are not and for many years this was not permitted. Problems involved in international equity ownership include settlement, withholding tax, voting rights and procedures, rights issues and disclosure requirements. Legal statutes in some countries place an obligation on shareholders to notify their ownership at a given percentage and to bid for the company as a whole after a certain limit is reached. Furthermore, there may still be some restriction on the proportion of shares owned by foreign investors in some countries.

Despite difficulties of information and procedure, for many years new equity issues have been distributed internationally, but usually where the overseas share ownership is a small proportion of the total. However, nowadays issues are underwritten and distributed by international syndicates wishing to establish a global ownership base, and some large domestic equity issues have an international element which is underwritten and distributed separately. This is carried out in a similar way to securities in the eurobond market, although the procedures and the clientele are different, and sales are often targeted to specific markets, based on geographical segmentation. However, one problem relating to euroequity issues which does not exist for eurobonds is called *flowback*, that is, the shares tend to flow back to the domestic market of issue, since that is generally the strongest and most active secondary market, and soon cease to be globally traded.

Two examples of UK euroequity issues are the British Gas and British Telecom privatisations. These were successful, despite potential difficulties in synchronising the underwriting arrangements in all the countries involved.

An example of a US euroequity issue is Benetton, who wished to expand the public ownership of their shares in 1989. Three syndicates were formed to underwrite and distribute equity to the US, Canada and elsewhere. The ordinary shares are listed on the European stock exchanges including Milan, Rome, Turin and Frankfurt as well as in Toronto SEAQ International. The issue was in the form of American depositary shares, and shares are still traded as American depositary receipts for simplicity.

This is a brief introduction to euroequity trading. A further discussion of international equity trading, including the methods of exchange and the difficulties facing the regulators is in Chapters 19 and 20.

12.7 Summary

The eurosecurity markets have become a major part of the financial markets. While many instruments appear to be similar to their domestic counterparts, the freedom from national regulations makes them particularly attractive. The very large debt issues are predominantly from the international and supranational organisations, and are arranged on an issuer-specific basis.

Notes

1. The effect of eurodollar transactions on the banking system is illustrated in the appendix to this chapter.
2. A further complication is that some financial institutions are actually located in a country, but officially designated offshore.
3. This is discussed in section 12.5 below.
4. Listings are normally obtained because some institutional investors are not allowed to purchase unquoted securities.

Further reading

Johnston, R. B. (1983), *The Economics of the Euro-Market*, Macmillan.
Scott-Quinn, B. (1990), *Investment Banking: Theory and practice*, Euromoney Books. Particularly for the eurobond market.

Questions

12.1 Why would a company issue debt in a eurocurrency rather than their domestic currency?
12.2 What is the difference between a eurobond and a foreign bond?
12.3 List some eurocurrency financial instruments.
12.4 Describe the main steps involved in the process of issuing eurobonds.

Appendix
How eurodollar transactions affect the banking system

As an example of how the eurodollar market works let us suppose that a Belgian export company (Company X) receives payment for goods which it has shipped to a customer (Company Y) in the USA or elsewhere. Since the dollar is the most frequently used vehicle of currency then it is likely that the payment will be made in dollars. The only way in which a payment can be made in dollars is by means of a cheque drawn on a US bank. Company X must therefore have an account with a US bank in order to receive payment. If we assume for the sake of simplification that both the importer and exporter hold their bank accounts with the same bank (Citybank) then we can follow through the transactions that might result with an initial payment of US$1,000,000.

Initial position

Citybank (US)

Assets	Demand deposit
US$1,000,000	to Co Y US$1,000,000

Changes

Citybank (US)

	Demand deposit
	to Co Y − US$1,000,000
	Demand deposit
	to Co X + US$1,000,000

The exporter now has US$1mn more in his account in New York than before, while the importer has US$1mn less. Total deposits in Citybank are unchanged.

Since the dollar is useful for trading purposes we assume that the Belgian exporter wishes to continue to hold dollars but would prefer to earn interest on them; and since his local bank in Belgium (Creditbank) offers to open an interest-bearing dollar account (a eurodollar account) he therefore instructs Citybank to transfer his US$1mn deposit to Creditbank.

Initial position

Creditbank (Brussels)	
Demand deposit to Citybank US$1,000,000	6-month deposit to Co X US$1,000,000

Changes

Citybank (US)	
	Demand deposit to Co X − $1,000,000
	Demand deposit to Creditbank + US$1,000,000

The result of transferring this deposit to a bank in Europe is not to reduce the deposits of Citybank. Only the ownership of the deposit is changed. It has now changed hands from Company Y to Company X to Creditbank. However, the result of transferring the deposit to a bank outside the US is to create a eurodollar deposit. Creditbank now has a non-earning asset (a demand deposit with a New York bank) and an interest-bearing liability (a eurodollar deposit). It must therefore lend out its deposit at Citybank at interest if it is going to be able to pay interest on its eurodollar deposit. If we assume that it has no non-bank customer who is in need of funds then it can simply on-lend the funds in the eurodollar inter-bank market where it will earn a fraction more interest than it has to pay on the deposit. It lends to a bank in London (Barclaybank) which needs the deposit since it has a non-bank customer who wants a eurodollar loan. At this stage we assume that Creditbank wishes to hold a 10 per cent cash reserve against its Eurodollar liability and thus lends only US$900,000.

Barclaybank has borrowed the deposit in order to lend it to a customer (Company Z). Assume once again that it decides to hold a 10 per cent reserve against the loan then the amount it will lend will be US$810,000. The way in which it makes this loan is by asking Citybank to credit Company Z's account with US$810,000 and correspondingly to debit its own account. Thus once again the deposit is simply transferred between owners without the deposits of Citybank changing in total.

Initial position

Barclaybank (London)	
Demand deposit at Citybank US$900,000	6-month eurodollar deposit to Creditbank US$900,000

Changes

Creditbank	
Demand deposit at Citybank − US$900,000 6-month eurodollar deposit with Barclaybank + US$900,000	

Citybank	
	Demand deposit to Creditbank − US$900,000 Demand deposit to Barclaybank + US$900,000

Changes

Barclaybank	
Demand deposit at Citybank − US$810,000 Loan to Co Z + US$810,000	

Citybank

	Demand deposit to Barclaybank − US$810,000 Demand deposit to Co Z + US$810,000

Final position

Citybank

Assets US$1,000,000	Demand deposit to Creditbank US$100,000 Demand deposit to Barclaybank US$90,000 Demand deposit to Co Z US$810,000
US$1,000,000	US$1,000,000

Creditbank

Demand deposit with Citybank US£100,000 6-month eurodollar deposit with Barclaybank US$900,000	6-month eurodollar deposit Co X US$1,000,000
US$1,000,000	US$1,000,000

Barclaybank

Demand deposit with Citybank US$90,000 Loan to Co Z US$810,000	6-month eurodollar deposit to Creditbank US$900,000
US$900,000	US$900,000

The end result of these transactions is that the initial deposit inflow of US$1mn into the eurodollar market has resulted in a total increase in eurodollar deposits of US$1.9mn. However, if we net-out inter-bank deposits of US$900.000, then the non-bank public has only acquired US$1mn of eurodollar deposits. When looked at in terms of the effect on world money supply, the increase in total dollar deposits outstanding to the non-bank public is only the amount of the final loan, that is US$810,000.

What Company Z does with this US$810,000 will determine whether or not there is a continuation of credit creation in the market. If it used the money to make purchases and the company receiving the deposit either pays the funds into a bank account in the US or else converts the dollars into domestic currency then the eurodollar credit creation will end there. This is in fact what is likely to happen.

This illustration was originally published in Einzig, P. and Scott-Quinn, B. *The Eurodollar System*, Macmillan 1977. The author is grateful to Brian Scott-Quinn for permission to produce it here.

The financial institutions

Introduction to Part III

Much investment in the capital markets, discussed in Part II, is undertaken by financial institutions. However, this investment activity is simply the result of the institutions managing their portfolios of securities in their role as intermediaries within the financial sector.

The retail and wholesale banks, and the building societies, insurance companies and pension funds, each undertakes financial transactions and provides products and services in their own right. The clearing and savings banks take deposits from savers and facilitate a payments mechanism, while the investment banks contribute to the functioning of a primary market for securities. The insurance market provides a level of security for the real sector, and pension funds enable small investors to make deposits now for future consumption, while both invest substantial amounts of funds in the financial sector. Part III examines in some detail the individual groups of institutions which make up the financial sector.

CHAPTER 13

Introduction to the financial institutions

13.1 Introduction

In Part I we examined the theory of financial intermediation and particularly the importance of the intermediary institutions in the reduction of transactions costs. This chapter considers the historical context of deposit-taking institutions and the growth of the banking industry's provision of safekeeping for small investors' cash to the financing of industry on an international level. To define the different roles of the institutions within the financial sector, a classification system is employed, although increasingly the organisations within this group offer a wide range of goods and services.

13.2 Historical perspective

As the European economies expanded, trade became more important. Precious metals, generally gold and silver or minted coins, provided a means of payment, but problems arose when the quantity and quality of such metals were inadequate to meet the needs of trade. Banking has its origins in the need to economise in hard currency. The traders who frequented the great medieval fairs developed means not only of offsetting mercantile debts, but also of assigning these debts by means of the bill of exchange.

By the mid-fourteenth century the Venetian money-changers had developed into recognised keepers of deposits, and not much later were settling the debts of their customers by book transfers of credit. These practices became commonplace in England with the expansion of trade in the latter part of the Tudor period. In the reigns of Elizabeth and James I certain English businessmen became recognised as money-lenders, money-changers, bullion-merchants, exchange specialists, and financial middlemen. Out of these activities, particularly those of the goldsmiths, the trade of banking emerged.

Rapid growth in trade, industry and colonialisation created a huge demand for capital. The banks became specialists in mobilising capital for trade and for the Exchequer. The growth of banking was rapid, but in times of absolute monarchism the establishment of a large joint-stock banking corporation was too risky to contemplate.[1] With the accession of William III, though, this kind of risk disappeared.

In 1694 the Bank of England was created, and in return for a £1,200,000 loan to the government to finance the war with France, the Bank received certain benefits, including the right to issue notes. Other banks were forced to operate as private partnerships, a restriction which, together with poor communications, limited banking in England largely to London. The needs of trade and the industrial revolution soon began to create a demand for banking facilities outside London, so an act was passed in 1826 permitting joint-stock banking with right of note issue. This proved a popular idea, and by 1836 100 joint stocks had been established.

By the mid-nineteenth century London had become the leading centre of European commerce. Like Amsterdam in the previous century, but in contrast with earlier commercial centres (e.g. Antwerp and Lyon), London was not only a centre of shipping and trade finance but also a major provider of long-term capital. London's rapid escalation to pre-eminence owed much to the way the Napoleonic wars had concentrated the world's trade in the British Empire and made Britain the country where capital might be invested safely. Amsterdam had been replaced by London as the financial and trading capital of Europe.

By the middle of the nineteenth century, Britain had become a major exporter and London was finding the short-term finance for this activity and providing a system for settling international payments. A good deal of this trade credit was provided by London's merchant banks and private banking companies. By the turn of the century, London was financing the bulk of the world's trade. Merchant banks, or acceptance houses, 'accepted' bills of exchange drawn on them by clients needing credit, with such payment guaranteed. No other centre was equipped for the financing of foreign trade to the same extent as London.

As the name implies, merchant banking has its origins in providing financing for merchants and supporting trade, particularly international business. For example, Barings were in wool and Morgans in cotton. Success in trade gave them the ability to back others, with their name alone often enough to guarantee success. In addition to financing trade by accepting bills of exchange, the merchant banks risked their own money by providing long-term venture capital for the development of industry domestically and overseas. Later, they introduced foreign government and industrial loans on the London capital market, and vast sums were raised in this way to finance railways, mines, plantations, harbours and utilities. This activity took place throughout the Empire, as well as in the Americas and in Europe.

The development of London as a financial centre was largely due to its prosperity as a port at the centre of a thriving Empire. The world's leading freight market, the Baltic Exchange, was based in London. This was not surprising, since Britain had built and operated the world's largest merchant fleet. Shipowners seeking a cargo and shippers and merchants wanting to transport cargoes around the world found it convenient to meet at the Baltic Exchange to do business. The proximity of excellent sources of trade credit, venture capital and a marine insurance market was, and still is, especially expedient.

Insurance itself is a complex and highly specialised trade. Knowledge and reputations acquired in marine insurance were readily adapted to other kinds of insurable risks. There are significant economies of scale in the writing of contracts, in the procurement of business and in the carrying of risks in the insurance business. The prompt payments of the numerous claims following the San Francisco earthquakes and fire consolidated London's reputation in this field.

London's role as the world's leading international insurance centre had a profound influence on its capital markets. Insurance companies receive large sums in premium income, much of it from abroad, which has to be invested. In the case of life assurance, the income is paid in contractual form on a predictable, continuing basis, so investment can be in long-term assets. In the nineteenth century, insurance companies were major holders of railway stock and the better class of foreign issues, but the overwhelming majority of stock exchange securities were held by the personal sector. Since the Second World War insurance, as well as pension funds, have been net acquirers of ordinary shares, because of the dramatic growth in the use of contractual saving by the personal sector.

The Industrial Revolution created the conditions in which there was a role for a new type of financial intermediary, the building society, which would satisfy two needs. First, it provided a safe place for the savings of the new urban workers and secondly, it made funds available for the financing of house purchases, at a time when the demand for housing was acute, especially in the new cities. In contrast to the banks and insurance companies, the building society movement did not commence life in London but rather in the Midlands and the north of England. The building society movement was established at a time when few banking firms existed outside London and when banks generally were primarily concerned with the issuance of notes, rather than providing a depository for excess funds. More recently, when banks did become deposit-taking institutions, they found considerable competition from the building societies, a situation which continues today.

The history of the development of Britain's financial institutions is a long and fascinating one. However, what is important for our purpose is to note the way in which intermediaries have come into being in order to smooth the flow of savings. Shifts in population and the expansion of trade provided the conditions in which specialist intermediaries such as building societies and merchant banks could operate. The proximity of different financial services with a common objective has reaped economies of scale, one example being shipping exchanges, sources of trade credit, and marine insurance to provide for international trade.

Advances in technology have played an important part as well. It is difficult to imagine that the great increases in international investment in the nineteenth century would have taken place on such a large scale if communications had not greatly improved – faster ships, the invention of the telegraph – with the resultant decrease in risks. The massive expansion of retail banking in the latter part of the twentieth century is due to a large extent to the economies of scale and scope made possible by computerisation. Improvements in technology account for the growth of all forms of intermediation since both increased access to information and decreasing costs allow financial institutions to narrow the spread between their borrowing and lending rates and hence become highly competitive.

Rapid changes are taking place at the present time in the financial sector, the most important being the implementation of further technology and deregulation of the financial sector which has prompted innovation in investment techniques and the continual introduction of new financial instruments. As far as financial intermediation is concerned, three developments can be identified as particularly important. These are first, the increase in the flow of funds between the international capital markets and the growth of international trade, along with the subsequently greater use by companies and governments of international credit and capital markets; secondly, the rapidly accelerating concentration and con-glomeration of financial intermediaries and other providers of financial services, illustrated by mergers between banks and leasing companies, between building societies, and between members of the securities industry. And finally, the entry by financial firms into other types of financial activities, for example, banks becoming involved with underwriting, insurance, investment services and real estate business.

13.3 Classification of institutions

There are an enormous range and variety among the financial institutions, and it is impossible to include them all here. But for clarity, institutions can be grouped together in some way, with some excluded altogether. There are a number of possible classification systems, but the one used for the remainder of Part III is based on two considerations which reflect the current organisation within the industry. The first defines the pattern of cash flows to the institution. This is a function of savings arising from contractual payment or in the form of deposits and the second is the regulatory structure, since this determines the source of competition and thus the interaction between the individual firms.

Such a system of classification would have been considerably different in the past, reflecting historical relationships between the corporate and the financial sectors. The early industrialisation in Britain required funds to be directed to the corporate sector, and these were supplied mostly from the banks. However, as the volume of capital increased, along with the separation of ownership from the management and control of the firm, funds from the capital markets in the form of financial securities became a major source of finance.

More recently, the decline in industrial and manufacturing activity in the UK has resulted in a shift of emphasis and the development of new markets, both for funds and financial restructuring. Beginning in the 1980s, the service industry has expanded, accompanied by changes in the underlying structure of the economy. The new markets facilitate the shift in corporate control, as ownership changes are determined by creating fresh alliances through takeovers and mergers. This has placed different demands on the financial institutions. Venture capital and credit markets have emerged as the evaluation of managerial performance within firms is not simply left to the shareholders as existing owners, but is also undertaken by potential managers wishing to make more productive use of the resources of inefficient firms. Competition to provide these services, and deregulation which allows participants from other sectors and other countries to enter the market, have resulted in a considerable restructuring of the financial system. Regulation, domestic and European, has also had considerable influence on the British financial services sector.

Differentiating deposit-taking institutions from the investing intermediaries is a recognition that savings are not the same for all groups in the economy. It is important to distinguish between *contractual* and *non-contractual* forms of savings, in order to understand the growth of non-bank intermediaries in recent years. Contractual saving arising from pension schemes is more usefully regarded as a form of remuneration than as saving. It is unresponsive to changes in economic factors such as interest rates, relative yields on financial securities, or inflation for the simple reason that it is based on standard contracts specifying the deductions to be made from employees' salaries and the contributions required of employers. The only external incentive to contractual saving is tax benefit, and thus it is not surprising that pension contributions grow proportionately with increases in income and wealth.

On the other hand, non-contractual savings are deposits which are much more volatile than pension deductions or insurance premiums, and are generally the excess funds after regular payments have been made. The nature of the cash flows has a major influence on the investment policies of deposit-taking institutions and the investing intermediaries. The deposit-taking banks' and building societies' policies are dominated by the need to be in a position to cover unpredictable outflows of deposits from instant access accounts, whereas the investing institutions can base theirs on predictable inflows and, in aggregate, models of expected outflows. Deposit-taking institutions invest heavily in short-term, money market securities, insurance companies and pension funds in equities and other long-term securities.

The reason for imposing any kind of system to classify a complex group of institutions is to attempt to give some order and form a basis for analysis. All classification schemes have their deficiencies and in this case, it may imply a neat and ordered set of relationships, where in fact there are large areas of overlap which arise because of the underlying nature of financial intermediation and the number of levels involved. Some institutions intermediate directly between surplus and deficit units, that is, savers and borrowers; others occupy a more distant position from one or both of these fundamental sectors. An example of a direct intermediary is a building society which borrows funds, in the form of deposits, from the personal sector and lends them to persons borrowing to finance house purchases. An example of indirect intermediation is to be found in the money markets, where discount houses borrow mainly from banks which have themselves borrowed from the personal sector, using the funds to purchase the short-term securities issued by the government, or the corporate sector. Many of these securities are acquired from other investors rather than from the original issuers. Thus, the deposit-taking institutions consist of direct as well as indirect intermediaries.

However, the imposition of a system of classification such as this helps to identify types of institution by the financial markets in which they conduct their business, and to recognise the regulatory constraints under which they operate.

13.4 Impact of government

Taxation, and the nature of the tax liability affecting different client groups, is a factor influencing the development of intermediaries. As noted in Chapter 1, the system of taxation is not neutral in its impact and the flow of savings has been directed into certain forms of investment at the expense of others. Two significant tax-induced distortions are to be found in the areas of (a) contractual savings schemes for individuals and (b) corporation financing.

The dismantling of the national health service in Great Britain and the encouragement for personal provision for health care and retirement income, have encouraged contractual saving. At the same time, the collapse of the market for rented property has resulted in heavy personal sector investment in owner-occupied housing. Both of these have been assisted by tax incentives, particularly directed at pension funds and life assurance, and now account, in aggregate, for almost the whole of net personal saving in the UK. The funds of building societies, insurance companies and pension funds have been growing very rapidly in consequence. The personal sector has been a net seller of government and company securities in every year since the Second World War. Insurance companies and pension funds have increased their holdings of these assets, to the point where investing institutions now hold about half of all government securities and more than half of the ordinary shares in issue.

The tax rules encourage forms of contractual saving in the following way. Owner-occupied housing is encouraged because interest paid on a proportion of loans for house purchase attracts tax relief, acting as a subsidy to house purchasers, while the enjoyment of occupancy (measured, say, in rent payments saved) and the capital gains on eventual resale escape tax. Investment in insurance policies was until the 1984 Budget encouraged, both by allowing some tax relief on premiums paid and by favourable treatment of the incomes earned by the insurance companies. Savings in the form of pension contributions are exempted from taxation.

In the corporate sector, tax regimes promote certain forms of company financing at the expense of others. The rapid growth of leasing in recent years was attributable in part to the fact that many companies accumulated large tax losses and leasing was the only way they could obtain tax benefits when acquiring plant and machinery. The leasing company was able to set the costs of acquiring the asset, including loan interest charges, against its rental income for tax assessment purposes, whereas the firm wanting to use the equipment had no taxable income against which to offset the equipment costs. The leasing company was therefore able to reduce the total tax bill incurred and to share these tax gains to the mutual benefit of both firms. Subsequent finance acts threaten these arrangements.

Government has influenced the development of intermediaries in other ways as well. The Bank of England's attempt to control the money supply has had the side-effect of causing a switch in deposits away from banks into building societies. The government has also come under extreme pressure to keep interest rates down in order to lower the cost of mortgage financing. Borrowers who have difficulty making monthly payments are offered as much assistance as possible, a system not paralleled by lenders in the non-mortgage market.

Governments have done much to try to ensure the smooth functioning of the financial system. These interventions take many forms, but they can be conveniently divided into two approaches, supervision and regulation. Supervision of the financial institutions has been made available by the Bank of England through the provision of *lender of last resort* facilities to the banks (via the discount houses); and by the launching of *lifeboats*, that is, the transfer of funds from an unsafe institution to a safe one, usually the clearing banks. Regulation is either direct or through self-regulatory organisations (SROs) and will be discussed later on.

Any imposed controls can sometimes damage the ability of institutions to compete, as illustrated by the banks' claim that they face problems in competing with building societies for deposits. An illustration of the advantages enjoyed by the absence of detailed controls is offered by the insurance industry. It has been argued that an important factor in London's success as an international insurance centre is the lack of governmental restrictions on its operations compared to other countries, enabling London insurers to invest funds more or less as they please and to pay claims without delay. A general examination of the structure of regulation encompassing all areas of financial activity is given in Chapter 19.

13.5 Competitive environment

Although it must be acknowledged that the growth and development of our financial institutions owe much to government actions, market factors and the increased level of international capital flows have played a large part as well. London's rise to pre-eminence as a financial centre began in times when the economy was not nearly as complex or dependent on the behaviour of foreign governments, and when taxation amounted to only a small proportion of the nation's income. London's past success had been due to its ability to economise in operations, thereby keeping the spreads between borrowing and lending rates as narrow as possible. There was little competition from other countries or from other institutions within the UK industry.

This is now far from the case. Competition is very intense, particularly among the deposit-taking intermediaries, and evident through advertising in the media and in the presence of a range of institutions in the High Street. Building societies increased their share of the personal deposit market at the expense of the savings banks, mainly, and also the commercial banks. This was initially due to a dichotomy between legislation on banks and that on building societies, although some of these are now closer. The institutions respond to each other by imitating competition with practices such as longer opening hours and Saturday trading. They also take advantage of the nature of financial innovation by updating the portfolio of products they offer.[2]

Apart from their rivalry with the building societies and with each other, the commercial banks face competition from foreign banks. In 1992, there were approximately 500 foreign banks in London, compared with 277 in Paris and 247 in Frankfurt. These foreign banks are overwhelmingly concentrated in London and many of them are principally concerned with foreign currency business. But some of them are very active in wholesale corporate lending and compete vigorously with UK-owned banks in this and other areas of domestic lending. Many banks offer investment management services to pension funds, unit trusts and to wealthy private individuals, and are in strong competition with other financial institutions in this area.

Insurance companies also operate in a competitive environment. Apart from competing among themselves, British insurance companies have to compete against foreign, notably American, rivals as well. Although the American market is larger in value terms than the UK one, a great deal of American business finds its way to London via the reinsurance market, whereby risk is divided up and spread among many firms. The life assurance companies compete not only among themselves but also with other institutions for savings, some of which also receive favourable tax treatment. Competition among life companies is largely concerned with premium rates and the payment of bonuses, which depends on their ability to minimise costs and to improve their long-run investment performance.

As reiterated a number of times already, intermediation incurs costs. The existence of competition cuts intermediation costs, since the most efficient institutions are able to undercut their less efficient rivals and so attract business from them. Regulation can weaken competition among institutions and hence push up the costs of intermediation. The purpose of the change in the method of monetary control introduced in 1971, known as competition and credit control, was to encourage competition among institutions by abandoning quantitative controls on credit and interest rates, and the policy was a success in this respect. Restrictive agreements also restrain competition and these have been largely eliminated.

13.6 Summary

In this chapter we have briefly recounted the development of the UK financial system. Institutions that exist today are still subject to market pressures and are very responsive to the economic environment. Taxation and government policy are shown to have played a major role in shaping the present structure of financial institutions. We concluded the chapter by reference to our classification of the types of institution and the structure of the sector in terms of domestic and foreign participants.

Notes

1. On one occasion, Charles I commandeered the bullion deposited by London merchants for safe custody in the Mint and released it only on receiving payment of £40,000 ransom!
2. The nature of financial innovation means that products and services are not patentable. Thus copying other firms' new inventions is extremely low-cost and the innovators cannot protect themselves from this.

Further reading

Buckle, M. and J. L. Thompson (1992), *The United Kingdom Financial System in Transition: Theory and practice*, Manchester University Press. Chapter 2 gives a fuller account of the development of the financial sector.

Cairncross, C. K. (1953), *Home and Foreign Investment, 1870–1913*, Cambridge University Press. A scholarly account of Britain's role in financing overseas development.

Richards, R. D. (1965), *The Early History of Banking in England*, Frank Cass & Co. This provides a fascinating explanation of the development of banking from pre-Tudor times through to the early nineteenth century.

Questions

13.1 Using a transaction cost framework, explain the rise of London as a financial centre in the nineteenth century.

13.2 Outline some of the ways in which the tax system affects savings and investment decisions in the economy.

13.3 Outline the major ways in which financial institutions are affecting the workings of financial markets. In what ways do intermediaries (a) encourage and (b) discourage savings and the use of savings?

CHAPTER 14

The banking sector

14.1 Introduction

This chapter considers the functions and operations of the institutions which make up the British banking sector. These include retail and wholesale banks and savings banks, which all take deposits, and discount houses which do not. We will consider the differences in their portfolio of activities and the diverse roles they play within the sector.

There are a number of broad categories of banks in the UK: the clearing banks, the savings banks, a group covered by the British Merchant Banking and Securities Houses Association, and those authorised institutions under the 1987 Banking Act which include all other banks, divided into British and non-British. This latter group includes the foreign subsidiaries of overseas banks, many of which may actually be retail banks in their home country.

Historically in the UK, there was a clear distinction between retail and wholesale institutions but this is becoming increasingly blurred. For our purposes, there is some advantage to considering them separately, since the strategy and risk management of a retail bank differ from the wholesale institutions being largely determined by the retail banks' clearing activities. The retail sector, therefore, comprises the clearing and savings banks, while wholesale business is generally the speciality of the remaining institutions. Therefore while in total they make up the banking sector, they can more accurately be described as indirect financing intermediaries.

There are approximately 500 authorised banks in the UK, although more than half of these are branches or subsidiaries of foreign banks. Since the deregulation in the UK, many more foreign banks are operating in London, a situation made attractive by European Community Banking Directives, noted in Chapter 5. Table 14.1 illustrates the relative size of the deposits in the different categories of banks. One important disparity to note is the proportion of deposits (liabilities) which are short-term sight deposits, compared with longer term time deposits.

The Bank of England recognises a bank, as set down by the 1979 Banking Act,

Table 14.1 Sterling and foreign currency deposits for banks in the UK (£m)

	Sterling		Foreign	
	Total	Sight deposits as % of total	Total	Share of foreign to sterling deposits
UK retail banks	304,750	46%	68,425	23%
UK merchant banks	34,837	20%	16,787	48%
Other British banks	39,025	8%	8,582	22%
American banks	18,656	22%	98,281	527%
Japanese banks	35,478	5%	205,144	578%
Other foreign banks	99,710	12%	278,738	280%
Discount houses	16,250	93%*	579	4%

*Percent of which call or overnight.

Note: End of March 1991.

Source: Bank of England Quarterly Bulletin, November 1992.

as an authorised institution which meets specific criteria including a capitalisation of at least £5 million. Another criterion is that they have an extensive branch network, and even though telephone banking is now established, these are subsidiaries of branch-based banks. In 1990, the Bank characterised twenty-one institutions as retail banks. In this group are the four clearing banks based in London, that is, Barclays, Lloyds, Midland and National Westminster, plus the Abbey National and the Trustee Savings Bank as well as the Scottish and Irish banks, the Bank of Scotland, the Clydesdale, the Royal Bank of Scotland, the Bank of Ireland, Northern Bank and Ulster Bank.

It is not possible to distinguish easily between the retail and wholesale sectors as the retail banks are heavily involved in wholesale business, with surpluses of funds arising from their retail operations commonly being placed in the wholesale market. This difficulty has resulted in a change in reporting format by the Bank of England, and from January 1993, the Bank reports the banking sector statistics in aggregate, that is, all the banks within the United Kingdom including the banking department of the Bank and UK branches of European authorised institutions.

A number of the clearing banks have imposed a corporate structure which separates their business into divisions reflecting their client base. Thus in most cases, there is a personal banking division, a strategic business unit dedicated to small and medium-sized firms and a purely wholesale department. In addition, some have an international section, whereas others transfer foreign business to specialist subsidiaries. Those institutions which cover all areas of banking activity are known as universal banks, and in reality, they are financial conglomerates.

14.2 Retail and clearing banks

Retail banks, or the retail division of universal banks, fulfil all the functions of financial intermediaries defined in Part I, that is, they act as brokers in bringing together borrowers and lenders, and they repackage funds from one group to match the needs of the other.

A subset of the retail banks also play an important role in providing the mechanism for the smooth processing of transactions between institutions, by clearing cheques written on any UK institution within the system. One of the costs of providing this payments service is the restrictions it imposes on bank portfolio decisions, since banks have to maintain a high proportion of funds in liquid assets if the payments system is to work without disruption.

This group have retail and commercial business divisions, with many branches throughout the UK and some overseas. Their clearing status is granted by the Bank of England, and they undertake to clear, or process, cheques for those institutions in the banking sector which do not have clearing provision.

The UK clearing banks are among the largest in the world in terms of market capitalisation, which is the value of share capital traded in the markets. On a domestic level they are largely measured in terms of assets on deposit, as shown in Table 14.2. While they are now multi-product institutions, they continue the traditional banking activities of taking deposits from savers, making loans to investors and providing a payment mechanism.

Within the retail banking category, most of the following products and services are offered to personal customers: savings and current accounts, mortgages and other loans, administration of estates, private trusts, investment services, unit trusts, life assurance, insurance broking, credit cards, hire purchase and consumer credit, personal advisory and agency services, foreign exchange and traveller's cheques.

In the commercial banking area, retail banks provide most of the services offered by the merchant banks, as well as their traditional lending activity, often with specialist divisions dealing with small businesses, the medium-sized corporate client or specific industrial sectors where they have built up a particular expertise. Recent acquisitions have taken the banks still further from their traditional business activities, illustrated by their move into ownership of travel agencies, life assurance brokerage firms, estate agencies and leasing companies. Also the 1986 reforms in the securities industry have allowed the banks to participate in securities trading, in most instances entering these markets by merging with or acquiring existing firms.

The savings banks are part of the retail banking sector and traditionally these institutions invested heavily in public sector securities, partly for historical reasons. The Trustee Savings Banks (TSBs) were originally sixteen unincorporated societies defined by geographical region, whose principal function was to encourage thrift, but which developed into an institution providing a full range of banking services to the personal sector. Having reached the point where they were

Table 14.2 UK clearing banks, 1993

Bank	Asset value (£)	Market capitalisation (£)
Barclays	138,108,000,000	8,769,000,000
National Westminster	122,569,000,000	7,844,000,000
Midland	59,408,000,000	13,521,000,000
Abbey National	57,405,000,000	6,292,000,000
Lloyds	51,306,000,000	7,478,000,000
Royal Bank of Scotland	32,165,600,000	3,438,000,000
Trustee Savings Bank	25,138,000,000	3,501,000,000
Standard Chartered	23,407,000,000	2,697,000,000
Bank of Scotland	22,095,200,000	2,223,000,000

Source: Bankers Almanac and *Financial Times*, January 1994.

Table 14.3 Summary balance sheet of banks in the UK (£m), May 1994

Liabilities		Assets	
Sterling deposits	545,605	Sterling assets:	633,642
Other currency deposits	807,532	Notes and coin	
Other liabilities	134,977	Balance with the Bank of England	
(Eligible liabilities:	426,164)	Market loans	
		Bills	
		Advances	
		Investments	
		Other currency assets:	854,472
		Market loans	
		Bills	
		Investment	
TOTAL	1,488,114	TOTAL	1,488,114

Source: Bank of England Quarterly Bulletin, Table 3, August 1994.

fully participating in the retail and wholesale markets, they acquired public company status, being privatised in 1986, but with the funds raised kept in-house rather than by the government as the other privatisations of the time.

The balance sheet information which follows is for banks in the UK. As noted above, the data available do not allow us to separate retail from wholesale activity. Table 14.3 shows the proportion of sterling currency business from that done in other currencies, both in borrowing and lending.

More detail about the composition of borrowing and lending is shown in Table 14.4. As can be seen from this table, the vast majority of the assets are in the form of loans to the private sector, most in sterling but some in other currencies. Also prominent is the non-sterling lending to the overseas sector, which accounts for the eurocurrency business discussed in Chapter 12. The domestic loans are not necessarily very liquid, although the individual banks' portfolios will be made up of debt with varying maturity. Other long-term securities are equity and debt, government and corporate, in which the bank invests on its own account.

Table 14.3 concentrates on deposits and loans, but on individual banks' balance sheet other items are also included. For example, there are values for the physical assets, property and capital equipment and other marketable securities. These can be quite extensive for retail banks with a wide-ranging branch network, and like the financial investments they are subject to changes in market prices.

Details of funds held show the most highly liquid assets are cash and notes, as well as funds invested in the money markets. These are either inter-bank loans or overnight loans to discount-houses. This is an important use of bank funds, and maintains a balance between the dealings of the banking system as a whole and the non-bank institutions. Finally, there is a small amount of cash held on behalf of each bank by the Bank of England, not as part of a supervisory reserve requirement, but simply a tax to finance certain activities of the Bank.

Liabilities are largely deposits from the public which are a combination of sight deposits or time deposits. They also include certificates of deposit, which are long-term deposits, of a minimum amount and with a fixed maturity date; some funds which are in transmission or still in the clearing system; and finally, there are some deposits in other currencies.

The structure of the balance sheet has to ensure that withdrawals can be met by sufficient funds. The actual composition of the portfolio of assets and liabilities partly reflects managerial judgements about the demand for liquid funds, but is also dependent on the requirements of the Bank of England. Minimum capital adequacy provisions are governed by international agreement, called the Basle Accord. This sets the ratio of cash reserves to assets a bank may hold. We will return to this issue later in the chapter.

In their role as intermediaries, retail banks provide a safe deposit for savers' funds and repackage those funds to households and firms that wish to borrow. But there are risks to the banks' solvency associated with these activities, which can be divided into liquidity risk and asset risk.

Liquidity risk arises when withdrawals from current accounts, and to some extent, savings accounts cannot be matched with cash or short-term assets. As we discussed in Part 1, one of the aspects of intermediation was maturity transformation, but this exposes the bank to liquidity risk. On the liabilities side of the balance sheet there is some degree of uncertainty about outflows of cash, even though managers can predict certain periods of higher cash demand, such as at Christmas, or when there is a large public share offering.

On the liabilities side, overdrafts are often the result of an unforeseen event. Risk of this kind is lessened by the bank having a large number of small accounts rather than fewer large ones. Then, in aggregate, cash inflows and outflows will be fairly balanced, and the uncertainty is minimised.

Table 14.4 Summary portfolios of banks in the UK (£m), 1987–93

Assets

	Total	Lending to public sector					Lending to private sector				Lending to overseas sector	
		Sterling				Other currencies	Sterling		Other currencies		Sterling	Other currencies
		Total		Central government	Other		Not seasonally adjusted	Seasonally adjusted	Not seasonally adjusted	Seasonally adjusted		
		Not seasonally adjusted	Seasonally adjusted									
	AEAA	AEBP	AEBS	AEBV	AEBY	AECB	AECE	AECH	AECK	AECN	AECP	AECS
1987	728,477	15,984	15,051	11,792	4,192	1,037	204,006	204,977	46,829	47,919	37,172	423,449
1988	816,792	14,711	13,884	10,753	3,958	442	260,866	261,693	56,733	57,246	41,466	442,574
1989	1,014,311	14,735	14,036	11,901	2,834	449	352,810	353,521	80,252	80,030	44,796	521,269
1990	1,031,239	14,651	14,071	12,133	2,518	447	398,387	398,968	72,626	71,900	47,947	497,181
1991	999,313	14,480	14,054	12,076	2,404	441	405,697	406,303	62,055	61,138	41,930	474,710
1992	1,143,029	14,544	14,147	11,009	3,535	5,437	407,126	407,769	68,988	68,161	50,906	596,028
1993	1,198,818	17,898	17,493	12,930	4,968	5,904	416,305	416,865	76,579	75,826	61,577	£20,555

Amounts outstanding at end of period

Liabilities

	Total	Domestic deposits									Overseas sector deposits		Non-deposit liabilities (net)
		Total		Public sector			Private sector				Sterling	Other currencies	
				Sterling		Other currencies	Sterling		Other currencies				
		Not seasonally adjusted	Seasonally adjusted	Not seasonally adjusted	Seasonally adjusted		Not seasonally adjusted	Seasonally adjusted	Not seasonally adjusted	Seasonally adjusted			
	AEAA	AEAD	AEAG	AEAJ	AEAM	AEAP	AEAS	AEAV	AGAK	AEBB	AEBD	AEBG	AEEJ
1987	728,477	211,478	211,088	7,786	7,456	304	171,869	172,289	31,519	31,060	48,218	425,456	43,325
1988	816,792	253,254	252,878	10,097	9,720	191	207,978	208,286	34,988	34,686	61,939	448,771	52,828
1989	1,014,311	337,427	337,413	9,967	9,573	193	278,804	279,066	48,463	48,575	73,406	534,756	68,721
1990	1,031,239	372,317	372,899	8,603	8,243	224	310,457	310,882	53,033	53,547	85,835	502,881	70,206
1991	999,313	365,400	366,509	6,041	5,741	237	321,712	322,419	37,410	38,117	74,926	487,183	71,805
1992	1,143,029	385,428	386,896	6,393	6,090	391	326,404	327,490	52,240	52,941	76,004	602,882	78,714
1993	1,198,818	411,840	413,262	7,906	7,587	346	345,957	347,029	57,631	58,316	76,756	625,435	84,787

Amount outstanding at end of period

Source: Financial Statistics, Table 4.2, CSO, 1994.

The difficulties in managing cash flows for a bank are not dissimilar to those for any firm with working capital requirements. However, banks do have the advantage of access to the inter-bank markets for short-term borrowing and lending quickly and at attractive rates. As a result retail banks have concentrated on managing their liabilities rather than their assets to maintain their liquidity. It should be noted that this does eliminate the need for banks to have reserves, but enables them to reduce their liquidity risk.

Asset risk is due to either default on loans by borrowers, or a fall in the price of marketable securities or other assets. Retail banks have earned a considerable reputation for credit assessment, and all applicants undergo strict credit checks before a loan is granted. Banks also attempt to reduce their risk by diversification, spreading their total risk exposure across a portfolio of individuals, businesses, industries and even countries. Another safeguard is the price of credit, and borrowers with a high risk of default tend to pay higher rates for their loans than those perceived as more secure.

Marketable securities, by definition, are exchanged in the market, and are priced according to supply and demand. Equity is selected on the basis of past profitability, while the value of government bonds is determined by the interest rate. The constituents of the bank's portfolio are taken into consideration by the Bank of England when determining the bank's solvency.

This independent evaluation of the risk profile of individual banks is important, since although the Basle Accord sets minimum capital reserve rates, UK banks are now assessed individually by the Bank of England and varying capital ratios are set. Even so, managers may choose to be still more cautious. There are considerable opportunity costs associated with excess capital, but a shortfall will lead to decreased spreads and diminished profits.

Finally, we should discuss the payments function of the retail banks, although they no longer are exclusive providers of this service. A payments system is simply a mechanism for keeping a record of transfers of ownership of assets which occurs in the settlement of debts incurred. This involves providing a medium of exchange following the acquisition of goods, a method of payment and a bridge between the time of purchase and the time of payment.

Banks provide all of these services, in the past by using cash and then cheques, and increasingly through other means as technology has made more choices available. Modern payment systems use credit cards, which are a medium of exchange allowing the purchase of goods. A cheque or a direct debit allows payment at an agreed date in the future, often several weeks after the purchaser has use of the goods, and with the ability to earn interest on the funds in the meantime. At the operations end of banking, electronic funds transfer systems allow the replacement of written cheques by processing accounting transfers electronically.

The increased blurring of retail and wholesale banking allows added value to the provision of a payments system. Excess funds in bank accounts may be too small for individuals to use, but in aggregate the intermediary can repackage them and lend them to investors. Thus intermediation can be a by-product of the payments service, and the profits from the intermediation contribute to the costs of the technology required to process transactions. Customer charges for account-related services are now very low or zero, funded by the banks' use of their residual funds.

The profitability of banks is through margins, that is, the spread between borrowing and lending rates. They also undertake investment of their own, but as discussed in an earlier chapter, the risk associated with this is undertaken with the knowledge that the Bank of England will set reserve requirements accordingly. Finally, they make further profits from fees and commissions from advice services, such as tax consulting, wills'and testaments, small business advisory, credit card provision and investment and brokerage services. Traditionally, the wholesale banks specialise in this area of business, particularly with corporate clients, and these will be addressed in the next section.

14.3 Wholesale banks

Sometimes called secondary banks, these are intermediaries dealing mainly in sizeable deposits; minimum sums involved tend to be from £250,000 upwards and with a smaller number of depositors and borrowers than the retail institutions. They also undertake inter-bank lending via the parallel money markets on a large scale. As mentioned in the introduction to this chapter, many retail banks are involved in the wholesale markets, but the reverse is not true. The banks in this sector do not have branch networks, although they do have a presence in many international locations.

Wholesale banks are sometimes divided into groups, such as the British merchant banks, other British banks, American banks, Japanese banks and other overseas banks, although these divisions are largely for data-reporting purposes, and there are many similarities between them. In practice, the name *investment bank* is used to cover a range of institutions undertaking merchant banking activities.

Merchant/investment banks

The British merchant banks, or acceptance houses, as they were known when first created, originated in the nineteenth century. They operated by first establishing a good name and reputation which they could then use to back bills of exchange for merchants engaged in international trade. Their role was to provide guarantees of payment at a time when delivery dates and capital transfers were much more lengthy and uncertain procedures than they are now. This business still continues, but they have extended their range of activities to advising on, arranging, placing and underwriting new capital issues, acting as intermediary between companies involved in mergers and acquisitions and acting as consultants with expertise in investments and portfolio management. This group are members of the British Merchant Bankers and Securities Houses Association (formally the London Accepting Houses Committee), and include institutions such as Morgan Grenfell, Schroders and Kleinwort Benson. Many of the clearing banks have merchant bank subsidiaries.

Although the British merchant banks are included under the generic label of investment banks, they are more likely to become involved in traditional accepting-house activities than other investment banks. This may include *bridge financing* where the bank is willing to finance part of a large transaction temporarily until it can be financed in the securities market, or perhaps taking an equity position with a company during a restructuring. This implies the acceptance of risk on the behalf of a client, very much reminiscent of the merchant banks' original role in the support of international trading companies. This deal-making culture may reflect a difference in approach which ensures that the overlap between the institutions will never be eradicated.

The balance sheet for a wholesale bank is composed of the same items as that of the retail banks, but with considerable differences in the relative shares of each item. Table 14.1 above shows two examples of these differences, the ratio of sight to time deposits, and particularly, the proportion of sterling to non-sterling deposits. Foreign currency business represents a large item on the balance sheet of banks in this segment of the industry.

International banks

The overseas banks in London undertake some sterling business, but operate largely in foreign currencies. The number of these institutions increased quickly following the relaxation of exchange controls in the UK in 1958. The largest banks are Japanese and American, although many countries are now represented in London. Rather like the early British banks overseas, they were initially established to provide services for their own nationals with trading activity in London, sometimes called correspondence banking, but now their main business is in the eurocurrency markets. As a result, many more foreign banks are located in London, and the eurocurrency markets have grown considerably, with a large share undertaken in eurodollars.

Eurocurrency relates to transactions in a currency other than that of the host country. Therefore, a bank located in London taking a deposit in dollars is eurocurrency, as is sterling deposited in a bank in Paris. Thus there is a separation of market and currency. This market grew largely as a result of regulatory advantages in London compared with the rest of the world, in particular the US since the majority of the business is in eurodollars, and also because of cost advantages of the wholesale banking sector.

Off balance sheet business is a major aspect of wholesale and international banking activity. This aspect of the business spreads income from purely financial intermediation to securities underwriting, arranging swaps customised to meet customers' specific requirements. Off balance sheet instruments are subject to risk valuation and this is included in the capital ratio levels set by the Bank of England. This risk was illustrated by the losses from local government swaps in which the banks have not considered the special legal status of the local authorities.

Discount houses

Another group in this sector are the discount houses. These are recognised banks under the 1979 Banking Act, but their specialised role is to ensure the smooth functioning of the secondary money markets, in particular, the market for Treasury bills. As such, they provide liquidity to the banking system as a whole, positioned between the monetary sector and the Bank of England. Their business is overwhelmingly in sterling, with very short-term liabilities to allow them to fulfil their role of providing liquidity for the retail banking sector. Their exposure to immediate recall of their liabilities is acceptable as the Bank assists them in times of especially high demand for funds. The activities of these banks are discussed in Chapter 11.

14.4 Summary

The banking sector in the UK is a large and important part of the financial sector. Restructuring of domestic banks, and entry by foreign banks, has changed the industry dramatically. While continuing to provide savings and investment facilities for retail customers, the clearing banks supply a payment system. The retail and wholesale activities are frequently carried out in parallel, although some specialist institutions still exist performing the merchant banking role.

Further reading

Gardener, E. and P. Molyneux (1990), *Changes in West European Banking*, Unwin Hyman.
Kaufman, G. (1992), *Banking Structures in Major Countries*, Kluwer Academic Publishers.
Lewis, M. K. and K. T. Davis (1987), *Domestic and International Banking*, Philip Allan.
Scott-Quinn, B. (1990), *Investment Banking: Theory and practice*, Euromoney Books.
    Excellent book on wholesale banking, with an international focus.
Struthers, J. and H. Speight (1986), *Money: Institutions, theory and policy*, Longman.

Questions

14.1 Explain what is meant by the term *deposit-taking*. What kind of markets for deposits exists and in what respects do they differ?

14.2 In what respects are the various kinds of deposit-taking institutions similar to and different from other kinds of businesses?

14.3 What is meant by the term *creditworthiness* in a banking context? In what ways can the lender try to minimise his or her risk?

14.4 Outline the profile of:
   (a) Retail banking clients
   (b) Wholesale banking clients.

14.5 List some of the innovations in products and services offered by retail banks during the 1990s.

CHAPTER 15

Non-bank deposit-taking institutions

15.1 Introduction

Deposit-taking institutions of the kind described in this chapter provide low-risk investment opportunities. They provide a similar service to retail banks, that is, taking deposits from individuals and households and making loans, largely to individuals and households. By far the largest group are the building societies. This chapter will begin by concentrating on the building societies, and also the reasons why some are seeking to become banks. We then discuss other savings institutions practising largely in the retail sector.

15.2 Building societies

The most important of the non-bank deposit-taking institutions are undoubtedly the building societies. The building societies are friendly societies and are owned by all account holders, known as shareholders, some of whom are borrowers, some lenders and some both. The societies developed at the end of the eighteenth century with the primary objectives of encouraging thrift and home-ownership, although more formal establishment was in 1836 with the first Building Society Act. Stated simply, the accumulated small savings of depositors are used to grant loans to individuals for house purchase, loans which are repaid steadily out of income.

Building society shareholders can be thought of as investing in a portfolio of property mortgages with the liquidity of their own stake effectively guaranteed. By maintaining a well-diversified portfolio of mortgage investments, a building society has a predictable and even flow of cash receipts with which to repay members when required. Furthermore, by charging borrowers a variable rate of interest a building society can increase its borrowing rate if necessary to stem any continued draining away of deposits. Through borrowing very short and lending very long, building societies are able to guarantee liquidity without holding a big proportion of funds in low-earning short-term assets.

The building society movement as a whole has grown very rapidly, especially in an environment such as that in the UK where private ownership of housing is so well established. From 1989 to 1993, total assets in the sector rose from £189.9 billion to £281.5 billion, and building societies now account for a greater proportion of total liquid assets of the personal sector than the banks. This rapid growth has been achieved partly by providing incentives for those wishing to borrow from them, such as low-start mortgages, and general help with house purchases.

The societies are major rivals of the commercial banks and the savings banks in the retail deposit market, accounting for over half of the personal deposit market. The societies are by far the largest providers of mortgage finance in the UK, although in recent years the commercial banks have moved into this field and are now providing the societies with stiff competition. They also compete with the retail banks in terms of their products, offering similar current accounts with cheque books, direct debit schemes and a variety of time deposit accounts. They open for longer and more convenient hours than the banks which are their closest competitors and have often higher-quality technology and funds transfer systems due to their later entry into automatic telling.

The building society sector has experienced a good deal of rationalisation of operations through mergers, the number of societies having fallen from over two thousand at the turn of the century to less than one hundred now. The movement's mortgage assets increased a thousandfold in monetary value during this period. The major increase in concentration has come through mergers among the medium-sized societies, and although the number of societies has fallen, the number of branches has remained stable.

The five largest societies account for over half of the movement's total assets. Lending by building societies to house-buyers now exceeds lending by the banks to the corporate sector, and the societies' business is still firmly in the retail rather than wholesale sector, although this is slowly changing (see Table 15.1). The emphasis on the personal sector is partly a result of their origins, but is also due to the way building society interest is taxed at source, discouraging many corporate investors. Aggregate balance sheet data for the building society sector are shown in Table 15.2. It is clear that the majority of the societies' assets are in mortgages, mostly to individuals and households.

There are still differences in the investment policies of banks compared with building societies, partly reflected in the spread between their borrowing and lending rates. Building societies hold less liquid assets than the retail banks since most of their assets are in loans to house-buyers, although they are keen competitors for funds in the retail deposit market. The reasons for the differences in asset structure are worth exploring.

We can view the managers of both banks and building societies as facing an asset composition and related financing problem. The objective of each is to select a portfolio of assets which offers the prospect of highest returns to savers and lower cost to borrowers, subject to meeting risk and other constraints. The

Table 15.1 Wholesale and retail business in UK building societies (£m)

	Wholesale	Retail	Other	Total	No mortgages
1989	27,728	142,629	19,497	189,854	1,729,000
1990	37,425	160,842	23,707	221,974	1,496,000
1991	43,803	178,934	25,653	248,390	1,380,000
1992	47,548	190,831	28,347	266,726	1,119,000
1993	50,277	201,057	30,165	281,499	1,126,000

Source: Financial Statistics, Table 4.3, CSO, 1994.

Table 15.2 Building society sector balance sheet (£m), 1993

Assets		Liabilities	
Mortgages	229,638	Retail shares and deposits	201,057
		Interest accrued	5,432
Cash and bank balances	31,525	Wholesale liabilities	50,277
Investments:		Other liabilities	24,733
Local authority	1,172		
British government	5,136		
Other	14,028		
TOTAL	281,499	TOTAL	281,499

Note: Other assets are: Bank bills, building society CDs, sterling Treasury bills, tax instruments, transit and suspense items and miscellaneous assets.
Source: Financial Statistics, Table 4.3, CSO, 1994.

manager has in mind a target level of liquid assets determined by prudential controls and experience with the kinds of borrowing and lending activities in which the bank or society specialises. As shown in Table 15.2, building societies are heavily invested in mortgages, over 80% of their assets being of this form. The next largest asset is their investment in short-term and miscellaneous assets, about 14% of which are in government securities. Thus the building society shareholders can be thought of as investing in a portfolio of property mortgages with the liquidity of their own stake effectively guaranteed.

The regulation of building societies is under the control of the Building Societies Commission. This includes levels of liquidity, reserves and general standards of conduct. There are also legal restrictions of the ownership of building societies, and societies' ownership of other financial institutions and on their permitted activities. Thus the role of the Commission is similar to that of the Bank of England's prudential and supervisory responsibilities concerning banks.

The structure of the industry has drastically changed in the last two decades, the small mutual society having been replaced by huge societies operating nationwide branch networks, while still maintaining their mutual status. The legal position of building societies differs from that of other financial institutions, banks in particular, and although there has been considerable debate about a number of societies changing their status, only the Abbey National Building Society has to date converted to a clearing bank, Abbey National plc.

The move into the wholesale sector is already taking place, and offering more traditionally non-retail products and services means societies can continue trading free of many of the restrictions under which banks operate, while they are themselves limited in some areas, most crucially, the amount of funds that they can raise from the wholesale money markets, and they are denied access to certain funding instruments. The historical difference between banks and building societies results in a general misunderstanding of societies in the international money markets, such that even if the restrictions are removed, they will not be readily understood by the financial community at large.

15.3 National Savings Bank

The National Savings Bank (NSB) is an institution similar to the Trustee Savings Bank before privatisation, but is outside the banking system. It is a public institution which operates through the Post Office branch network, and is used for collecting personal savings, much of which goes towards financing public sector borrowing. It provides demand and time deposit accounts and a variety of other financial products. Interest earned on deposit has always been paid tax free, although tax is liable, and subsequently rates of interest have been lower than other deposit-taking institutions.[1]

There are no assets to match liabilities, and thus no liquidity or capital adequacy regulations to comply with. National Savings are purely a safe depository. They neither make loans nor extend overdrafts, but do facilitate the sale of government debt and are therefore risk-free intermediaries, supported by Treasury guarantees. This is the part of public sector borrowing which is financed by non-marketable debt.

Table 15.3 shows the range of business undertaken by National Savings. Deposits in savings accounts are transferred to the National Debt Commissioners,

Table 15.3 National Savings instruments: selected instruments (£m), 1993

National Savings certificates:	
Index-linked	
Index-linked or bonus	1,204
Principal	6,765
Fixed interest	
Interest	1,994
Principal	7,782
Premium savings bonds	3,038
Capital bonds	2,058
Children's bonus bonds	340
Investment account	9,180
Income bonds	10,565
Other securities, including those no longer on sale	4,876
TOTAL – Administered by National Savings	47,802

Source: Financial Statistics, Table 1.2, CSO, 1994.

and invested in government securities. For statistical reasons, National Savings Bank accounts are considered in the national financial accounts as part of central government, and deposits with these accounts are treated as directly financing the central government borrowing requirement. At the end of 1993, £46,351 million of National Savings contributed to funding the PSBR.

Finally, we should mention the Post Office Giro, which is not a deposit-taking institution, but a means of making payments. All Giro accounts are held in a central office, which became part of the London Clearing Bankers House in 1981. It has been used increasingly as government makes payments to individuals who do not have bank accounts, although the UK experience of this method of distribution is low compared with other European countries where Giro accounts are much more popular.

15.4 Finance houses

There are a large number of finance houses, which although now designated as banks, interact between the retail and wholesale markets, providing loans to both the personal and commercial sectors. These are often subsidiaries of UK or foreign banks although sometimes they are independent institutions. Their main activity is the provision of instalment loans, but they also undertake *leasing* and *factoring*:

Leasing requires the finance house to purchase physical assets which are then leased for an agreed period to a firm, in return for rents on those assets. At the end of the term, the asset is retained by the firm or returned to the finance house, depending on the contract. This method is used extensively by small and medium-sized businesses, and will be discussed further in Chapter 17.

Factoring is the purchase of a loan by the finance house, priced according to the risk of default of the debtor company. Finance houses obtain their own funds from banks, and thus act as intermediaries undertaking risk transformation to a greater extent than retail banks would be prepared to do. Their liabilities are low-risk bank funds while their assets are high-risk consumer credit.

Finance houses traditionally specialised in instalment lending, that is, hire purchase financing to consumers and to business firms to finance the purchase of durable assets. Now they provide personal loans and offer leasing, factoring, stocking loans and block discounting to the commercial and industrial sector.[2] The method by which hire purchase finance is made available is not by direct contact between the borrower and the finance house, as is the case with other financial institutions, but between the buyer and the retailer.

The advantage of this arrangement is that it (a) allows the retailer to use the financing dimension as part of his or her marketing strategy, and (b) reduces search costs for the borrower/customer. Against these savings and economies have to be set the problems of high default rates brought about by the enthusiasm of the retailers to make a sale, often to customers whose credit rating is too low for them to obtain finance from any other source. The interest rates charged for hire purchase are correspondingly high.

There is considerable competition for the finance houses, from the banks and building societies for the individual household and small business sectors, and from industry financing for the larger commercial and industrial sectors. As shown in Table 15.4, their assets are largely made up of credit, particularly to the personal sector, while liabilities are short- and long-term borrowings with some commercial bills. They generally borrow from banks, but are also able to take advantage of low-cost funds in the wholesale money markets. Most of their loans are made on fixed rate terms, and therefore they can suffer if the interest rate changes, and along with it, the cost of their short-term funds. Finance houses are regulated by the Consumer Credit Act of 1974 and the Director of Fair Trading.

The finance houses have been included in this section because their lending activities are highly specialised. It should be noted however that many of the finance houses are subsidiaries of banks, and as such their liabilities are included in the official money supply statistics.

15.5 Summary

This chapter has shown that building societies offer similar services to banks, particularly in the retail sector, but are still predominantly providers of mortgages.

Table 15.4 Finance houses and non-bank credit institutions

Assets		Liabilities	
Cash and balances with banks	99	Commercial bills	737
Certificates of deposit	0	Loans from banks	
Other current assets	869	Short-term	4,154
		Long-term	2,219
Loans and advances		Other UK	231
Finance leases	1,322	Overseas	44
UK industrial and commercial	1,753	Non-bank	51
Personal sector	6,296		
Other financial	54	Other current liabilities	467
Other physical	156	Capital issues	1,457
		Reserves	1,189
TOTAL	10,549	TOTAL	10,549

Source: Financial Statistics, Table 5.2, CSO, 1994.

The National Savings Department offers a number of financial instruments for savers, and contributes considerable funds to finance the PSBR. Other institutions also offer borrowing arrangements to industry, especially to small and medium-sized firms, and frequently on a leasing arrangement.

Notes

1. Rates are notoriously sticky: for example, the interest on a savings account was 3.5% from 1861 to 1970!
2. These facilities are either discussed in Chapter 17 or defined in the glossary.

Further reading

Drake, L. M. (1989), *The Building Society Industry in Transition*, Macmillan.

Llewellyn, D. (1992), 'Competition, diversification, and structural change in the British financial system', Chapter 9 in G. Kaufman (ed.), *Banking Structures in Major Countries*, Kluwer Academic Publishers.

McKillop, D., Ferguson, C. and J. Glass (1993), *Building Societies: Structure, performance and change*, Graham & Trotman.

Questions

15.1 What is a building society? Explain why they have been so successful in attracting deposits from the personal sector.

15.2 In what ways do banks and building societies differ? What are the advantages and disadvantages of each?

15.3 Describe some of the main sources of finance available to companies.

CHAPTER 16

Insurance, pension funds and investment institutions

16.1 Introduction

This chapter is primarily concerned with insurance and pensions. The insurance companies and pension funds are important for two reasons. First, they provide financial security, whether this is to claim funds following damage or an accident, or as a provision for income in the future. But secondly, they have an enormous impact on patterns of investment in the securities markets because of the volume of funds at their disposal. We shall concentrate more on their primary activities in this chapter, although their market presence will be discussed later.

The explanations of some of the products offered in the field of insurance and pensions are best understood by analysing the products' characteristics in financial terms. We have covered only the simpler policies and other services here, but have provided a more technical discussion of the actuarial aspects in the appendix.

16.2 Insurance

Insurance is designed to protect a policyholder against the financial loss arising from some specified event. One way to categorise insurance is by the type of event being insured against, examples of which are personal accident, fire or theft. Another important division is between long-term or general insurance. This distinction is made for a number of reasons but follows directly from legal constraints which require long-term and short-term insurance business to be separated, as is defined by the 1982 Insurance Companies Act. In practice, this is not always simple since it has to accommodate those companies which have traditionally carried out both long-term and general insurance business.

The category of business is important, as it has considerable effect on the way in which cash flows in to the company, and also in the way risk is dealt with. For example, general insurance involves a single payment which may or may not be repeated in subsequent years, but long-term policies are contractual, and ensure a payment annually for many years. However, although there is a distinction between general (short-term) and life (long-term) insurance, there are two common features. One of these is that both types of insurance involve risk reduction through the aggregation of independent events, and the other is that all insurance provides against financial loss.

Life insurance

Life insurance is a long-term contract offering cover against death, injury or incapacity. It is to ensure some financial support for dependants in the event of death or of loss of earnings following injury. However, life insurance policies are also designed to provide an investment in the form of capital security after a specified term. These are generally known as assurance, and are similar to pensions.

Payments to life assurance are contractual and therefore any decision made regarding the premiums may affect the profitability of the company for many years in the future. In reacting to this problem, companies have created long-term policies in which some of the uncertainty about the value of the eventual claim is passed on to the policyholder.

In life business, an insurance company can analyse the incidence of death from its previous policyholders and arrive at an estimate of the likely number of claims to be met in the following years. For example, it will be obvious that the chance of a person aged 82 surviving five years is considerably lower than that of a 25-year-old surviving a similar period. Consequently, the estimated claims arising from a group of 82-year-old customers would be greater than the claims from a younger client group. Therefore there is a strong emphasis on linking a statistical analysis of the probable events with the determination of the premiums at which the insurance contracts are offered.

As stated, many longer-term insurance contracts are equivalent to a pension,

Table 16.1 Premiums received by British insurance companies (£m), 1991

Sector	UK	Overseas	Total	% share
Ordinary life	38,246	7,468	45,714	97.1
Industrial life	1,378		1,378	2.9
Total life	39,624	7,468	47,092	100.0
Motor	5,209	3,870	9,079	33.3
Fire and accident	10,229	6,172	16,401	60.1
Marine, aviation and transport	1,369	421	1,790	6.6
Total general	16,807	10,463	27,270	100.0

Source: Insurance Statistics, Association of British Insurers.

and such insurance policies allow individuals to contribute during their working life and receive payments on retirement until their death. The insurance company is faced with estimating the cost of providing payments from the date of retirement until the date of death, similar to the calculations faced by pension funds discussed below. Another common feature of life policies and pensions is the need to minimise risk. One method of doing so is to match the characteristics of assets and liabilities, and both do invest their assets in long-term investments which match the long-term liabilities represented by the outstanding policies. Given the similarity of managing cash flows for life assurance and pension funds, the overall approach is examined later in this chapter.

General insurance

The sectors of insurance business are variously classified for statistical purposes. One such classification used by the British Insurance Association is by (a) Fire and Accident, (b) Motor Vehicle and (c) Marine, Aviation and Transport. Some indication of the relative size of each of these sectors, relative to life, is given in Table 16.1.

The nature of general insurance is that it is contingent on a particular event, and claims occur if the event takes place and not otherwise. To see how premiums are set, we can consider a general insurance policy written on property. The insurer accepts that of the total number of buildings covered by its policies, some buildings will be damaged each year. By careful analysis of the historical data, the insurance company will arrive at an estimated number of buildings and a subsequent figure for the compensation that it will be required to pay. In the long run, therefore, the company fixes its premiums to exceed its estimated claims by an amount sufficient to cover its administration and operating costs, and include the required profit margin. Year-by-year fluctuations in actual losses may exceed actual premiums but the company expects that a satisfactory profit will be achieved in the long run.

The position is complicated by the fact that insurance companies receive the premiums months or even years before they pay out claims. During the intervening period, they will have the use of the premium money which can be invested to earn a return. It is possible therefore that an insurance company would have a very small profit or even a loss between its claims and expenses and its premiums but still make a viable return when its investment income is taken into account.

One difficulty facing insurers as a result of the mismatching of premiums and claims is price changes, and for this reason, many policies are index-linked. For example, motor insurance is one kind of general insurance where companies have found that the cost of settling claims has tended to rise year by year partly because of inflation and changes in the type of claim, and partly because of an increase in the frequency of claims. Because of this change, insurance companies have raised their premiums in an effort to ensure that total premiums match total claims. This is only possible in general insurance where policies are renewed each year, and although they may lose some customers to other insurers, they will gain others. Life policies, by comparison, present inflexible contracts, and insurance companies are unable to alter the premiums of policies for existing policyholders.

Some companies in the general insurance business are classified as composite insurers since they undertake long-term and shorter term business. These composite insurance companies include firms such as Royal, Eagle Star and Commercial Union and they dominate the insurance company market in the UK, although they face increasing competition. In the commercial market this has been exacerbated by the increasing trend of large industrial companies to make their own arrangements for insurance, usually by setting up subsidiary or 'captive' insurance companies. Expansion of overseas insurance companies, including those in the US, has led to the current oversupply of insurers with the inevitable reduction in profits made by insurance companies.

The important conclusion from this is that institutions engaged in short-term insurance business are often heavily dependent on their investment activities for their profitability. Hence their importance as institutional investors in the securities markets.

Lloyd's of London

Probably the most famous institution in the insurance sector is Lloyd's of London.[1] This is a Society, incorporated under an Act of Parliament in 1871 called the Lloyd's Act and known formally as the Corporation of Lloyd's. The Society provides the premises, administrative staff and other facilities, including the handling of claims, which enable Lloyd's to function as an insurance market. Within this market any risk, with very few exceptions, can be placed with Lloyd's underwriters.

The origins of Lloyd's of London can be traced back to 1688 with the first known reference to Edward Lloyd's Coffee House in Tower Street, London, where wealthy traders and shipowners used to meet to discuss shipping business and agree to insure, or underwrite, each other's voyages. This involved the payment of a premium in return for the promise of payment to cover losses if the vessel or her cargo were lost at sea. Thus risk was transferred from the assured to the underwriter, in return for the payment of a premium.

As ships and cargoes became too valuable for one insurer to take on, syndicates were formed so the risk could be diversified across a number of underwriters. All those in the syndicate who were prepared to insure a particular risk wrote their *name* under that of the lead underwriter. Lloyd's Names provide the capital upon which Lloyd's is based. They are the ultimate beneficiaries of any profits generated, and are liable for any losses, to the full extent of their personal wealth.

All business is conducted in a trading area within the Lloyd's building known as the *Room*. Each syndicate has its own allocated area, called an underwriting box, at which the active underwriter from each syndicate evaluates, and then

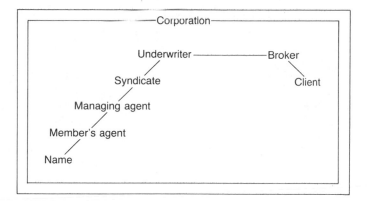

Figure 16.1   Relationships of Lloyd's entities.

accepts or rejects business from licensed brokers on behalf of the syndicate. Figure 16.1 illustrates the relationship between the various participants.

Lloyd's is active in many areas of insurance business, as shown in Table 16.2.[2] It can be seen that the legacy of marine insurance is continued, with this being the largest share of business. Over half of all business accepted is recontracted to other insurers, a practice known as reinsurance. More generally, the term is applied whenever one insurer passes on some part of the risk to another insurer. This can be seen in a detail from Lloyd's financial position, shown in Table 16.3.

A large insurance contract may involve many syndicates, each underwriting a small proportion of the risk, but the premium for the contract will be determined by the leading underwriter who initially evaluates and accepts that risk. In 1991, there were over 400 syndicates with 34,146 members in total. The Names must each be able to demonstrate considerable financial resources before they are accepted as members. Members receive any profit from the underwriting (and the associated investment income) at the end of a three-year account. Thus the surplus from premiums received on policies covering 1990 are finally distributed to members (after paying claims and expenses and reserving for outstanding claims) at the end of 1992.

The profitability of membership varies considerably from one type of insurance to another, and from one syndicate to another, but increasing competition has depressed profits and emphasised the importance of income earned from the short-term investment of premiums. In general liability business, for example, Lloyd's underwriters consistently made losses from underwriting in the period 1976 to 1980, and by 1980 an overall loss was made as the underwriting loss of £119 million exceeded the investment income. The impact of this loss might not be as dramatic as at first it appears because of the special tax considerations which attract high tax-payers to become members of Lloyd's, for example the facility to carry forward losses to offset against future tax liability on underwriting profits.

The variability of profit between types of business is matched by the various

Table 16.2 Lloyd's principal markets

Marine	35.0%
Property damage	22.2%
General liability	16.1%
Motor	12.3%
Aviation	10.2%
Accident and health	4.1%
Life	0.1%

Source: Lloyd's of London Statistics, September 1990[3].

Table 16.3 Lloyd's insurance markets, 1990

	£million
Income	
Premiums	3,653
Investment profit	399
Total income	4,052
Expenditure	
Reinsurance premiums	2,113
Claims	1,518
Other expenses	157
Total profit	264

Source: Lloyd's of London.

syndicates' results. In some years, one syndicate may report a profit, while another made a loss. Names can diversify their own risk by becoming a member of more than one syndicate, but they are required to spread their underwriting capacity between them. All syndicates are legally required to disband and reform each year, which means that certain types of business are not suited to Lloyd's, such as life insurance or other long-term risk.

Lloyd's brokers compete with other insurance broking companies. Insurance brokers act as intermediaries between clients and insurers and place the business with insurance companies or with Lloyd's. The brokers' income is earned in commission and investment income from funds held prior to paying insurers. In addition to advising clients on their insurance business, brokers may also manage insurance on their own account. Other insurance intermediaries include the insurance agents who sell insurance, mainly to individuals, on a commission or fee basis for insurance businesses.

Risk management

In taking on insurance business, insurers have to minimise their total risk. One way is by reinsurance discussed above. In other cases, insurers can try to reduce the risk either by imposing conditions under which the risk is accepted or by taking on only certain types of policy. Insurers will also try to find out all the relevant information in considering a proposal and may, if they think fit, refuse to cover a risk. The difficulty in managing risk in insurance on highly uncertain events is not helped by the problems of *moral hazard* and *adverse selection*, two conditions which should be defined.

Moral hazard may arise after the insurance policy has been issued. This is a situation where the policyholder behaves differently once they have transferred the risk to the insurance company. Householders who are less careful about their belongings or are more cavalier about security if they know they can be reimbursed when property is stolen, have transferred a higher level of risk to the insurance company than the insurer anticipated when setting the premium.

An associated problem is that of *adverse selection*. This occurs when the demand for insurance is biased towards those who are particularly high risk. These may be people who smoke or are employed in particularly dangerous professions which change their life expectancy, and some markets are dominated by particularly high-risk participants. A classic example is where individuals take out private health insurance. Such insurance might attract people who are not the most healthy members of society or who have high-risk hobbies such as sky-diving.

This is quite different from firms who knowingly take on high risk, such as young drivers or those with previous motoring convictions. While the probability of claims from this biased sample might be difficult to forecast, and therefore gives the insurer a higher risk profile, appropriately high premiums will correct for this. The majority of more risk-averse firms preferring to avoid this type of business can choose to do so.

An economic analysis of the effects of both moral hazard and adverse selection would focus on the welfare implications. These two examples of mismeasured risk, that is, a change of behaviour when insured and the individual with a high-risk lifestyle, incur higher premiums for those who are truly low risk. In both these cases, the problem is due to asymmetric information, that is, the insured has more knowledge about the extent of the risk than the insurer. Insurance companies try to reduce the incentives for the applicant to conceal information which might lead to a policy being refused or issued only on punitive terms. The most common response of the company is to refuse to pay out any claims if full and accurate information is not disclosed at the time at which the policy is issued, although there are still imperfections in these markets.

In most types of insurance, the insurer will aim merely to provide indemnity. This implies that on settlement of a claim, a policyholder should not be in a better financial position than before the incident leading to the claim. This principle could be particularly important in setting fire policies. For example, if it was found that a fire has *accidentally* destroyed a warehouse full of stock which might in any case have been unsaleable, the insurance company would, on the basis of indemnity, be justified in paying no compensation for the valueless stock. An exception to this principle can be found in the area of household contents insurance, since there has been a tendency for insurers to offer 'good as new' policies. Thus, for example, a damaged or stolen outdated television will be replaced by a new one.

16.3 Pension funds

Pensions are organised in Britain both by the state and through schemes based on the occupation of the individual, although increasingly, they are the joint responsibility of the employer and the individual. Just under half of the British workforce are members of an occupational pension scheme. The state scheme provides a basic flat-rate benefit payable on retirement and an additional payment related to earnings.

Private occupation-based pensions can be either funded or unfunded. Unfunded pensions provide benefits for existing pensioners from the contributions paid by the employer and existing employees. Funded pension schemes, on the other hand, operate by setting up an investment fund into which contributions are paid by employees and the employer. These funds can be invested with any profits enjoyed either as income or capital gain, and benefit by the exemption from any tax liability. Thus for the pension fund contributor they represent a very efficient method of deferring income. On retirement, the employees will receive a pension generated from the investment contributions.

In the private sector, most pensions are funded with the employer paying more into the fund than the employee, although some operate on a non-contributory basis in which the employee is not required to contribute anything. In the public sector, pensions such as those which cover policemen and civil servants are technically unfunded although some public sector pensions including teachers' pensions are funded.

One policy issue affecting the provision of pensions, is that related to the transfer of pension benefits associated with a change of employer. It has been the practice in some pension schemes that employees merely had their contributions returned to them on leaving the firm's employment. A more equitable treatment exists for a fund which preserves the pension of an early leaver. Thus a pension scheme which provides 1/80 of the final salary for every year of service would pay a pension of 1/2 of the final salary for an employee who worked for forty years. The same scheme would provide a pension of 1/4 of the final salary for an employee who left after only twenty years. On the assumption that the leaver worked for another firm for a further twenty years, at retirement, this individual would receive two pensions, one from each employer.

If the salary were the same at the end of each twenty-year period, the leaver's pension rights would be unaffected. However, if the salary increases during the time spent with the second firm, which is the most likely situation, the leaver may be worse off at retirement. Consider the following example:

> Suppose an employee works for firm A for twenty years, leaving with a final salary of £10,000, and then joins firm B, retiring after a further twenty years with a salary of £20,000. Further suppose that the final salary received from firm B is the same as it would have been with firm A, the whole of the forty years would be computed at the £20,000 point on the scale.
>
> The pensions from A and B together would amount to

$$\{(20)(1/80)(£10,000)\} + \{(20)(1/80)(£20,000)\} = £7,500$$

> If there had been no change in employment, the pension would amount to

$$\{(40)(1/80)(£20,000)\} = £10,000$$

Thus the pension derived from the two firms would be considerably below that at the termination of continued employment with the same firm.

The distinction between funded and unfunded pensions not only affects the cost of administering the scheme but also differs in impact on the capital markets. With unfunded schemes, there need be little if any financial investment since the contributions received will be almost immediately paid out in benefits. With funded schemes the contributions paid into the fund may not be required for a number of years into the future and there will be correspondingly large sums invested for long periods of time in order to ensure that adequate pensions can be paid.

The investment decisions required in administering a pension scheme are considerable and often crucial in determining the level of contributions. For small pension schemes it may be difficult to acquire the professional expertise for this task and thus many corporate schemes are run by insurance companies offering specialist help in this area. Larger schemes may administer the benefits and contributions internally but hand over the investment decisions to professional investment advisers, including merchant banks (such as Barings or Warburgs), stockbrokers (such as Grieveson Grant or Fielding Newson-Smith) or insurance companies (Legal & General or Prudential). Very large funds, such as that of the Post Office pension fund, may employ several professional managers each with instructions to manage part of their investment portfolios.

16.4 Common characteristics of life assurance and pensions

The long-term nature of life and pension business means that substantial funds are available for investment, and these are considerably in excess of the funds generated by short-term insurance. Whereas general insurers hope that claims will total less than premiums in any one period, long-term insurers are more concerned that the valuation of their existing fund will adequately cover the estimated liabilities at some future date. Often the liability is known in advance or can be identified shortly before it becomes due. Pensions, for example, are usually calculated on the basis of years of service and average or final salary levels.

On the basis of forecasting the number of years from retirement to death, the fund manager can calculate the amount that will be required to provide the pension. One variable which causes difficulty in this estimation is the expected rate of inflation. Others are the final salary at retirement and the investment returns. During the 1970s and the latter part of the 1980s, for example, many salaries increased dramatically with the unexpected inflation. Unfortunately this was not accompanied by an associated rise in the returns from investment so that in some cases actuaries found that the future liabilities of the long-term funds substantially exceeded the anticipated asset value. Consequently, funding con-tributions were increased in order to save the long-term fund from insolvency.

We discuss the investment implications of this problem later in this chapter and look more closely at the actuarial problems in the appendix to this chapter. With long-term funds, premiums may not always be paid over many years. Single-premium policies have been successfully marketed by insurance companies either to provide annuities or lump-sum cash payments at the end of the specified period (or on death if earlier). This business is referred to as industrial life insurance and a number of insurance companies and friendly societies specialise in this service.

There is a variety of long-term insurance policies which provides another type of cover to individuals. Term policies provide *pure* insurance cover against death within a specified period of, say, five to ten years. The insured individual pays the premium for the period. If the holder survives no benefit is paid. On death in the period covered, a specified amount of cash is paid to the family or surviving dependants of the insured.

In other cases, the policy contains a substantial savings element, and the benefits may accrue either to the insured or their dependants. In the case of the whole-life policy, the term is not specified but the insurance fund will always pay benefit on death of the insured whenever this occurs. The premiums for this contract, of course, will be substantially higher than for the term policy because in every whole-life policy the insurer will be committed to pay the agreed sum insured.

A policy which has become popular with individuals, particularly those purchasing property, is the endowment policy which combines the pure insur-ance feature of the term policy with the guaranteed payment of the whole-life. Endowment policies cover a fixed period. If the insured person dies before the policy matures, the insurance policy pays the benefit. If the insured survives, the promised amount will be paid when the policy matures. Usually this type of policy is taken out on a 'with-profits' basis, by which the total amount payable rises over the period at a rate dependent upon the profitability of the insurance company.

Alternatively, a policy may be linked to a specific investment fund so that the insured individual can monitor the value of the insurance payment over the life of the policy. This type of policy is called 'unit-linked' since the fund is sometimes set up as a unit trust, which is discussed below. In other cases, the investment is linked to an internal fund managed by the company.

The other major type of policy is the annuity which provides an income from a specified date until the death of the insured person. In some cases the payments can be made as long as either of two named people survive. Thus two people can arrange for an annuity to continue for as long as either survive. The premiums for this policy can be paid either as a single cash sum or as a series of payments over a number of years, in which case it is called a deferred annuity. This type of policy is usually sold as part of a pension scheme because there are substantial tax savings for this arrangement. Annuities can also be set up to contribute to charity or to endow a university chair or scholarship.

16.5 Principles of investment management

In order to safeguard the payment of pensions many years in the future, the funds generated either from pension schemes or from long-term insurance policies must be invested efficiently. In the case of pensions, actuaries regularly check that the value of the fund, containing accrued contributions and reinvested income, is sufficient to cover all the expected future benefits. To carry out this task, a number of assumptions have to be made since both the future contributions and benefits to be paid are uncertain. Typically, actuaries will assume specific rates of interest to be earned by the fund and also specific rates of inflation, growth rates of earnings to determine both the future contributions and benefits, and mortality rates.

One way in which investment managers can minimise the uncertainty of achieving a return is by investing all the funds in fixed interest government bonds. This investment would clearly not be risky in the sense that the government is unlikely to default on the interest or capital repayment. However, if inflation suddenly accelerates the wisdom of investing in fixed term bonds would be questionable. Indexed bonds are attractive specifically to pension funds since the value of the interest payments increases when inflation rises. Indexed bonds provide the pension funds with an extremely secure return against which it can evaluate its investment policy, assuming the investments are long term and in sufficient quantity.

With large funds, investors believe that by diversifying among different types of investment, substantially greater returns can be achieved without incurring greater degrees of risk. This property of portfolio diversification is central to the investment management of long-term funds and has led to investment in assets as wide ranging as antiques, paintings and gold.

Table 16.4 Investments of life and general insurance companies, 1990–1

Funds/assets	Life insurance				General insurance			
	1990		1991		1990		1991	
	£m	%	£m	%	£m	%	£m	%
British government authority securities	30,987	12.2	36,157	12.0	5,376	11.6	6,016	12.1
Foreign and Commonwealth government, provincial and municipal stocks	7,504	2.9	17,163	5.7	7,537	16.2	9,261	18.7
Debentures, loan stocks, preference and guaranteed stocks and shares	23,155	9.1	24,900	8.2	6,753	14.6	8,008	16.1
Ordinary stocks and shares	123,031	48.3	154,944	51.4	12,727	27.4	13,087	26.4
Mortgages	13,372	5.2	14,805	4.9	2,113	4.6	1,242	2.5
Real property and ground rents	37,754	14.8	34,808	11.5	4,093	8.8	3,947	7.9
Other investments	19,197	7.5	18,894	6.3	7,788	16.8	8,098	16.3
Total invested assets	255,000	100.0	301,671	100.00	46,387	100.0	49,659	100.0
Net current assets	2,104		618		6,007		6,438	
Total	257,104		302,289		52,394		56,097	

In general, the investment portfolios of the long-term funds are classified into categories, as shown in Table 16.4. This illustrates differences in investment patterns between life and general insurance, reflecting the nature of the liabilities incurred.

As might be expected, the short-term investors, that is, general insurance funds, hold much larger proportions of their funds in the form of short-term assets. It is noted also that pension funds hold about 50% of their assets in ordinary shares. In fact, the figures presented in the table understate the importance of bond-type investments held by insurance funds, since it would be fair to include the mortgages and real property with the government, local authority and corporate debt as they all have the same characteristics as bonds.

Life insurance funds have traditionally held property in their portfolios and over recent years they have invested consistently more in property than the pension funds. Critics of this involvement in the property market have argued that it has diverted resources away from more productive uses. From a financial viewpoint, however, the property market has provided very profitable investment opportunities for the institutions, although during the recent property slump the market was shown to be riskier than many investors had previously believed.

In common with many large investors, the relaxation of foreign currency restrictions has led to overseas investment. As discussed in Chapter 7, the need to minimise transactions costs initially encouraged participation in international equity markets, and more recent pressure is due to competition in the industry.

Because of the wide choice of assets open to fund managers it might seem difficult to monitor the efficiency of their investment decisions. In fact, the evaluation of investment performance is an important activity and has considerable influence on investment policies. There are several consulting actuarial firms and other specialist institutions which offer a performance evaluation service to institutional investors. Usually, the funds are analysed on the basis of asset-types. An example is the case of an ordinary share portfolio, where the proportion of shares held in the various industrial sectors will be identified. For each asset-type, an average index is constructed and the hypothetical return from investing in the index is estimated. The fund's performance is then allocated to its constituent assets and each component's return is compared with that estimated for the appropriate index. There are thus two main criteria by which fund management can be judged, timing and selection.

For example, suppose a fund manager misjudges the potential profitability of investing in oil company shares. Consequently, the fund may be holding little or no oil company shares during a period in which the oil sector rises in value, and the fund underperforms because of the mistake in timing.

Selection concerns the identification of individual companies or specific investments. Thus fund managers may correctly foresee that the shares of computer-based companies will rise in value but be unfortunate in buying the least profitable companies' shares. Similarly, a fund manager may recognise that office properties will generally rise in value but be unfortunate in buying particular offices that remain unaffected by the trend.

The quality of the investment performance of the fund manager can directly influence the competitive terms offered by the company on insurance policies, as well as having obvious implications for the provision of pensions by pension funds. Consider for example an individual who wishes to take out a life insurance policy covering a period of twenty years. The cheapest type of policy is, as discussed above, a term policy which might provide £15,000 payable on the event of death of the insured within the insured period. The premiums quoted by the insurance company will take into account its assessment of the probable date of death of the insured, as well as the operating and administrative costs. However, when these factors are taken into account, the insurance contract will still effectively consist of a series of cash inflows terminated by one cash outflow. In setting its premiums, the company will have to take into account the rate at which the premiums will accumulate. In other words, the company must assess the rate of return that it expects to earn on its investments, and the more successful the investment returns, the more competitive can be the premiums quoted.

This issue is particularly important for insurance policies which contain a large savings element. For instance, an endowment insurance policy may be offered to a 35-year-old man which would mature in ten years' time. For a guaranteed insured sum of £2,000, the premiums might be in the region of £15 monthly. But in addition to the guaranteed sum of £2,000, the maturity value of the policy will be linked to the profitability of the fund in which the premiums are invested. Estimations of the maturity value of the policies may be very variable but it is quite conceivable that the estimates would range from £2,500 to £3,500. To the insured individual, the investment performance of the fund manager could be vitally important in assessing the policy to be taken out.

We can see this using the following example.

> Suppose the cost of providing £3,500 life cover during the same period amounts to monthly premiums of less than £1. The savings or investment component of the endowment policy, obtained from the net monthly premiums (£15 less the term policy premium of £1) paid over ten years, is the estimated terminal value (TV) of £3,500. This is evaluated by compounding the annuity of £14 per month for a ten-year period and equating the terminal value of the annuity with the final sum.[4]

The implied return of the investment component (if the insured survives) is given by i in the expression

$$14s_{\overline{120}|\,i} = 3500$$

or in the general form derived in Chapter 5,

$$ms_{\overline{n}|\,i} = TV_n$$

where n = the number of months; m = the monthly premium; TV_n = the estimated terminal value of the policy, and $s_{\overline{n}|\,i}$ = the TV of an ordinary annuity.

By trial and error, the monthly return is found to be 1.12% which implies an effective annual rate of over 14%. Even without taking into account the effect of taxation, this calculation provides the individual with some measure of the expectations of the various insurance companies. Bearing in mind the spread of investment between the types of assets held by the long-term fund, this investment can be compared with the performance which the individual could otherwise hope to achieve by investing directly in funds such as unit trusts and in National Savings or building societies.

Another comparison can be made between policies which offer only a specified sum and those which offer a 'with profits' payment. In the latter case, the insured is paying a higher premium in exchange for a benefit which will partly depend on the investment performance of the long-term funds.

One other point which should briefly be mentioned in discussing investment performance concerns the methods used in estimating returns. The problem arises because during the course of any period, the fund will receive cash inflows from premiums paid, or from pension contributions, and will make cash payments (outflows) in the form of pension or insurance policy benefits. The value of the fund will therefore fluctuate simply because of the patterns of those cash flows which are beyond the control of the fund manager. From the investor's viewpoint, the investment performance can be assessed in the same way as any other investment project by finding the rate of return which equates the cash flows. This approach which was identified in Chapter 6 as calculating the internal rate of return is referred to in the investment literature as the money-weighted return.

For the fund manager, the more critical question concerns the performance of those aspects which can be controlled. In practice, the performance would be assessed by calculating the average return earned over each interval of time in which no cash flows were received or paid. Thus if a fund was valued on 1 January and received cash on 31 January and made cash payments on 1 June, we might calculate the return for the period by averaging the change in the value of the fund over the periods 1 January to 31 January, 31 January to 1 June, and 1 June to 31 December. In this way, the returns are calculated for periods, determined by the payment or receipt of cash. This method is implicit in the comparison of the fund with market indicators discussed earlier, and is called the time-weighted return. Differences between the two methods may be substantial and most obvious when the returns are variable.

A simple demonstration of this is the following case of a fund initially valued (at 1 January) at £100 million.

Date	Cash flow (£m)	Value of fund (£m)
1 January		100
31 January	+100	200
28 February		300
31 March		200
30 April	−100	100
30 May	+100	250

Estimating first the money-weighted return, we solve for i in the following expression

$$100(1 + i)^5 + 100(1 + i)^4 - 100(1 + i) + 100 = 250$$

The first £100 is invested for five months, the second cash flow of £100 is invested for four months whilst the third cash outflow occurs only one month before the end of the period. The final cash inflow of £100 occurs on the date at which the final valuation is made. Thus the final valuation can be thought of as the largest possible final cash outflow

$$i = 0.056 \text{ or } 5.6\% \text{ per month}$$

Notice that in this example, the value of the fund is only taken into account at the beginning and end of the measurement period.

To find the time-weighted return we first calculate the return for the period between each time at which cash is received or paid. The return for each of these sub-intervals is given by

$$i_t = \frac{\text{value at } (t+1) - \text{value at } t - \text{net cash inflows}}{\text{value at } t}$$

in which the value at the end of the period includes any cash received or paid out on that date. Thus

$$i_{\text{Jan}} = \frac{200 - 100 - 100}{100} = 0\%$$

$$i_{\text{Feb}} = \frac{300 - 200}{200} = 50\%$$

$$i_{\text{Mar}} = \frac{200 - 300}{300} = -33.3\%$$

$$i_{\text{Apr}} = \frac{100 - 200 + 100}{200} = 0\%$$

$$i_{\text{May}} = \frac{250 - 100 - 100}{100} = 50\%$$

The average of these sub-interval returns is 13.33% per month which is nearly three times greater than the money-weighted return, but which, when analysed on a month-by-month basis, reveals the variability of the investment performance of the fund. Thus, from the trustee's point of view the time-weighted return may be a more useful check on the fund management's portfolio decisions than the money-weighted return.

Measurement of investment performance is an integral part of portfolio management. Although fund managers might argue that there is too much emphasis on short-term considerations, few would deny that some monitoring is essential. The importance of measuring the returns made by fund managers is even greater when investment is predominantly an institutional activity. Hence, the increase in interest shown in performance measurement is a direct consequence of the development of institutional investors and is reflected most clearly in the area of life and pension business.

16.6 Investment institutions

Other institutions act as investment intermediaries and contribute to the efficiency of the financial sector by providing new information which is rapidly transmitted from one sector to another. The most important of these are unit trusts and investment trusts, and we shall consider these next.

Unit trusts

Unit trusts are one group of institutions operating as investment intermediaries. They are open-ended funds, that is, the size of the fund and the number of shares issued depend directly upon the investors. If investors wish to place more money in the fund, the managers of the unit trust have to create and sell more shares, or units as they are called. The price at which the units are sold or bought by the managers is dictated by the value of the fund. Thus to give a very simple example, if a unit trust is valued at £10 million and has 10 million units outstanding, further units will be offered for sale at, or slightly above, 100p each whilst units will be bought back by the management at slightly below 100p. If a further million units are sold to new investors, the value of the fund will be £11 million but the number of units issued will also have increased to 11 million and so the price of each unit will in principle remain unchanged by this transaction.

There will be administrative charges and legal costs which will lower the price at which units will be bought and raise the price at which units will be sold. Managers usually have some discretion in the method of calculating the price of units so that like the bid/offer quotation of the stock market, the bid/offer prices of the unit trust will reflect the views and current stock position of the management. The bid prices will usually differ by about 5% to 7% from the offer prices.

The organisation of the unit trust involves two institutions, the management and the trustees. The role of the trustee is to safeguard the interests of the unit holders and to ensure that the trust is operating on the lines laid down by the trust deed which has to be drawn up before the unit trust is established. The role of the management company is to invest the assets of the unit holders. The assets will usually be invested in ordinary shares although some unit trusts invest in bonds and other securities. Sometimes the management company of the unit trust will act on the trustee's behalf in maintaining the register of unit holders, but in other cases the registration is carried out by companies which specialise in providing the register service.

The management company also advertises the sale of units, although the terms and claims made in the advertisement are monitored by the trustee to ensure that no misleading information is given to the investing public. There are units which are not allowed to advertise, and these may be formed for specialist investment or for a group of private investors wishing to pool their resources. To distinguish between the types of unit trust, the term *authorised* is used in respect of those trusts whose activities have been authorised by the Department of Trade and

Industry. Authorisation involves acceptance of restraints on investment policy as regards the concentration of assets in one investment or the type of asset held.

Unit trusts are designed to provide an opportunity for individuals to invest relatively small amounts of money in a diversified portfolio. The managements of the unit trusts will sometimes be provided by banks such as Midland or Lloyd's which offer investment advice to their personal customers. Other unit trusts are managed by companies which sell unit-linked life insurance policies. The value of the sum paid when the policy matures will be determined by the price of the units. Managers of this type of trust include the Scottish Widows Fund Management and the Legal & General group. There are several general management groups such as M&G and Save and Prosper which manage a large number of unit trust funds created for a variety of different purposes and which offer specialist funds for investment overseas or in particular sectors or markets. Some of these have a specific flavour, such as environmental or ethnic content. Finally, stockbroking firms such as James Capel and Grieveson Grant also form unit trusts to provide a service for individual investors with relatively small portfolios.

The development of unit trusts has been very successful. Initiated in the 1930s, their size and number grew slowly until the early 1960s when, because of less restrictive legislation and buoyant equity markets, their growth accelerated. By the beginning of the 1970s there were over two hundred trusts with funds valued at nearly £1,500 million. By 1980, the value of funds had more than trebled to nearly £5,000 million and by 1992 the number of trusts reached 1456 spread between 151 individual firms, managing funds valued at £63.874 billion.

This represents a very wide choice to individual investors. Besides the various types of management group, unit trusts differ in their investment objectives. A number of categories are publicised and an indication of the range of specialities can be seen in Table 16.5.

Although unit trusts have been established with a wide range of objectives, their portfolios in aggregate show a heavy proportion of ordinary shares. Table 16.6 compares their main holdings with those of the investment trusts. A large proportion of the total portfolio is held in equity, split between UK and overseas companies.

Investment trusts

Investment trusts are companies which issue shares and fixed interest securities, investing the proceeds in a managed portfolio. They are closed-end funds, which means investors wishing to buy investment trust shares have to find other investors willing to sell. No new shares are created since the investment trust is not directly involved in the buying and selling of its securities after the primary issue has been made. Correspondingly, the price of the investment trust shares does not depend directly on the value of the assets held by the investment trust. In practice, the share price will usually be considerably below the corresponding value of the assets: a feature which is referred to as the investment trust discount.

Table 16.5 Market value of unit trusts, by sector

Sector	Fund value £ May 1993
1 UK general	16,985,786,030
2 UK growth	9,063,253,624
3 UK equity income	7,911,651,818
4 International growth	6,695,473,054
5 Europe	6,167,030,915
6 Exempt	4,396,207,836
7 North America	3,876,510,460
8 Far East excluding Japan	3,458,728,404
9 Japan	3,148,199,016
10 UK smaller companies	3,133,370,134
11 Far East including Japan	1,893,615,698
12 UK balanced	1,353,286,956
13 International balanced	1,212,906,964
14 UK gilt and fixed interest	984,527,002
15 Fund of funds	905,611,402
16 International fixed interest	854,296,464
17 Investment trust units	816,648,888
18 Money market	500,388,265
19 Financial and property	477,469,371
20 International equity income	303,763,488
21 Commodity and energy	284,881,685
22 Convertibles	125,830,496
23 Australasia	76,858,387
24 Pensions	65,058,949
All sectors	73,785,743,904

Table 16.6 Portfolio composition of unit and investment trusts (£m), 1992

	UK securities		Overseas securities		
	Government	Private	Government	Private	Total
Unit trusts	660 (1%)	34,616 (60%)		22,657 (39%)	58,096
Investment trusts	2,139 (4%)	12,600 (48%)	941 (3%)	12,457 (44%)	28,137

Source: Financial Statistics, Table 5.2, 1994.

Investment trusts were first formed in the nineteenth century and have always emphasised the international aspects of investment. As can be seen from Table 16.6, their holdings of overseas securities account for over 40% of their portfolios, rather more than unit trusts. Many of the restrictions imposed on unit trusts do not apply to investment trusts, and they are more likely to invest in a wider range of assets including property and unlisted securities.

Some investment trusts have emphasised this feature in recent years. Like the unit trusts, investment trusts are administered by a group of managers. Although each investment trust is a separate company, many are controlled by management groups not unlike those controlling unit trusts. Among these management groups may be found Touche Remnant, Investment Trust Services and Kleinwort Benson. There has also been a strong Scottish emphasis in the investment trust sector which has long traditions in both Edinburgh and Glasgow.

Investment trusts differ from unit trusts in a number of ways. One of the more obvious differences is the ability to borrow money. The effect of this borrowing is to increase the potential profitability but at an additional level of risk. For example, if the investment trust borrows money at 10%, the shareholders will receive proportionately more if the achieved profit is more than 10%, but greatly reduced profits if the investment trust earns less than 10% of its investment. This gearing effect is a potential benefit to private investors since the result is to gear up the performance of their investment in a way which could otherwise only be achieved by borrowing money in order to buy shares. Provided the trust can borrow at rates of interest below those available to the investor, gearing may be of considerable benefit.

Historically, the investment trust companies were aimed at individual investors but their shares have also attracted the attention of insurance companies and pension funds. These institutions have come increasingly to dominate the ownership of the investment trusts, and partly because the institutions already own diversified portfolios, there has been a shift in popularity towards more specialised investment trusts and away from trusts aiming for a general portfolio. In some cases, the management groups have responded by changing their investment policies. Touche Remnant, for example, announced in 1982 that nine of its eleven investment trusts were to be given more specialised objectives. It was hoped that in responding to the institutional preferences, the popularity of the trusts' shares would increase and the discount would thereby fall.

Predictably, if the discount becomes too large, it would be reasonable to expect a demand for the trust to be liquidated in order to realise the full value of the underlying assets. In the past this has not occurred. One explanation for this is that investors may fear high liquidation costs. Furthermore, a small group of investors might find it prohibitively expensive to buy enough shares to gain control in order to push through the decision to liquidate. Certainly any news of possible liquidation tends to cause the share price to move quite sharply.

Liquidation has occurred to some extent though, in that some investment trusts have been unitised, that is, converted into unit trusts. The effect of this change is that the shareholders become unit holders, and the price of the shares (units) is no longer determined by supply and demand but by the trust management. This is done in accordance with the agreed procedures, and generally involves estimating the equivalent asset value for each unit issued. Alternatively, as in the case of

British Investment Trust, an institutional shareholder makes an open bid for the shares and gains control of the trust. Although the trust shares are still listed at a discount to the underlying assets, the controlling shareholder can now influence the investment and dividend policy of the trust towards its own interests.

Property-based funds

As stated above, investment trusts are able to invest in a wider range of assets than the authorised unit trusts. In particular, some investment trusts resemble property companies which issue shares and debt, and invest the proceeds in land and buildings. The shares of property companies are not normally regarded in quite the same way as investment trusts since property companies emphasise their role as developers rather than as portfolio managers.

These companies do however have a unit trust equivalent in the property unit trusts, which provide an opportunity for tax-exempt institutional investors to invest in property. Property unit trusts became popular for smaller pension funds in the late 1960s during a period in which property investment by large funds increased dramatically. Thus the first major property unit trust, the Pension Fund Property Unit Trust, was established in 1966 and four other trusts were established within twelve months.

The property unit trusts respond more sensitively to the wishes of their unit holders than do other unit trusts, a responsiveness which stems partly from the smaller number of unit holders in each trust. This concentration of interest in a few institutional hands thus enables much closer contact between the management of the trust and the unit holders. Another reason for the close link is the illiquidity of the underlying property asset which effectively prevents too large a proportion of unit holders from liquidating their unit holdings. Property unit trust holders therefore will always wish to have current information about the investments held by their management group.

The management group will try to avoid a situation in which they have to sell property in order to buy units from investors and may impose conditions about the length of notice required before buying back units. They may also impose other conditions that restrain the ease with which unit holders can realise their cash.

The value of funds within the property unit trust sector varies considerably, but not surprisingly, fluctuates with property prices. In 1988 the outstanding value at market prices was £1,124 million, but fell to £597 million in 1992. Over recent years, the proportion of the sector's portfolio invested in property has been around 95%, so there is almost no diversification.

For private investors, there are open-ended funds which invest in property. These funds are called property bonds and are invariably linked to a life insurance policy. This linkage minimises the risk of unexpected liquidation demands from the management group's viewpoint. Like the property unit trusts, however, the property bond funds minimise the risk of having to sell their property by maintaining a reserve of liquid assets. In some cases the proportion of liquid assets can exceed 50%. Thus if bond holders wish to cancel their insurance policies and withdraw their investment, the managers can repurchase the bond without difficulty.

One facet of the illiquidity of the underlying property investment is illustrated in the valuation of the property bond funds. Unlike unit trusts which have to value their investments by reference to their current market prices, the property bonds can assess the value of the property only if it is valued by professional property valuers. Since such an exercise is necessarily expensive, it is carried out at rather infrequent intervals. Thus if property values are rising, investors wishing to cash in their investments may not receive the full value since the transaction will reflect the valuation at an earlier date.

Another feature which exacerbates the liquidity problem is the need to invest large sums of cash in property. Property investors have traditionally placed great emphasis on buying prime property, which has usually implied offices or shops in central city areas. However, such properties have often been developed on a large scale and their purchase has necessarily involved several millions of pounds. As a result, property funds have had to buy prime property at the cost of diversification. In smaller funds, one property may account for 20% or 30% of the portfolios. The investment performance of the fund therefore may be more risky than might be expected from the size of the fund.

Other managed funds

More flexibility is offered to private investors in the form of managed bonds. With these funds the management has the discretion to switch the investment from one asset-type to another. Alternatively, the investor may specify the asset in which his or her money is invested and can change the type of asset held during the course of the year. Managed bonds, like property bonds, are invariably linked to insurance contracts and represent just one of a number of different types of investment scheme which are promoted by or in association with insurance companies.

Other examples include equity bonds, international bonds, fixed interest bonds and money bonds, the last of these specifically for very liquid investments. In principle they fulfil the same function, offering opportunities for individuals to save in a tax-efficient way but with an insurance element included.

Apart from the specialist investment intermediaries described, there are a large number of funds established overseas. These off-shore funds may be registered in the Channel Islands, the Isle of Man, Bermuda or other areas in which their registration entails low or zero taxation. They are usually subject to less stringent accounting requirements than funds registered within the UK, and the valuation of their assets may be accomplished in terms of US dollars, Swiss francs or sterling. It is therefore especially difficult to reach any estimate of the size of the off-shore sector with any degree of confidence.

16.7 Supervision

Historically, the insurance industry has been closely supervised, because of the consequences to premium holders if a company fails. The Life Assurance Companies Act of 1870 first required minimum deposits for companies in this area of business, and formal supervision of general insurance began with the Assurance Companies Act in 1909. Most recently, legislation is contained in the Insurance Companies Act of 1982 which requires that institutions must follow strict principles to ensure they are managed by reputable persons who carry out insurance business properly, and that capital reserves are adequate, especially in the light of the uncertain nature of insurance claims.

Pension funds are bound by trust legislation and therefore not so heavily regulated as insurance companies. They do have to be recognised by the division of the Inland Revenue because of the tax implications of their investments. The National Association of Pension Funds has no regulatory powers, but acts on behalf of the pension industry in its interaction with government. There is no self-regulatory organisation in existence for the pension industry, exceptionally within the financial services sector, although European Community directives do include these funds in reciprocity agreements.

Finally, other investment and unit trusts are self-regulatory and will be discussed further in Chapter 19, although both have a lobbying organisation with no formal regulatory powers. These are the Association of Investment Trust Companies and the Unit Trust Association, respectively.

16.8 Summary

This chapter has discussed aspects of insurance and pension business and has shown how simple policies can be evaluated. The growth of the long-term insurance and pension funds has created a huge investing sector at the same time as providing a means of compensation for accident or disaster and a scheme for long-term saving.

Notes

1. Unfortunately, much of the recent attention on Lloyd's has been negative. We shall discuss this in Chapter 19.
2. Note that Tables 2 and 3 report 1990 data. This is because Lloyd's accounts are traditionally presented three years in arrears.
3. The formula for the annuity is given in the appendix of Chapter 5.

Further reading

Arnaud, A. A. (1983), *Investment Trusts Explained*, Woodhead-Faulkner. This is an account of the investment trust sector concentrating on the institutional features of the companies as a method of investment.

Ayres, F. (1963), *Mathematics of Finance*, McGraw-Hill. This book contains five chapters dealing with the derivation and application of insurance and annuity valuation equations.

Dodds, J. C. (1987), *The Investment Behaviour of British Life Insurance Companies*, Croom Helm.

Franklin, P. J. and G. Woodhead (1980), *The UK Life Assurance Industry*, Croom Helm. This rigorous and authoritative text provides an analysis of the microeconomics of life insurance.

Goacher, D. J. and P. J. Curwen (1987), *British Non-Bank Financial Intermediaries*, Allen and Unwin.

Minns, R. (1980), *Pension Funds and British Capitalism*, Heinemann Educational Books. This stimulating study of the relationship between the financial and industrial sectors of the economy examines the informal and formal control of pension fund portfolio investment. The author presents arguments for the direction of investment into British industrial activity.

Pawley, M., Winstone, D. and P. Bentley (1991), *UK Financial Institutions and Markets*, Macmillan. Chapters 6 and 7 give considerable detail on products and also regulation of insurance and pension and investment funds.

Questions

16.1 Consider the costs of operating unfunded and funded pension schemes. In what circumstances will the unfunded scheme be (a) cheaper and (b) dearer in providing identical benefits? (Hint: you might first consider setting up a pension scheme for a company which experiences no net change in the number of its employees.)

16.2 Ms A is a 30-year-old single parent of two children aged 4 and 6. What sort of factors do you think she ought to take into account in deciding whether she should take out a term insurance or whole-life policy?

16.3 Why do you think there is such a large difference in the premiums quoted by competing firms in the life insurance business?

16.4 There have been increasing merger activity and discussions between financial institutions of all types. In the light of this trend consider the similarities between insurance companies and (a) banks and (b) investment trusts.

Problems

16.5 Evaluate the investment return on the endowment implied by the following policies on the assumption that the insured survives the term (sum assured = £11,000, assume annual premiums paid at end of each year):

(a) A fifteen-year term policy for a 45-year-old man; annual premium = £60

(b) A fifteen-year endowment (non-profit) policy for the same person; annual premium = £486

16.6 A 30-year-old woman is quoted the following premiums, on the assumption that she will die in forty-five years' time. Estimate the return that is implicit in the with profits component of the life policy:

(a) Whole-life, sum assured £5,000, annual premium £30 (payable at the end of each year)

(b) Whole-life with profit, sum assured £5,000, expected total maturity value £24,300, annual premium £100 (payable at the end of each year)

16.7 A 75-year-old woman can buy an annuity of £1,940 (half-yearly in arrears) for £10,000. If she can invest the £10,000 in a bond at a nominal yield of 12%, to what age would she have to survive before the annuity was the preferable investment? (Ignore the effect of taxation.)

16.8 A woman started employment on her twenty-first birthday and after fifteen years was earning £8,000 per year. She then left and worked for another firm for ten years at £16,000 per year, after which she moved to a third firm at a salary of £24,000. Just before she retired at the age of 61 she heard from a friend working for her first employer that her graded salary would now have been £20,000 had she still been working for the firm.

Calculate her present pension if each firm operated a contributory pension scheme in which the benefits amounted to 1/80 of the final salary for each year of service. Would her pension have been greater had she stayed with her original employer?

16.9 A fund manager receives £100 million on the first day of January, February, March, April and May. On the last day of each month the fund is valued at £120m, £280m, £280m, £320m and £600m. Estimate the money-weighted and time-weighted returns for the fund. Compare this performance with the market if the index moved from 100 on 1 January to 110, 132, 125, 120, 140 on the last day of successive months.

Appendix
Actuarial Calculations

In the text it was stated that insurance companies analysed the statistics of mortality rates and adjusted their premiums so that a surplus was generated from their portfolios of policies. In this appendix, we illustrate how these statistics might be used in valuing simple policies.

If l_x = the number of people living at age x, then l_{x+1} will be the number of those surviving for more than a year from the age x. The number of people dying within the year will therefore be given by $d_x = l_x - l_{x+1}$. Similarly, the proportion of people dying within the year will be given by d_x/l_x, whereas the proportion of people surviving for at least one year will be given by l_{x+1}/l_x.

Mortality tables are published but in this example we construct hypothetical statistics for a group of 18-year-olds.

Age x	Number living l_x	Number dying d_x
18	1000	3
19	997	3
20	994	3
21	991	3
22	988	3
23	985	3

Of the 1000 18-year-old people, 997 should be alive a year later. The probability therefore that an 18-year-old will survive a year is 997/1000 or 0.997. Similarly, the probability that an 18-year-old will survive two years will be 994/1000 or 0.994.

Temporary annuity

Consider first an annuity which pays £1,000 per annum to an 18-year-old for a period of three years or until death (whichever is the earlier). Assume that payments are received at the end of each year, but that the single premium is paid at the beginning.

Thus the payments for a group of policyholders will depend on the numbers living at the end of the first and second years. From the table we expect that the proportion of 18-year-olds who survive will be 997/100 (one year) and 994/1000 (two years). If all policyholders were certain to survive for two years, the present value of successive payments of £1 for two years would be

$$a_{\overline{2}|\,i} = \frac{1}{1+i} + \frac{1}{(1+i)^2}$$

If we weight these £1 payments by the chances of their occurring we get

$$a_{\overline{x:2}|} = \left[\frac{l_{x+1}}{l_x} \frac{1}{(1+i)} \right] + \left[\frac{l_{x+2}}{l_x} \frac{1}{(1+i)^2} \right] \tag{16A.1}$$

where

$a_{\overline{x:n}|}$ = single premium for an n-year temporary life annuity of £1 per year for an individual aged x years

l_x = the number living at age x

i = the investment (discount) rate

If we take the investment rate i to be 5% then

$$a_{\overline{18:2}|} = 0.9495 + 0.9016$$
$$= £1.851$$

Thus to provide a £1 annuity for two years to an 18-year-old, a premium of at least £1.851 would be required (ignoring the expenses of commission, etc.). In general, the single premium for an n-year temporary life annuity of £1 per year for an individual aged x years will be given by

$$a_{\overline{x:n}|} = \sum_{t=1}^{n} \frac{l_{x+t}}{l_x} \frac{1}{(1+i)^t} \tag{16A.2}$$

The premium required to pay the annuity of £1 for three years can be found to be

$$\left[\frac{997}{100} \frac{1}{1.05} \right] + \left[\frac{994}{1000} \frac{1}{(1.05)^2} \right] + \left[\frac{991}{1000} \frac{1}{(1.05)^3} \right] = £2.71$$

The value of a whole life annuity can be found simply by extending the range of n to encompass the maximum expected life span of individuals covered by the policy. In fact in producing statistics of mortality, actuaries will usually construct tables summing the series

$$\frac{l_{x+1}}{(1+i)^1}, \ldots, \frac{l_{x+n}}{(1+i)^n}$$

over the remaining life span of prospective customers, for selected rates of interest i.

Term insurance

A term policy pays out the insured sum if the individual dies within a specified term. Thus the expected probabilities will be given by

$$\frac{d_x}{l_x}, \frac{d_{x+1}}{l_x}, \ldots$$

when d_x is the number of people dying between the ages of x and $x + 1$. Taking into account the time value of the funds, the necessary single premium for a term of n years will be given by

$$A_{\overline{x:n}} = \left[\frac{d_x}{l_x}\right]\left[\frac{1}{(1+i)}\right] + \left[\frac{d_{x+1}}{l_x}\right]\left[\frac{1}{(1+i)^2}\right]$$

$$+ \ldots + \left[\frac{d_{x+n-1}}{l_x}\right]\left[\frac{1}{(1+i)^n}\right] \tag{16A.3}$$

For 18-year-olds, a two-year policy would be valued at

$$A_{\overline{18:2}} = \frac{3}{1000}\frac{1}{1.05} + \frac{3}{1000}\frac{1}{(1.05)^2}$$

Thus, single premium = £0.00558 for a £1 policy, £5.58 for a £1,000 policy.

For a whole-life insurance policy, this series can be extended over the expected life span of the insured. As with the annuity calculations, tables include information which facilitates the estimation of life insurance premiums.

Complications start to enter the actuarial calculation when evaluating policies for which annual premiums are payable. But we can illustrate the method by considering the evaluation of a term policy insurance promising £1 on death on which the premiums are paid annually at the beginning of each year.

At the start of the period the annual premium P will be paid by l_x individuals. At the end of the first year, d_x will be paid out and the premium will become due for the surviving l_{x1} individuals. We therefore have

$$\left[\frac{l_x}{l_x}\right]P + \left[\frac{l_{x+1}}{l_x}\right]\frac{P}{(1+i)} + \left[\frac{l_{x+2}}{l_x}\right]\frac{P}{(1+i)^2}$$

$$+\ldots+ \left[\frac{l_{x+n}}{l_x}\right]\left[\frac{P}{(1+i)^n}\right] = \left[\frac{d_x}{l_x}\right]\left[\frac{1}{(1+i)}\right] + \left[\frac{d_{x+1}}{l_x}\right]\left[\frac{1}{(1+i)^2}\right]$$

$$+\ldots+ \left[\frac{d_{x+n-1}}{l_x}\right]\left[\frac{1}{(1+i)^n}\right] \tag{16A.4}$$

But the left-hand side of the equation is similar to the expression (16A.2), the single premium for an n-year temporary life annuity. It can be rewritten in the form

$$P(1 + a_{\overline{x:n}})$$

Similarly, the right-hand side can be seen to be like (16A.3) and can be written A x:n. So

$$P(1 + a_{\overline{x:n}}) = A_{\overline{x:n}}$$

or

$$P^1{}_{\overline{x:n}} = \frac{A_{\overline{x:n}}}{(1 + a_{\overline{x:n}}{}^{-1})}$$

where

$P^1{}_{\overline{x:n}}$ = net annual premium for an ordinary n-year term insurance policy
$A_{\overline{x:n}}$ = net single premium for an n-year term insurance policy
$a_{\overline{x:n}}$ = net single premium for an n-year term life annuity

These expressions may be used in building and evaluating more complicated policies – students should refer to the actuarial texts for more comprehensive and realistic applications.

PART IV

Governance and regulation

Introduction to Part IV

The section is concerned not with the structure of the financial sector markets but with some of the issues facing practitioners both within and outside the institutions. The relationship between the financial sector and industry is not always an easy one, and national government and the international organisations sometimes intervene, both to smooth access to capital markets, and also to regulate them.

Chapter 17 focuses on an increasingly important segment of the market for funds, the small and medium-sized businesses. The special needs and practices of these firms require alternative methods of raising capital and this is sometimes achieved by indirect routes, such as through the venture capital agencies, or by leasing arrangements.

The separation of the management of a firm from its shareholders, and hence the owners of the firm, has been investigated at length in the economics and finance literature. This is generally within the framework of principal and agent theory, a relationship introduced in Chapter 7 in the context of brokers and investors. Here, the owners of the firm are the principals and the managers are the agents. Additional complications can arise when the principal is an investing intermediary with large amounts of capital at its disposal. Finally, alternative models of the interactions of providers and users of funds are presented. These topics are addressed in Chapter 18.

Finally, in Part IV we consider the supervision and regulation of financial markets. This is mainly from a UK perspective, but given there is an increasing need for convergence with other national systems, some comments on the international harmonisation of regulation are also included.

Small business finance

17.1 Introduction

The process of intermediation inherently requires a flexible response to any allocative or operational market inefficiencies. This can be illustrated by the number of specialist institutions, usually from the commercial sector, but sometimes directly from government or even from the international agencies, aimed at the market for venture capital and to other borrowers who find mainstream financing difficult. One particularly important group, in terms of the number of firms involved, are those in the small and medium-sized firm sector.

In this chapter we examine the funding available to this group, as well as some of the institutions which act as intermediaries in channelling finance to borrowing institutions, or to industry directly. These are generally specialist organisations aiming at a particular market or class of risk. We shall also consider alternative ways for firms to invest in new projects, such as financial and operating leases.

17.2 Funding small and medium-sized enterprises

Historically, it has been suggested that small companies have been hampered in their attempts to expand by their lack of financing opportunities. Very small companies can borrow money from banks in their normal course of business, in the same way as individuals and households do. Large companies can use the capital markets, issuing debt or equity on the Stock Exchange. But it is small and medium-sized firms which find it more difficult to borrow or raise funds.

Concern over the small-firm sector is not new. The first major review of the imperfections in the finance market relating to small firms was carried out by the Macmillan Committee in 1931, concluding that there was a shortage of long-term capital for this sector. The Industrial and Commercial Finance Corporation was established in 1945, as a consequence of this report, providing loans and particularly equity capital for small firms. In 1971, the Bolton Committee found this *equity gap* for small firms still existed, although special schemes were recommended. Finally, in 1979, the Wilson Committee found that small firms still lacked suitable long-term funding, and this time did support the creation of a loan guarantee scheme for smaller firms, which was implemented in 1981.

There are a number of ways in which small firms differ from larger ones with respect to their desirability as investment vehicles for lenders. These include:

1. A higher failure rate. Empirically, failure rates are clearly related to size.
2. Greater uncertainty. Irregular cash flows and a greater vulnerability to changing economic conditions usually face a small firm. This is not necessarily a problem for the lender; as we have stated earlier, higher risk investments attract higher returns. The difficulty is the evaluation of risk. Many small firms are recently registered, have little history and fewer disclosure requirements. Therefore any judgement about the extent of associated risk is inevitably subjective.
3. Volatile performance. Small firms can often be characterised as a limited number of managers producing a modest range of products. There is little scope for diversification of any kind, and rarely are there any additional resources to draw on if necessary.

There have been numerous responses to this identified gap in the market. Individual banks have set up subsidiary companies with the prime objective of developing financing links with expanding companies. Clearly, if a potentially successful small firm can be identified, they are very attractive to the financial sector. As they expand, the demand for additional products and services will grow, eventually to include pension and insurance plans for owners and managers, possibly specialist advice on exporting, and maybe a quotation on the Stock Exchange.

This financing can take various forms including loans made for periods of up to five or seven years, instalment credit, leasing and loans made on the strength of trade debtors. The sums involved are usually between £50,000 and £250,000 but can involve larger sums for companies which can offer more security against the loan or which are estimated to have superior growth opportunities.

There are also similar institutions which specialise in offering finance in the form of participating equity. Again flexibility is emphasised in the packages of finance offered but may consist of, perhaps, £200,000 taken first as a preference share but with an option of converting into an ordinary share at some further date. This arrangement safeguards the income of the lending company in the short term but ensures that if the debtor firm performs as well as anticipated, the lender will be able to share in the increased wealth generated by it.

With respect to the investing intermediaries, specialist funds have been set up by the pension and long-term insurance funds as well as by those investment trusts which have the necessary discretion in investing their funds. Because of the long time horizon taken by these institutions, it is not surprising that they tend to take more equity interest than their banking counterparts. One approach for a long-term fund wishing to provide finance for new or expanding firms is to buy the property used by the company, which then repays the fund by renting the property back. This type of financing is called 'sale and leaseback' since the borrower effectively obtains finance by leasing back a property previously owned. We shall return to leasing arrangements later in this chapter.

17.3 Venture capital organisations

One growth area for banks in recent years is that of venture capital. Funds are used for start-up ventures, expansion and growth in an unquoted company. In the UK during 1982, the industry made around 300 investments totalling £110 million, and in 1989, over 1,300 investments totalling £1,400 million. Many of these were buyouts and therefore did not assist completely new firms to become established, but this investment did help to facilitate changes of ownership and continued commercial activity in a number of cases.

There are two formal sources of venture capital in the UK. An example of the first is a financial institution with relevant expertise, the Investors in Industry plc otherwise known as the 3i Group, often called a *captive* fund. This was set up by a group of institutions including the Bank of England, the clearing banks and long-term investors: The 3i Group offers a number of specialist financing services, including the provision of capital to companies expecting to expand very quickly. This venture capital division undertakes to provide finance to small and medium-sized businesses in the form either of loans or by buying shares.

The 3i Group is a publicly quoted company and obtains finance through the capital markets. In addition, the group accepts deposits for periods of between one and ten years. Because it has more than £1,000 million lent or invested, the group has access to large-scale economies that might be unavailable to the smaller firms that it finances. In this respect it is a very successful example of financial intermediation. The group also has expertise in helping to finance management buyouts in which the management of a company or a division of a company effectively takes control from the previous owners. In the case of a division separating from its parent, a new company is created. Management buyouts were quite popular during the 1980s, partly as a response to correct overambitious diversification in previous years, although they have since lost their appeal.

The other major source of funds is independent firms exclusively concerned with the provision of venture capital. These include subsidiaries of US organisations and smaller UK groups specialising in certain sectors of the market, such as regional funds, for example, Northern Venture Managers. Their firms generally compete for institutional funds from the pensions and insurance companies, where many of the investing intermediaries and banks allocate capital, especially for venture capital projects.

17.4 Public sector enterprise schemes

As well as the many intermediaries set up by the private sector, there are a number of institutions and schemes that have been established by and on behalf of the government. In some cases they have been designed to take investment decisions that would not otherwise be considered acceptable by private sector institutions. Thus, for example, the National Research and Development Corporation (NRDC) was established specifically to provide funds for technological innovation.

The NRDC and the National Enterprise Board (NEB) are now linked under a common partnership, known as the British Technology Group. The group's role has changed substantially in response to current political views. When it was established in 1975, it was viewed as being a major channel through which public funds could be directed towards industrial companies. The British Technology Group was privatised in 1992, and is now controlled by a consortium of ten UK financial institutions and the venture capital division of the British Coal pension funds. An additional twelve UK universities are also involved.

Other public sector financial services include a range of regionally-based financial facilities, such as the Derbyshire Enterprise Board. These are generally administered by central or local government and are required to be registered as financial intermediaries, even though capital is not raised from market sources. In addition, the Enterprise Investment Scheme, named the *business angels project* is another government initiative designed to channel funds into small companies.

17.5 International institutions

The enormous growth in the number of overseas banks participating in the UK financial markets has led to a substantial increase in intermediation between British institutions and overseas suppliers of investment funds.

Besides the large number of overseas banks which now operate in the UK, some of which have a particular focus, there are a number of agencies set up under international agreements. Most of these, such as the International Monetary Fund, operate by lending currency to countries. The funds for these loans are provided by subscriptions from member countries and so do not come within our consideration. In some cases, such as the problems arising from the effect of oil revenues accruing to a small number of countries, the solution has involved the cooperation of market-orientated institutions (including banks) with the IMF and the member governments. In this instance the excess supply of dollars accruing to the oil-exporting countries was recycled into the world investment markets (including the UK stock and monetary markets).

In other cases, the IMF has, with the agreement of its members, created extra liquidity in the world monetary markets by issuing the special drawing right (SDR), introduced in Chapter 6. The aim was to effect the same kind of changes in the international sphere as the introduction of bank credit had within the domestic financial system, that is, to increase the efficient operation of the system.

Another international agency which has acted as an intermediary affecting operations in the UK markets, is the European Investment Bank (EIB). The EIB was set up in 1958 with capital subscribed from the members of the European Community and with the power to raise capital on domestic and international capital markets. Most of the loans made by the EIB help to finance regional development projects and concern 'infra-structure' such as the provision of roads, water supply and sewage treatment; they also finance small and medium-sized tourism enterprises.

The economic significance of operations such as the EIB is that the projects financed can be very large, and are financed by an international intermediary raising capital from domestic markets with the security provided by the institution rather than the specific project. It is almost impossible to categorise large projects into domestic, international, private or public since a prominent feature of this type of intermediation is cooperation between different types of institution. The EIB can cooperate with private sector intermediaries and may lend sterling, dollars or mixtures of currencies as the specific case requires. Loans may involve fixed or floating interest rates and be repaid in a single currency or a range of specified currencies.

17.6 Leasing

Leasing is a contract between the lessor who retains ownership of an asset and the lessee who has exclusive use of that asset. Therefore a leasing agreement requires the permanent separation of ownership and use, which is central to the concept of equipment leasing, and which differentiates it from hire-purchasing where the lessee does eventually take title to the goods.

The UK leasing industry has grown dramatically in the past few years, with about 10% of all investment in equipment leased in 1978 to 24% in 1992. The most common items of capital equipment leased include plant, machinery, vehicles and computer hardware.

Particularly for small firms, finance for asset acquisition has traditionally been raised from the clearing banks, but leasing can offer a very attractive alternative source of funds. We shall briefly consider the advantages and disadvantages of leasing compared with outright ownership of the equipment, but first we should consider the tax effects, since these may be a benefit or a cost.

Tax effects

The first effect is a positive one, as the entire lease repayment can be offset against taxable profit, as an expense. This contrasts with other forms of finance where only the interest element is allowed as an expense against profit for tax purposes. Thus, leasing can provide a greater tax benefit than an interest-bearing loan.

But at the same time, the lessee is not the owner of the asset, and so capital allowances may not be claimed. So, unlike direct ownership, or eventual ownership through hire-purchase, there may be a disincentive associated with leasing.

Cash flow benefits

Leasing can positively influence the firm's cash flow position. Maintaining liquidity is a constant difficulty for small firms, and can frequently be the cause of failure. The known, regular pattern of payments can be easier to deal with than single large payments, and businesses subject to seasonality can match their cash payments to their cash receipts.

Protection against obsolescence

This is an increasingly important benefit for firms using high levels of technology, and particularly affects computer and office equipment. Leasing can provide the opportunity to replace the asset with an updated version easily, whereas although there is a secondary market for machines, the prices generally reflect a high loss on the original investment. As well as upgrading, many leasing firms provide service and maintenance for the asset.

Ownership of the asset

One constraint to leasing is that, by definition, the asset is not owned, now or in the future. Apart from the inability to claim capital allowance, the value of the firm overall is reduced if the equipment is leased and not owned. This is only an issue if the firm is to be sold, or if the assets are to be sold to pay outstanding debts.

It is also apparent from a number of surveys of small firms to discover their preferences with respect to leasing that the benefits of outright ownership do seem to be driven by non-economic rationale, and mistrust of leasing.

Relative costs

Perceptions that leasing is costly may be unfounded, although this is difficult to discuss in general terms since each leasing agreement is specific to the lessee and the lessor. However, comparative costs are difficult to compute given the tax effects must be included, and the costs of acquiring finance from another source.

Certainly in general, small firms experiencing the equity gap may look to other sources of funding, and leasing may be cost-effective. Particularly very new companies which do not have any financial history may find the cost of debt to finance new equipment is very high. Instead finance companies may be prepared to provide lease finance.

17.7 Summary

The needs of special industry groups, such as small or medium-sized firms or new enterprises, are addressed by both commercial lenders and government initiatives. The costs and benefits of leasing are not necessarily a sufficiently strong argument for new entrepreneurs, although they may be adequate for finance companies.

Further reading

Barber, J., Metcalfe, J. S. and M. Porteous (1989), *Barriers to Growth in Small Firms*, Routledge.
Department of Employment (1989), *Small Firms in Britain*, Department of Employment.

Government reports on the special funds requirements of small firms:
Bolton Committee (1971), *Report on the Committee of Enquiry on Small Firms*, Cmnd 4811, HMSO.
Macmillan Committee (1931), *Report of the Committee on Finance and Industry*, Cmnd 3897, HMSO.
Wilson Committee (1979), *The Financing of Small Firms*, Interim Report of the Committee to Review the Functioning of Financial Institutions, Cmnd 7503, HMSO.

Questions

17.1 What makes small firms inherently risky?
17.2 Outline the arguments for and against leasing.
17.3 Describe some of the main sources of finance available to small and medium-sized firms.

CHAPTER 18

Finance, industry and governance

18.1 Introduction

This chapter discusses the ways in which industry and the financial sector interact. It is generally accepted that industry is responsible for funding itself, having an obligation to shareholders to undertake the most profitable investment projects, while acquiring the lowest cost funds available from the financial sector with which to do it. But these two groups are not entirely independent.

We shall begin by examining some of the conflicts between the industrial and financial sectors, particularly in the light of the increasing power of the institutional investors in the capital markets. An investigation into the financial aspects of corporate governance, undertaken by the Cadbury Committee, has highlighted the respective responsibilities of managers and of shareholders, with the recognition that institutional shareholders may have different objectives than private shareholders. This report will be discussed only in this context.

Finally, a comparison of alternative models of the relationship of government, the financial institutions and industry illustrates that aspects of investment practice differ between the UK and other countries.

18.2 Corporate versus institutional governance

Corporate governance is the system by which companies are directed and controlled. Clearly an important aspect of this is the investment strategy of the management and the methods they use to raise the necessary funds. However, this book has deliberately avoided any discussion of investment decisions by firms or individuals, and has concentrated solely on the intermediary role of the institutions in allocating funds, in a market which is assumed to price assets efficiently.

However, in the discussion of the equity clientele effect in Chapter 7, we saw how the market price of securities could be distorted by the block trades of the institutional investors. This is increasingly the case, since the value of UK and overseas equity controlled by insurance companies and pension funds increased from £221 billion in 1983 to over £417 billion in 1993. Additional consequences of this enormous spending power include possible political and allocational effects, and considerable unease about the nature of governance. We shall now consider the main issues of importance here.

Shareholder influence

One way in which this investment power might be expected to be asserted is in influencing the management policies of the companies in which the insurance and pension funds hold shares. For example, in some firms an insurance company may be the single most important shareholder, while in others a small group of institutional funds may jointly hold more than half the issued share capital and thus dominate the voting on any issue which affects shareholder interests. Critics of this potential power argue that the fund managers are in a position to exploit their specific interests, citing names of directors of insurance companies who also appear on the board of other companies in which shares are held. These interlocking directorships and other less formal links may adversely affect the interests of private shareholders since decisions may be forced through the board more in the interests of the long-term insurance or pension funds and against the interests of the less knowledgeable private investors.

A more positive view is that the institutions are a welcome countervailing force to the policies and decisions made by the management of the company. Without institutional investors, the private shareholders of any large company might be far too weak and badly organised to safeguard their own interests. Management would then be in a position to maintain inefficient policies which could never be effectively questioned. In this case, the institutional investors are helping to maintain high levels of efficiency and are able to remove any manager not acting in a way most beneficial to shareholders.

The above argument fails if the investing institutions are passive. Passivity on the part of the investing intermediaries will not question incompetent managers, nor will it monitor them. It is sometimes argued that institutional investors should intervene more in the managerial affairs of the companies in which they hold shares, although the empirical evidence is that there is a low level of active participation with respect to exercising voting rights at firms' annual general meetings. When investors do exert pressure, they may reverse poor performance, but if they are not committed to long-term investment, preferring to transfer their funds elsewhere, the company situation may be worsened by their leaving.

Short-termism

That decisions often lack a sufficient time-horizon is a criticism frequently levelled at British industry, and often associated with the impact of institutional investors. The argument is more persuasive when based on the method of remuneration, both of company executives and fund managers. In the case of the former group, accounting-based bonuses may result in short-horizon outcomes taking precedence over long-term investment decisions. In real terms, many investment projects in industry which would be expected to give an acceptable return to shareholders are of a much longer duration.

Clearly, the involvement of the fund managers adds further complexity to the principal and agent problem, in that there are two agents: the firm's managers and the fund managers. Firms may have long investment horizons, and so may the providers of capital, particularly in the case of pension fund contributors. Thus, the principal and agent may agree, but between these two actors are the fund managers, whose personal incentives are not compatible with long-term perform-ance measurement, if their remuneration depends on short-term results.

Contrary to these criticisms is the view that, in an efficient stock market, the mismatch of horizons is of no consequence because share prices capture long-term expectations of corporate performance. However, it is worth remembering Keynes' comment that success on the stock market depends on outguessing the other guessers rather than having any particular skills at valuing real assets.

Reallocation of funds

We have argued earlier that takeover bids made for a poorly run company may contribute to the allocative efficiency of the market. This can be done more easily if several large institutional investors approve of the proposed new management and redistribute funds from inefficient to efficient firms. Capital is more readily available to ease the transition and restructuring within the organisation, if the change is supported by the fund managers.

Ethical investment

One positive aspect of the size of the institutional investors' portfolios is the influence that can be exerted over the behaviour of firms in the area of environmental and ethical responsibility. Institutional fund managers responsible to a client-group that is concerned over a particular issue have an incentive to seek investments in companies with a sufficiently high record of performance in this area. The growth of ethical investment funds during the past decade confirms that many individual investors who would have no power at all on their own are able to exert pressure on fund managers, and the institutional investors appear to be increasingly prepared to listen.

18.3 The financial aspects of corporate governance

General disquiet about the effectiveness of financing UK industry is not new. The Wilson Committee was set up in 1980 to investigate an area of long-standing concern, namely the ways in which the markets and institutions channel funds to industry and commerce, including the small-business recommendations referred to in Chapter 17.

At that time it was suggested that an agency be created for directing investment, particularly to ensure that some proportion of the institutional investors' cash flow be used to stimulate investment in the UK. This was intended to encourage long-term investment projects, with the investing institutions being rewarded with a guaranteed minimum rate of return equal to the gilt-edged rate. The proposal was rejected on the basis that the existing institutions and markets were sufficiently efficient and flexible to deal with the appraisal of any potentially profitable projects, and a subsidised institution would inevitably encourage investment in less successful projects.

The current political and economic environment supporting deregulation within the financial sector, including the removal of any restrictions on international capital flows, is clearly contrary to any attempt to legislate in this area. Freedom of choice has emerged as the clear rule for investment and the construction of portfolios, be they individual, corporate or institutional. Certainly, since the publication of the Wilson Report, there has been no further movement towards directing investment.

However, for some time, considerable disquiet has been expressed about standards of corporate behaviour, particularly with respect to financial accountability, and this has been heightened by a number of major company failures and also examples of misconduct and fraud, some of which are illustrated in the next chapter. As a response to this concern, the Cadbury Committee was set up in May 1991, jointly by the Financial Reporting Council, the London Stock Exchange and the accountancy profession, to address the financial aspects of corporate governance specifically related to financial reporting and accountability.

The committee's recommendations were presented as a Code of Best Practice, to be monitored by the London Stock Exchange. The Exchange requires companies, as a continuing obligation of listing, to state whether they are complying with the Code and to give reasons for non-compliance. However, like other Stock Exchange rules, there are no legal powers of enforcement although a formal statement of censure would be very detrimental to continued trading.

The arguments presented for adhering to the Code were twofold. First it was thought that a clear understanding of the responsibilities of managers and an openness with regard to strategies would gain support from shareholders and also would assist the efficient operations of capital markets. It was hoped that this would increase confidence in individual firms and the financial sector as a whole. Secondly, if standards of financial reporting and business activity generally did not improve, more regulation would be required rather than the continued deregulation or self-regulation of the financial sector.

The report of the Cadbury Committee included a review of the structure and responsibilities of boards of directors, the role of auditors and the form and content of financial accounts. But in addition it also dealt with the rights and responsibilities of institutional and private shareholders. This last point is of particular interest in the context of this chapter.

It is recognised that the proportion of shares held by individuals and by institutions has broadly reversed over the last thirty years, although the institutional shareholding is held on behalf of individuals as fund members. Therefore there is a common interest between these groups, in particular in the standards of financial reporting and governance in the companies in which they have invested. The Cadbury Committee claimed that all shareholders should use their power to influence the standards, as it is their responsibility as owners to bring about changes in companies when necessary, rather than selling their shares. However, the fund managers have an added responsibility in this regard because of their specialist knowledge of the industry and their familiarity with financial statements, and they are required to clarify more complex details to the fund contributors to ensure parity between shareholders.

Some final comments on the Committee's report relate to the importance of shareholder communications and price-sensitive information. We will address the topic of insider information in the next chapter, but it is interesting to note here that there is a mutual responsibility in this area. If price-sensitive information is made available to shareholders, as it should be if they are to be involved in a long-term relationship with the company, they must be prepared to accept the short-term constraints to share dealing until that information is made public.

This Code of Conduct recommended by the Cadbury Committee attempts to ensure high standards of governance, by placing the responsibility on maintaining good practice on the management of the firm, their financial advisers and auditors and the shareholders alike. The emphasis is on accountability rather than increased regulation.

18.4 Relationship of the financial sector to industry

The final topic in this chapter continues with the theme of corporate performance and the role of the financial sector, although now we concentrate on the role of the banks rather than the investing intermediaries. This is an area in which the UK differs significantly from a number of other countries. While the legal framework may have accounted for these differences historically, custom and practice have caused them to become established as part of the organisational culture of corporations and financial institutions.

A number of factors can be used to structure country comparisons, such as regulation, competition and customer relations, including those between banks and corporations in financial distress. Regulation will be discussed first, since it has an impact on the other issues.

One of the most important aspects of national regulation is the degree to which the financial sector institutions are required to be specialist rather than general, and therefore are restricted in their activities. Although specialist banks still exist in many countries, particularly in Europe, the move towards universal banking has accelerated during the last few years. For example, banks in Germany and the UK undertake a wide variety of activities, including retail and wholesale banking, insurance and the provision of investment advice and brokerage services. Differences between the way German and British banks conduct their securities trading remain. For example, the Germans operate through subsidiaries, while the British include these activities directly, but within the overall organisation all of these financial activities are permissible.

On the other hand, in the US and Japan there are more restrictions on the activities of banks, and these countries both prohibit securities trading, underwriting of corporate equity and insurance entirely.

Another important national distinction is whether banks are allowed to hold equity in non-financial firms or not, a difference which has major implications for corporate control. American and Japanese banks face restrictions in this regard, although with very different results. Japanese banks have their ownership of individual companies limited to 5%, with several banks holding a small share in most companies, while in the US corporate ownership is held directly by individuals and investment funds, spread over many investors, but with no banks or other financial institutions being represented. In the UK, banks hold little or no corporate equity, most of which is under the control of the investing institutions.

Conversely, banks in Germany, France and Spain have a considerable financial interest in corporations, sometimes as direct owners of equity and sometimes as custodians of the shares held by private investors. The relationship between bank and corporation is very close in Germany, frequently with a bank representative being in a senior position on the supervisory board of the company.

The level of competition in the banking sector differs from the highly concentrated UK, Japanese and German models to the highly fragmented US system, although the one-state banking regulation in the US is undergoing considerable reform. The large number of private firms within the US banking sector has resulted in a variable risk profile and high bankruptcy rate for banks. As a consequence, the relationship between banking and industry is sometimes threatened, which is a special problem in an area where confidence in the security of the banking sector in general is a very important factor.

One measure of this relationship between banks and corporate clients is shown by the reaction of banks to customers who are performing poorly. In Germany, the banks are used to having the role of arbiter in issues of financial control, and they intervene both in their own right, and as custodians on behalf of other shareholders. In Japan, complex systems of networks exist between firms and banks, and the structure of cross-shareholding means decisions are often collective ones. In each of these countries, banks will intervene to restructure firms to resolve financial distress by informal rescue arrangements.

Rather than the close association enjoyed by German and Japanese banks with their customers, the US and UK experience is one of increasing distance and loss of long-term commitment. There has been a shift from an on-going relationship to a series of market-based transactions using short-term contracts. Legislation in the UK has forbidden banks to intervene to demand an internal restructuring to avoid bankruptcy, and the US restricts or discourages insider support for financially distressed firms.

The advantage of relationship banking is that banks can enter into implicit contracts with firms. One such contract may be an agreement that banks can refinance the company or reduce lending margins if they are experiencing distress, on the understanding that they can get higher margins when this has been resolved. It does require countercyclical adjustment which can only be done under flexible loan rates, but the bank can offer rescheduling of debt if needed, whereas at present, banks widen margins to compensate for higher default risks in recessions and to narrow them in a recovery, that is, act pro-cyclically. This can emphasise the business cycle rather than reducing it, and exacerbate the already high cost of capital in the UK compared with Japanese and German counterparts.

18.5 Summary

Changes in the pattern of investment, with greater financial power being held by the investing intermediaries and less by private individuals, have shifted the balance of control in the market for capital. As a consequence, a redefining of roles and responsibilities has occurred, in a search for a mutually satisfactory model of corporate governance. This relationship between the providers and users of funds is important in the financial sector as a whole, and we have considered the part played by the banks and the investment institutions in the provision of funding to industry. Comparisons with Japan and Germany show that the closer involvement of banks with individual firms has some advantages, and relationship banking may be the model of choice if long-term investment programmes are to succeed.

Further reading

Details of the recommendations included in the Cadbury Report:
Bank of England Quarterly Bulletin (1994), *The Bank and Corporate Governance: Past, present and future*, November, pp. 388–91.
Report on the Committee on *The Financial Aspects of Corporate Governance* (1992), Gee and Co.

Relationship banking and comparative systems:
Gardener, E. P. and P. Molyneux (1990), *Changes in Western European Banking*, Unwin Hyman.
Kaufman, G. A. (ed.) (1992), *Banking Structure in Major Countries*, Kluwer Academic Publishers.

Questions

18.1 Outline the responsibilities defined by the Cadbury Report, with respect to:
   (a) Managers
   (b) Private shareholders
   (c) Institutional shareholders
18.2 What do you understand by *relationship banking*? Discuss the different approaches of bank lending to industry in the UK and Germany.

CHAPTER 19

Regulation and international harmonisation

19.1 Introduction

Throughout this book, we have discussed supervision and regulation in very general terms, but have not considered its impact on individual markets. This chapter begins by taking a critical perspective of regulation and puts it into an economic framework. We then map the structure of regulation imposed by the authorities, including the self-regulatory organisations charged with maintaining levels of conduct conducive to efficient market performance and practice. Some recent cases are used as illustrations of fraud, and finally, we shall examine some of the steps already taken in the harmonisation of financial practice in the European Union and internationally.

19.2 Perspectives on regulation

The financial sector is probably one of the most highly regulated industries in the UK, and most other countries. Even the frequent references to the liberal environment in the City of London imply a degree of reregulation, as changes have been designed to encourage rather than restrict activities. It has been suggested that much of the regulation introduced into the financial sector during the last few years has been prompted as much by the wish to create a climate free of restrictions as by the need to respond to a scandal or crisis. Indeed the debate on the type and extent of regulation in financial markets recurs during any period in which the markets are seen to be disturbed, whether by economic pressures or sudden development.

The regulatory environment in the UK still attracts criticism, even from the supporters of the 1984 Gower Report on Investor Protection which is the basis of much of the present structure. The motivation for regulation of the financial sector comes from a number of sources. A political, rather than technical, factor is the need for the markets to be seen to be fair, with undesirable elements promptly removed from the financial community. The expulsion of those seen to be acting fraudulently, as well as the exclusion of those considered to be unsuitable to manage investors' funds are both part of the necessary supervision and regulation of the sector. This follows from the premiss that there is a difference between financial and other economic activity. Hence the failure of a financial institution has wide-ranging effects beyond that firm's own customers and the individuals employed by them, compared with the consequences following the collapse of non-financial firms.

Another feature of financial institutions, especially banks and investment funds, is that they have very large numbers of customers who are often unfamiliar with the industry and the products and services offered and who are generally unsophisticated about financial activities. Thus an aspect of consumer protection is involved.

The introduction of new products and a wave of financial innovation, accompanied by massive changes in the financial sector, prompted further debate about an appropriate level of regulation. The incentives for many of the innovations were to evade existing regulation, while at the same time, new entrants to the markets offering traditional financial sector services (such as Marks & Spencer loans) were not under the same supervision as established financial institutions.

The final factor leading to a reappraisal of the regulatory system was the increasing international nature of financial markets, with a call for international standards in excess of the informal arrangements through the Bank for International Settlements, or some level of harmonisation.

While these factors support a degree of regulation, arguments against it are based primarily on costs, incurred by both the regulator and the regulated. There are also efficiency arguments, centred on the threat to competition posed by restrictions and the stifling of financial and technical innovation, and the fear that institutions will capture the regulators with a view to biasing the regulations in their own favour or distorting the markets in some way.

The current system of regulation attempts to account for many of the issues raised in the discussion above, with that result that three themes dominate legislation: authorisation, supervision and compensation. First, licensing authorities only allow financial business to be undertaken by suitable individuals who are competent and qualified – that is, they are *fit and proper persons*. To engage in business without authorisation is a criminal offence. Secondly, supervision, including reporting and disclosure and the monitoring of financial institutions, is carried out as frequently as required by the supervising body. If this is not satisfactory, the licence to operate is withdrawn. Finally, compensation for private individuals is available in the case of failure. This is specifically to aid unknowing investors in the event of fraud or other misconduct, and not simply to repay the loss incurred in a risky investment.

19.3 The structure of regulation

The activities within the financial sector are regulated quite differently. In some cases economic controls are imposed and in some prudential supervision includes granting a licence prior to operation. There has traditionally been a strong reliance on self-regulation in the UK securities markets, and this worked well while the investment community was small, trading was carried out face to face, and participants generally knew each other. But over the last few years personal contact and mutual responsibility have diminished and the sheer increase in the number of participants in the London markets has meant that moral suasion is no longer adequate and external agencies have been forced to intervene.

Formal legislation is now in place, involving the Department of Trade and Industry, the Serious Fraud Squad and the Director of Public Prosecutions, as well as the Bank of England which has effectively stepped in from time to time to supervise market operations.

All of the broad areas of activity covered in this book are regulated through Acts of Parliament. The Bank of England is responsible for the banking sector, as well as the gilt-edged security and money markets, and the Building Societies Commission for building societies, under the 1987 Banking Act and 1986 Building Societies Act respectively.

The insurance sector is the responsibility of the Department of Trade and Industry, under the 1982 Insurance Companies Act, although there are exceptions to this. The most notable is Lloyd's who retained the right to supervise itself under a separate statute, the 1982 Lloyd's Act. However, this statute has caused considerable controversy for some time, in many cases arising from the practice of reinsurance. Re-insurance has the beneficial aspect of spreading the risk; it has also been the basis of some institutional problems suffered by Lloyd's over the past decade. However, because of the freedom with which underwriters have been able to transact reinsurance business with companies registered outside Lloyd's and outside the insurance regulations of the UK, individual underwriters setting up reinsurance contracts may face conflicts of interest. During the early 1980s, the self-regulatory system of Lloyd's received some harsh criticism and changes were made but there is still considerable debate in this area.

Finally, the Securities and Investment Board (SIB) is responsible for a whole range of investment activities under the 1986 Financial Services Act, although this has been delegated to a number of individual bodies, known as self-regulatory organisations (SROs). The act also gave powers to the Trade Secretary to initiate investigations into insider dealing.

The principle of self-regulation was instituted for a number of reasons. Since it was acknowledged that financial markets are continually developing, a flexible form of regulation and control is quicker to implement and clearly preferable to a highly complex legal structure which may be slow to react to new demands. Also the involvement of practitioners in both formulating and enforcing the rules encourages compliance and the maintenance of high standards of conduct as well as providing the opportunity for closer scrutiny of fellow professionals. Finally, it was considered beneficial for there to be a degree of separation between government and the routine regulation of the markets.

Therefore the SIB does not regulate directly but monitors the effectiveness of the SROs. Currently there are five SROs, covering different investment activities:

FIMBRA – The Financial Intermediaries, Managers and Brokers Regulatory Association. This is for independent intermediaries advising on and arranging deals in investments, mainly life assurance and unit trusts, or providing investment advisory and management services to retail customers.

IMRO – The Investment Management Regulatory Organisation. This is for investment managers and advisers, particularly institutional funds, unit trust and pension fund managers.

LAUTRO – The Life Assurance and Unit Trust Regulatory Organisation. This is concerned only with the marketing associated with life assurance and unit trust products. Membership of this SRO will not necessarily authorise a firm to carry on investment business, as this only occurs through recognition by FIMBRA or IMRO.

SFA – The Securities and Futures Authority. This was formed by mergers between a number of entities. Its members are those institutions dealing or arranging deals in securities and derivatives, including bonds, equities, gilts, eurosecurities, commodity and financial options and futures. Also covered by this organisation are those advising on corporate finance activity, such as mergers and acquisitions.

PIA – The Personal Investment Authority. This is the most recent SRO and is concerned with retail investment.

The Securities and Investment Board also acknowledges certain recognised investment exchanges (RIEs) and recognised professional bodies (RPBs), all of which have approved resources and codes of practice. The responsibilities of the SIB are shown in Figure 19.1. In addition, there is the Takeover Panel, which is concerned with setting rules and overseeing the conduct of takeovers and other issues.

Some of the difficulty with this system of regulation, constructed as it is on an activity-specific framework, is that many organisations are involved in a wide range of activities, and so there is considerable overlap. If we consider the jurisdiction of the SIB only, one firm may be responsible to more than one SRO. This becomes more complex still when other supervisory authorities are also involved. For example, the clearing banks are supervised primarily by the Bank of England, but they also offer many investment services covered by the Financial Services Act. This is clearly inefficient, as well as increasing the cost of regulation which is carried by the firms, and inevitably the customers.

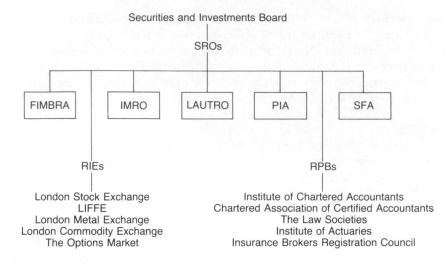

Figure 19.1 Regulatory structure of UK financial markets.

The Companies Securities Act (1985), and aspects of the Financial Services Act, covers a number of activities associated with securities including the problem of insider dealing. The problem of insider dealing arises at its simplest when an employee of a company sells confidential information to an investor. In other cases, any individual who is professionally related to a company may be able to use some confidential information for speculating in the shares of the company. This has become increasingly difficult to monitor since the Big Bang restructuring and the emergence of institutions which undertake a variety of investment activities. In the era of single capacity trading, one firm was not involved in the spread of services including brokerage, investment advice and corporate finance business. Now that this does happen, distinctions have to be made between members of the same organisations engaged in activities which may present opportunities for conflict of interest. The somewhat artificial barriers constructed within organisations are known as 'Chinese walls'. The costs of monitoring these activities are high, but the loss of confidence in the financial sector is the inevitable result of not doing this.

Regulation in the derivatives markets is fairly rigorous, and is made easier since the markets are in clearly defined physical locations, e.g. LIFFE in London and the Chicago Board of Trade in the US. Brokers and traders are under the control of the Exchange itself, the regulatory authority (the Securities and Investment Board in the UK) and the self-regulatory Securities and Futures Authority. But although regulation is easier to impose, the opportunities for fraudulent practice are clear, since the complexity of the market instruments means that investors are especially vulnerable.[1]

In other countries, the equivalent body to the Securities and Investment Board (e.g. the US Securities and Exchange Commission) has to cover the dealing and trading practices in a wide range of financial/investment markets located in many different parts of the country, and in these circumstances it may be beneficial if the authority has official status and the possession of significant powers to enforce compliance with regulations.

19.4 Non-compliance and fraud in the financial sector

Regulation and supervision are in place to protect investors and maintain confidence in the financial system as a whole. But however prudent a supervisor, or risk-averse a manager, organisations fail, usually as a result of fraud. The Serious Fraud Office investigates alleged frauds of £5 million or more, and during 1992, nearly sixty cases were under investigation.

Examples of violation of regulation and of fraud can be drawn from all sections of the financial sector, and the following illustrations are just a few of a number of recent well-publicised cases.

Concern over bank supervision can be illustrated by the collapse of *Johnson Matthey Bankers* in 1985. The Bank loaned £134 million to attempt to save this institution as part of the 'lifeboat' scheme which was supposed to neutralise the damage of one failing bank by redirecting its funds into safer ones, such as the clearing banks. But the plan failed, and Johnson Matthey lost £248 million. Following this, the bank auditors were investigated, and the Bank of England was criticised for failing to supervise effectively.

More recently, the failure of the *Bank of Credit and Commerce International* (BCCI) in 1991 has attracted considerable attention. Following the Second Banking Directive, responsibility for the primary supervision of the bank belonged to the central bank of the home country, Institut Monetaire Luxembourgeois, although auditors reporting to the Bank of England expressed increasing concern. The damage to the bank following criminal proceedings relating to drug trafficking and money-laundering in Florida was so great that even though shareholders contributed £400 million for restructuring, the bank went into liquidation.

In another area of financial activity, *Barlow Clowes* was an investment fraud of massive proportions. Investors, 96% of whom were UK residents, were induced to invest money by a series of mispresentations and their money subsequently misappropriated. The company was based in Gibraltar to take advantage of the liberal regulatory environment and claimed to be involved in the investment and management of gilt-edged securities on behalf of clients. However, much of the money was simply diverted through an elaborate network of offshore companies; some was spent on houses, yachts, cars and antique furniture, or put into companies owned by the Clowes family. That which was invested, was not in government-backed securities, but high-risk assets.

Elaborate manoeuvres concealed these transactions from professional advisers, although in 1987 concern was expressed and the company was investigated. The Securities and Investment Board petitioned for a full inquiry, and the company was placed in compulsory liquidation in 1988. The Department of Trade and Industry was considered negligent for allowing Clowes to continue trading after being warned earlier about his activities, and the government agreed to reimburse investors almost all of their money.

An illustration of illegal dealing in the wholesale banking sector is that of the *Blue Arrow* share issue in 1987. Blue Arrow discussed with its advisers, including County NatWest and Phillips & Drew Securities Ltd, their plans to acquire an American company, Manpower Inc. A finance package of £837 million was required and was funded by a rights issue of new shares to existing shareholders, underwritten predominantly by both advising institutions. However, the take-up figure on the rights issue was a disappointing 38.4%, making the placement of the rest on the market very difficult, and leaving the underwriters with a large number of unwanted shares. To avoid this situation, the underwriting institutions purchased sufficient of the outstanding issue without disclosing their involvement in order to conceal the *true rate* of take-up, thereby misleading the market's view of the attractiveness of the shares.

The Bank of England reported their concern to the Department of Trade and Industry, and the Serious Fraud Squad investigated the affair. This is clearly different from the previous two examples, since no one received any personal gain. However, the importance attached to protecting the integrity of the market is maintained, irrespective of the rights of individual investors, none of whom has made any complaint.

Our final example of another violation of the 1985 Companies Act also arises from the wholesale banking sector, and concerns the circumstances surrounding the takeover offer by *Guinness* for Distillers. The illegal activity was based on a share support operation where the objective was to raise the share price of Guinness, making its shares-for-shares offer for Distillers more attractive than it actually was. Those purchasing shares on the understanding that they would be indemnified against losses and costs, and paid a bonus if the acquisition was successful, would be guilty of creating a false market. The argument was that if these conditions of purchase had been generally known, the market would have discounted the impact on the share price. Those involved were convicted of conspiracy to defraud and theft, although the case is now again under review.

While these cases in no sense exhaust the recent fraud and illegal activity in the financial sector, they provide examples of how the regulatory authorities attempt to exert control to maintain confidence in the fairness of the industry. Some cases have already been concluded, such as Ivan Boesky and Michael Milken in the US both of whom used inside information on takeovers to buy underpriced securities. Many others continue, such as the Maxwell pension fund dispute, with further insider dealing investigations and the Lloyd's controversy still under review.

19.5 Regulatory harmonisation

Legislation concerning the financial sector is being developed at a time of increasing globalisation of the market for financial services. The introduction of new products and services and ways of delivering them through technology has increased the need for regulation at an international level. In the 1970s, the Basle Accord was an endeavour by bank supervisors to erode national differences by introducing uniform minimum capital requirements for banks involved in cross-border business.

The European Union programme of legislation is qualitatively different from previous international regulation since its objective is to achieve internal financial integration within the community, as set out in the Single European Act. All the UK legislation has to be consistent with EC law, as seen for example in the directives governing the listing requirements for securities, the solvency requirements for banks and investor protection embodied in the Investment Services Directives.

The framework for insurance reflects those of the banking directives, where supervision and mutual recognition are the objectives. In the non-life insurance sector, types of risk are defined as large or mass risk, large being that relating to large firms and all types of marine and aviation, and mass is almost everything else, including retail domestic and car insurance. The large risk market is becoming increasingly competitive on an international scale. Life insurance is not included in the legislation.

The regulation of the financial sector is contained in the Second Banking Directive, which was discussed in some detail in Chapter 14, and the Investment Services Directive. These are based on the model of universal banking with no separation of investment and commercial activity. For the European Union, the goal is to create a single, unified market by removing barriers to the provision of services across borders: the establishment of branches or subsidiaries of financial institutions throughout the member countries.

The general approach of a single licence through mutual recognition and the assurance of minimum standards on prudential supervision have been implemented. Total harmonisation is unlikely, but one solution reached was the recognition of the laws, regulation and practices of other countries as equivalent to its own, thereby precluding the use of differences in national rules to restrict access. The only exception to this is in cases where national security, or undue risk to consumers or investors, is threatened.

On an international level, differences in regulation still persist. The gap between highly regulated financial sectors and those with a more liberalised regime inevitably results in capital flows moving towards deregulated markets. Investors and firms participating in international markets need to become more knowledgeable, while national regulators struggle to agree on acceptable standards of practice which do not threaten the confidence necessary for the financial sector to function well.

19.6 Summary

Many arguments exist for and against regulation of the financial sector. The general aims of regulation are: to grant authorisation to reputable institutions, and rescind this if there is any misconduct; to supervise and monitor institutions regularly; and to compensate investors in the case of loss due to fraud. Regulation is costly and possibly inhibits competition, but generally provides confidence in the financial sector as a whole.

Note

1. It should be noted that by its nature, derivatives trading may result in an institution suffering huge losses, not due to fraud within the derivatives markets, but rather to overexposure in those markets. The 1995 collapse of Barings Bank followed a high level of activity in derivatives trading unsupported by the firm's total capitalisation.

Further reading

Clarke, M. (1986), *Regulating the City – Competition, Scandal and Reform*, Open University Press.

Gowland, D. (1990), *The Regulation of Financial Markets in the 1990s*, Edward Elgar.

Seldon, A. (ed.) (1988), *Financial Regulation – Or Over Regulation?*, Institute of Economic Affairs.

Stonham, P. (1987), *Global Stock Market Reforms*, Gower Studies in Finance and Investment, Gower.

The Bank of England Quarterly Bulletin has many articles and notes on regulation. In addition a number of government papers on regulatory issues include:

Gower, J. (1982), *Review of Investor Protection – A Discussion Document*, HMSO.

Regulatory Arrangements at Lloyd's: Report of the Committee of Inquiry, Cm 59, HMSO, 1987.

The Royal Commission on Criminal Justice (1993), *The Investigation, Prosecution and Trial of Serious Fraud*, Research Report No. 14, HMSO.

Questions

19.1 Some markets are closely regulated and some not. What is the rationale for regulating the banking sector and not the housing sector?

19.2 Discuss the difference between *regulation* and *supervision*.

19.3 Is harmonisation of regulation a good thing in a trading area such as the European Community? How is this different from an international system of regulation?

19.4 Is self-regulation by practitioners in the financial sector appropriate?

International perspectives and future trends

Introduction to Part V

Chapter 20 of this book covers a topic which has arisen a number of times earlier: the international aspects of financial flows and the differences between trading systems in a number of major global markets. Finally, the concluding remarks highlight some aspects of the financial sector for which change is expected in the new competitive and regulatory environment.

An overview of international financial systems

20.1 Introduction

This book has provided an introduction to the organisations which comprise the financial sector, and has been set firmly in the framework of UK financial markets operating within the British economy. However, it is increasingly obvious that these are simply part of a global network, and this raises a number of issues, of which we will examine only two. The first concerns the threat of competition facing UK markets from other financial centres, and the other is the danger of such an internationally integrated system to the stability of the markets as a whole.

The advantage to London of being in between the major markets of New York and Tokyo with respect to time zones is now being undermined by the other European centres, particularly Paris and Frankfurt. London has been established as a major centre for international equity trading since 1986, and at present the amount of international equity trading in London far exceeds that in other financial centres. SEAQ International is a system parallel to the screen-based pricing and transaction system used for domestic trading, SEAQ, and this accounts for about half of the turnover, with the remaining international business carried in the over-the-counter markets. Table 20.1 shows some details of this activity.

But we cannot assume that this situation will continue and therefore we should consider how these other markets operate, and the threats they may pose to London. We will also comment briefly on some of the newly emerging financial markets and on the direction of their development, since they present opportunities for increased involvement of established financial centres.

All markets are concerned with the exchange of goods and services, and intermediaries exist everywhere to enable these transactions to take place. Both national customs and regulation affect the nature of these intermediaries, although the theory on which the activity is based is a common one. But in general terms, the more developed the country's economy, the greater the complexity of its financial markets. Clearly, as wealth increases, individuals have a greater demand

Table 20.1 International equity trading in London, 1991

	Number of international companies listed	Share of turnover of international equity	London, as % of domestic
US	187	—	—
Japan	114	26.5%	—
South Africa	96	—	—
Canada	36	—	—
France	43	11.8%	29.5
Netherlands	35	8.3%	52.9
Germany	22	23.2%	—
Sweden	21	—	45.0
Switzerland	—	—	35.5

Source: Bank of England (1991, p. 248) and *Stock Exchange Quarterly* with *Quality of Markets Reviews*, July–Sept 1991, pp. 84–5.

for financial securities as there is an excess of funds over that required for immediate consumption, and also the possibility of a diversity of investment projects in which to invest. There is then a need for allocational efficiency for the best promotion of growth and development.

However, while it is not surprising that a positive relationship exists between gross national product per capita and the sophistication of the financial system, this does not dictate how that financial system is organised. As we saw in Chapter 17, there are differences in the relationship between the financial sector and industry, and this difference also affects the structure and importance of the capital markets. Consequently, it can be claimed that the UK, the US, Canada and Japan all have highly developed securities markets, while France and Germany emphasise financial intermediation.

Other differences arise from ideology, as in the centrally planned economies where state ownership of productive resources nullified the need for individuals to participate in markets for tradable securities. A different political system may include a policy which actively promotes the small investor, which by its nature necessitates financial intermediation.

The divergence of financial systems has been reduced in the light of deregulation and the liberalisation of capital flows. Private capital from those countries with less developed capital markets has gravitated to markets abroad, either directly, or through the eurocurrency markets. Indeed, national regulation can now be easily avoided in this way; for example, Japanese interest rate control resulted in a transfer of capital to the US to obtain a higher market return.

But although the markets are in many ways becoming more similar and integrated, differences still persist, and there are a couple of reasons why these are of interest. First, it is useful to highlight areas of competitive pressure for the UK financial sector, and highlight some of the continuing advantages enjoyed by the City of London. Secondly, since some countries are now only beginning to develop financial markets, it is useful to consider the appropriateness of available systems in the context of national requirements.

The remainder of this chapter briefly considers the central features of a number of national financial systems, some of which are highly developed while others are not fully established. Inevitably, in such a comparison we should include the United States and Japan, since they form the two arms of the global time-zone triangle, and also the major European exchanges, as they provide the third.

20.2 The United States

The United States is the largest economy in the world, and this is reflected in the size and diversity of its financial markets. The majority of these markets are located in New York and the American stock exchanges in New York City, although some trading takes place in Los Angeles and some in Midwest cities, such as Chicago. The derivatives markets are much more spread throughout the country, with Chicago and Philadelphia as well as New York trading in a large number of financial and commodity contracts. Apart from these formal markets, over-the-counter trading takes place through the National Association of Securities Dealers Automated Quotations (NASDAQ) system.

The New York Stock Exchange (NYSE) is the largest in the US, and about 80% in dollar value of securities is traded on it. Nearly 2000 firms are listed there, and although there are some foreign firms listed on the New York Stock Exchange, listing is costly; there are strict regulations about the quality of disclosure.

Trading takes place on the floor of the Exchange, unlike the dealing-rooms in the UK. Each security is traded at a specific trading-post where there is a specialist in a fixed number of securities. Any broker wishing to buy or sell goes to that location on the floor. Present and recent pricing information is presented, but the specialist will only give the bid/ask spread rather than the specific bid or offer price. This is a system of continuous trading, but with open outcry, which makes the market transparent. Orders can be left with the specialist, so that the broker does not have to wait for a coincidental matching between buy and sell trades, with transactions costs having to be paid to the specialist as well as the brokers. This use of the specialist can easily be transferred to a computer, to be a system of programmed trading.

Specialists became increasingly important since this system began and in 1934 Congress passed the Securities and Exchange Act which stated that specialists must *maintain a fair and orderly market*, a condition now included as Stock Exchange Rule 103. It is interesting to note that this was never in the remit of London Stock Exchange dealers, even when the single capacity trading system placed the jobber in a similar role to that of the specialist.

The American Stock Exchange (AMEX)[1] is considerably smaller than the NYSE, taking about 4% of business by dollar value. Listing requirements are less stringent, and firms are generally smaller. Several listed companies move to the NYSE when they are sufficiently highly capitalised. Trading mechanisms reflect those of the NYSE, with specialist brokers, and the administration of transactions is done through a mutual clearing house and technical and computing facilities are shared.

Unlike the fortnightly account system in place in London until very recent changes, settlement in the US is on a rolling five-day basis. Customers are required to deposit a proportion of the purchase value with the broker, in a margin account. The size of this margin varies, although at times of high uncertainty this has reached 100%.

Ownership of company equity is the subject of considerable debate in the US as it is in the UK. The investing intermediaries are heavily involved in equity holdings, although there is a more commonly accepted principle of securities trading by individuals in the US, and legislation protected this, encouraging the large funds to invest in bonds instead. However, personal ownership of shares has fallen, with the proportion of equity held by individuals decreasing from 83% in 1970 to 65% in 1988.[2]

20.3 Japan

Three exchanges, Tokyo, Osaka and Nagoya, account for 99% of securities trading in Japan. Domestic and foreign firms are listed, and by market capitalisation, Tokyo is the largest exchange in the world. Membership to the exchange is very restricted, and to foreigners extremely so, but pressures are now resulting in a slightly more open environment and the advantage of reciprocal membership is recognised. Other foreign financial institutions are also entering the Japanese markets, and there are mutual and pension funds as well as banks and insurance companies active in Japan.

The securities markets are divided into those for fully listed companies and those for smaller, maybe newer, companies, but in a less formal way than in the UK or the US. Trading is by continuous auction, such as in New York, with trading-posts and specialists. The most active shares are traded on the floor of the exchange, and the remainder by computer. Price information and other market data are communicated through the Tokyo Market Information Service monitors. Financial futures are traded in both Osaka and Tokyo, and futures and options contracts are listed on the Singapore International Monetary Exchange.

As in the US, Japanese settlement following transactions is carried out on a rolling basis, in this case, of three days. Purchasers contribute to a margin account of 30% minimum, but this can be increased by the government if necessary.

Institutional investment patterns again reflect those of the UK and the US. The proportion of equity held by individuals fell from 61% in 1950 to 24% in 1987, although funds available for investment are high, due to high disposable incomes and the propensity to save referred to earlier. Banks and insurance companies also increased their holdings during this time, but the cross-holdings of shares between the financial institutions and industry discussed in Chapter 17 imply a high level of participation in the equity markets.

Markets in Japan have been more stable than those of many other countries. This may be due to legislation which restricts daily price movements to particular limits, but also the willingness of the authorities to advise large shareholders on particular aspects of their trading, and the corporate and banking relationship structure may reduce volatility in the markets.

20.4 Europe

Many of the European securities markets have undergone a similar series of reforms and subsequent restructuring as occurred in London during the past few years. Initially, this was to stem the flow of business to London, which had been deregulated for some time, particularly with respect to capital movements. Reforms on the scale of London's Big Bang have occurred in many European countries, in particular in France. Change in the trading mechanism has been in the direction of continuous trading, and in the removal of non-competitive trading practices and minimum commissions, all three reflecting those in London.

The Paris Bourse began operations in 1563. Brokers were given the exclusive right to deal in equities and bonds. This monopoly lasted, as in the UK, until the mid-1980s. Reform has included the introduction of continuous computerised order matching. The MATIF, the options and futures market, was opened in 1985, and now has a number of financial and commodity contracts. This was thought initially to be a major threat to the derivatives markets in London, but the merger of the markets for financial contracts has proved beneficial in countering this competition.

Markets designed for small and medium-sized firms have been developed in Europe in parallel with the USM in London. The *Second Marche* in France and the *Geregelter Markt* (second segment) in Germany are both specialist markets to cater for new companies at a lower price and with less demanding listing requirements.

The German markets in general are very segmented, with several regional exchanges for securities trading. The major exchange is in Frankfurt, but computerised trading and an integrated series of markets will be in operation in the future. However, this has still not been fully implemented as the smaller exchanges are attempting to maintain their own autonomy. Options and futures contracts are traded in Denmark, the Netherlands, Sweden and Switzerland.

Considerable debate has taken place about a common trading system within the European Union, but so far is unresolved. One proposal is that the preferred model is for one market to be the central trading area, with all other markets accessible from it, but obvious controversy has arisen over the choice of the central market.

20.5 Emerging financial markets

Countries in transition and newly developing market economies have many common problems in establishing a capitalist financial system. One of the major difficulties is knowing quite where to start, if one considers the hugely complex and interrelated structure of a financial secor such as that in the UK.

A major influence in the choice of organisational structure is the existing industry and any other resources of the country. In privatisation programmes, such as those taking place in Eastern and Central Europe, the transfer of ownership of productive capacity by issuing shares to any purchaser with the necessary funds may result in a very disparate collection of equity holders. Much of the ownership may move to foreign investors which may be detrimental to the growth of the domestic economy. The establishment of a market economy is a fairly slow process, and short-term profitability which is then exported, may not be very useful. A system where the banking sector, with supervisory or equity involvement as in the German or Japanese structure, has a prominent role may be more sympathetic with emerging industries than an equity-based capital provision.

Developing countries also have the task of undertaking the allocation of assets and the creation of ownership. Until these issues are resolved, the funding of investment projects cannot take place. The banking sector in many developing countries is well established, generally as a legacy of colonialism, and through proliferation of banks as subsidiaries of domestic banks. On the other hand, securities markets are very expensive in terms of the funds and expertise required to develop and put in place a well-regulated and efficient trading system. Regulation is necessary, in terms of investor protection and the disclosure of information on investment, and this requires not only legislation but also training of the professionals to carry this out. A more efficient introduction to equity trading may be for firms to acquire listing on regional exchanges. This has been the case in Southern Africa, where many of the expanding economies in Africa have chosen to use the Johannesburg markets as a base for raising capital.

However, the above comments have been made with respect to the establishment of a financial system. If emerging markets are considered from an investor's point of view, there is an increasing trend in investment in growing economies. In particular, investment funds and unit trusts are becoming available for UK investors, frequently earning high returns. This trend is partly to diversify across markets which are not too closely related to the UK economic cycle. In this way, investments which would appear to be high risk contribute to a well-balanced portfolio. Also, new economies tend to experience high growth in the early stages, much as new companies do, and these two factors have recently resulted in high performance.

20.6 The hazards of cross-border trading

The benefits of understanding differences in various national financial systems allow us to recognise some potential dangers in the structure as a whole. One example of a negative effect from international networks of financial markets is the contagious effect of rapid price changes. The 1987 crash has provided an example of a fall in prices which spread through the world at considerable speed, although no reason has satisfactorily accounted for this in terms of parallel national economic circumstances, but rather the use of both technology and programmed trading techniques.

The individual impact of these two features of twentieth-century trading should be clearly separated. The introduction of technology for use in the mechanics of trading securities as well as for settlement and confirmation of ownership is continuing in established markets and is the assumed starting-point for developing ones. But the programmed trading systems which use preset price levels to trigger buying and selling have been found to be detrimental to stability and are now controlled.

20.7 Summary

All countries have undergone changes in the structure of their financial markets, in many cases as a response to the increase in international capital flows. Also common is the rise in the proportion of investment activity carried out by investing intermediaries compared with that of private individuals. This has put increasing pressure on exchanges to be competitive with respect to prices, although the introduction of the support and information systems necessary for global trading has been very costly. Extreme volatility and the contagious effect of panic buying and selling throughout the global financial system have been controlled to some extent by mutual agreement on trading practices.

Notes

1. AMEX was only granted its present name in the early 1950s. Previously it was known as the New York Curb Exchange as it started as an outside market before it was moved to a permanent structure in the 1920s (Sobel, 1972).
2. Source: Flow of Funds Accounts, 1989, Federal Reserve System.

Further reading

For an explanation of programmed trading see:
Hill, J. and F. Jones (1988), 'Equity trading, program trading, portfolio insurance, computer trading and all that', *Financial Analysts Journal*, July.

For a discussion of the possible causes of the 1987 crash see:
Roll, R. (1988), 'The international crash of October 1987', *Financial Analysts Journal*, September.

For a discussion of the regulatory response to the 1987 crash see:
Gowland, D. (1990), *The Regulation of Financial Markets in the 1990s*, Edward Elgar, Chapter 6.
Sakakibara *et al.*, S. (1988), *The Japanese Stock Market: Pricing systems and accounting information*, Praeger.
Sobel, R. (1972), *AMEX: A history of the American Stock Exchange 1921–1971*, Weybright & Talley.
Sobel, R. (1975), *NYSE: A history of the New York Stock Exchange 1935–1975*, Weybright & Talley.
Spicer and Oppenheim (1977), *Guide to Stock Markets Across the World*, Spicer & Oppenheim.

CHAPTER 21

New developments in the financial system

It is impossible to be completely up to date in any book on the financial sector, given the dynamic nature of the markets and the economic environment in which they operate. Indeed, many of the topics which were to be included in these concluding comments have either been incorporated into other chapters as they have become established practice or rejected as no longer interesting. Therefore this final section addresses some central issues relevant to the financial markets in the future, although no doubt these will be superseded by other events before very long.

To begin with the domestic markets, there are a number of factors of importance to the future of the financial sector. A central one is the future membership of the European Monetary Union, an issue which for Britain is still unresolved. In Chapter 6, we referred to the convergence criteria demanded by the Maastricht Treaty, before the next stage of monetary union can be achieved. Progress has so far been slow, and by the end of 1994 these conditions had not been met in full by any country with the exception of Luxembourg. Table 21.1 shows the relative positions of member countries and of candidate nations. There is still time for a change in these positions, but delay seems almost inevitable.

However, regardless of the status of Britain's membership of the European Monetary Union, if sufficient member states do meet the convergence criteria, and the third stage of the plan is implemented, there are implications for UK financial markets. One market which will definitely be affected is derivatives trading, which has experienced very high growth rates in London during the past decade. Although LIFFE is the largest market of its kind in the European time zone, it is inevitable that the choice of available contracts will fall, even though the volume of trade may not. The creation of a single currency in January 1999, common and inflexible interest rates, and the possible emergence of a single, dominant issuer of government debt across the European Union will restrict the product range.

The effects of European Monetary Union on monetary and fiscal policy is still the subject of considerable debate, particularly the amount of freedom of action assigned to individual governments. The establishment of a European Central

Table 21.1 Convergence situation of potential EMU members

Convergence criteria
1. The average inflation rate (CPI) in the twelve months prior to the assessment date not exceeding the average of the three best performing member states by more than 1.5%.
2. General public sector budget deficit not greater than 3% of GDP.
3. Total public sector debt not greater than 60% of GDP.
4. The average nominal interest rate (long-term government bond yields) may not be more than 2% above the average of the three countries with the lowest CPI rate.
5. The exchange rate has to be kept within the normal EMS bands two years before the assessment date.

	Inflation rate		Budget balance as % of GDP		Debt as % of GDP		Long-term interest rate	ERM band
							12 months	
	1993	1994	1993	1994	1992	1993	to July 1994	
Germany	4.2	**3.0**	−3.3	−3.1	**44.4**	**48.6**	6.2	15.0
France	**2.1**	**1.7**	−5.8	−5.4	**39.5**	**44.1**	6.4	15.0
Italy	4.2	3.8	−9.5	−9.2	108.4	118.6	8.3	free floating
UK	**1.6**	**2.5**	−7.2	−5.3	**41.8**	**48.8**	7.3	free floating
Spain	4.6	4.8	−7.2	−6.1	**48.8**	**55.6**	9.0	15.0
Netherlands	**2.6**	**2.6**	−2.9	−3.0	79.6	80.8	6.2	15.0
Belgium	**2.8**	**2.7**	−7.2	−5.3	131.9	138.4	7.2	15.0
Denmark	**1.3**	**2.1**	−4.5	−4.4	68.9	79.9	6.9	15.0
Portugal	6.5	5.8	−7.8	−6.5	61.7	66.7	7.7	15.0
Greece	14.4	10.8	−15.5	−16.0	110.2	120.4	19.6	free floating
Ireland	**1.5**	**2.4**	−2.5	−2.5	91.6	92.9	7.3	15.0
Luxembourg	3.6	**2.8**	−2.5	−2.2	7.3	**10.0**	7.8	15.0

Switzerland and EU candidates

Switzerland	3.3	**1.0**	−4.5	−4.2	**38.0**	**43.0**	4.8	free floating
Austria	3.6	**2.8**	−4.7	−4.6	**56.3**	62.6	6.5	tied to the DEM
Sweden	4.7	**2.5**	−12.9	−11.0	70.1	83.0	8.1	free floating
Norway	**2.3**	**1.3**	−2.7	−2.6	**41.3**	**42.2**	6.4	free floating
Finland	**2.2**	**1.2**	−7.9	−6.0	**44.0**	58.5	7.9	free floating

Source: Deutsche Bank, reported in *The Guardian*, 10 October 1994.
Key: Criteria matched in bold.

Bank will create an institution with full responsibility for monetary policy across Europe. It will be independent of political interference from any single country, and so no individual government will have the power to finance their budget deficits by printing money.

Clearly, the establishment of a European Central Bank will have a direct effect on the future status of the Bank of England. An independent, national central bank would be a sequential condition of European monetary union, although it would be wrong to assume that this is the only aspect in favour of an independent Bank of England. Proposals for an independent central bank in the UK have been debated for several years, usually modelled on the Deutsche Bundesbank, on which the European Central Bank is based, or the Reserve Bank of New Zealand.

This debate has recently been revived. The current view seems to be that whatever the institutional and structural arrangements required for independence, the objective should be the reduction of inflation, and the elimination of the often conflicting goals of short-term monetary policy with long-term price stability. The control of inflation is still the primary motivating factor, and it is suggested that this may be best achieved by the Bank and not by the government setting monetary targets. A policy of price stability can then be achieved, rather than giving this responsibility to governments who are always open to the temptation to create money.

The implications of an independent mandate for the Bank does imply that it should relinquish its role as banker to the government while still being accountable to the Treasury, although the responsibility for the supervision of the banking system may be transferred to another body, as has already occurred in other areas of financial regulation and control. The only remaining question is the degree of independence, and how the government can regain control if the need arises. This model of an independent Bank is substantially different from those operating in other European countries, but is more easily adaptable to a move to the Bundesbank structure if the United Kingdom were to join the monetary union.

The ability of the City of London to maintain its status as a European financial centre is another issue which exists independently from any eventual Monetary Union, but is none the less more important because of it. London does have many established advantages including: a long history of being a major financial centre; a time zone centrally poised between New York and Tokyo; the English language; a clear legal framework; and open financial markets with a benign regulatory environment. If London can also add to these factors new trading mechanisms, and particularly the settlement and non-paper-based transfer systems, it will increase the competitiveness of security markets, but it is crucial that cost advantages can also be achieved. Some competitor markets have achieved this; for example, France moved to a full electronic system, as has Germany, although markets in both of these countries are considerably less complicated than those in the UK.

Possible threats to London as a centre are the liberalisation of markets abroad and particularly the growth of Asian regional banking centres. Uncertain economic growth rates in Eastern and Central Europe may make Frankfurt look increasingly attractive, especially since this is the chosen location of the European Monetary Institute and eventually the European Central Bank. However, the move by European financial institutions to establish the centre of their global investments in London supports the view that the expertise and business environment in London are beneficial to global investment activity.

The final point to be made about the organisations within the UK financial system is related to the degree of restructuring of firms and institutions in the industry. Many of these changes are largely dependent on the close links already established with other countries. In some cases these links have been prompted by the wish for closer involvement with European member states, and a wish to take advantage of the single market for financial services by those outside the Union. For example, entry to the European Union by acquisition has occurred in the building society and banking sectors already.

Moving finally to those issues common to all financial markets, the increased use of technology, process and product innovation and a liberalised system of regulation have shaped the industry during the past decade, and it is hard to believe they will not continue to do so. These have been themes throughout the book, and we have returned to them with respect to capital markets, banking and the investing institutions on a number of occasions. But it is important to note that much of the analysis in this book is not affected by the detail of the current products and services. The valuation of assets and the importance of market efficiency are essential, and remain a central underlying factor in understanding the financial system and the practices within it.

Glossary

Acceptance credit A type of bill of exchange created by an institution or company owing money.

Accepting houses Banks which have the distinctive function of guaranteeing or *accepting* bills of exchange.

American depository receipt (ADR) Receipts issued by American securities houses or banks against their own holdings of overseas shares. ADRs are traded in dollars and holders receive dividend payments in dollars, so they represent a convenient way for US residents to deal in overseas securities.

American option A derivative instrument that can be exercised before or at the expiry date. See Option and European option.

Annual percentage rate The effective interest rate, allowing for compounding. This is considerably less than a flat rate quoted on a loan where interest is compounded.

Annuity A series of cash flows paid at the end of each of a specified number of periods. The cash flows may be equal each period or they may grow or decline in a mathematically regular fashion.

Arbitrage Buying and selling securities in order to profit from price differences without incurring risk.

Ask price The price at which a dealer is prepared to sell a security.

Asset stripping The practice of taking over a company and selling some or all of its assets. The term has been mainly used in a pejorative sense.

Bank bill A bill of exchange guaranteed or accepted by a bank.

Bank of England The central bank of the UK, responsible for carrying out the government's monetary policy and regulating the British financial system.

Barter The process of exchanging goods or services without using money.

Basis point One hundredth of one percent or 0.01%.

Bear An investor who trades on the expectation that prices in the market will fall. A bear market is used to describe a period in which prices have fallen.

Beta A measure of risk of a security: the covariance between the returns from the security and the returns from a market index.

333

Bid price The price at which a dealer is prepared to buy a security.

Bill of exchange A certificate containing a promise to pay a specified amount of money, which is created by the creditor company or institution and *accepted* by or on behalf of the debtor. It can subsequently be traded as a financial asset.

Bond rating The classification of a bond into risk categories denoted by alphabetical characters.

Broker An individual or firm acting as an agent on behalf of an investor to buy or sell securities or other assets.

Building society A financial institution which borrows and accepts deposits with the objective of providing loans for house purchase.

Bull An investor who trades in the expectation that prices in the market will rise. A bull market is used to describe a period in which prices have risen.

Bulldog bond A type of foreign bond, denominated in sterling, issued on behalf of foreign companies or institutions.

Call market Trading is discrete, such as an auction. See Continuous market.

Call option A derivative instrument which gives the holder the right to buy an underlying security at a specified price before or at the expiry date.

Call over A system of trading on securities markets in which securities are traded during specific periods by dealers trading directly with each other.

Capital budgeting The process by which a firm identifies and chooses capital investments to hold – usually involving the purchase of real assets, e.g. machinery, property.

Capitalisation issue Process whereby a company turns accumulated reserves into new shares and is a bookkeeping transaction only. Also called scrip or bonus issue.

Capitalisation rate A multiplier, used to derive a valuation by applying it to a current benefits flow, e.g. dividends or profits.

Captive insurance companies Subsidiaries of industrial or commercial groups established to handle the insurance needs of the group.

Certificate of deposit A security traded in the short-term financial markets and created by a bank certifying that a specified sum of money has been deposited and will be repaid with interest at a specific date.

Clearing bank A retail bank accepting deposits from the personal and corporate sectors and offering a wide range of financial services to individual customers. These banks are part of the national cheque-clearing system.

Commercial bank A financial institution that borrows money or accepts deposits which are invested in financial markets or lent to borrowers. See also Accepting house, Clearing bank.

Commercial bill Bill of exchange issued either by a commercial or financial institution.

Composite rate An average rate of tax deducted at source by building societies and banks on interest earned by depositors. The composite rate is determined by reference to the average tax liability of depositors.

Compound interest The amount by which a sum of money will grow in each of a number of periods when the amount deposited plus the interest already earned attract interest at a given rate.

Consols Certain UK government stocks for which no date by which they will be redeemed is specified. The term is sometimes used as a general description for any undated or irredeemable bonds.

Continuous market Markets which occur anytime a buy and sell order coincide. See Call market.

Convertible stock Fixed interest loans or preference shares which can be converted at some specified time into ordinary shares of the same company.

Coupon The interest payable on a fixed interest investment, the rate of interest payable being specified in terms of the nominal value of a security.

Covered call The combination of writing a call option while also owning the underlying security.

Cum div With dividend. See Ex div.

Debenture stock A type of fixed interest bond which effectively acts as a mortgage on assets owned by the issuer.

Derivative An instrument which derives its value from an underlying security, e.g. option, future, swap.

Discount house A company which specialises in trading in money market instruments and has lender-of-last-resort facilities at the Bank of England.

Discount market The market in which bills of exchange and Treasury bills are bought and sold.

Discount rate The amount over £1 which £1 now is deemed to be worth one period hence. Can be expressed either in terms of present value or future value.

Disintermediation (of the banking system) The move of the main business of financial intermediation away from the banks, and towards the investment institutions.

Dividend Cash paid to shareholders, usually twice a year – interim dividend and final dividend.

Dividend yield Dividends divided by the share price.

Drop-lock A bond in which the interest rate is initially variable but which in specified circumstances is *locked* into a fixed rate.

Earnings yield The profits available for shareholders divided by the share price.

Effective rate of interest The rate of interest earned over the course of a year taking into account any compounding of interest that might be appropriate.

Efficient market hypothesis The view that the market price of securities reflects information instantaneously.

Endowment policy An insurance policy offering a payment at the end of the contracted period or on death of the insured, if earlier.

Entity A company, institution, individual or group which can be distinguished from its economic environment for the purpose of analysis. A legal entity has the capacity to enter into contracts.

Equity In the context of capital markets, equity refers to an ordinary share. In accounting and legal terms, it refers to the financial interest in a firm's assets after prior claims have been met.

Eurobond An international bond that may be issued in any currency and subsequently traded in international markets – usually by dealers buying and selling on their own or clients' accounts. London is an important centre for eurobond trading.

Eurocurrency Any currency which is traded, lent or repaid by market participants outside the country of origin.

Eurodollars Dollar-denominated eurocurrency.

European option A derivative instrument that can be exercised only at the expiry date. See Option and American option.

Ex div Shares (bonds) are traded ex div shortly before dividends (interest) are due to be paid. The purchase of an ex div security does not entitle the purchaser to receive the next dividend (interest) payment which accordingly is paid to the seller of the share (bond).

Exercise price The specified price at which options can be taken up or exercised. Also called the Strike price.

Expectations hypothesis A model of the term structure of interest rates that predicts that the future short-term rates of interest can be estimated by reference to the differences between current long-term interest rates.

Export Credits Guarantee Department A government-established institution providing insurance in international trade (especially to UK exporters).

Factoring Raising finance either by selling trade debts or using them as security for borrowing.

FIMBRA The Financial Intermediaries, Managers and Brokers Regulatory Association, the SRO for independent intermediaries providing investment advisory and management services to retail customers of insurance and unit trusts.

Finance house (Finance company) A financial institution which accepts deposits and finances leasing and hire-purchase agreements.

Financial futures A standardised financial security enabling investors to contract a future investment at a specified price or rate.

Fiscal policy Government policy concerned with taxation and public spending.

Flow of funds Analysis of economic activity based on the movements of financial assets and liabilities between entities and sectors in the economy.

Flowback The tendency of internationally traded securities to return to the home country, since the domestic market presents the strongest secondary trading conditions. Generally applies to equity.

Focal date A point in time, chosen for convenient estimation, to which future (or past) cash flows are discounted (or compounded).

Foreign bond A security issued by a borrower in a domestic capital market other than their own, denominated in the currency of the market.

Forward-forward Trading in financial futures so as to arbitrage with exchange or interest rates in a later period.

Forward rate The rate of interest covering a period which is implied by the current prices of securities of the same type. Thus a two-year and a three-year bond can together imply a forward one-year rate between the second and third years.

Fundamental analysis The valuation of shares based on the analysis of corporate and economic information.

Fund manager Individual who manages monies placed with an investment fund.

Futures Standardised contracts involving either commodities or financial assets (or indices). See Financial futures.

Gearing Level of borrowing. Measured by ratio of debt to debt plus equity. (Also called leverage.)

Gilt, gilt-edged A security issued on behalf of (or backed up by) the government.

Hedging The avoidance of risk by arranging a contract at specified prices which will yield a known return.

Hire-purchase The purchase of an asset by a formal agreement involving a number of payments spread out over a period.

IMRO The Investment Management Regulatory Organisation, the SRO for investment managers and advisers, particularly institutional funds, unit trust and pension fund managers.

Indemnity The principle of replacing in an insurance claim only the value of what has been lost.

Index An indicator of the general movements in prices, quantities or values of goods or services. Used extensively in reporting of prices in financial markets.

Index fund A fund or unit trust that aims to maintain a portfolio that will match the investment performance of a broad-based stock market index such as the ET Actuaries All-Share Index.

Index-linked gilt A government bond for which the interest and redemption value are directly linked to the Index of Retail Prices.

Insider A person who has access to unpublished or privileged information and who uses it to trade at unfair advantage in the capital market.

Insurance company A financial institution which is involved in general and/or long-term insurance business. In general insurance the insurance company will compensate their insured clients for loss caused by specific accidents or events. Long-term business mainly concerns *life* or pension provision.

Inter-bank Usually refers to the short-term loans traded between banks on the parallel money markets.

Intermediary An intermediary links borrowers and lenders either by acting as an agent, or by bringing together potential traders, or by acting in place of a market.

Internal rate of return A measure of profitability of an investment project.

Introduction A method by which existing securities become traded on the Stock Exchange.

Investment trust A company which performs the task of fund manager on behalf of its shareholders.

Irredeemable A security which does not specify to holders any date at which it will be redeemed (repaid) by the issuer.

Issuing house A financial institution (e.g. bank, stockbroker) which advises on and arranges the issuance of securities.

LAUTRO The Life Assurance and Unit Trust Regulatory Organisation, the SRO concerned with the marketing associated with life assurance and unit trust products.

Lease A method of obtaining the use of an asset by contracting a series of payments (e.g. rents) over a specified period.

Lender of last resort The understanding that the Bank of England will always stand ready to lend money to a limited number of financial institutions if they are unable to obtain finance from market sources.

Lessee The entity, in a lease, which agrees to pay the leasing payments in exchange for use of the asset.

Lessor The entity, in a lease, which finances the purchase of the asset in return for receipt of leasing payments.

Lifeboat An operation, set up by the Bank of England, designed to save a number of financially embarrassed institutions.

LIFFE The London International Financial Futures Exchange.

Limit order An order to buy or sell securities at a price specified to be above or below the current prices quoted in the market.

Liquid asset An asset which may easily be turned into cash at short notice.

Liquidity preference The explanation of the term structure of interest rates based on the assumption that lenders prefer securities which have shorter maturities (i.e. which are more liquid). The preference will be reflected in the lower returns on short-term securities.

Listed securities Securities which are authorised to be traded on a particular financial market.

Lloyd's A market for insurance.

Loan stock A long-term bond issued by a company or public sector body.

Margin The proportion or amount of funds that has to be deposited by an investor when trading options or futures contracts.

Maturity The length of time elapsing before a debt is to be redeemed by the issuer.

Merchant bank A wholesale bank which will provide funds, arrange and advise on corporate finance.

Merger The combination of two or more firms into a single entity.

Minimum lending rate A specified rate of interest at which the Bank of England might offer assistance to the discount market.

Monetary policy Economic policy acting through the supply of money, interest rates and the availability of credit within the economy.

Money market A short-term financial market usually involving assets with less than a year to maturity.

Money multiplier The extent to which the financial system can create credit from its reserve assets (e.g. cash and government short-term securities).

Money-weighted return A measure of investment performance equivalent to the internal rate of return in a fund over a specified period.

Moral hazard The problem caused by the incentive of the insured (a) to mislead the insurer by providing false information or making false claims and (b) to take little care to avoid loss.

Negotiable securities Securities which, when traded, give the buyer the same rights as those previously enjoyed by the seller.

Net present value (NPV) The value of an investment's cash flows discounted to a focal date at the beginning of the project.

Net terminal value (NTV) The value of an investment's cash flows compounded to a focal date at the end of the project.

Net worth Book value of a company's equity, plus retained earnings.

Nominal interest The calculation of interest which assumes that interest accrues only at the end of each year.

Nominal value The price which was denominated for coupon payment purposes at the time of issue – not necessarily the issue price. With bonds which are to be redeemed, the nominal value will generally coincide with the redemption price.

Numeraire A commodity (such as money) which is used to express the values of other commodities or services.

Offer for sale A method of issuing securities by offering to potential investors a specified number of securities at a specified price.

Offer price The price at which a dealer is prepared to sell securities.

Open outcry System of trading where participants signal and shout prices to each other on the trading-floor.

Opportunity cost The benefits forgone by the adoption of a particular action, e.g. the opportunity costs of investing in a project is the return that could have been obtained in the best comparable investment.

Option The right to undertake a transaction on pre-specified terms. Thus traded options give the right to buy or sell an underlying security at a known price. See Call and Put options.

Ordinary share The security representing the claim to the residual ownership of a company. See Equity.

Overdraft The facility to obtain credit from a bank by withdrawing more from the bank account than has been previously deposited.

Overfunding The policy of selling long-term government bonds in excess of the amount required to finance the public sector borrowing requirement.

Over-the-counter (OTC) market An informal dealer-based market.

Par (bond) The nominal value of a bond, or a bond which is currently quoted at a price equal to its nominal value.

Parallel markets A number of markets in which short-term instruments are traded without lender-of-last-resort facilities.

Pension fund An institution or arrangement which accepts contributions from members in order to pay out pensions on retirement.

Perpetuity An endless annuity.

PIA The Personal Investment Authority, the SRO for retail investment intermediaries.

Placing A method of selling securities, subsequently to be traded in the secondary market, by selling the securities to a selected number of investors.

Preference share A share which pays a fixed dividend and ranks prior to the ordinary shares in liquidation.

Price/earnings (P/E) ratio The ratio of the price of a share to either the most recent or forecasted profits per share.

Primary market A market in which securities are traded between issuers and investors, thereby raising additional funds for the issuing entity.

Prime (property) Property which, by nature of its size, location and tenants, affords the owner a very secure growth in rental income.

Property bond A fund, linked to insurance schemes, which invests the net premiums in property.

Prospectus The advertisement, used in issuing shares, carrying financial and investment details of interest to potential investors.

Public sector borrowing requirement (PSBR) The amount of money required by the public sector, not otherwise raised by taxation.

Published accounts Financial statements circulated by companies giving the latest balance sheet (details of their assets, liabilities and equities) and profit and loss statement, and various other data on their operations and prospects.

Put-call parity theorem A relationship based on the principles of arbitrage, relating the prices of the call option, the put option, the rate of interest and the price of the underlying share.

Put option A derivative instrument which gives the writer the right to sell an underlying security before or at the expiry date.

Random walk In the context of share price behaviour, prices follow a random walk if past changes are of no help in predicting future changes.

Real return The return on an investment after taking into account the effects of changes in purchasing power.

Redemption (maturity) The repayment of a stock at a specified date and price.

Redemption yield An indicator of the return earned on buying a stock and holding it until maturity.

Reinsurance The practice of reducing the risks of bearing insurance by recontracting some, or all, of the insurance with another insurer.

Reserve assets Financial assets, such as cash, Treasury bills and deposits at the Bank of England, required to be held by banks.

Rights issue The offer by a company of additional shares to its existing shareholders at a specially low price.

Riskless, risk-free, rate A return which is certain to materialise if a security is bought and held over a specified investment horizon (e.g. Treasury bills bought and held over their three-month lives).

Roll-over An agreement whereby a loan is prolonged at specified terms.

Round-tripping A type of arbitrage trade involving borrowing from one source and lending in another market at a higher rate of interest.

Running yield Bond interest divided by price.

Sale and leaseback The provision of finance whereby a company sells a property to an institution on the agreement that it can lease the premises, thereby converting a capital value into an immediate cash inflow at the cost of future lease payments.

Savings bank An incorporated society providing savings facilities for the personal sector.

Scrip issue The issuing, without charge, of additional shares to existing shareholders.

Secondary market The market in which existing securities and financial claims are bought and sold.

Segmentation hypothesis The explanation of the term structure of interest rates by identification of investors/borrowers with specific investment horizons.

Seniority (of debt) Debt which must be repaid before *subordinated* debt receives any payment, in case of bankruptcy.

SFA The Securities and Futures Authority, the SRO for those institutions dealing or arranging deals in securities and derivatives, including bonds, equities, gilts, eurosecurities, commodity and financial options and futures. Also covered by this organisation are those advising on corporate finance activity, such as mergers and acquisitions.

Short A bond with less than five years to run before maturity.

Short sale Sale of a security that the investor does not own.

Simple interest The calculation of simple interest allows only for interest to be charged on the principal sum, not on any interest accruing from previous periods.

Specialist A member of the New York Stock Exchange whose responsibility is to maintain an orderly market by dealing and monitoring share transactions in particular stocks.

Specie-price model Exchange rate parity system based on a precious metal, usually gold.

Spot market Transactions where a commodity is priced at the current price, and it is paid for and delivered now (on the spot) rather than at some future date.

Spot rate The rate of interest to maturity currently offered on a particular class of bond or bill.

Stag An investor who applies for securities at the time of issue on the expectation that the market price will be greater than the price at which they are issued.

Stockbroker A member (firm or individual) of the Stock Exchange who deals on behalf of clients.

Straddle A combination of options, comprising a put and a call, with common expiry price and date.

Strap A combination of options, comprising two calls and a put, with common expiry price and date.

Striking price The price at which securities will be sold as a result of an issue by tender. Sometimes also used to describe the exercise price of an option.

Strip A combination of options, comprising two puts and a call, with common expiry price and date.

Swap A private agreement between two parties to exchange cash flows at prearranged times in the future.

Syndicate The groups into which the underwriting members of Lloyd's are organised, and on whose behalf the underwriting agents accept insurance business. Now also used for similar groups involved in underwriting and distributing eurobonds and euroequity issues.

Tender An issue of securities for which the issue price is determined by the various prices offered by investors wishing to buy the stock.

Term insurance A life policy which expires worthless if the insured survives the term covered by the policy.

Term structure of interest rates The pattern of interest rates currently available for bonds of different maturities (terms).

Tick size The smallest price change permitted by the exchange on a particular futures contract.

Time-weighted return The average rate of return earned on an investment between the receipt or payment of cash flows.

Trade bill A Bill of Exchange issued by a company and accepted by another company (not a bank).

Transfer payment A payment or gift of money made without a corresponding service or commodity.

Transmutation of claims The change in form or maturity of one financial claim into another.

Treasury bill A short-term loan taken out by the government in the form of a bill of exchange.

Trustee Savings Bank (TSB) Banks which evolved from institutions set up to channel personal savings into financing the PSBR, but which now operate in a commercial framework.

Underwriter An individual or institution agreeing either to buy or insure an event such as a share issue or a range of insurance risks.

Unit trust An open-ended fund which sells units to investors and invests the proceeds in a range of investments (usually equities).

Unlisted security A security which is traded by dealers but not listed (quoted) on the Stock Exchange.

Warrant A security which gives the holder the right to buy, during a specified period, a number of ordinary shares in the issuing company at a specified price.

Whole-life An insurance contract paying a specified sum of money at death of the insured in return for a regular premium.

Yield A rate of return.

Yield curve A curve describing the pattern of redemption yields of similar bonds of differing maturities.

Zero coupon bond A bond which offers return only in the form of capital gain. (Usually seen in practice only for short-term issues, e.g. Treasury bills.)

Financial Tables

Present value of £1

Period % Interest rate per period

Period	1	2	3	4	5	6	7	8	9	10	11	12
1	.9901	.9804	.9709	.9615	.9524	.9434	.9346	.9259	.9174	.9091	.9009	.8929
2	.9803	.9612	.9426	.9246	.9070	.8900	.8734	.8573	.8417	.8264	.8116	.7972
3	.9706	.9423	.9151	.8890	.8638	.8396	.8163	.7938	.7722	.7513	.7312	.7118
4	.9610	.9238	.8885	.8548	.8227	.7921	.7629	.7350	.7084	.6830	.6587	.6355
5	.9515	.9057	.8626	.8219	.7835	.7473	.7130	.6806	.6499	.6209	.5935	.5674
6	.9420	.8880	.8375	.7903	.7462	.7050	.6663	.6302	.5963	.5645	.5346	.5066
7	.9327	.8706	.8131	.7599	.7107	.6651	.6227	.5835	.5470	.5132	.4817	.4523
8	.9235	.8535	.7894	.7307	.6768	.6274	.5820	.5403	.5019	.4665	.4339	.4039
9	.9143	.8368	.7664	.7026	.6446	.5919	.5439	.5002	.4604	.4241	.3909	.3606
10	.9053	.8203	.7441	.6756	.6139	.5584	.5083	.4632	.4224	.3855	.3522	.3220
11	.8963	.8043	.7224	.6496	.5847	.5268	.4751	.4289	.3875	.3505	.3173	.2875
12	.8874	.7885	.7014	.6246	.5568	.4970	.4440	.3971	.3555	.3186	.2858	.2567
13	.8787	.7730	.6810	.6006	.5303	.4688	.4150	.3677	.3262	.2897	.2575	.2292
14	.8700	.7579	.6611	.5775	.5051	.4423	.3878	.3405	.2992	.2633	.2320	.2046
15	.8613	.7430	.6419	.5553	.4810	.4173	.3624	.3152	.2745	.2394	.2090	.1827
16	.8528	.7284	.6232	.5339	.4581	.3936	.3387	.2919	.2519	.2176	.1883	.1631
17	.8444	.7142	.6050	.5134	.4363	.3714	.3166	.2703	.2311	.1978	.1696	.1456
18	.8360	.7002	.5874	.4936	.4155	.3503	.2959	.2502	.2120	.1799	.1528	.1300
19	.8277	.6864	.5703	.4746	.3957	.3305	.2765	.2317	.1945	.1635	.1377	.1161
20	.8195	.6730	.5537	.4564	.3769	.3118	.2584	.2145	.1784	.1486	.1240	.1037
21	.8114	.6598	.5375	.4388	.3589	.2942	.2415	.1987	.1637	.1351	.1117	.0926
22	.8034	.6468	.5219	.4220	.3418	.2775	.2257	.1839	.1502	.1228	.1007	.0826
23	.7954	.6342	.5067	.4057	.3256	.2618	.2109	.1703	.1378	.1117	.0907	.0738
24	.7876	.6217	.4919	.3901	.3101	.2470	.1971	.1577	.1264	.1015	.0817	.0659
25	.7798	.6095	.4776	.3751	.2953	.2330	.1842	.1460	.1160	.0923	.0736	.0588
26	.7720	.5976	.4637	.3607	.2812	.2198	.1722	.1352	.1064	.0839	.0663	.0525
27	.7644	.5859	.4502	.3468	.2678	.2074	.1609	.1252	.0976	.0763	.0597	.0469
28	.7568	.5744	.4371	.3335	.2551	.1956	.1504	.1159	.0895	.0693	.0538	.0419
29	.7493	.5631	.4243	.3207	.2429	.1846	.1406	.1073	.0822	.0630	.0485	.0374
30	.7419	.5521	.4120	.3083	.2314	.1741	.1314	.0994	.0754	.0573	.0437	.0334
31	.7346	.5412	.4000	.2965	.2204	.1643	.1228	.0920	.0691	.0521	.0394	.0298
32	.7273	.5306	.3883	.2851	.2099	.1550	.1147	.0852	.0634	.0474	.0355	.0266
33	.7201	.5202	.3770	.2741	.1999	.1462	.1072	.0789	.0582	.0431	.0319	.0238
34	.7130	.5100	.3660	.2636	.1904	.1379	.1002	.0730	.0534	.0391	.0288	.0212
35	.7059	.5000	.3554	.2534	.1813	.1301	.0937	.0676	.0490	.0356	.0259	.0189

1. Present value of £1
2. Present value of £1 per period
3. Terminal value of £1 per period

Present value of £1

Period	% Interest rate per period											
	13	14	15	16	18	20	22	24	26	28	30	35
1	.8850	.8772	.8696	.8621	.8475	.8333	.8197	.8065	.7937	.7813	.7692	.7407
2	.7831	.7695	.7561	.7432	.7182	.6944	.6719	.6504	.6299	.6104	.5917	.5487
3	.6931	.6750	.6575	.6407	.6086	.5787	.5507	.5245	.4999	.4768	.4552	.4064
4	.6133	.5921	.5718	.5523	.5158	.4823	.4514	.4230	.3968	.3725	.3501	.3011
5	.5428	.5194	.4972	.4761	.4371	.4019	.3700	.3411	.3149	.2910	.2693	.2230
6	.4803	.4556	.4323	.4104	.3704	.3349	.3033	.2751	.2499	.2274	.2072	.1652
7	.4251	.3996	.3759	.3538	.3139	.2791	.2486	.2218	.1983	.1776	.1594	.1224
8	.3762	.3506	.3269	.3050	.2660	.2326	.2038	.1789	.1574	.1388	.1226	.0906
9	.3329	.3075	.2843	.2630	.2255	.1938	.1670	.1443	.1249	.1084	.0943	.0671
10	.2946	.2697	.2472	.2267	.1911	.1615	.1369	.1164	.0992	.0847	.0725	.0497
11	.2607	.2366	.2149	.1954	.1619	.1346	.1122	.0938	.0787	.0662	.0558	.0368
12	.2307	.2076	.1869	.1685	.1372	.1122	.0920	.0757	.0625	.0517	.0429	.0273
13	.2042	.1821	.1625	.1452	.1163	.0935	.0754	.0610	.0496	.0404	.0330	.0202
14	.1807	.1597	.1413	.1252	.0985	.0779	.0618	.0492	.0393	.0316	.0254	.0150
15	.1599	.1401	.1229	.1079	.0835	.0649	.0507	.0397	.0312	.0247	.0195	.0111
16	.1415	.1229	.1069	.0930	.0708	.0541	.0415	.0320	.0248	.0193	.0150	.0082
17	.1252	.1078	.0929	.0802	.0600	.0451	.0340	.0258	.0197	.0150	.0116	.0061
18	.1108	.0946	.0808	.0691	.0508	.0376	.0279	.0208	.0156	.0118	.0089	.0045
19	.0981	.0829	.0703	.0596	.0431	.0313	.0229	.0168	.0124	.0092	.0068	.0033
20	.0868	.0728	.0611	.0514	.0365	.0261	.0187	.0135	.0098	.0072	.0053	.0025
21	.0768	.0638	.0531	.0443	.0309	.0217	.0154	.0109	.0078	.0056	.0040	.0018
22	.0680	.0560	.0462	.0382	.0262	.0181	.0126	.0088	.0062	.0044	.0031	.0014
23	.0601	.0491	.0402	.0329	.0222	.0151	.0103	.0071	.0049	.0034	.0024	.0010
24	.0532	.0431	.0349	.0284	.0188	.0126	.0085	.0057	.0039	.0027	.0018	.0007
25	.0471	.0378	.0304	.0245	.0160	.0105	.0069	.0046	.0031	.0021	.0014	.0006
26	.0417	.0331	.0264	.0211	.0135	.0087	.0057	.0037	.0025	.0016	.0011	.0004
27	.0369	.0291	.0230	.0182	.0115	.0073	.0047	.0030	.0019	.0013	.0008	.0003
28	.0326	.0255	.0200	.0157	.0097	.0061	.0038	.0024	.0015	.0010	.0006	.0002
29	.0289	.0224	.0174	.0135	.0082	.0051	.0031	.0020	.0012	.0008	.0005	.0002
30	.0256	.0196	.0151	.0116	.0070	.0042	.0026	.0016	.0010	.0006	.0004	.0001
31	.0226	.0172	.0131	.0100	.0059	.0035	.0021	.0013	.0008	.0005	.0003	.0001
32	.0200	.0151	.0114	.0087	.0050	.0029	.0017	.0010	.0006	.0004	.0002	.0001
33	.0177	.0132	.0099	.0075	.0042	.0024	.0014	.0008	.0005	.0003	.0002	.0001
34	.0157	.0116	.0086	.0064	.0036	.0020	.0012	.0007	.0004	.0002	.0001	.0000
35	.0139	.0102	.0075	.0055	.0030	.0017	.0009	.0005	.0003	.0002	.0001	.0000

Present value of £1 per period

Period	% Interest rate per period											
	1	2	3	4	5	6	7	8	9	10	11	12
1	0.990	0.980	0.971	0.962	0.952	0.943	0.935	0.926	0.917	0.909	0.901	0.893
2	1.970	1.942	1.913	1.886	1.859	1.833	1.808	1.783	1.759	1.736	1.713	1.690
3	2.941	2.884	2.829	2.775	2.723	2.673	2.624	2.577	2.531	2.487	2.444	2.402
4	3.902	3.808	3.717	3.630	3.546	3.465	3.387	3.312	3.240	3.170	3.102	3.037
5	4.853	4.713	4.580	4.452	4.329	4.212	4.100	3.993	3.890	3.791	3.696	3.605
6	5.795	5.601	5.417	5.242	5.076	4.917	4.767	4.623	4.486	4.355	4.231	4.111
7	6.778	6.472	6.230	6.002	5.786	5.582	5.389	5.206	5.033	4.868	4.712	4.564
8	7.652	7.325	7.020	6.733	6.463	6.210	5.971	5.747	5.535	5.335	5.146	4.968
9	8.566	8.162	7.786	7.435	7.108	6.802	6.515	6.247	5.995	5.759	5.537	5.328
10	9.470	8.983	8.530	8.111	7.722	7.360	7.024	6.710	6.418	6.145	5.889	5.650
11	10.37	9.790	9.250	8.760	8.306	7.887	7.499	7.139	6.805	6.495	6.207	5.938
12	11.26	10.58	9.950	9.390	8.863	8.384	7.943	7.536	7.161	6.814	6.492	6.194
13	12.13	11.35	10.63	9.990	9.390	8.853	8.358	7.904	7.487	7.103	6.750	6.424
14	13.00	12.11	11.30	10.56	9.900	9.290	8.745	8.244	7.786	7.367	6.982	6.628
15	13.87	12.85	11.94	11.12	10.38	9.710	9.110	8.559	8.061	7.606	7.191	6.811
16	14.72	13.58	12.56	11.65	10.84	10.11	9.450	8.851	8.313	7.824	7.379	6.974
17	15.56	14.29	13.17	12.17	11.27	10.48	9.760	9.120	8.544	8.022	7.549	7.120
18	16.40	14.99	13.75	12.66	11.69	10.83	10.06	9.370	8.756	8.201	7.702	7.250
19	17.23	15.68	14.32	13.13	12.09	11.16	10.34	9.600	8.950	8.365	7.839	7.366
20	18.05	16.35	14.88	13.59	12.46	11.47	10.59	9.820	9.130	8.514	7.963	7.469
21	18.86	17.01	15.42	14.03	12.82	11.76	10.84	10.02	9.290	8.649	8.075	7.562
22	19.66	17.66	15.94	14.45	13.16	12.04	11.06	10.20	9.440	8.772	8.176	7.645
23	20.46	18.29	16.44	14.86	13.49	12.30	11.27	10.37	9.580	8.883	8.266	7.718
24	21.24	18.91	16.94	15.25	13.80	12.55	11.47	10.53	9.710	8.985	8.348	7.784
25	22.02	19.52	17.41	15.62	14.09	12.78	11.65	10.67	9.820	9.080	8.422	7.843
26	22.80	20.12	17.88	15.98	14.38	13.00	11.83	10.81	9.930	9.160	8.488	7.896
27	23.56	20.71	18.33	16.33	14.64	13.21	11.99	10.94	10.03	9.240	8.548	7.943
28	24.32	21.28	18.76	16.66	14.90	13.41	12.14	11.05	10.12	9.310	8.602	7.984
29	25.07	21.84	19.19	16.98	15.14	13.59	12.28	11.16	10.20	9.370	8.650	8.022
30	25.81	22.40	19.60	17.29	15.37	13.76	12.41	11.26	10.27	9.430	8.694	8.055
31	26.54	22.94	20.00	17.59	15.59	13.93	12.53	11.35	10.34	9.480	8.733	8.085
32	27.27	23.47	20.39	17.87	15.80	14.08	12.65	11.43	10.41	9.530	8.769	8.112
33	27.99	23.99	20.77	18.15	16.00	14.23	12.75	11.51	10.46	9.570	8.801	8.135
34	28.70	24.50	21.13	18.41	16.19	14.37	12.85	11.59	10.52	9.610	8.829	8.157
35	29.41	25.00	21.49	18.66	16.37	14.50	12.95	11.65	10.57	9.640	8.855	8.176

Present value of £1 per period

Period	% Interest rate per period											
	13	14	15	16	18	20	22	24	26	28	30	35
1	0.885	0.877	0.870	0.862	0.847	0.833	0.820	0.806	0.794	0.781	0.769	0.741
2	1.668	1.647	1.626	1.605	1.566	1.528	1.492	1.457	1.424	1.392	1.361	1.289
3	2.361	2.322	2.283	2.246	2.174	2.106	2.042	1.981	1.923	1.868	1.816	1.696
4	2.974	2.914	2.855	2.798	2.690	2.589	2.494	2.404	2.320	2.241	2.166	1.997
5	3.517	3.433	3.352	3.274	3.127	2.991	2.864	2.745	2.635	2.532	2.436	2.220
6	3.998	3.889	3.784	3.685	3.498	3.326	3.167	3.020	2.885	2.759	2.643	2.385
7	4.423	4.288	4.160	4.039	3.812	3.605	3.416	3.242	3.083	2.937	2.802	2.508
8	4.799	4.639	4.487	4.344	4.078	3.837	3.619	3.421	3.241	3.076	2.925	2.598
9	5.132	4.946	4.772	4.607	4.303	4.031	3.786	3.566	3.366	3.184	3.019	2.665
10	5.426	5.216	5.019	4.833	4.494	4.192	3.923	3.682	3.465	3.269	3.092	2.715
11	5.687	5.453	5.234	5.029	4.656	4.327	4.035	3.776	3.543	3.335	3.147	2.752
12	5.918	5.660	5.421	5.197	4.793	4.439	4.127	3.851	3.606	3.387	3.190	2.779
13	6.122	5.842	5.583	5.342	4.910	4.533	4.203	3.912	3.656	3.427	3.223	2.799
14	6.302	6.002	5.724	5.468	5.008	4.611	4.265	3.962	3.695	3.459	3.249	2.814
15	6.462	6.142	5.847	5.575	5.092	4.675	4.315	4.001	3.726	3.483	3.268	2.825
16	6.604	6.265	5.954	5.668	5.162	4.730	4.357	4.033	3.751	3.503	3.283	2.834
17	6.729	6.373	6.047	5.749	5.222	4.775	4.391	4.059	3.771	3.518	3.295	2.840
18	6.840	6.467	6.128	5.818	5.273	4.812	4.419	4.080	3.786	3.529	3.304	2.844
19	6.938	6.550	6.198	5.877	5.316	4.843	4.442	4.097	3.799	3.539	3.311	2.848
20	7.025	6.623	6.259	5.929	5.353	4.870	4.460	4.110	3.808	3.546	3.316	2.850
21	7.102	6.687	6.312	5.973	5.384	4.891	4.476	4.121	3.816	3.551	3.320	2.852
22	7.170	6.743	6.359	6.011	5.410	4.909	4.488	4.130	3.822	3.556	3.323	2.853
23	7.230	6.792	6.399	6.044	5.432	4.925	4.499	4.137	3.827	3.559	3.325	2.854
24	7.283	6.835	6.434	6.073	5.451	4.937	4.507	4.143	3.831	3.562	3.327	2.855
25	7.330	6.873	6.464	6.097	5.467	4.948	4.514	4.147	3.834	3.564	3.329	2.856
26	7.372	6.906	6.491	6.118	5.480	4.956	4.520	4.151	3.837	3.566	3.330	2.856
27	7.409	6.935	6.514	6.136	5.492	4.964	4.524	4.154	3.839	3.567	3.331	2.856
28	7.441	6.961	6.534	6.152	5.502	4.970	4.528	4.157	3.840	3.568	3.331	2.857
29	7.470	6.983	6.551	6.166	5.510	4.975	4.531	4.159	3.841	3.569	3.332	2.857
30	7.496	7.003	6.566	6.177	5.517	4.979	4.534	4.160	3.842	3.569	3.332	2.857
31	7.518	7.020	6.579	6.187	5.523	4.982	4.536	4.161	3.843	3.570	3.332	2.857
32	7.538	7.035	6.591	6.196	5.528	4.985	4.538	4.162	3.844	3.570	3.333	2.857
33	7.556	7.048	6.600	6.203	5.532	4.988	4.539	4.163	3.844	3.570	3.333	2.857
34	7.572	7.060	6.609	6.210	5.536	4.990	4.540	4.164	3.845	3.571	3.333	2.857
35	7.586	7.070	6.617	6.215	5.539	4.992	4.541	4.164	3.845	3.571	3.333	2.857

Financial tables

Terminal value of £1 per period

Period	% Interest rate per period											
	1	2	3	4	5	6	7	8	9	10	11	12
1	1.000	1.000	1.000	1.000	1.000	1.000	1.000	1.000	1.000	1.000	1.000	1.000
2	2.010	2.020	2.030	2.040	2.050	2.060	2.070	2.080	2.090	2.100	2.110	2.120
3	3.030	3.060	3.091	3.122	3.152	3.184	3.215	3.246	3.278	3.310	3.342	3.374
4	4.060	4.122	4.184	4.246	4.310	4.375	4.440	4.506	4.573	4.641	4.710	4.779
5	5.101	5.204	5.309	5.416	5.526	5.637	5.751	5.867	5.985	6.105	6.228	6.353
6	6.152	6.308	6.468	6.633	6.802	6.975	7.153	7.336	7.523	7.716	7.913	8.115
7	7.214	7.434	7.662	7.898	8.142	8.394	8.654	8.923	9.200	9.487	9.783	10.09
8	8.286	8.583	8.892	9.214	9.549	9.897	10.26	10.64	11.03	11.44	11.86	12.30
9	9.369	9.755	10.16	10.58	11.03	11.49	11.98	12.49	13.02	13.58	14.16	14.78
10	10.46	10.95	11.46	12.01	12.58	13.18	13.82	14.49	15.19	15.94	16.72	17.55
11	11.57	12.17	12.81	13.49	14.21	14.97	15.78	16.65	17.56	18.53	19.56	20.65
12	12.68	13.41	14.19	15.03	15.92	16.87	17.89	18.98	20.14	21.38	22.71	24.13
13	13.81	14.68	15.62	16.63	17.71	18.88	20.14	21.50	22.95	24.52	26.21	28.03
14	14.95	15.97	17.09	18.29	19.60	21.02	22.55	24.21	26.02	27.97	30.09	32.39
15	16.10	17.29	18.60	20.02	21.58	23.28	25.13	27.15	29.36	31.77	34.41	37.28
16	17.26	18.64	20.16	21.82	23.66	25.67	27.89	30.32	33.00	35.95	39.19	42.75
17	18.43	20.01	21.76	23.70	25.84	28.21	30.84	33.75	36.97	40.54	44.50	48.88
18	19.61	21.41	23.41	25.65	28.13	30.91	34.00	37.45	41.30	45.60	50.40	55.75
19	20.81	22.84	25.12	27.67	30.54	33.76	37.38	41.45	46.02	51.16	56.94	63.44
20	22.02	24.30	26.87	29.78	33.07	36.79	41.00	45.76	51.16	57.27	64.20	72.05
21	23.24	25.78	28.68	31.97	35.72	39.99	44.87	50.42	56.76	64.00	72.27	81.70
22	24.47	27.30	30.54	34.25	38.51	43.39	49.01	55.46	62.87	71.40	81.21	92.50
23	25.72	28.84	32.45	36.62	41.43	47.00	53.44	60.89	69.53	79.54	91.15	104.6
24	26.97	30.42	34.43	39.08	44.50	50.82	58.18	66.76	76.79	88.50	102.2	118.2
25	28.24	32.03	36.46	41.65	47.73	54.86	63.25	73.11	84.70	98.35	114.4	133.3
26	29.53	33.67	38.55	44.31	51.11	59.16	68.68	79.95	93.32	109.2	128.0	150.3
27	30.82	35.34	40.71	47.08	54.67	63.71	74.48	87.35	102.7	121.1	143.1	169.4
28	32.13	37.05	42.93	49.97	58.40	68.53	80.70	95.34	113.0	134.2	159.8	190.7
29	33.45	38.79	45.22	52.97	62.32	73.64	87.35	104.0	124.1	148.6	178.4	214.6
30	34.78	40.57	47.58	56.08	66.44	79.06	94.46	113.3	136.3	164.5	199.0	241.3
31	36.13	42.38	50.00	59.33	70.76	84.80	102.1	123.3	149.6	181.9	221.9	271.3
32	37.49	44.23	52.50	62.70	75.30	90.89	110.2	134.2	164.0	201.1	247.3	304.8
33	38.87	46.11	55.08	66.21	80.06	97.34	118.9	146.0	179.8	222.3	275.5	342.4
34	40.26	48.03	57.73	69.86	85.07	104.2	128.3	158.6	197.0	245.5	306.8	384.5
35	41.66	49.99	60.46	73.65	90.32	111.4	138.2	172.3	215.7	271.0	341.6	431.7

Terminal value of £1 per period

Period	% Interest rate per period											
	13	14	15	16	18	20	22	24	26	28	30	35
1	1.000	1.000	1.000	1.000	1.000	1.000	1.000	1.000	1.000	1.000	1.000	1.000
2	2.130	2.140	2.150	2.160	2.180	2.200	2.220	2.240	2.260	2.280	2.300	2.350
3	3.407	3.440	3.472	3.506	3.572	3.640	3.708	3.778	3.848	3.918	3.990	4.173
4	4.850	4.921	4.993	5.066	5.215	5.368	5.524	5.684	5.848	6.016	6.187	6.633
5	6.480	6.610	6.742	6.877	7.154	7.442	7.740	8.048	8.368	8.700	9.043	9.954
6	8.323	8.536	8.754	8.977	9.442	9.930	10.44	10.98	11.54	12.14	12.76	14.44
7	10.40	10.73	11.07	11.41	12.14	12.92	13.74	14.62	15.55	16.53	17.58	20.49
8	12.76	13.23	13.73	14.24	15.33	16.50	17.76	19.12	20.59	22.16	23.86	28.66
9	15.42	16.09	16.79	17.52	19.09	20.80	22.67	24.71	26.94	29.37	32.01	39.70
10	18.42	19.34	20.30	21.32	23.52	25.96	28.66	31.64	34.94	38.59	42.62	54.59
11	21.81	23.04	24.35	25.73	28.76	32.15	35.96	40.24	45.03	50.40	56.41	74.70
12	25.65	27.27	29.00	30.85	34.93	39.58	44.87	50.89	57.74	65.51	74.33	101.8
13	29.98	32.09	34.35	36.79	42.22	48.50	55.75	64.11	73.75	84.85	97.63	138.5
14	34.88	37.58	40.50	43.67	50.82	59.20	69.01	80.50	93.93	109.6	127.9	188.0
15	40.42	43.84	47.58	51.66	60.97	72.04	85.19	100.8	119.3	141.3	167.3	254.7
16	46.67	50.98	55.72	60.93	72.94	87.44	104.9	126.0	151.4	181.9	218.5	344.9
17	53.74	59.12	65.08	71.67	87.07	105.9	129.0	157.3	191.7	233.8	285.0	466.6
18	61.73	68.39	75.84	84.14	103.7	128.1	158.4	196.0	242.6	300.3	371.5	630.9
19	70.75	78.97	88.21	98.60	123.4	154.7	194.3	244.0	306.7	385.3	484.0	852.7
20	80.95	91.02	102.4	115.4	146.6	186.7	238.0	303.6	387.4	494.2	630.2	1152
21	92.47	104.8	118.8	134.8	174.0	225.0	291.3	377.5	489.1	633.6	820.2	1556
22	105.5	120.4	137.6	157.4	206.3	271.0	356.4	469.1	617.3	812.0	1067	2102
23	120.2	138.3	159.3	183.6	244.5	326.2	435.9	582.6	778.8	1040	1388	2839
24	136.8	158.7	184.2	214.0	289.5	392.5	532.8	723.5	982.3	1332	1806	3833
25	155.6	181.9	212.8	249.2	342.6	472.0	651.0	898.1	1238	1706	2348	5176
26	176.9	208.3	245.7	290.1	405.3	567.4	795.2	1114	1561	2185	3054	6989
27	200.8	238.5	283.6	337.5	479.2	681.9	971.1	1383	1968	2798	3971	9436
28	227.9	272.9	327.1	392.5	566.5	819.2	1185	1716	2481	3583	5164	–
29	258.6	312.1	377.2	456.3	669.4	984.1	1447	2128	3127	4587	6714	–
30	293.2	356.8	434.7	530.3	790.9	1181	1767	2640	3942	5873	8729	–
31	332.3	407.7	501.0	616.2	934.3	1419	2156	3275	4967	7518	–	–
32	376.5	465.8	577.1	715.7	1103	1704	2632	4062	6260	9624	–	–
33	426.5	532.0	664.7	831.3	1303	2045	3212	5039	7889	–	–	–
34	482.9	607.5	765.4	965.3	1538	2456	3920	6249	9941	–	–	–
35	546.7	693.6	881.2	1120	1816	2948	4783	7750	–	–	–	–

Index